Vegas at Odds

STUDIES IN INDUSTRY AND SOCIETY

Philip B. Scranton, *Series Editor*

Published with the assistance of
the Hagley Museum and Library

Vegas at Odds

Labor Conflict in a Leisure Economy,
1960–1985

JAMES P. KRAFT

The Johns Hopkins University Press
Baltimore

The Johns Hopkins University Press
2715 North Charles Street
Baltimore, Maryland 21218-4363
www.press.jhu.edu

Library of Congress Cataloging-in-Publication Data

Kraft, James P.
Vegas at odds : labor conflict in a leisure economy, 1960–1985 /
James P. Kraft.
p. cm.—(Studies in industry and society)
Includes bibliographical references and index.
ISBN-13: 978-0-8018-9357-5 (hardcover : alk. paper)
ISBN-10: 0-8018-9357-7 (hardcover : alk. paper)
1. Labor movement—Nevada—Las Vegas—History—20th century.
2. Labor—Nevada—Las Vegas—History—20th century.   3. Las
Vegas (Nev.)—Economic conditions—20th century.   I. Title.
HD8085.L373K73 2009
331.7'6179509793135—dc22
2009007043

A catalog record for this book is available from the British Library.

Special discounts are available for bulk purchases of this book.
For more information, please contact Special Sales at 410-516-6936
or specialsales@press.jhu.edu.

To Renée

Contents

Acknowledgments   *ix*

Introduction   1

1 The Rise of Corporate Resorts   9

2 Working in Las Vegas   33

3 The First Work Stoppages   53

4 The Struggle for the Casinos   73

5 Workplace Incidents   96

6 Fighting for Equal Rights   117

7 The Spirit of '76   139

8 Management Digs In, 1982–1984   159

9 The Strike of 1984–1985   180

Afterword   200

Notes   *209*
Essay on Sources   *257*
Index   *265*

Illustrations follow page 72

Acknowledgments

Many generous and thoughtful people contributed to this study, the results of which loom large in the finished product. Philip Scranton expressed an early interest in the study at a meeting of the Business History Association in Glasgow, Scotland, and ten years later supported its publication at Johns Hopkins University Press. In the intervening years, I discussed the project often with Edwin J. Perkins, my mentor at the University of Southern California, and benefited immensely from his advice. I also benefited from the frequent counsel of two former colleagues at the University of Hawaii, Idus Newby and Robert Locke, who read multiple drafts of the study and made me aware of many sentences and paragraphs that needed rethinking and rewriting. Mansel Blackford, a former colleague at the Ohio State University, also critiqued a draft of the work in ways that sharpened my focus. Margot Henriksen and Timothy Minchin read multiple chapters of the work to my advantage, and Howell John Harris, Hal Rothman, Louise McReynolds, Peter Hoffenberg, Christopher Yeh, and Chris Bohner offered useful comments on more specific parts.

Union officers and resort managers helped me address specific questions and issues. I offer special thanks to Thom Pastor of the Las Vegas Musicians Union, who introduced me to many of the city's former labor leaders. Interviews with Mark Massagli, Walt Elliot, Claude "Blackie" Evans, Dick Thomas, Dennis Kist, Jeff McColl, Alan Ware, Terry Greenwald, Mike Werner, Sam Savali, and Jim Bonaventure proved invaluable. So did conversations with Jim Arnold, Dee Taylor, Courtney Alexander, Julie Perlman, Mike Magnani, Cheryl Thomas, Mike Russell, Rob Rovere, Max Price, Leslie Curtis, Robert Trombetta, and other union officials. Resort managers who helped with the study include Bill Champion, Bill Davis, Bill Moore, Dan Riechart, Marilyn Seay, Nancy Macaulay, Ginny Murphy, and Elaine Tackley. Attorneys who represented either unions or resorts during the period under study were also helpful, especially Dennis Sabbath, Gary Moss, and Kevin Efroymson.

Archivists and librarians helped me greatly as well. At the Department of Special Collections in the Lied Library at the University of Nevada, Las Vegas, I benefited from the assistance of Joyce Marshall-Moore, Sue Kim Chung, Claytee White, Peter Michel, David Swartz, Jonnie Kennedy, and Kathy War. At the Nevada State Library and Archives in Carson City, Joyce Cox, Jeffrey Kintop, Christopher Driggs, Guy Louis Rocha, Susan Searcy, and C. Mitch Ison were especially generous with their time. Eric Moody, Marta Gonzalez-Collins, Michael Mahar, and Mella Rothwell Harmon at the Nevada Historical Society in nearby Reno were also helpful, as was Mary Larson of the University of Nevada Reno, Oral History Program.

Other individuals pointed me to additional sources. I am especially grateful to the legal team of Greg Smith and Malani Kotchaka, and to their professional staff of Patricia Affleck, Thomas Blankenship, Rosalie Garcia, Nancy Pirie, Rose Marie Reynolds, Sandra Thompson, and James Whitmire. I also wish to thank Cathlyn Baird of the Conrad Hilton Archives in Houston, Texas; Nathan Albright and Michael Chavez of the National Labor Relations Board in Las Vegas; George Knapp at KLAS TV in Las Vegas; Vince Eade at the University of Nevada, Las Vegas; and Joyce McNeill of the Nevada Resort Association. Still others helped me find sources at the Federal Bureau of Investigation in Washington, D.C., and at the National Archives in College Park, Maryland, including Traci Wits, Sarah Didiwick, Debbie Lopes, Richard Peuser, and Janis Wiggins. For help in collecting photographs, I am grateful to Rebecca Clifford-Cruz and Joan Whitely at the *Las Vegas Sun* and Padmini Pai, Pamela Busse, and Bob Katelle at the *Las Vegas Review-Journal*. I would also like to thank Dave Millman of the Nevada State Museum and Historical Society, and Karen Siveroli of the Las Vegas Convention and Visitors Authority.

My debts and obligations are greater than these acknowledgments indicate. To complete this project, I received financial assistance from the University of Hawaii as well as the National Endowment for the Humanities. I also received expert advice from Robert J. Brugger's superb editorial team at the Johns Hopkins University Press. On a more personal level, I benefited from the camaraderie of many colleagues, friends, and family members. I extend a special aloha and mahalo to Robb Navrides, Rocky Jackson, Harold McCarthur, Susan Reid, Arthur Verge, Patrick Patterson, Karen Mead, Jennifer Isernhagen, Robert, Cinda, and Kathryn Kraft, and my parents Marion and Hubert Kraft. I have dedicated this book to the most important person in my life, my wife Renée Arnold, whom I had the good fortune of meeting twenty years ago. How time flies!

Vegas at Odds

Introduction

It is a striking city, especially at night. Glitzy neon signs light up the Strip, hawking everything from Hollywood headliners to the "best steaks in town." Posh hotels and casinos spread ancient pyramids, medieval castles, and other improbabilities across the landscape. Pagan statues line the entrances to Caesars Palace, swashbuckling pirates dangle from a frigate at Treasure Island, a mammoth lion guards the MGM Grand. Each new mega-resort dazzles more brightly than the last. At the $1.5 billion Venetian, guests ride gondolas along imagined eighteenth-century Italian canals; at the Paris, they climb the Eiffel Tower; at the Mandalay Bay, they surf the beach or enjoy a fine vintage fetched by a "wine angel" from a four-story wine rack.

The recently renovated downtown is equally impressive. There, casinos and hotels have attracted tourists since the 1930s, when the Golden Nail opened at Fremont and Main Streets. The Golden Nail is still there, dwarfed by behemoths with names like the Golden Nugget and the Union Plaza. The older heart of the city is now a veritable amusement park, its main thoroughfare, Fremont Street, closed to vehicular traffic since imaginative civic leaders erected a "space frame" above it to protect tourists from desert sun by day and to enthrall them with high-tech light displays by night. The area resembles old Coney Island more than the center of a modern metropolis, especially on weekends and holidays, when musical groups, mimes, and others perform on the sidewalks.

Swank resorts and carnival glitz have made Las Vegas a world-class tourist destination. Travelers flock not just to gamble but to experience a unique mixture of gaming, entertainment, and other forms of self-indulgence that divert them from the cares or routines of everyday life. At the beginning of the new millennium, more than thirty-three million people visited the city annually, spending perhaps $7 billion gambling and five times that amount on other forms of diversion and entertainment. The resorts at which they relaxed and indulged themselves employed a third of the workforce in Las Vegas, and other tourist-related businesses accounted for the livelihoods of another third. The largest resorts in the area each employed six thousand to eight thousand workers, more than many of the nation's steel mills and textile factories once employed.

The transition to the phenomenon of modern Las Vegas has been studied sketchily and is imperfectly understood. Much of what is known of the city comes from journalists and other popular writers whose works, though often interesting and informative, are episodic and incomplete as historical narratives, or distorting because of their focus on spectacular events or larger-than-life personalities. The bulk of this literature portrays Las Vegas as "Sin City," a place where people indulge in illicit, problematic, or otherwise socially suspect activities. The rest of it describes Las Vegas as a secular "Mecca" to which people trek for their own kinds of rejuvenation, or as a "Camelot" to which they escape to search, vainly, for their own paradise. This literature further leaves the impression that larger-than-life entrepreneurs like Howard Hughes and Steve Wynn built the city by themselves, with little or no help from the thousands of others, including wageworkers, who did most of the actual labor. It also suggests that trade unions and their leaders played little if any role in shaping the city's history.[1]

Movies reinforce these images and stereotypes. Though not all films about Las Vegas fall into these categories, many portray the city as a moral testing ground where evil forces challenge decency, integrity, and even common sense. Others contradictorily picture it as a "benign oasis," a postmodern city that has transcended the social ills that plagued modern metropolises. The flashing neon, rapid-action-filled gaming tables, and other evident pulsations, in these accounts, become a kind of new reality where everything is glamorized. These films typically infer that men and women who labor long hours for modest wages in ostensibly glamorous settings are comfortable and contented, and relatively passive players in the social and economic history of this leisure metropolis.[2]

Insiders with their own needs have also shaped perceptions of Las Vegas. In the mid-twentieth century, many businesses attracted tourists to Las Vegas by linking the city to the wild and wooly West of a bygone day. Their efforts fed on myths of moral license, cowboy freedom, and six-gun justice, as did the dress of their employees. By 1975, corporate business leaders began to tidy up images of Las Vegas.

They renamed gambling "gaming" and marketed the city as a vacation spot for families with children of all ages, as if it were a national forest, theme park, or public beach. More recently, they resurrected Las Vegas's reputation as a place where adults cavort. The Las Vegas Convention and Visitors Authority adopted the slogan "What happens here, stays here" to suggest that the city is wonderfully risqué and its workers discreet and accommodating.[3]

These conflicting images show the extent to which "reading" Las Vegas is a function of language. In poststructural terms, the city, like everything else, is a text to be read, and the reading an exercise in reader subjectivity. The city in this formulation becomes a set of signifiers to which individuals assign the signifieds to validate their needs or purposes. To put it too simply, perhaps, Las Vegas is largely what people want it to be. Those who find it a modern-day Gomorrah are impressed by or concerned about one set of issues they find there, and the same applies, *mutatis mutandis*, to those who find something else. There seems to be little point in trying to resolve these contradictions or to insist on a definitive depiction of the city. Like all modern metropolises it is a complex social phenomenon, and no doubt most of whatever has been said about it is true or misleading or incomplete to one degree or another.

This book explores one aspect of the recent history of greater Las Vegas—work, workers, and labor relations in the area's resort industry during the eventful and often-stressful quarter century that ended in the mid-1980s. In the early part of this period, Las Vegas resorts had traditional structures of business ownership based on proprietorships or small partnerships. Though no two resorts were the same, and some had ties to organized crime, most embraced paternalistic concepts of management modeled on old forms of business enterprise and maintained relatively good, stable relations with workers and trade unions. In the late 1960s, new state laws permitted publicly traded corporations to enter the Nevada gaming business, which opened the resort industry to vast new capital resources and managerial forms. Resorts thus grew larger and larger, their management more rational and hierarchical, and their labor relations more complex, impersonal, and confrontational. By 1985, after successfully facing down a massive industry-wide strike, highly capitalized corporations dominated the area's leisure economy, and professionally trained managers directed its workforce. A basic concern of this study is how these and related developments affected resort workers and their unions, and how and with what success workers and unions responded to the changes in ownership and management.

As a contribution to labor history, this study sheds light on workers and work experiences in the service sector of the nation's economy. Since the mid-twentieth century, the numbers of American workers in service industries have risen steadily while those in agriculture, manufacturing, and other traditional forms of employment have declined. In some parts of the country, the service sector has become the primary engine of economic growth, generating the bulk of new jobs. That was true in postwar Southern Nevada, where the proliferation of resorts and related leisure enterprises brought employment to people in a wide variety of services and entertainment. Labor historians have not ignored workers in service industries, but they have privileged their counterparts in manufacturing and extractive industries. Thus, we know relatively little of the history of workers in an increasingly important area of economic life. What did those workers do on a daily basis? How did they cope with changes and challenges in the workplace? What were their attitudes about their jobs and careers? Addressing these and similar questions, this study explores the work experiences of a wide range of service workers. It looks at the occupational hierarchies of a service-oriented industry and the institutional bases of that industry. Most notably, it explores the complex relationship between labor and management.

Workers in tourism and businesses dependent upon tourism in Las Vegas lived in a world that differed greatly from the one the resorts created for tourists. As residents, they were no doubt less impressed by the outward appearance of the city than were tourists. They punched time clocks rather than slot machines, at least during work hours. Many worked behind the scenes: they made beds, cooked meals, repaired machines, or safeguarded public order. Others had a more public role and interacted with the tourists, including those who dealt cards or counted money, parked cars, served drinks, took reservations, or handled luggage. A few of them performed in showrooms or lounges, as headliners or (far more often) as unknowns in musical or theatrical groups. The tourist industry is labor intensive; most of the jobs it creates require limited skills and routine work and are poorly paid. Others, of course, demand considerable skill, some even real talent and creativity, and are thus unusually challenging and highly compensated. This variety is a central factor in the labor history of Las Vegas, for it affects not only the workplace environment and the work experience but also the attitudes of most workers toward their work.

Collectively, casino workers approached their jobs not unlike workers in other industries; whether they were more satisfied or content is difficult to say. What is clear is that the workplace for resort workers in Las Vegas was substantively distinctive from that of, say, textile workers in North Carolina, steel mill workers in Indiana, coal miners in West Virginia, or agricultural laborers in the Imperial Valley of California. It is essential, though, not to idealize that difference. Although many Las Vegas resort workers enjoyed their jobs, most of them also belonged voluntarily to trade unions that worked conscientiously to protect and advance their interests and economic well-being vis-à-vis management. They also—and this is a vital point—invariably supported their unions when union leaders told them to confront management even to the point of going on strike. Conflict between labor and management arose over many issues, but mostly over wages, conditions of employment, and management prerogatives.

Las Vegas at times was more battleground than playground. Over the period of this study, resorts sought to make their employees more efficient, which meant more productive, and that in turn meant increasing management control of the workplace. Workers and their unions resisted these developments, seeking instead to retain traditional practices or to induce changes to their advantage. In the resulting confrontations, workers went on strike on several occasions and showed remarkable solidarity when doing so. In 1976 thirteen thousand workers struck more than a dozen major resorts, shutting down much of the Las Vegas resort industry for two weeks. When an even larger number went on strike in 1984, an even greater dislocation resulted. The growing scope and intensity of work stoppages in the years of this study suggest that the corporatization of the resort industry made for more adversarial labor relations.

These stoppages speak pointedly to the impact of corporate development in Las Vegas, but to focus on them entirely is to make the history of work and workers in the area episodic and uneven. More indicative of the day-to-day quality and substance of labor-management relations were the routine, perhaps daily, confrontations between individual resort workers and their immediate supervisors, which centered on issues from the evidently trivial to the quite substantial. To illustrate the quality of labor relations in the workplace, this study draws upon surviving records of union organizing campaigns, employee grievances, and efforts to end discriminatory practices. These records show not only that workers encountered management on different levels and often in a confrontational manner but also how workers and groups of workers related to one another and how internal conflict could result when what was good for one group was sometimes costly to others. Workplace conflict has typically been analyzed in terms of labor versus management, but actualities were more nuanced than that approach implies. Workers interacted with one another as well as with managers, and in ways that determined wages and working conditions as well as the extent of trade union organization, the rights of workers, and the composition of the labor force.

In this study, I have sought consciously to avoid romanticizing work in "old" and "glamorous" Las Vegas or reducing workers to victims of overbearing managers or exploitative entrepreneurs. In recognizing the importance of entrepreneurs and management in the resort industry, I have tried to understand the binary nature of management and labor. Competition is a central fact of the resort business; in highly competitive markets, managers must contain labor costs just as workers must strive for better pay and benefits. Individual workers, no less than individual managers, were occasionally irresponsible or unnecessarily troublesome, and sometimes untrustworthy, an especially problematic quality in an industry where so many employees handled money. The same variety of character existed among union leaders, who were generally dedicated to improving the lives of the workers they represented, but who were sometimes men with criminal records and underworld ties.

Labor-management conflict in Las Vegas arose largely from the contrasting social being of employers and employees, which generated contrasting values and interests. Even the most union-friendly managers in resorts always assumed that labor was subordinate to capital and that employees had no legitimate voice in arranging fundamental matters about work and the allocation of resources. Corporate executives regarded union demands, whether on matters of cost items or workplace control, as assaults on their prerogatives. They generally considered themselves responsible for the success of Las Vegas tourism and viewed unions and labor militancy as threats to that success. "The Southern Nevada economy depends on [our] being able to continue the aggressive promotional, publicity, sales and entertainment campaigns which have built the number of visitors to more than nine million each year," one of them told striking workers in 1976. "Union demands would impair our ability to continue these successful practices."[4] Of course, their views on how to handle the unions varied. When their workers went on strike, some were more willing than others to compromise.

For their part, workers and unions had no quarrel with popular notions of private property, free enterprise, and individual responsibility. They recognized that management played an indispensable role in the functioning of the industry in which they worked. But they challenged management's view of labor's proper role in the capitalist order. Corporate leaders, they seemed to believe, failed to appreciate how much workers contributed to the functioning and success of the industry, or refused to acknowledge the challenges workers faced in performing and holding their jobs. Management, they insisted, had a moral responsibility to pay decent wages and ensure job security for decent performance, maintain proper working conditions, and provide accustomed fringe benefits.

Most of them saw unions as instruments for securing these objectives and took pride in their union membership. "You cannot work in this town without a union," a former hotel maid explained. "That's just like having the cops on the street. You cannot live here without the police."[5] Of course, not all workers shared these views; some rejected the basic principles of trade unionism, and some even staffed vacated positions during strikes. Nonetheless, the perspectives of workers and managers were sufficiently different to provoke discord daily in the workplace and to prompt periodic confrontations in contractual negotiations.

The confrontations reflected broader patterns of American life. In the 1950s and early 1960s, the United States underwent a surge of unparalleled economic growth, which helped unionized workers make substantial gains in real income, fringe benefits, and job security. By the 1970s, this growth subsided, and the bargaining strength of unions in most industries, including Las Vegas tourism, eroded. The production of many manufactured goods began to outpace demand for them, unemployment increased, and the proportion of unionized workers in the national workforce began to decline. In many industries, traditional bargaining practices and understandings disappeared, bargaining itself became more confrontational, and workers lost some of the gains made in the preceding decades. By the mid-1980s, jobs in once vital industries like steel and textiles were declining rapidly in the face of global competition and new laborsaving technologies, which further sapped the strength of organized labor. Postwar "social accords" that had stabilized labor relations had broken down, and many once proud unions all but collapsed.

The history of unions in Las Vegas followed these general patterns but with variations of its own. Unions established themselves in Las Vegas before the appearance of large resorts or the corporatization of resort ownership, when employers were still basically entrepreneurs and gamblers and often had ties to organized crime. Though these employers adamantly opposed the unionization of casino dealers and security guards, they acquiesced in the unionization of other employees. Unlike American manufacturers, they could not easily outsource or mechanize the work of their employees. At a time when the demand for labor almost always outstripped the supply, and Las Vegas itself was a remote and still emerging city, employers came to rely on union hiring halls to staff their workforce. Some even borrowed from union retirement funds to raise capital to build or improve their resorts. By the late 1960s, when national corporations began investing in Las Vegas, resort workers already had relatively high pay and benefits, as well as stronger unions than workers of comparable skill and experience in other cities, including other tourist destinations. In the 1970s and 1980s, they began to lose this relative advantage. The unions did not wither away; rather, they adapted.

Vegas at Odds, then, challenges a few common assumptions about work and labor relations in modern America. To begin with, it suggests that service work is a more complex phenomenon than often assumed and that service workers are not necessarily unskilled, docile, or difficult to organize. Occupational groups like cocktail servers and maids do not usually come to mind when one thinks of people with abilities and job responsibilities, or of striking workers on picket lines. Yet all jobs in the resort industry required some level of training and dexterity, and labor relations in the industry hinged on power. Workers and employers in Las Vegas resorts no less than in Chicago meatpacking plants had different priorities and interests. Employers in all industries have often pushed workers beyond what seemed appropriate and necessary, regardless of whether profits were up or down. Work environments in Las Vegas were often as tense and volatile as those in major manufacturing centers. Like all groups of wage earners, workers in tourism had countless ways of resisting managerial initiatives. Their unions did not always respond understandingly to their concerns, or avoid demoralizing defeats, but they fought power with power. The unions became more confrontational in the 1970s and early 1980s and, in doing so, kept Las Vegas a "union town."

Las Vegas is, I believe, a good place to study service workers and their unions. The city has never been a true manufacturing, transportation, or trans-shipment center, or a center of agricultural or mining activity. Economic life in Las Vegas has always revolved around service activities. Although businesses in most Sunbelt cities have shown a deep hostility to organized labor, trade unions in Las Vegas have a long history of organizing workers and winning contracts with decent wages and benefits; and their activities have reflected broad patterns and trends in American society. Las Vegas is also one of the newest cities in the nation, and thus its history is relatively easy to understand. In the years under study, the population of greater Las Vegas jumped from 50,000 to 600,000, paralleling the equally spectacular growth of tourism in the area. By 1985 Las Vegas was not only a major tourist destination but an early example of a postindustrial society. Indeed, as the late Hal Rothman noted, perhaps no other city in the world had such a fully developed service economy.[6]

The Rise of Corporate Resorts

Modern systems of water distribution and air-conditioning have turned many desert towns into thriving urban complexes. Las Vegas's rise, however, was unique. In the quarter century after World War II, its population grew at a faster rate than that of any other city in the nation. Warm weather, low taxes, affordable housing, and employment opportunities attracted residents; gaming, entertainment, and other leisure activities enticed tourists. The construction and then the operation of new hotels and casinos created thousands of jobs. By the 1970s, hotels and casinos in the metropolitan area employed about thirty thousand people, a third of the workforce, and other tourist-related businesses another third.

Entrepreneurs as well as public policies facilitated this development. The collaboration between entrepreneurs and bureaucrats, including government agencies at the national, state, and local levels, bestowed a sense of legitimacy on a category of business activity that many Americans still saw as questionable or undesirable, if not sinful. That legitimacy encouraged industrial development and soon ushered in a new age of enterprise in which large corporations had distinct business and economic advantages. The advent of corporate structures and corporate control, though not apparent to tourists, loomed large in the eyes of resort workers. By the mid-1970s, corporations occupied the vital center in the story of tourism and tourist work in Las Vegas.

In 1950 Nevada was a sparsely populated agricultural and mining state in the Great Basin, an arid region of the American West stretching from the Sierra

Nevadas to the Rocky Mountains. Its agriculture centered on stock raising and hay production, the expansion of which was limited by lack of water and irrigation systems. Mining centered on copper, zinc, and lead production. Gold and silver production was also important to the state's economy, but largely a by-product of other mining operations. Nevada's small population and isolated location inhibited development in other sectors of the economy. The state's population was 160,000, that of its largest city, Reno, 32,000.[1]

Political leaders were already hard at work to change these circumstances. Among the earliest of these was Charles Russell, the first Republican to hold the governorship in the postwar period. After assuming office in 1951, Russell wrote personal letters to business leaders across the country, boasting of Nevada's warm climate, low taxes, and improving transportation systems, describing the state as a "strategic center" in the rapidly growing West, and thus a "logical place" to locate new distributive and manufacturing facilities. He also drew attention to opportunities in recreation and leisure. "Nevada is growing steadily in prestige as one of the West's foremost recreation states," Russell wrote, "and its varied types of entertainment are unexcelled anywhere."[2]

By this time, the business of providing accommodations, transportation, and other services to tourists was the most dynamic sector of Nevada's economy. Like other western states, Nevada benefited handsomely from the postwar surge in vacation and recreational spending.[3] Camping grounds and other indoor and outdoor recreational facilities drew tens of thousands of people to Lake Tahoe in northern Nevada, and to Lake Mead in the south, where the chief attraction remained the still relatively new Hoover Dam, "the great pyramid of the American West." Harnessing the fast-moving waters of the Colorado River, that dam provided much needed water and energy to the West. Built in the 1930s, the dam was a massive engineering phenomenon. Some 400,000 people took guided tours of it in 1950, a figure that increased steadily thereafter.[4]

Legalized gambling, however, was already Nevada's greatest attraction to outsiders. Gambling had been a way of life in Nevada since the nineteenth century, when mining camps and boomtowns were major centers of economic activity. It was legal from 1869 to 1909, when reform-minded citizens succeeded in outlawing it and other "immoral" activities. The state removed the ban in 1931, however, and at midcentury gambling was the driving force behind the state's emerging tourist industry and a major source of tax revenue. Gross gambling income in Nevada topped $50 million in 1951, which exceeded the value of all minerals produced in the state. About 3 percent of that money went into the state's tax coffers.[5]

Public officials often portrayed gambling as one part of the state's larger recreation and leisure economy, as though it fit in the mainstream of American business activity. But gambling was an unusual industry. The firms engaged in it were unlike the state's other businesses, including those in other tourist-oriented activities. In the early postwar years, legalized gambling as often as not took place in dingy bars, pool halls, or characterless commercial buildings. Even glitzy gambling locales looked more like saloons than modern casinos. Most operated twenty-four hours a day, seven days a week, and were patronized almost exclusively by men. Although these establishments were supposed to be licensed, it was a challenge for public officials to check their paperwork or their books. They had difficulty detecting "skimming" and the resulting tax fraud in such places, or even ensuring they were properly licensed. Such establishments often served as gathering places for alcoholics, hoodlums, and prostitutes and might even admit minors with money to lose. They were constantly under attack by opponents of gambling, who hoped once again to outlaw the activity.[6]

The popularity of gambling reflected the interest many people had in playing slot machines and table games like blackjack and poker, knowing—or suspecting—that the odds of winning were tilted against them. Slot machines, which one operated by inserting coins into a slot and pulling down a handle on the side, were typically programmed to retain 5 to 10 percent of the money inserted. Though an occasional player beat the machines out of a meaningful sum of money, almost no one beat them over a long period of time. The odds of winning table games were not much better. Experienced players had a much better chance of winning than amateurs, but "the house" always had an advantage. The house—the proprietors—treated the lucky few who won "jackpots" as celebrities, which only encouraged other would-be jackpot winners.[7]

By the early 1950s, gambling in Las Vegas, a fledgling city on the southern tip of the state, was centered downtown. The city originated near springs of fresh water in a large valley in which indigenous Native Americans and then Spanish-speaking settlers had once lived, and in which Mormon missionaries later canvassed. It was little more than a whistle stop on the Union Pacific Railroad until the late 1920s, when President Herbert Hoover approved construction of the nearby dam that bears his name. Only twenty-five miles southeast of Las Vegas, the construction site attracted thousands of job-hungry Americans during the worst years of the Great Depression. Many of the job seekers brought their families with them, and many of these settled in Las Vegas.[8] The population of the area surged again during World War II, when the federal government funded construction of a huge magnesium processing plant south of Las Vegas, powered by energy from Hoover Dam. The plant employed more than two thousand people, more than any mining operation in the state. Its presence encouraged construction of new housing and creation of new service activities in and around the city.[9]

By midcentury, Las Vegas was a bustling municipality of twenty-five thousand people, surrounded by several thousand more in nearby Henderson, Boulder City, and North Las Vegas, and in such suburbs as Paradise City and Winchester. The population of Clark County, which encompassed these areas, topped fifty thousand.[10] Economically, the area benefited from new manufacturing enterprises as well as new wholesale and retail outlets, and from an especially dynamic construction industry. Between 1950 and 1954, the value of new construction in greater Las Vegas quadrupled over that of the previous five years, from $15 million to $60 million.[11]

The construction of several large hotels and casinos along a three-mile stretch of highway just outside the Las Vegas city limits, which came to be known as the "Strip," spearheaded this construction boom. The first gaming properties appeared outside the city limits in the early 1930s, when city officials limited gambling in the city to a few downtown "clubs." The largest and most lavish of these out-of-the-city establishments, the Meadows Club, opened on the road to Hoover Dam only months after Nevada legalized gambling in 1931. But it was El Rancho, which opened in 1941 on Highway 91 a mile south of downtown, that ushered in the new age of development on the Strip. The Last Frontier opened near El Rancho a year later, and the Flamingo and the Thunderbird soon thereafter. Like their downtown counterparts, these Strip properties kept their casinos open twenty-four hours a day, seven days a week.[12]

Strip properties had distinct advantages over their downtown competitors. Their location made them the first places motorists from Los Angeles reached in the area and enabled them to avoid city taxes and land prices. They were also more than gaming houses, or gaming houses with facilities for overnight guests. They were resorts, upscale hotels with varieties of recreational facilities and leisure services for vacationers as well as gamblers. The Flamingo, the most glamorous of them, had not only a large gambling casino but more than a hundred hotel rooms, an unusually large swimming pool surrounded by lush gardens and palm trees, a gym and steam room, as well as badminton, handball, squash, and tennis courts, a stable of forty riding horses, even a trap-shooting range. Its waiters and dealers wore tuxedos and treated customers as guests after the fashion of comparable establishments in Monte Carlo.[13]

The Thunderbird seemed modest by comparison, but its Navaho Indian motif gave it a distinctive character and charm, as did its fine-dining restaurant, which featured not only rich, red carpeting, crystal chandeliers, and spectacular views of the swimming pool and surrounding garden but gourmet food as well. Guests who found this or an equally elegant Oyster Bar too formal or expensive could patronize a smart coffee shop just off the casino floor, open around the clock. Twice a day, the shop featured a "chuck wagon" buffet that offered popular dining favorites, such as prime roast beef and southern fried chicken.[14]

In the early 1950s, after Clark County officials blocked Las Vegas's efforts to annex the Strip, the resorts there increased in size and number and in the economic level and cultural sophistication of their appeal. The Desert Inn, which opened in 1950, was perhaps the most impressive of the new resorts in these respects. Spread over seventeen acres, it boasted three hundred air-conditioned hotel rooms with individual thermostats and a 2,400-square-foot casino, the largest in the state. It also featured an eighteen-hole golf course that hosted professional tournaments. The Sahara and the Sands opened two years later, followed soon by the Dunes, the Riviera, the Tropicana, and the Stardust. Each seemed to reach new heights in resort development. The Stardust, for example, had more hotel rooms—one thousand—than any of its competitors, as well as the supreme status symbol, the largest neon sign on the Strip. Some 216 feet long and 27 feet high, the sign was the first Las Vegas image motorists saw as they approached the Strip from the west, that is, from Southern California.[15]

Because these resorts were newer, larger, and more elegant than downtown properties, the Strip soon acquired an atmosphere of its own. Sensing this, entrepreneurs soon remade downtown in the image of the Strip. A refurbished and enlarged Golden Nugget, which had opened there in 1945 at Fremont and Second streets, had the most hotel rooms and the largest, most glamorous casino downtown. It also had a gourmet restaurant, and the city's tallest neon sign, which soared a hundred feet in the air. It likewise had a distinctive motif, a romanticized re-creation of old San Francisco and the Barbary Coast. Construction of the Fremont Hotel soon further changed the downtown landscape. At fifteen stories, with chips of quartz on its exterior sparkling in the sun, the Fremont was the tallest structure in the state, and one of the most visually dazzling. The $6 million spent to construct and furnish it was a staggering sum at the time. Despite these improvements, the downtown area remained less glamorous than the Strip through the postwar years. Its hotels and casinos never matched the elegance of the Strip and offered less in terms of dining and entertainment facilities, catering as they did largely to slot machine players.[16]

This first wave of remaking Las Vegas ended in the late 1950s. By then, the Strip boasted a dozen multimillion-dollar resorts, all of them with extravagant

features and services, including live stage shows and fine dining, and downtown hotels had attractions of their own. Collectively, the resorts and hotels in
the two areas had become the cornerstone of the Las Vegas economy, attracting
millions of tourists and gamblers. In 1960 nearly ten million people visited the
area and spent an estimated $250 million, including $100 million on gambling.[17] These figures continued to rise rapidly, especially after McCarran Airport expanded to accommodate jet aircraft, which shrank flight times from the
East Coast by half.[18]

In 1964, when Nevada celebrated its one-hundredth anniversary of statehood,
Governor Grant Sawyer took the opportunity to boast of these transformations.
"We no longer are a rustic Western outpost with our eyes turned to the age of
cattle kings and mining barons," Sawyer proclaimed, "[but] a modern, progressive state." The governor, a Democrat, had made his own notable contribution to
this development. A year earlier, Sawyer had sent a thirty-seven-person "Sell
Nevada" delegation on a three-week tour of Europe to discuss investment in
the state with business and civic leaders in six European nations. His mood was
celebratory. From 1950 to 1960, the state's population had increased from
160,000 to 285,000, giving Nevada the fastest growth rate in the nation.[19] This
growth was transforming Las Vegas into a metropolis. In 1960, 130,000 people
lived in and around the city, constituting more than a third of the state's population. Most of them enjoyed the conveniences of modern living, from decent
housing and medical facilities to an expanding education system and a vigorous
community life, as well as a rapidly expanding labor market.[20]

Tourism was at an all-time high and growing. A new convention center, one of
the nation's first facilities designed specifically for conventions and exhibitions,
hosted more than a hundred conventions with more than sixty thousand delegates
during its first year of operation. The annual tourist count in Clark County sur-
passed twelve million in 1964, when tourist spending topped $360 million, hav-
ing more than doubled in ten years. Gambling in the county that year accounted
for more than half the state's gross gaming income. Las Vegas had become the
gaming capital of Nevada, the nation, and the Western Hemisphere.[21]

Organized crime played an important role in some of these developments. In the
early 1930s, when Nevada legalized gambling, criminal gangs in the East and
Midwest were deeply involved in gambling activity as well as black-market operations that included smuggling alcohol and narcotics into the country. The gangs
were distinguished from other criminal groups by their centralized and authori-

tarian structures of control and the utter ruthlessness of their enforcement methods and mechanizations. Their crimes included intimidation, extortion, kidnapping, smuggling, robbery, and murder. Relations between the several "families" in the gangs depended on many things but often hinged on understandings between leaders, many of whom lived as ostensibly conventional businessmen and whose influence often extended into political circles and law enforcement agencies. Many of them were Italian Americans from southern Italy or Sicily, where the "Mafiosi" had extended unofficial and largely sub-rosa structures of power and patronage.[22]

By the 1950s illegal gambling in cities like New York, Chicago, and Miami had, under the patronage of such men, become a major source of income for organized crime. According to the Federal Bureau of Investigation (FBI), which monitored such activity, there were in Chicago alone more than ten thousand locations where illicit gambling took place at that time. These included underground casinos much like those operating aboveground in Nevada but, more typically, myriad smaller places all the way down to newsstands, cigar stores, and lowlife watering holes where individual "bookies" accepted bets. There, clients put money on everything from the outcome of sporting events to political elections, even on future weather conditions. Like the owners of Las Vegas casinos, the men who financed the bookies made money by calculating the odds of winning or losing bets to their advantage.[23]

As the Nevada gambling industry matured, some of the notorious personalities who operated in this underworld invested in the state's casinos. A few of them moved to Las Vegas as owners or proprietors of gambling enterprises, including hotels and later resorts, and contracted with legitimate service firms and trade unions to operate the legitimate aspects of their business. Others sent associates-in-crime to oversee the management of their properties. A few leased out the hotel side of their enterprises to independent firms like the United Hotel Company and themselves managed only their gambling casinos. The latter arrangement enabled their "skimming" operations, that is, the withholding of moneys from casino receipts before calculating a total for accounting and tax purposes. This evidently common practice of raking money "off the top" gave owners and investors a lucrative source of tax-free income and enabled them to pay off "hidden interests" in their illicit activities.[24]

The Flamingo's owners skimmed money from their casino throughout the postwar period. One of the resort's managers, Jerry Gordon, later admitted to participating in such operations and, in doing so, explained how the operations worked. Gordon and two of his associates collected money in the Flamingo's casino three times a day and added it up in a private "counting room." "My usual function was to record the amounts counted," Gordon explained. Concerned that FBI agents might be listening in on their conversations by means of a "wiretap," the men used hand signals to communicate with one another. "Where the currency was sufficient, the counter would call out an amount less than what he had actually counted and would indicate to me by hand signal the amount held out. I would record the amount on the 'stiff sheet' and the counter would give me the amount held out, usually in $100 bills, which I would put under the clipboard." Gordon then transferred the money to a safe-deposit box in the back of the cashier's cage and later gave it to owners of the resort. For his participation in the operation, Gordon said he was paid money "over and above the salary paid me and reported for income tax purposes."[25]

Authorities had difficulty knowing the extent of such activities because of their inability to infiltrate agents into the circles of individuals privy to such information and practices. "Only the most trusted employees take part in the 'first count' of receipts at which the 'skimming' takes place," an informant explained to FBI director J. Edgar Hoover.[26] Authorities even had trouble understanding how casinos worked. "The insidious nature of organized crime was not understood in the 1950s," the Las Vegas Sheriff's Department later admitted. "Few persons outside of the casinos possessed the working knowledge needed to control the cash flow and keep the operators honest."[27] No reliable estimate of the amount of gambling revenue skimmed from Las Vegas casinos in the postwar years has ever been established, but FBI agents suggested that casino owners skimmed perhaps a third of their gambling revenues.[28]

Benjamin "Bugsy" Siegel, whom the FBI linked to murder and bootlegging in New York, helped work out ways of hiding money as well as financing resort development. Siegel had moved to Southern California in the late 1930s to help associates extend their illegal gambling operations there. He first went to Las Vegas in 1941 to oversee the installation of racing wire services in cooperating casinos, services which became an essential link in nationwide betting on horseracing. Low costs and strong-armed tactics enabled Siegel and his partners to monopolize this market, and they used the monopoly to extort money from illegal bookmakers across the country. They used at least some of the extorted money to purchase a controlling interest in the Flamingo, then being constructed on the Strip just beyond El Rancho and the Last Frontier. After spending a million dollars of his own money on the construction of the Flamingo, Siegel borrowed another $3 million to finish it. He did so largely by selling blocks of stock in the Flamingo for $50,000 each. Though he miscalculated the cost of constructing the Flamingo, Siegel's method of raising capital worked. When unidentified gun-men murdered him in his Southern California residence in 1941, the Flamingo had already opened.[29]

These patterns of financing became institutionalized with the Desert Inn. The Strip's fifth resort was the progeny of Wilbur Clark, a former dealer and bar-tender on gambling boats off the coast of Southern California. By the 1940s Clark had investments in more than a dozen bars in Southern California, the earnings from which he used to purchase a share of El Rancho in Las Vegas. In 1945 he bought a large tract of land on the Strip which he envisioned as the site of his own luxury resort similar to one he had seen in Palms Springs. Clark had difficulty finding the money to build his Desert Inn until 1948, when a group of Cleveland businessmen led by Morris "Moe" Dalitz, a one-time rumrunner who had muscled his way into various "rackets" in the Midwest, lent him more than $1 million to finance his project. In return, Clark gave Dalitz's group a control-ling share in the property, thereby becoming the group's "front man," a locally respected businessman who had little control over gaming activity in the resort he ostensibly owned. Several of the Cleveland investors, including Dalitz, moved to Las Vegas in the early 1950s to oversee casino operations at the Desert Inn while employing others to run the hotel side of the enterprise.[30]

This pattern of investment, ownership, and management appeared also at the Sands, another new Strip resort. One of the original investors in this property, Charlie "Babe" Barron, was a former Chicago bookmaker with two arrests in cases involving gangland-style murders, for which he was once on the U.S. Treasury Department's list of most important criminals. He also once managed a gambling establishment, Hotel Riviera, in Havana, which federal authorities linked to orga-nized crime. The principal owner of that establishment, Meyer Lansky, another investor in the Sands, was according to the FBI a major figure in the American Mafia. Lansky had worked closely with Siegel at the Flamingo in Las Vegas and reportedly controlled gambling syndicates in Florida, Louisiana, Michigan, and other states. FBI informants linked him and other investors in the Sands in Las Vegas to illegal gambling operations in Houston, Minneapolis, Palm Springs, and St. Louis.[31]

If mob figures in Las Vegas behaved as they did in other cities, where bloody factional fighting was common, reform-minded Nevadans might once again have outlawed gambling. But men like Meyer Lansky knew the importance of appeasing the local electorate and insisted on keeping the city a relatively pleas-ant place to live. Las Vegas was what one former police officer called an "open city," where warring factions from across the country shared in the gambling industry's profits. "This was not the mob that had terrorized the cities of the East," the officer explained. "This was the mob on its best behavior. This was a mob that was careful to offend no one among the townspeople, and, in fact, made every effort to endear itself to the population."[32] If mobsters wanted to kill someone, they normally waited until the person was away from Las Vegas, as the case of "Bugsy" Siegel reveals.

♠ ♣ ♥ ♦

The ability of underworld figures to shape resort development in Las Vegas was never controlling, and it declined as legitimate lending institutions began funding casinos and resorts in the city. Local business leaders, along with Salt Lake City bankers, opened one of the city's first investment institutions, the Bank of Las Vegas, in 1955. Headed by E. Parry Thomas, a Utah Mormon and a longtime investor in Nevada real estate, the bank's initial capitalization was $250 million. Under Thomas's direction, the bank financed the construction or expansion of several resorts along the Strip, including the Desert Inn, the Dunes, the Riviera, the Sahara, and the Sands. Its profits from its Las Vegas ventures made it one of the area's largest financial institutions in the 1960s, when it changed its name to the Valley Bank of Nevada.[33]

Another important source of funding for resorts and casinos was the Teamsters Central States Pension Fund. Created in 1955 by the nation's largest trade union, which had a sizable membership in Las Vegas and Clark County, the Teamsters used the huge resources of this fund to finance enterprises that created jobs for union members. This included tourist resorts in Florida, Southern California, and other locales, including Las Vegas. The union began investing in Las Vegas in 1959, when it made a loan to Moe Dalitz and his associates to build the Sunrise Hotel. Dalitz and his partners tapped the fund again in 1960 to acquire the Fremont Hotel and the Stardust. Over the ensuing decade, the Teamsters fund helped build or improve more than a dozen of the Las Vegas area resorts, including the Aladdin, Caesars Palace, Circus Circus, the Dunes, the Four Queens, the Landmark, and the Sahara.[34]

These new capital sources, while vital to the development of the resort industry, were limited and tainted by popular as well as FBI association with organized crime.[35] In the late 1950s, a congressional investigating committee headed by Senator John McClellan of Arkansas uncovered numerous cases of corruption and political chicanery involving a number of labor unions, including the Teamsters, and the revelations led to the downfall of Teamsters' president James P. Hoffa, who had helped establish the Central States Fund. By 1967, when Hoffa went to prison for jury tampering, federal investigators had linked organized crime to the fund and concluded that criminals had used it to gain some control of casino operations at Caesars Palace, the Landmark, and the Stardust. The Teamsters had channeled suspect money into Las Vegas through the Bank of Nevada.[36]

Revelation of these developments over a number of years generated public pressure to remove the men and influences of organized crime from the Las Vegas tourist industry. This encouraged Nevada officials, if reluctantly and gradually at first, to impose regulations on the industry. In 1945 the Nevada Tax Commission assumed responsibility for licensing and taxing gambling establishments, though it lacked the power or the will to confront organized crime in the industry. This began to change in the early 1950s after federal investigators demonstrated conclusively that "skimming" operations were not only financing criminal activity in other parts of the country but cheating state and local governments of tax revenues. In 1955 the state created a Gaming Control Board to remedy this situation by acting as an investigative and enforcement branch of the Tax Commission. The continued rapid expansion of the gaming industry plus budgetary and other constraints on the board, including perhaps its own lack of assertive leadership in novel circumstances, overburdened or otherwise compromised the agency and rendered it ineffective. This failure, as well as mounting public concerns, caused the state legislature in 1959 to create the Nevada Gaming Commission with the Control Board as its investigative and enforcement arm.[37]

These agencies took increasingly effective steps to curtail the presence of criminals and criminal activities in Las Vegas tourism. They made extensive background checks on applicants for casino licenses and denied licenses to anyone with underworld ties. They also distributed a list of persons excluded from the industry, known as the "Black Book," and warned casino owners that business contacts with anyone in the book could result in the revocation of gaming licenses. In 1962 a federal court rejected challenges to the Black Book, ruling that the "good people" of Nevada were dependent on gaming and therefore justified in taking extraordinary measures to keep the undesirable individuals out of the gaming business. If Nevada gaming authorities believed individual casino owners were ignoring the Black Book, the courts ruled, the individual owner could defend his actions before the Nevada Gaming Commission, which had the power to revoke gaming licenses.[38]

Singer Frank Sinatra was one of the first to lose his gaming license as a result of this ruling. Sinatra's widely publicized fight with gaming regulators showed how Nevada was working to clean up the industry. In 1963 state gaming regulators learned that Sam Giancana, one of the men listed in the original Black Book, had recently stayed for more than a week at Sinatra's Cal Neva Lodge at Lake Tahoe. To the regulators Giancana was a mafia figure, and his presence at the lodge evidence of Sinatra's association with organized crime. Federal agents were already aware of incidents of violence at the lodge and of allegations concerning the interstate transportation of prostitutes there. Giancana's visit to Sinatra's lodge thus violated requirements the Gaming Control Board imposed on its licensees. The board therefore subpoenaed several employees of Sinatra's lodge and, on the basis of their testimony, recommended the revocation of Sinatra's gaming license. The singer quickly surrendered the license and sold his interests in gaming enterprises.[39]

Nevada regulators took other steps to fight organized crime. They standardized methods for counting casino moneys and surveilled counting rooms. They prohibited casino owners themselves from counting money. They also placed new restrictions on the activities of "junketeers" who received heavily discounted room rates from hotels in return for bringing groups of gamblers to Nevada. In concert with the Internal Revenue Service, the regulators suspected junketeers of lending money to gamblers at exorbitant rates of interest and channeling interest payments to crime families in the East. A new state licensing process helped regulators identify the junketeers' financial ties and kept some of them out of gaming.[40]

It was the threat of federal intervention that prompted the state to take these actions. Nevada officials and resort owners alike had long worried that Congress might use the linkage to organize crime to regulate or even outlaw gaming. Proposed laws to do just that had been before Congress since the early 1950s, when a congressional committee headed by Senator Estes Kefauver of Tennessee had investigated criminal activity in Nevada. The Kefauver Committee, whose hearings were broadcast nationally, proposed that the federal government shut down gambling in Nevada unless the state got rid of the criminal elements infesting it. The U.S. Supreme Court hinted at the likelihood of federal prohibition of gambling in Nevada when, in 1962, it upheld the state's right to revoke the gambling licenses of casinos owned by or otherwise connected with anyone listed in the Black Book. If Nevada failed to eliminate known criminals from its gambling industry, the Court ruled, "the federal government would be pressured to move in." If that happened, the Court continued, "licensed gambling in Nevada would come to an end with ever greater celerity than that which saw the end of polygamy in Utah."[41] By the late 1960s, after a notable investigation of mob-related activities in Nevada by the Justice Department, all opponents of federal regulation saw the necessity of cleaning up the state's gambling industry.

Whether the industry could survive such a shakeout was not clear. The men who ran casinos in Las Vegas knew as much or perhaps even more about the intricacies of operating and managing gambling enterprises than anyone else in the country. They understood how cards were "stacked," slot machines "rigged," and books "cooked." Recognizing this, Robbins Cahill, the original chairman of the Gaming Control Board, suggested that such men were "too valuable to lose" for the industry and perhaps even for the Control Board, provided the board could tap into their expertise. "They're keen businessmen, they're competitive, and they know the business," Cahill explained.[42] Other industry insiders agreed. "We couldn't learn in a lifetime what some of these 'old-timers' know almost instinctively, like when to give a high roller more credit and when to shut him off," one of them said. "No one else knows as much about running gambling operations."[43] These men were among those who had pioneered the ways of doing business that shaped the tourist industry and made it successful and, in the process, had defined the city and its economic success.

It would be inaccurate to suggest that the mob made Las Vegas what it had become by the 1960s or that there had been no "clean" businessmen in the gambling and resort business before federal officials pressured the state to rid the business of their ties to organized crime. The line between legitimate and illegitimate casino owners seems always to have been blurred. Some individuals with shadowy pasts in gambling were no doubt more businessmen than anything else, and no doubt some ostensibly legitimate businessmen had questionable or even mob connections. The two groups coexisted in Las Vegas with little evident friction, and both contributed to the development of the tourist industry and thus to the city. Many aboveboard entrepreneurs and developers had deep understandings of even arcane aspects of gambling, from table games to horseracing. Like "first movers" in other industries, they had goals of their own and the desire and resources to realize them. At a time when gaming was an open market in which individuals with limited resources could invest, they saw opportunities and seized them. Business acumen and personal connections were critical to their success. They forged partnerships with one another, and worked closely with political, civic, and union leaders to promote their own interests and the interests of their industry. They often relied on relatives to make their enterprises, most of them small, function successfully. They dealt with workers and unions as they had to. Gambling was a risky business. The turnover among owners and managers in the gambling industry in the early postwar years was perhaps as high as the turnover among low-skilled employees.

Sam Boyd, who came to control three major downtown resorts, was evidently an entrepreneur without ties to organized crime. Boyd entered the gaming industry in the early 1930s, running bingo games on a ship off the coast of California. He moved to Las Vegas during World War II, as a penny roulette dealer in a small downtown casino. After the war he became a "pit boss" at El Rancho and then at the Thunderbird, supervising the work of dealers and other casino workers. In 1952, at the age of forty-two, Boyd became an owner of the Sahara, a new Strip property, investing $6,000 of his own money and another $10,000 borrowed from a friend. He worked as a "shift boss" in the casino there for five years before purchasing 3 percent of the new Mint Hotel downtown, where he soon became vice president and general manager.[44] Like many other men in the industry whose careers paralleled his own, Boyd was a workaholic. "His day would usually start with a function around 7 a.m.," one of his secretaries later recalled. "Then he'd work till 3 p.m., maybe go home or take a nap for an hour, or just rest on the sofa in his office, then shower and change clothes and work until two or three in the morning. He'd sleep for a couple more hours, then start his day again." Boyd kept this schedule seven days a week, "and thought everyone else should too." By the 1970s, Boyd had investments in two additional downtown resorts, the Union Plaza and the California Hotel.[45]

Mel Exber and Jackie Gaughan, longtime business partners, were others who began with limited resources and became successful through hard work and resourceful management. The two men came to know each other in the late 1940s through sports betting. Exber, who then managed a sports book in Las Vegas, took bets from Gaughan, who lived in Omaha, Nebraska. The men worked together after Gaughan moved to Las Vegas in the 1950s, and in 1961 they pooled their resources to buy the Las Vegas Club, a shuttered downtown casino once run by L. B. "Benny" Binion, a gambler who also owned the nearby Horseshoe Club. To turn the property into a successful business, Exber and Gaughan put in race and sports books, introduced table games like faro, and raised betting limits. "We dealt the highest limit craps in town," Exber recalled. "Ten cents to a thousand dollars."[46] They also opened a small restaurant, its walls plastered with caricatures of major league baseball players. "It drew in people with kids," Exber said of the caricaturing. The men also curried favor with townsfolk through such well-publicized activities as purchasing Girl Scout cookies and distributing them to the public. Their resourcefulness and success enabled them to buy additional downtown establishments, including the Union Plaza and El Cortez.[47]

Such entrepreneurs turned Las Vegas into an entertainment Mecca. As early as the 1930s, gambling clubs began booking nationally known entertainers such as Judy Garland, who performed at the Meadows Club shortly after it opened. By the 1940s, live entertainment had become a regular attraction at the resorts. Pianist and comedian Jimmy Durante performed at the Flamingo when the hotel opened, and other popular entertainers followed him, including Abbot and Costello, the Andrews Sisters, Pearl Bailey, and Xavier Cugat.[48] Jacob "Jake" Kozloff, a Pennsylvania brewer who purchased the Last Frontier in 1951, showcased such performers as Liberace, Sammy Davis Jr., Nat "King" Cole, and Lena Horne. Such stars added glamour to the emerging marvel already called "Vegas!"[49]

Jack Entratter, one of the original investors in the Sands, played a vital role in this development. Part owner of the Copacabana Nightclub in New York, Entratter moved to the Sands when it opened in 1952 and, by featuring such stars as Martin and Lewis, Paul Anka, and Frank Sinatra, made the Sands a major venue for Las Vegas entertainment. He coaxed such entertainers to perform through multiyear contracts at high pay. He also hired some of the nation's best songwriters, among them Jule Styne, Sammy Cahn, and Jimmy Van Heusen, to write original music for his productions. A dozen or so "Copa Girls," whom Entratter billed as "the most beautiful girls in the world," appeared on stage with the entertainers.[50] Like baseball caricatures at the Las Vegas Club, the girls helped offset the image of Las Vegas as "Sin City." They were young, under twenty-three years of age, and had what the Sands called a "wholesome" look. All were new in show business, which helped sustain an image of innocence to match their beauty.[51] Like other Strip properties, the Sands made its showgirls a centerpiece of its marketing campaigns, featuring photos of the "girls" in advertisements across the country. The eroticized photos caught the attention of female as well as male readers, helping to cement the public image of Las Vegas as well as the Sands as one of glamour and excitement.[52]

Warren Bayley, who opened his Hacienda Hotel at the southern end of the Strip in 1956, was equally innovative. Bayley had run a company with investments in several California hotels, but he saw himself as a "country boy" and shaped the Hacienda in his own image. The resort was cozier and more family-friendly than other Strip properties. Its hotel rooms were better furnished and decorated than those of its competitors. Its swimming pool, shaped like the letter Z, was Nevada's largest; its night-lighted golf course was unique in Nevada, as was its miniature racetrack around which children drove "pee-wee" race cars. Bayley's management strategy, described on the cover of Hacienda matchbooks, was to do "everything possible" for his guests. "It is our pleasure to be of service," the matchbooks read. This was the "Hacienda Way." It was also what Las Vegas resorts were increasingly offering tourists and gamblers.[53]

The Hacienda's marketing campaigns were impressive as well as representative. The resort offered some of the industry's first "packaged" vacation plans. A basic "Hacienda Holiday" included a deluxe room for $16 a night and $10 in poker chips. More expensive plans not only included these bargains but added tours of Las Vegas and environs, via chartered bus, airplane, and/or helicopter, as the tourist chose. The Hacienda's general manager, Richard Taylor, came up with an especially innovative promotional stunt after being denied permission to erect a billboard advertising the Hacienda at a major highway intersection where cars heading to Las Vegas from Bakersfield, California, merged with those traveling to the same destination from Los Angeles. Taylor paid two attractive cocktail waitresses to stand at another intersection on the highway where traffic stopped because of a construction project and distribute coupons for free drinks at the Hacienda. One man who received a coupon later testified to the effectiveness of the campaign, which lasted more than a year. "Coming upon a pretty girl in western tights and tassels is something of a surprise," he said, "especially when she starts moving toward your car."[54]

The opening of Jay Sarno's Caesars Palace in 1966 marked another milestone in the evolution of the ownership and management of Las Vegas resorts. Sarno was a building contractor who in the 1950s had used money borrowed from the Teamsters pension fund to build a motel chain in the southeastern United States. With still more money from the Teamsters and several business partners, Sarno built Caesars Palace with such architectural flair as to make the resort itself a tourist attraction foreshadowing a later major feature of Las Vegas tourism. Caesars featured an egged-shaped casino surrounded by Romanesque fountains and statues that included a mammoth inside frieze depicting the Roman battle at Etruscan Hills and an oversized floating lounge called Cleopatra's Barge. In one of its five restaurants, "wine goddesses" massaged male diners as they ate, while its main showroom, the eight-hundred-seat Circus Maximus, was a miniature of the Roman Colosseum. The hotel itself, a fourteen-story, crescent-shaped Greco-Roman structure, was similarly eye-catching.[55] The immediate success of Caesars Palace led Sarno soon thereafter to borrow still more money from the Teamsters to open another spectacular property on the Strip across from the Riviera, which he named Circus Circus. Its tent-shaped casino included carnival games, sideshows, and a baby elephant, Tanya, who pulled the handle of a giant slot machine.[56]

Such places made resorts much more than hotels with gambling facilities. When tourists stepped into them, they entered a world of make-believe, of relaxation and diversion, whose regnant values and permissible behaviors were new to middle-class Americans. Everything in sight seemed to mock traditional values. The atmosphere itself spurned bourgeois social conformities even to the point of ridiculing the prudence and moral constraints most Americans used to contour their social lives and public deeds. The aura itself encouraged people to squander money by creating a setting in which squandering was more fun than frugality, an environment that challenged social conventionality and even traditional norms of personal modesty and that privileged indulgence over restraint. In short, Las Vegas entrepreneurs created a breathing space in the American world in which ingrained habits and values could be questioned and, if one were not careful, loosened and even suspended. This was perhaps the entrepreneurs' most significant accomplishment. They turned Las Vegas into the ultimate destination for adult entertainment.[57]

Basic changes in American culture assisted this effort. Social and political developments in the 1960s transformed popular mores and values in ways that validated the accomplishment just noted. Popular culture became more tolerant of casual dress and relaxed codes of public discourse and activities, which in turn permeated public entertainment. Proponents of women's liberation promoted relaxed standards of social and sexual behavior, while comedians and other entertainers, many of them African Americans, helped further loosen the standards of permissible public speech. By the early 1970s, as George Carlin noted in one of his famous comedy routines, there were only seven "dirty" words a person could not say on the public airwaves. Las Vegas's special contribution to these developments was to transform gambling—heretofore variously illegal, sinful, or antisocial behavior—into gaming, an acceptable social diversion.[58]

The shift in control of gambling casinos from entrepreneurs and men associated with organized crime to publicly traded corporations facilitated this transformation. Before the 1960s, the closest example to a modern corporation involving itself in Las Vegas gaming was perhaps Warren Bayley's ownership and management of the Hacienda Hotel. Bayley raised capital to build the Hacienda through Standard Motels, one of the first publicly owned motel and hotel chains in the nation, of which he was chairman of the board. However, while Standard Motels owned and operated the Hacienda Hotel, Bayley and a few close business associates owned and operated the hotel's casino.[59] Del Webb, a businessman who made his fortune in construction, entered the gaming business in a similar way. In 1960, the year stock in the Del Webb Corporation was first publicly traded, the corporation built the Sahara Hotel for associates of Alfred Winter (who once ran an illegal gambling operation in Portland, Oregon). A year later, Webb's company purchased and operated the Sahara and subsequently invested in the Thunderbird, the Mint, and the Lucky Club.[60]

Corporate investment in gaming was at this point impossible because Nevada law required the Gaming Control Board to investigate anyone with any investment in the industry for ties to organized crime. Because the state interpreted that requirement to include anyone who owned any stock in a licensed gaming corporation, it functioned to keep modern corporations out of the industry. The Gaming Control Board could not possibly run background checks on all stockholders in such corporations, even if the stockholders agreed to be investigated. Warren Bayley and Del Webb had circumvented this requirement by creating subsidiaries of their own to own and operate gaming operations in their hotels. Only men who qualified for gaming licenses invested in these subsidiaries.[61]

By 1966, when Republican Paul Laxalt became governor, many Nevada officials, including Laxalt, recognized that the state's regulatory system had not only failed to exclude men with "mob" connections from the Las Vegas gaming industry but functioned to deter investment in the industry by corporations. The result of this recognition was passage of two corporate gaming acts by the state legislature in 1967 and 1969. The acts amended the state's gaming codes by opening the industry to the capital resources of American business enterprise. They accomplished this by limiting the requirement for background investigations of corporate stockholders to those who owned more than 5 percent of a corporation applying for a gaming license. The legislation, which Laxalt called the "salvation of Nevada gaming," opened the door to corporate ownership of gaming properties because the capital resources of major national corporations dwarfed those of "mobsters," thus putting the latter at a distinct competitive disadvantage. No individuals or syndicate in the underworld could match the financial resources of any such corporation. Once corporations with access to national capital markets began purchasing gaming casinos, often at inflated prices, "mobsters" began disappearing from the industry.[62]

Howard Hughes, the son of an inventor and businessman who made a fortune in oil and toolmaking, played a symbolic role in the resulting revolution in the ownership and control of Las Vegas gaming. Hughes began investing in mining and real estate in Nevada before he moved to Las Vegas in 1966. On

Thanksgiving evening of that year, the reclusive billionaire slipped into Las Vegas and moved into a suite on the top floor of the Desert Inn, a property long associated with organized crime. Cloistered there, he presently applied for a gaming license to buy the property. Governor Laxalt, whose election Hughes had supported, endorsed the application, seeing Hughes as a business leader whose investments and charities would promote the state and its economy.[63] His application approved, Hughes bought five Strip properties over the next three years—the Desert Inn, the Sands, the Castaways, the Silver Slipper, and the Frontier. He also tried to buy Caesars Palace, the Stardust, and other resorts, but the federal government blocked his effort on the grounds that the purchases would give him a monopoly on lodging in Las Vegas. He nonetheless added the thirty-one-story Landmark Hotel to his empire in 1969, by which time Hughes controlled about a seventh of Nevada's gaming revenue, including a quarter of all revenue generated on the Strip.[64]

Hughes's entrance into the resort industry had long-term implications. Hughes was different from other men who invested in Las Vegas gaming. He not only had access to far more capital than any of the others but had no ties to organized crime and a positive public image. For all his eccentricities, he was a respectable, enterprising entrepreneur whom the press described variously as a "gentleman," a "genius," even a "hero." Because of this image and his vast wealth, his purchases of Las Vegas casinos enhanced the glamour as well as the legitimacy of the gaming business itself. By 1970, when he moved from Las Vegas to the Bahamas, he had a reputation as the man who had chased the "mob" out of Las Vegas. The image was undeserved, but as his business partner Robert Maheu said, Hughes did try to "clean up" Las Vegas. The fact that he purchased resorts long associated with organized crime, Maheu explained, was part of that effort. Hughes managed his properties through his Hughes Tool Company, a Houston-based corporation with extensive holdings in aerospace and airlines, the top executives of which were major operators in national and international enterprises.[65]

Conrad Hilton and his son Barron played a similar though less overwhelming role in the advent of corporate control in Las Vegas. Conrad Hilton, founder of Hilton Hotels, was a respected businessman who had built his first luxury hotel in Dallas, Texas, in 1925. Shortly after World War II, he formed the public corporation that still bears his name, the first hotel firm listed on the New York Stock Exchange. By the time Hughes began investing in Southern Nevada, the corporation owned upscale hotels across the nation, including properties in the Caribbean with large casinos. The son became chief executive officer of the company in 1966 and was one of the men who urged Nevada officials to reform the state's gaming laws. In 1970 the corporation purchased a controlling interest in the International Hotel, a huge, modern Y-shaped property that had recently opened east of the Strip, as well as the older Flamingo, and two years later it took full control of those properties. Like Webb and Hughes, the Hiltons lent a new aura of respectability to the gaming industry, and soon other large corporations began investing in Las Vegas, among them Holiday Inn, Hyatt Corporation, and Ramada Inn.[66]

The entry of these high-profile national chains into Las Vegas consolidated the public impression that the area's gambling establishments were now entirely legitimate enterprises offering equally legitimate leisure experiences to growing hordes of American tourists. Of course, a number of independently owned resorts remained, but they too adopted corporate forms of organization and operation and continued under the control of local businessmen whose stock was closely held. Incorporation offered such men access to new capital and limited their financial liabilities in case of failure. It also prevented the death or whims of individual owners from forcing the dissolution of the firm. Once they adopted the corporate form, owners of these small enterprises sold only enough stock to raise sufficient capital to enable them to renovate and expand their properties to the extent necessary to survive the competition from national chains. Individual owners of these places often maintained operational control of their incorporated properties by owning enough of their stock to do so.[67]

Steve Wynn exemplified the continuing importance of these individual entrepreneurs. Wynn owned part of the Frontier Hotel before Howard Hughes bought it and began buying stock in the Golden Nugget when its shares became available to public investors in the late 1960s. Wynn became a member of the Nugget's corporate office in 1973, by which time he owned 5 percent of the resort's stock. He continued to purchase the stock and used the resulting leverage to become president and chief executive officer of the resort. By the time he owned 13 percent of the company, he raised money to remodel the Nugget's casino and add a tower of hotel rooms. His strategies paid off handsomely. From 1972 to 1976, pretax profits at the Golden Nugget jumped from $1 million to $7.5 million. The increase reflected Wynn's entrepreneurial talents as well as the ability of independent resorts to cope with changing conditions in the industry prompted by the entry of national corporations.[68]

With the triumph of the corporation, ownership and management of the resort industry increasingly resembled those of other American industries. Management became concentrated in the hands of corporate officers elected and responsible to stockholders. Corporate leaders focused not on daily operations but on long-term policy and planning and on the bottom line of profitability. Barron Hilton's description of his own role in company affairs underscores the point. "I'm not involved in the day-to-day operations of our hotels," Hilton told public officials in these years; "I monitor the profit and loss statements of the hotel." Unlike earlier investors in Las Vegas, Hilton took what he called a "truly long-term outlook." "We are not now and never have been seekers of the quick return," he explained.[69] Men like Hilton were attuned to rationalizing practices that enhanced efficiency and profitability. Advised by financial and legal staffs, they employed nationwide marketing strategies, streamlined accounting, auditing, and money-handling procedures, and systems for extending credit to gamblers.[70] They also developed and applied systematic personnel and employment policies. In the words of Jack Pieper, general manager of Howard Hughes's Frontier, the advent of corporate control introduced "updated management-by-objective techniques." Those techniques, Pieper said, enabled him to manage the Frontier "in an orderly and organized manner with carefully defined parameters of predictability and control."[71]

A day in the life of Henri Lewin, a vice-president of the Hilton Corporation in these years, typified these patterns. Lewin, who had worked in the lodging industry for more than a quarter century, had the responsibility of overseeing hotel operations in nearly a dozen Hilton resorts spread over California, Oregon, and other western states. From his office in the Las Vegas Hilton, Lewin scrutinized all aspects of hotel services.[72] "I must know every single thing," he told a journalist when describing the scope of his activities, "I must be involved at every level."[73] Like leaders at other large corporations, Lewin demanded frequent reports from every department head and supervisor he oversaw. He enforced scores of administrative rules and regulations, including one that dictated that every letter he received be answered the same day. He telephoned the managers of the properties he oversaw, often three or four times a workday, which typically began at seven o'clock in the morning and might not end until midnight. Lewin's chief concerns were profitability, long-term planning, and handling complaints from those above and below him in the corporate chain of command. He looked for ways to improve all aspects of resort operations and wanted the best of everything for the public as well as the corporation he thought of himself as serving. "If Elvis Presley is the best star, then I have to hire him for your entertainment," Lewin explained. "If the oldest elevator makes the best elevator, then I must get it."[74]

The reorganization of the Hughes Las Vegas holdings in these years epitomized the transformed resort industry in which Henri Lewin operated. In 1972 Hughes sold his oil and toolmaking business, in which he had built his fortune, and created the Summa Corporation to house his remaining investments, which included not only resorts and additional real estate in Southern Nevada but an airline and other businesses. Hughes had little to do with the operation of Summa, which he left to a five-member board of directors and its executive officers. Like Lewin and his peers and supervisors at Hilton, these few men controlled a giant, profit-oriented corporate structure. Summa was then the largest owner of Las Vegas gaming and resort properties. Each of its score of resorts generated millions of dollars in annual revenue, for a combined total of more than $1 billion a year, which amounted to perhaps three-quarters of the income for all properties on the Strip.[75]

The management of other large resorts, such as the new MGM Grand at Flamingo Road on the Strip, also epitomized the new patterns in the management of the Las Vegas gaming business. When it opened in 1973, the MGM advertised itself as the world's largest hotel. The resort itself encompassed 2.5 million square feet of covered space and cost $160 million to build. It was part of a business empire run by Kirk Kerkorian, who made his fortune in the airline industry. Kerkorian financed the construction by creating his own publicly traded corporation, which he funded in part by selling his interests in the Flamingo and the International. Like the International, the MGM was a Y-shaped structure with three towers of rooms with views of the city and the surrounding desert. Its casino housed a thousand slot machines and a hundred gaming tables. Its main showroom sat nine hundred people, and its seven kitchens could serve thirty thousand meals a day. There were also swimming pools, tennis courts, and a spa. The resort employed forty-five hundred people, more than twice as many as the average resort in the area.[76]

The MGM also pioneered new changes in resort management in Las Vegas. Its management structure was even more structured than those of Summa or Hilton, consisting as it did of a board of seven corporate officers, nine "senior directors," and fifty-seven lower-level managers and supervisors. The lines of authority and communication between these levels were minutely detailed, as were the responsibilities of each position. The duties of the nine senior directors illustrate the pattern. One director managed separate departments of purchasing, engineering, warehousing, and security, each of which had its own manager and cadre of supervisors. Another director was in charge of promotion, advertising, and public relations; and still another oversaw personnel policies. A food and beverage director was responsible for the management of all restaurants, banquet rooms, and room service. Other directors dealt with convention sales, hotel operations, entertainment, and casino operations. The director of casino operations administered the work of two dozen subordinate supervisors, from card room supervisors and credit department managers to the head of the slot department.[77]

MGM personnel policies were thus as minutely specified as any in the industry. When the resort hired a new employee, it gave him or her a pamphlet signed by President Alvin Benedict, which spelled out management's "objectives and philosophy." Though designed to instill a sense of confidence and trust in management, employees likely read it from a perspective of their own. Many no doubt recognized the pamphlet's subliminal message and purpose. It defined employees as "subordinates" with "potential" who should work according to rules. "You will be attending sessions on company familiarization," the pamphlet explained. "You will be given a list of rules that contain your responsibilities regarding conduct of work." The handout told employees they were part of a "family," though they were unlikely to be on family terms with managers above their immediate supervisor. "It is impossible at this point in time to introduce you personally to each officer and senior department head," the pamphlet read, "but you should be able to recognize them and know their positions when you see them." To help with that, the handout included photographs of each of the resort's corporate officers and senior directors.[78]

Other passages in the pamphlet reflected management's concern to "rationalize" the workplace. Despite the differences of social being between labor and management, the pamphlet suggested that workers and employers shared similar interests in making the MGM a success. "The secret of a successful organization is teamwork, where people work together for common interests and goals," the pamphlet explained. Employees would receive competitive wages and job security "insofar as practicable." "Exceptional achievement" on the part of employees would result in "positive personal recognition." In the language of the new era of affirmative action, employees were assured that race and gender were "never factors in employment," a statement that might equally have been read cynically, with traditional patterns of discrimination in mind, or hopefully, with the efforts just then underway in the industry to rectify those patterns. Read either way on this sensitive matter, the pamphlet displayed the impersonal face of management in the new age of corporate control of the Las Vegas tourist business.[79]

By 1975 Las Vegas had become "Fun City." Its promoters no longer promoted it as a refuge for seekers of gambling, booze, and "broads"; it was instead a vacation destination for families, with something for everyone from five to ninety-five. This was a purposeful change designed by new corporate interests to appeal to middle Americans, including women and children. Las Vegas and its leisure-based economy had matured. About 300,000 people now lived in and around the city, which upwards of ten million tourists visited annually. The local economy in and out of the gaming and resort business was booming. "Everywhere you look," the president of the Chamber of Commerce said, "Las Vegas is expanding up and out, bulging and straining to keep up with the demands."[80] Industrial development was phenomenal. In less than a generation, the informalities and human scale of traditional forms of business enterprise had given way to large-scale rationalization and bureaucratization. The period of this profound transition was so brief that thousands of workers experienced the whole of it.[81]

Working in Las Vegas

It is tempting to view service workers as unskilled, often transient laborers, who have little or no influence over their work experiences and even less impact on larger economic matters. While much of the work in Las Vegas resorts did in fact involve tedious, repetitive tasks for low wages by low-skilled employees, the overall picture of work in resorts was much more varied and interesting than that scenario allows. A great deal of it was in fact challenging, skilled, and remunerative. Even the jobs of many resort workers who performed "menial" tasks were vital to the success of the resort industry. In addition, many of these workers performed tasks that required training, dexterity, and experience. The evidence is convincing that people in both of these categories saw their jobs in terms more positive than negative given the circumstances of their lives. Many showed commitment to and interest in their work. More than a few, including workers at the bottom of the job hierarchy, considered themselves participants in a larger-than-life enterprise capped at the top by the dazzling wealth, glamour, and extravagance of Las Vegas tourism and entertainment.

This is an episode, an experience, difficult to locate in the conventionalities of American labor history. Resort workers in Las Vegas were largely service workers, but they were certainly not apathetic about matters relating to their wages, workplace circumstance, or social being; nor were they passive players in the history of their industry. Most of them belonged to relatively strong trade unions that won them meaningful pay raises and increasing job security through the period of this study. Generally the unions were democratic and pragmatic, and some of their leaders had influence in state and local politics. The unions also had considerable control over the local labor force. Although they were autonomous organizations at the local level, they had of necessity to work with each other as well as their own national organizations. Their success depended on their ability to confront realistically the economic and institutional challenges they faced.

♠   ♣   ♥   ♦

Through the postwar years, Las Vegas hotels and casinos employed more than a quarter of the local workforce. In 1955, for example, about 8,000 of the area's 30,000 wage earners worked in hotels and casinos, and some 6,000 of those in the ten largest resorts on the Strip.[1] Twenty years later, hotels and casinos employed about 40,000 of the area's 150,000 wage earners, concentrated in increasingly large resorts. In 1975 the Desert Inn and the Sahara each employed about 1,200 people and Caesars Palace more than 2,000, while the mammoth MGM Grand employed 4,500, more workers than all manufacturing firms in the area combined. By 1973 the annual payrolls of hotels and casinos in and around Las Vegas amounted to more than $300 million.[2]

With their sizable workforces, the resorts offered guests an astonishing variety of services, from pedicures and rubdowns to banking and security. They housed them, entertained them, wined and dined them, and transported them; and the most lavish of them otherwise sought to satisfy their every need and whim. To illustrate the scale of all this, the Las Vegas Hilton included three towers of hotel rooms, a thirty-thousand-square-foot casino, multiple bars and lounges, a two-thousand-seat showroom, a "legitimate" theater, a dance hall, and an outdoor recreation area with badminton and tennis courts, table tennis, swimming pools, health spa, golf driving range, and an eighteen-hole golf course. It also included six restaurants and a large coffee shop, as well as clothing stores and souvenir shops and other retail outlets.[3]

There were four general categories of wage employees in resorts, the lines between which were loose and overlapping. The first category consisted of professional and semiprofessional people, who had training and often considerable experience in jobs that demanded administrative or technological knowledge and creativity as well as the ability to work with other people. A few of them, such as executive chefs and orchestra leaders, received individually negotiated salaries and supervised the work of other employees, though in the employment hierarchy they were well below the circle of executives who managed the resorts. A second, larger category included white-collar workers—secretaries, clerks, and switchboard operators, whose jobs required technical training, tact, and judgment and who had varying degrees of autonomy and independence in the execution of their tasks. A third and still-larger category incorporated blue-collar workers, who typically worked outdoors tending gardens, or parking cars, for example, or indoors repairing slot machines, operating surveillance systems, or guarding property.[4]

The fourth and largest category of employees encompassed workers who had direct contact with customers—bartenders and wait people, for example, and casino dealers, luggage handlers, and housekeepers. Though jobs in this category were relatively low skilled and involved little individual innovativeness, even the most menial required some skill and initiative. Workers who dealt directly with customers or guests had to deliver services dependably, correctly, and courteously. Moreover, they had to project an image that reinforced management's ideas of what attracted customers to Las Vegas. Employees must smile and speak courteously while accommodating customers' every demand and need.[5]

Resorts had house rules regulating the appearance and demeanor of employees who dealt with customers. The Landmark Hotel, for example, required its security guards to keep their uniforms "clean and neatly pressed," and their shoes or boots "highly polished." It permitted them short mustaches but no beards or goatees, and required them to keep their hair "clean and neatly trimmed." The guards must also "maintain vigilance and alertness at all time," which meant keeping their hands out of their pockets and minimizing interaction with guests and other employees. Conversations in the workplace must be "impersonal"; and off-the-job guards must maintain a good image: the Landmark, for example, required them to conduct their private affairs "in such a manner as to cause no derogatory reflection on the Landmark's Hotel or the Security Department."[6]

The variety of occupations in resorts makes it difficult to speak generally about resort workers, but some conclusions seem evident. In the postwar years, most hotel and casino workers were newcomers to Las Vegas and to the types of work they did. They were also disproportionately young, male, and white, and in all of these characteristics they mirrored patterns in the state's workforce. According to census reports, a third of Nevada's population in 1960 had lived outside the state five years earlier, and the state as a whole had proportionately more young and middle-aged adults than the nation as a whole. About a third of recent arrivals came from California and another third from Texas and elsewhere in the Southwest. A quarter or so had lived east of the Mississippi River, and many of the rest were from the Northern Plains. The ratio of men to women in the state's workforce was about two to one, and most workers held relatively low-skilled and low-paying jobs.[7] Turnover in the job market was consequently high, especially in the resort industry. In areas of employment like kitchen work and housekeeping, resorts often replaced more than a fifth of their workforce annually. The turnover problem was even greater in the field of security, where some resorts replaced more than a third of their workforce annually. Because this lack of stability in security could compromise services, it was a constant source of concern for management.[8]

Both custom and law segmented the labor market. The best jobs—those involving power, authority, creativity, or high pay—were almost invariably reserved for white men. Public ordinances barred women from working as bartenders and dealers in the city limits, and attitudes and customs discouraged them from applying—or being considered by union stewards—for those and other male-dominated jobs along the Strip. By custom as well as preference, resorts restricted African Americans, who accounted for about 9 percent of Clark Countians in the early 1960s and 15 percent of the city population, to work in areas of housekeeping and cleaning.

These patterns reflected those in the larger society. Businesses in all industries discriminated against women and minorities before the civil rights laws of the 1960s had an effect. Until then, racial segregation was the rule in all aspects of life in Las Vegas. Resorts generally refused to accept black guests, many of them prominently displaying signs with some variation of the words, "No colored trade solicited." Those that did accept black guests limited their numbers and excluded them from their dining, gambling, and swimming facilities.[9]

The persistence of discrimination reflected the strength of social custom as well as racism in Las Vegas and its resort industry. Racial equality was not part of the image resorts sought to project. If they thought about it at all, it was probably to fear that desegregation would drive away white customers. Owners and managers did not really know the racial views of their customers, but they were no doubt correct in assuming that their views were those conventional among white Americans in the 1950s and early 1960s. Those views, of course, discouraged any thought of racial equality.

Although wageworkers who began at the bottom of the wage scale in Las Vegas resorts rose to the ranks of well-paying positions no more frequently than did their counterparts in other similar industries, they did change jobs and even job classifications often, not least because of the rapid growth of the industry and thus of job openings in it. Bellhops became bell captains; busboys became banquet servers; and blackjack dealers became pit bosses. Similarly, change girls became head clerks, and hairdressers heads of wardrobe departments. Dissatisfied, disgruntled, or venturesome employees seem often to have moved to a newly opened resort down the street or on the Strip. In the unionized workforce, employers hired workers according to collective bargaining agreements, which encouraged continuity and promotions. The agreements required management to hire union workers and give preference to experienced applicants. Promotions kept employees in the same area of employment and involved modest pay hikes. In 1970 employees in housekeeping departments in the resorts earned $15 to $22 a day regardless of their responsibilities, and those in dining room services $15 to $25.[10]

Because many early Las Vegas entrepreneurs were Italian Americans or Jewish Americans, it might have been the case that men of Italian and Jewish ancestry had better chances of moving up the occupational ladder from the 1930s to the 1950s than did those of other ethnicities. Men in these groups were probably disproportionately involved in illegal gambling in the East, and their skills and personal connections helped at least some of them secure employment and investment opportunities in those years in Las Vegas. Once that occurred, they turned to experienced and trusted friends to help build their enterprises. It was thus no coincidence that a disproportionate share of casino bosses, showroom captains, maitre d's, and other midlevel managers, as well as dealers, had Italian or Jewish surnames before and after 1950. So, too, did many entertainers. Italian American singers and entertainers were popular across the country in those years, but the prevalence of their names on marquees along the Strip suggests a certain degree of ethnic favoring. Like the *padrones* who employed Italian migrant laborers in turn-of-the-century Chicago and New York, the men who pioneered gambling in Las Vegas privileged their own ethnic groups.[11]

The service-oriented nature of resort work safeguarded employees from some of the dislocations workers in manufacturing began facing in the 1960s and 1970s, when new technologies simplified or eliminated jobs, or when the onset of globalization began "outsourcing" manufacturing jobs overseas. Even musicians, whose jobs across the country had been rendered superfluous in theaters and other venues by the introduction of new recording technologies, continued to have steady work in Las Vegas. Yet work patterns in resorts were never static, and technological changes there did indeed simplify many jobs and thus reduce skill levels. New automated beverage dispensers that released premeasured amounts of liquor, for example, simplified the tasks of bartenders, just as dishwashing machines, microwave ovens, and prepackaged meals affected the skill levels necessary for kitchen work.

♠ ♣ ♥ ♦

Recollections of employees reveal some of the variety in these patterns. They also indicate something of the nature and structure of the workforce and of workers' attitudes toward their jobs. Many of the reminiscing workers were new-comers who sought work in Las Vegas in the postwar years, and perhaps excite-ment too. This was especially true of workers in the field of entertainment.

The memories of Mark Massagli, who was for years a lounge musician in Las Vegas before becoming a union leader in the mid-1960s, illustrate this pattern. Massagli grew up in Southern California, where he learned to play the upright bass. In 1957, when he was twenty-one, he moved to Las Vegas as a member of the Hank Penny Band. The city made an immediate, positive impression on him. "Boy, I thought, what a wonderful place," he recalled, "a musician working in Las Vegas, all this glamour and glitter and music everywhere."[12] After a while, Mas-sagli left the Penny band to work for the Sawyer Sisters, who performed at major properties along the Strip. Job opportunities for musicians, Massagli recalled, were plentiful. In addition to orchestra musicians who accompanied headline acts in principal showrooms, or supported stars or acts in production shows, hundreds of musicians like Massagli worked in casino or hotel lounges. "There used to be three or four hundred jobs in lounges," he remembered. "They would have entertainment that would start like at ten in the morning and go until four in the morning. That would leave them six hours to clean up the lounge . . . and it would start all over again, seven days a week." At a time when a loaf of bread cost about a quarter and soft drinks were a dime, Massagli earned nearly $200 a week.[13]

Denise Miller's experience paralleled Massagli's. Miller was a professional dancer who moved to Las Vegas at midcentury at age eighteen to work at the Fla-mingo. She had earlier worked as a dancer in Chicago before moving to Los An-geles, only to find her career floundering there. "I was starving to death in Los Angeles," she recalled. "I had decided to work as a secretary but I couldn't make a living." A chance to work at the Flamingo was therefore appealing: "I was offered a job to come to Las Vegas, and I snatched at it because it was twice the pay that I was making as a secretary." The city impressed her instantly. "When I found Las Vegas," she recollected, "I thought I found paradise. It was a little town that had the hotels so I could work at my trade. I really thought I had found heaven." Miller worked six weeks at the Flamingo and then a year at the Last Frontier with the

Katherine Duffy Dancers. When the producer moved the group to the Thunderbird, Miller went along and worked there more than a year.[14]

Her work required dedication and long hours. Miller worked two shows a night six nights a week, and spent countless daytime hours rehearsing. The Duffy Dancers changed their routines every few weeks, which meant Miller often rehearsed "all day" and danced at night. "A new set of muscles were always hurting," she recounted. Dancers had to learn new routines quickly and show versatility in performing them. "We danced to everything imaginable," Miller said. "You had to do a can-can one week and a true ballet dance the following week. You had to be able to do a minstrel show, work a tambourine, beat a snare drum, work on roller skates, rubber balls, and jump rope through hoops." Miller took pride in her work and enjoyed it. "I wouldn't have traded it for anything," she said. Unfortunately, jobs like Miller's were for the young only; Miller's dance career lasted less than a decade.[15]

Reminiscences of Julie Menard, who worked as a showgirl at the Tropicana in these years, breathed a similar excitement and commitment to work, and spoke to the relevance of gender in the workplace. The gender typing of some jobs worked to the advantage of young women like Menard. Showgirls were not professionals by any traditional definition. Most of them did little more than trip across the stage in highly choreographed patterns while scantily and revealingly clad. Their presence lent beauty and glamour to shows and thus to the tourist's Las Vegas experience. Showgirls were young, in their late teens or twenties, tall, nice looking, and white. The only African American showgirls in Las Vegas in these years worked at a short-lived resort named the Moulin Rouge, northwest of the railroad station in the predominantly black section of Las Vegas.[16]

Menard moved to Las Vegas from Los Angeles in 1964, at the age of twenty-one. She had studied modeling, had a striking profile (nearly six feet tall, long blond hair, and size 38D brassiere), and quickly landed a job in the "Folies Bergere." This was a fast-paced dance show featuring more than a dozen "girls" in sequined bikinis and feathered headpieces. She typically performed two shows a night, for six nights a week, for which she earned about $200 a week. Her job was more difficult than audiences imagined. She had to wear uncomfortably high heels and a tall, cumbersome headdress, and to get from her dressing room to her backstage position, she had to climb up a steep, potentially dangerous ladder. On stage, she had to walk down another steep staircase without handrails, with extended arms and eyes on the audience. She nonetheless liked the job, as did most showgirls. "A lot of it was a lot of fun," Menard recalled. "You're like a celebrity." Indeed, showgirls were often treated as such. Casino managers gave them money to wander through the crowds and gamble after the show, and let them keep their winnings. "We were treated well, everything was nice," Menard recalled.[17]

Hundreds of women had less glamorous jobs in the resort industry as wardrobe workers. Every large resort employed a dozen or more seamstresses and costume makers, even those that purchased ready-made costumes from outside sources. These skilled women worked in rooms directly behind the stage, fitting or repairing or decorating costumes with sequins, rhinestones, or other trim. As the occasion demanded, they also redesigned costumes, turning long gowns into short ones, for example, or changing plantation outfits into western wear. They also made emergency repairs during shows, replacing elastic in tights, perhaps, or replacing zippers. Wardrobe workers also helped dress performers for shows and assisted them with quick changes of clothing during performances. Some of these showtime assistants worked in dressing rooms near the stage, others in designated spots where they met entertainers coming off stage. The latter especially worked on rigid time schedules that they rehearsed with the casts of the shows. In the rehearsals, they learned to follow designated "cues" that signaled the onset of their tasks. They often had additional duties as makeup artists and hairdressers, for example.[18]

The reflections of Mae Burke, a longtime time head wardrobe mistress at the Tropicana, show the patterns of employment among such workers and offer an example of a worker's success story in Las Vegas. Burke moved to the city from Buffalo, New York, after the war, with no thought of a career in wardrobing. Trained as a nurse, Burke could also sew, and through friends found a part-time job as a wardrobe worker at El Rancho. She later took a similar job at the Royal Nevada and then at the Tropicana when it opened in 1957. There, she began taking on supervisory responsibilities and eventually became head of the wardrobing department. In the latter capacity, she worked five nights and an afternoon or two a week, earning about 50 percent more than each of the twenty employees she supervised. Before each nightly show, Burke checked costumes and assigned workers to positions offstage. She oversaw the workers during performances, assisting or reassigning them as needed. After each show, she inventoried the wardrobe, and ordered repairs or supplies as necessary. In addition, she prepared work schedules, distributed payroll checks, and dealt with grievances. Her biggest challenge, she later recalled, was a problem endemic to supervisors in all the resorts—dealing with the rapid turnover in her workforce. "When there's a change in the cast," she explained, "we alter costumes. Then we buy new shoes. There's a constant turnover—it's quite a chore to keep up with changes in the cast."[19]

Stagehands were another skilled group of entertainment employees. Their tasks were to prepare sets for showrooms, operate equipment during performances, and "strike" sets for later performances. Set construction entailed carpentry, the most important skill involved in the craft, and occasionally welding skills, if the construction of stage props involved steel. Lighted sets required the skills of electricians. Less-skilled stagehands hung curtains to rise and fall from "fly lofts" or roll quickly off stage. Others operated spotlights, soundboards, special effects equipment, and a variety of other devices, including video and motion picture equipment, to create whatever effects the show at hand necessitated. Like orchestra musicians in resorts, they typically worked six nights a week, for which they earned perhaps $250 to $300 a week in the late 1960s.[20]

Joe Moll, a stagehand at the Sands in these years, recounted the story of his long-term employment in the industry. Moll moved to Las Vegas from California in 1952, after a stint in the Air Force. He had studied electrical engineering and worked as a movie projectionist, which enabled him to get a job at the Sands operating sound and lighting equipment, from which he moved into positions of greater responsibility. Still at the Sands twenty-five years later, Moll was then head of the stagehands department. When a local newspaper ran a story commemorating his long tenure at the resort, Moll emphasized the positive aspects of his own work and that of his fellow stagehands. "It's always been a well paid profession," he explained. His routines were interesting and challenging. "I haven't been bored one day in the whole time," he said. "It's a challenging, exciting job," he added. "Shows change frequently, and even if the incoming act is one you've worked with for ten years, his show is always different."[21]

The life of Virgil Kist further highlights the abilities, ambitions, and mobility of workers in this category. Kist grew up on a farm in Iowa and joined the Ringling Brothers Circus as a teenager in the 1930s. He had learned mechanical skills on the farm and then how to "rig" and "strike" stages in the circus. After serving in the army during World War II, he sought work as a stagehand in New York, without luck. He relocated to Las Vegas in 1960 and found steady work there as a stagehand. By the mid-1970s he had worked at various resorts on the Strip, including the Thunderbird, the Desert Inn, the Tropicana, and the Dunes, in such varied capacities as rigger, carpenter, welder, and electrician. One of his sons, Dennis, remembered his father as one who "could do a little of everything." The fact that Virgil Kist had a wife and five children to support partly explained his willingness to take on all jobs.[22]

♠ ♣ ♥ ♦

Workers' recollections about other sectors of employment are equally revealing. Many of the industry's employees worked in fast-paced casinos, where to some of them the excitement seemed never to stop. In 1970 major resorts along the Strip employed between one hundred and two hundred dealers. They operated card or dice games, such as poker, twenty-one, baccarat, or craps; spun roulette wheels; or ran bingo games. Still others were keno writers or took bets on sporting events.[23] Each of these activities involved its own expertise and even language, and the rapid pace required experience, concentration, and swift execution. In a single hour, a dealer might make hundreds of mathematical calculations while relying on tools unique to each game, such as sticks, markers, and buttons and dice.[24] In the early 1970s, dealers were still overwhelmingly white men. The only black dealers in Las Vegas at that time worked in gambling clubs in the "colored" section of town.

The story of Marvin Vallone illustrates these patterns. Vallone, an Italian American from New York, learned to play table games as a child. "We used to shoot craps behind the store, and play cards," he reminisced. Vallone moved to Las Vegas in 1956 to get away from cold weather. "When I came here in the winter time and there was no snow and no rain, I said this is where I wanted to live," he recalled. "I really like it." Married with children when he moved to the city, Vallone rented a two-bedroom apartment in Las Vegas and, with help from a relative who already lived in the city, found a job as a "shill" at the Boulder Club downtown. For $8 a day, he sat at a gaming table making bets with house money, acting the part of an involved gambler in order to attract other gamblers. When business was slow, other employees taught him the finer points of casino games. "When there was nothing to do," he recalled, "they would give you a chance to break-in. They would teach you." This break-in system was mutually beneficial. It provided management cheap labor and workers job training.[25]

The training set Vallone on his career path, which ultimately enabled him to achieve middle-class living standards. In 1958 he became a craps dealer at the Horseshoe, earning $25 a day in wages, plus gratuities. Two years later, he moved to the Showboat, where the tips were better, and where he made "$30 to $35 a day." A former supervisor from the Boulder Club hired him at the Tropicana in 1966, where "tokes," as tips were known, averaged about $50 a day. Though Vallone remembered that wages and working conditions at the Tropicana were "excellent," he nonetheless moved to Caesars Palace the following year. By 1973, when he moved to the new MGM Grand, Vallone had been in gaming for more than fifteen years and had seen his income rise steadily; by then he owned his own home with a swimming pool. This outcome was the result not only of Vallone's work and skills but of the rapid growth of the resort industry and the attendant availability of good jobs for experienced workers at ever-increasing wages. It seems that Vallone's success was typical for reliable workers who persisted in the resort industry after acquiring the skills the industry needed and rewarded.[26]

Yvonne Mattes, a switchboard operator at the Sands in these years, suggested that workers in less exhilarating jobs could also find their work satisfying, that they too saw something exciting about working in Las Vegas. Mattes arrived from Bakersfield, California, in 1962, after her husband accepted a job with the Las Vegas Police Department. Her experience as a telephone operator at Edwards Air Force Base in California helped her get a similar job at the Mint Hotel downtown. After a few months there, she moved to the Sands, where she received a "big jump" in pay to $18 a shift. Mattes remembered working in ten-woman crews, six of whom answered incoming calls while three handled show reservations and the other one made wake-up calls. Mattes rejected the notion that work at the switchboard was low skilled or uninteresting. "Everybody thinks operators are stupid, but it's not true," she said. "It's mind-boggling what they have to know, what they have to remember." Among those bits of information were requests from hotel guests, seating arrangements in showrooms, and directions in and around Las Vegas. One of her major challenges was to stay calm when dealing with angry or demanding callers. "We had to lie sometimes," Mattes recalled, "if people said to say they weren't there. We always had to be nice." Mattes had no complaints about the work. "I liked my job, really liked it," she said. "It was never boring." One source of excitement, she remembered, was talking to personalities like Dean Martin and Frank Sinatra. "I liked seeing them."[27]

Workers in food and beverage services generally recalled their work in less enthusiastic terms, yet their attitudes about working in Las Vegas varied widely. Cary Petersen, who moved to Las Vegas from Chicago, offered testimony about a general pattern in which jobs were readily available. Petersen began working as a busboy at the Union Plaza, at the age of fifteen, but he soon became a dishwasher and "worked his way up" into the ranks of cooks. He learned new cooking skills on the job, by watching others. "I started watching the cooks," he later explained. "They gave me a chance to get in the pantry. It was right next to the egg station and this guy taught me how to do eggs, how to flip them." "Little by little," Petersen learned the tasks of a broiler chef, for which he earned more money. He found the work challenging, even exciting at times. "I always thought cooking was kinda neat," he later said, "not boring."[28]

Jeanne Mead's memories of her work as a waitress in the city suggest something similar. Mead, with several years of experience as a waitress, moved to Las

Vegas from Colorado in 1956. As a single mother of two, Mead needed a job immediately. She found one in a downtown coffee shop. "I went to the union not long after I came to town, and I got a job that day," she remembered. It was a "non-stop" job, however, and Mead found the constant work tiring. Within a year, she moved to the new Hacienda Hotel on the Strip, where she felt "more relaxed." "I liked it from the start," she said of the job, "I liked it very much." Tips were better at the Hacienda, and the "atmosphere" was too. The dining room in which Mead worked overlooked a swimming pool and a garden, which made her work environment "very pleasant." She also liked the owners of the Hacienda, Warren and Judy Bayley, whom she remembered as "fair" and "kind." "I got along well with management," she recalled.[29]

Other food and beverage servers were more critical of their jobs and supervisors. Overbearing managers and difficult co-workers seem to have been numerous in this area of work, though there is no way to quantify that observation. Waiting was typically busy and stressful work, and wait people were usually exhausted at the end of their shifts, from aching backs or feet, if not from dealing with demanding customers or supervisors or uncooperative co-workers. They had little time to be friendly with customers, or to provide them with the kind of service many guests expected. They often worked without breaks, either from concern for customers or co-workers or from fear of falling behind in their work. Cocktail waitresses often had to wear uncomfortable or skimpy costumes and deal with groping or rowdy customers. "I'm sick and tired of being pinched like a tomato," one of them complained. Some waitresses developed strategies to ward off such attention. "The first thing I did when I got my first job was to buy a wedding ring," one of them recalled. "Nothing would cool a pass quicker than to wave that band before a guy and tell him my man's a security guard."[30] Another longtime waiter summed up his attitude about waiting when he advised young co-workers to quit their jobs. "Get your education and get out," he warned, "because you get stuck in this business if you don't."[31]

The recollections of Alma Whitney, a housekeeper at the Desert Inn for thirty-five years, spoke to the challenge of working the jobs low-skilled workers were obliged to take. Whitney was an African American who thus faced special challenges in Las Vegas, where most housekeepers in the industry were blacks. Whitney moved to Las Vegas from Tallulah, Louisiana, in 1952, at the age of sixteen. Like many other African Americans, she left family and friends to find a better life. "I had a little girl," she explained, "and I came [to Las Vegas] to work, so I could help support her." She traveled to Las Vegas in the automobile of a man who made his living driving poor black southerners to jobs in other parts of the country, stopping only for gas. "At that time, you couldn't stop, no place, you know, not blacks," Whitney explained.[32] The grueling, three-day trip was one small sign of the problems African Americans faced in the age of segregation.

In Las Vegas, Whitney found a job as a maid at a motel off the Strip. Six months later she got work at the Desert Inn. At both places, she was responsible for cleaning about a dozen rooms a day, six days a week. She thought the workload reasonable, but cleaning windows and tubs was difficult. "I had a glass that went from wall to wall and from floor to ceiling," she remembered. "You got a great big tub that you had to get in and try to do," she added. Whitney's difficulties varied with the habits of hotel guests. Guests who left their rooms a mess created problems for housekeepers. "Some of those people leave those rooms in a hell of a fix," Whitney explained. "Some of them, you'd almost hate to go in them." Children presented special problems. Not only did they often leave messes to be cleaned up, but they slept on roll-away beds which had to be stripped, folded, and put outside for porters to carry away. "I would hate for summer to come, when they come up with those kids." It was "pretty rough," she said of her job.[33]

Like other resort workers, Whitney saw gaming and related activities as her own means of realizing the American dream. Her ardor and perseverance reflected her personal ambitions, which grew out of her background and family obligations. She viewed her job in Las Vegas against the backdrop of her previous hopeless poverty in Louisiana. She had been accustomed to physical work but not to steady wages or job benefits. A job that offered those advantages was a veritable boon to her. Las Vegas thus represented opportunity, a way of making it for herself and her child. That might not have seemed like much to most Americans then or now, but the perspective that mattered most for understanding Whitney's situation was hers, not ours. The same might be said of the Italian American Marvin Vallone, who was willing to take an $8-a-day job as a shill to begin his journey of "making it" in Las Vegas on the way to a comfortable middle-class lifestyle. For Whitney no less than Vallone, the life story as it relates to employment in the Las Vegas resort industry was a marvelous success story.

Security employees were among the most essential workers in resorts. Their chief concern was thievery, the opportunity for which was everywhere. A million dollars in cash might pass daily through a sizable resort casino, some of it literally spilling on the floor around slot machines. Resorts invested heavily in security, against armed bandits as well as individuals trying to rig casino games or tamper with slot machines. Employee theft was also a large and constant problem. Workers who handled cash, luggage, and other valuable property had chances to help themselves to what they handled, and when they did so, they harmed their employers.

The size and structure of security forces varied from place to place. Most resorts employed a security chief and provided him a staff of assistants and uniformed guards. At the Aladdin in 1973, for example, a chief and his lieutenant had responsibility for policing the resort and enforcing security policies. They were assisted by three sergeants and sixteen guards. The sergeants were middle managers or foremen in the security operation, assigning guards to posts and moving them around as necessary. They also evaluated the work of guards in written reports that commented on, among other items, their reliability and skills. Sergeants lacked the authority to fire guards, but they could suspend them pending investigation by the chief. Sergeants also delegated responsibilities to experienced and trusted guards. These "shift leaders" made sure guards manned their posts and handled incidents properly.[34]

The duties of guards at resorts included patrolling designated areas. Patrols often worked in teams of two, walking in opposite directions from one other, while guards usually worked alone. After responding to "incidents," both wrote brief reports, or completed standard forms answering prepared questions. Every on-duty security person had the power to detain unruly or violent guests and guests suspected of illegal behavior. Most detentions involved individuals who had been "drinking to excess" or were "obviously drunk." Each resort also assigned guards to entrances at which employees reported for work and punched time clocks. These "time keepers" protected the clocks and punch cards and prevented nonemployees from using the entrance. They also inspected the bags of departing employees to prevent the stealing of resort property. The area in which these guards worked was the "time office," which also served as home base for security workers. There, their supervisors had offices, their work schedules were posted, and they encountered each other at the beginning and ending of shifts. Like security guards in other service industries, they wore uniforms issued by employers, including identification badges and handcuffs, but not firearms, which the guards themselves furnished according to employer specifications.[35]

The backgrounds of security guards varied considerably. Resorts preferred experienced workers, but sometimes settled for whomever they could get. A few guards at the Four Queens in these years had previously worked in security at other resorts; prior experience in security work for most of them, however, was at such places as airports and retail stores. Some had been police officers outside Las Vegas, and a few had been military police. Several had no experience in the field. Frequent turnover of security employees, which in some resorts exceeded

50 percent annually, threatened and even compromised security services and was a constant source of anxiety for management officials. Low levels of pay largely accounted for the turnover problem. Sergeants and guards made little more than the minimum wage.[36]

After interviewing George Rahas, director of security at the Sahara in the 1970s, a local journalist in Las Vegas concluded that security work at the resort was difficult and complex. Officers at the Sahara, he found, patrolled more than twenty-seven acres of land, the site of a one-thousand-room hotel, dozens of hallways and stairwells, and a popular casino that never closed. According to Rahas, it took experienced, well-trained officers to keep the Sahara safe. "We hire only ex-police officers for our security force," he explained in the article. "If an applicant has been trained as a policeman, we can give him the other training necessary for hotel and gaming security." The additional training was in areas of public safety and assistance specific to resorts and in the operation of the resort's televised surveillance systems. It also included training in how to recognize cheating scams involving electronic devices, special counters, and dishonest dealers and how to detect suspicious persons and behavior. Rahas maintained a file on more than thirty-five hundred people who had in the past threatened, or who might in the future threaten, the well-being of the resort, including car thieves, pimps, and prostitutes as well as gambling cheats. "We add eighty photos and descriptions a month," said Rahas, whose own background reflected the experience and skills necessary for his position. Before moving to Las Vegas, Rahas had attended Brooklyn Law School, served in the U.S. Army intelligence in Germany, and worked as a federal narcotics agent in New York City.[37]

The introduction of new surveillance systems demonstrated how technological innovations could affect work routines as well as the balance of power between labor and management. In the postwar years, security employees generally detected theft in casinos by observing dealers and gamblers, often from "catwalks" in casino ceilings. By the 1970s, however, security employees worked in surveillance monitoring rooms, where they operated "smart" cameras which they glided along ceiling rails and "zoomed-in" on suspicious activity or on workers or players suspected of cheating. When the employees saw something suspicious, they switched on machines to film the event and record the conversations of participants. The installation, operation, and maintenance of such equipment significantly increased the skill requirements for security personnel while they eliminated the jobs of many traditional security workers. The new equipment not only helped employers identify dishonest dealers but enhanced their ability to supervise and evaluate other employees. Management used the equipment to detect employees who performed poorly and to improve work routines. As resorts grew in size, management committed more and more resources to these systems. The surveillance of work therefore increased, especially in casinos, which had the most comprehensive surveillance equipment. The days when "bosses" ruled casinos gave way to an era of technological oversight.[38]

♠　♣　♥　♦

There is little evidence to suggest that resort workers came to Las Vegas with a sense of group consciousness, but most joined trade unions once they were there. Unions have had a relatively strong and successful presence in Las Vegas since the early twentieth century, when the Union Pacific Railroad set up repair shops and supply yards just north of downtown. During construction of Hoover Dam in the 1930s, several unions in the building trades organized local affiliates and created circumstances in which other unions could thrive. By midcentury, Las Vegas was a "union town," and a few unions were well established in the resorts, representing workers in every major occupational category except casino dealing and security.[39] By the 1970s, about two-thirds of the area's resort workers belonged to unions, including such diverse groups as bartenders, desk clerks, maids, musicians, stagehands, waiters, and waitresses.

Most of the unions were craft based, that is, they included employees in a single occupational group or craft. They were also generally affiliates of national unions and subordinate to the nationals in various ways. The local unions were democratic to the extent that their effective operating heads were elected, and administrative functions were in the hands of people responsible to the elected head. Members had opportunities to influence policy making in business meetings and through strike-authorization votes. In all areas of employment where employees were unionized, workers were required to join the union and pay their dues to secure employment and maintain their jobs. Participation in union meetings was typically low. Top officials in the unions in the postwar period were experienced craftsmen who had worked their way up through the union hierarchy. All of them were salaried and had staffs of salaried assistants. The most powerful individual in each union was typically the secretary-treasurer, who usually held office for an extended period of time, not the president, a largely honorary official. The secretary-treasurer oversaw the administration of union business and had traditionally headed the collective bargaining team. By the 1970s, however, the chief union negotiators had become union lawyers.

Like the union members they represented, Las Vegas labor leaders were not Marxists bent on transforming capitalist relations of production in the resort industry. Instead, they were practical-minded men of affairs who wanted a bigger piece of the capitalist pie for themselves and the workers they represented. "Our chief long-range goal," as one of them said, "is to improve the wages, hours and working conditions of our members and organize the unorganized wherever they may be."[40] As long as the real income of union members improved and their circumstances in the workplace were tolerable, these men gave employers a free hand in other aspects of management. In collective bargaining, in other words, jobs, wages, and benefits trumped liberal concerns about industrial democracy, gender and racial equality, and other social reforms. When the Vietnam War became the most controversial issue in domestic affairs, union leaders in Las Vegas had little to say about it, at least in public, or about American foreign policy generally, or antiwar protest. Many, perhaps most of them, had served in the armed forces during World War II, and that experience no doubt modeled their ideas about the nation and patriotism. Positions of union leadership were caps on their careers, not platforms from which they sought to reform the nation or the world.

Union leaders operated within the constraints of federal law and bureaucracy. They benefited from provisions of the National Labor Relations Act of 1935, which required employers to recognize legitimately established unions and bargain with them in good faith. That act created the National Labor Relations Board (NLRB), a generally union-friendly bureaucracy, to enforce its provisions. The Taft-Hartley Act of 1948 restricted some of the union-friendly provisions of the earlier act. Among other things, it outlawed spur-of-the-moment "wildcat" strikes and made it easier for employers to restrict picketing activity during strikes and to decertify established unions. The act also declared arbitration the "most de-sirable" method for settling workplace disputes, a process that often benefited unions. During World War II, the federal government established rules for arbitrating labor disputes, recognized groups of arbitrators to settle them, and made their findings binding on parties to an arbitrated dispute. After the war, arbitrators developed their own professional association and code of ethics and made their services available to employers and unions across the country. In the period of this study, labor and management in the Las Vegas resort industry routinely relied on arbitration to resolve a wide range of disagreements over everything from collective bargaining itself to the meaning of the language in contracts already in effect.

A major source of union power in postwar America was the ability to control the labor supply, at least in unionized locales. In Las Vegas, unions found vari-ous ways to do that. Some limited the number of people who could train locally for certain jobs, and required experienced workers who moved to Las Vegas to wait out "transfer periods," during which time they could not accept full-time unionized jobs. In most states, unions also controlled the labor supply by establishing "closed shops," that is, by requiring employers to hire only union members. In Nevada, however, voters approved a right-to-work initiative in 1952, which outlawed that practice. Specifically, the initiative prohibited labor organizations and their officers from compelling people to join a union or to strike against their will, and it prevented employers from discriminating against non-union workers in hiring. The Taft-Hartley Act of 1948 had earlier imposed restrictions on the closed shop and permitted states to impose additional restrictions. By 1952 more than a dozen states had done so in so-called right-to-work laws, either by statute or by constitutional amendment.[41]

The right-to-work movement amounted to a public and political backlash against the gains organized labor had made under the New Deal in the 1930s, and against the costly wave of strikes that afflicted American industry in 1945–46. In Nevada, however, the movement was chiefly an effort to restrain labor costs and a means of attracting new businesses to the state. It began not in Las Vegas but in Reno, where in the late 1940s business and civic leaders invoked the language and tactics of open-shop advocates to resist union organizing efforts in the warehousing and tourist industries. They called unions "coercive," "un-American" institutions that raised wages above their "natural" levels and thus discouraged business development.[42] The movement gained momentum after July 4, 1949, when unions in Reno struck local restaurants and hotels at the height of the tourist season. The strike, which lasted six days, ended in a settlement that brought tourism workers higher wages and benefits but convinced many residents that unions harmed the public interest. In the aftermath of the strike, business and community leaders in Reno formed the Nevada Citizens Committee to circulate petitions for a ballot initiative to outlaw the closed shop. Narrowly, voters approved the initiative in 1952 and rejected referenda to repeal it in 1954 and 1956. Unions abandoned the effort to repeal the law in 1958, when Nevada made it more difficult to put initiatives on the ballot.[43]

Over the years, the right-to-work law was a source of political acrimony that had little effect on the Las Vegas resort industry. By 1952 resort owners there already recognized and dealt with the unions that represented most of their employees. They also hired most of their workers through union hiring halls, a practice that amounted to a closed shop. Owners continued this practice after the state outlawed compulsory union membership, not just to placate the unions but because it was an effective way of finding new workers in their rapidly expanding industry. Job seekers established their qualifications and joined the appropriate union at the hiring halls, and union agents referred qualified workers to employers who requested them. In this process, the agents seem to have functioned as screeners for management. They had no incentive to recommend unqualified applicants or otherwise disturb the working relationships they had with industry managers. In return, employers agreed to hire union members and pay them union wages and benefits. In this regard, labor and management were partners in the rapidly expanding resort industry in Las Vegas.[44]

The unions' chief source of power in the industry was their ability to stop work, which explains why employers cooperated with them in such areas as hiring practices. Work stoppages always hurt the industry, but they were dangerous weapons and often harmful to workers as well. Neither labor nor management ever desired a strike; but each on occasion concluded that a strike was the lesser of the evil choices it believed it faced. Though strikes were always about money matters first, they usually also involved fundamental concerns of workers' rights and management prerogatives. Threats to strike were basic parts of collective bargaining and typically occurred in the late stages of bargaining, just before labor contracts expired. In this process, both sides played bluffing games, and, more often than not, one side effectively called the other's bluff and a work stoppage was averted. When that was not the case, it was because union leaders, with the approval of union members by secret ballot in widely publicized elections, concluded that a strike was necessary. National unions, which helped provide strike benefits to workers, also usually approved the strike.[45]

Union strength also derived from the services unions provided their members. By the 1960s in the Las Vegas resort industry, these services included health and welfare programs to which employers contributed. The programs provided medical services, retirement pensions, and life or disability insurance. They also offered a host of lesser services, from counseling and legal assistance to low-interest loans and special credit card rates. Union headquarters sometimes served as centers of social activity where workers met new friends. During work stoppages, the headquarters became gathering places where union leaders disseminated information and set up rudimentary child-care and picketer-care centers as well as "strike kitchens."

The Clark County Central Labor Council oversaw union activity in and around Las Vegas. The council included representatives of every major union in the county and functioned to encourage labor solidarity and joint union activity. It had no executive authority over affiliated unions and no role in collective bargaining; it did, however, sanction strikes and encourage its affiliates to honor the picket lines of striking workers. The council also had political and educational functions, endorsing political candidates who supported organized labor, and training union representatives in contract negotiations and labor law.[46] In doing so, the council cooperated with the Nevada State Federation of Labor. The federation's annual conventions provided opportunities for resort workers and their unions to air their problems and concerns. Unions in the building trades generally dominated the federation, especially in the early postwar years, though those in the resort industry became more influential over the period of this study. The federation served primarily to keep member unions abreast of legislative bills affecting organized labor and identifying political candidates friendly to labor.[47]

Service workers constitute a diverse and complex group of workers, and their jobs are likewise complex and varied. Intricate patterns lay behind their work in Las Vegas tourism. Their skills varied as did the demands and rewards of their work. The rapid turnover among them suggests that work, especially perhaps among women, was less central to their lives than other things such as family. Work was for most a necessity but for some a choice. And among the choices many of the workers made was where to work. The lure of one of the nation's fastest-growing and most fascinating cities, and of work in one of its most expansive and distinctive industries, cannot be gainsaid in explaining the story of work in Las Vegas in the period of this study. "People was very encouraged to come to Las Vegas cause it was somewhere to come to," a former maid in the industry recalled. "Las Vegas was hopping, you hear me?"[48]

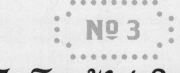

The First Work Stoppages

For more than two decades after World War II, when Las Vegas resorts operated as proprietorships or small partnerships, employers and unions enjoyed generally amicable relationships. Employers offered union workers steady pay raises, increasing job security, and expanding benefits in return for labor peace. By the late 1960s and early 1970s the corporate form of ownership was rapidly displacing proprietorships and partnerships, and as that transformation occurred, new patterns in industrial relations emerged. Outlooks on both sides of the workplace also began to change. Corporate employers soon organized a vigorous trade association to advance their mutual interests and took increasingly aggressive and calculating stances in collective bargaining. In response, workers and unions had to fight with unaccustomed assiduity to protect and improve what they already had in wages and benefits and to preserve important prerogatives in the workplace. The results of the rising tensions and antagonisms in these circumstances were the first strikes in the Las Vegas resort industry.

The timing of the first strikes reflected not only structural changes in the Las Vegas resort industry but also larger patterns of change in American economic life. In the postwar years after 1946–47, union workers across the country negotiated long-term contracts that meaningfully boosted income and encouraged a sense of security and well-being among them. Though the ups and downs of business cycles were periodically troubling, industrial relations remained relatively harmonious. Strikes were typically short and peaceful and seldom took a heavy toll on workers. By the late 1960s, however, changing economic and political realities began to threaten this equilibrium to the disadvantage of union workers. Established understandings in collective bargaining, what historians call postwar "social accords," began to break down. Work environments and bargaining processes turned volatile. In the 1970s and 1980s, work stoppages often hurt workers materially and emotionally. These trends even affected the story of labor relations in "boom towns" like Las Vegas.

♠ ♣ ♥ ♦

In postwar Las Vegas, when places like the Sands and the Stardust opened on the Strip, resort owners and their employees interacted in a workplace that was relatively relaxed and free of systematic tensions. The basic circumstance of their interaction was familiar enough. Owners wanted to maximize profits without generating labor disputes; and employees wanted higher wages, as much say-so as they could get in the workplace, and job security. Both groups had measures of control over the work process, which they used to whatever advantages they could get. The situation varied from resort to resort, but everywhere compromise typically trumped conflict, and most resorts were relatively free of structured workplace tensions.

Management systems and attitudes largely explained this situation. Though owners delegated the day-to-day supervision of wage earners to salaried assistants, they often came into contact with employees. Whenever they did, they tended to act more like paternal figures than profit-minded businessmen. Though some were more accessible than others, most knew the names of their longtime employees, even the names of their spouses and children. Like southern textile owners of an earlier day, many of whom were looked up to by their employees as tolerable paternalists, resort owners in postwar Las Vegas treated wage earners in human rather than categorical terms. They asked employees about their health and family life, gave them flowers or other tokens of personal concern on special occasions, and might hand out Christmas-time bonuses or certificates for things like hams and turkeys. "It all depends on how long you had worked there," one former maid at the Desert Inn explained of the Christmas presents. "Some of us who had worked there about two or three weeks, they would give us between $25 and $50 bonus, and some of them that had been there longer, they got more," she recalled. "I had enough I could get my kids all their toys."[1] Though attitudes toward individual employees depended on a wide range of circumstances, the divide between owners and workers was muted by acts of paternal concern that workers appreciated.

The recollections of Jeanne Mead, a former waitress at the Hacienda illustrate this sense of intimacy and paternalism. They also suggest that workers appreciated this style of management. "When the Bayleys had the Hacienda it was a real nice place to work," Mead said of Warren Bayley and his wife Judy (who ran the resort for several years after her husband died in 1964). "They were beautiful people to work for," Mead recalled. "If you were sick they sent flowers. If you had a sick child or something they might inquire about him. You felt that they cared and consequently you wanted to do your best for them too." "It was a family-like hotel," she added.[2] Mead's perspective on management showed the kind of give-and-take that often characterized the postwar work environment. It revealed how employers could lift the spirit and morale of their employees by simple and inexpensive acts of concern and, in doing so, enhance a feeling of fealty toward themselves. "I had pride in the hotel," Mead recalled.[3] Owners like the Bayleys were not distant stockholders who knew little of the day-to-day operations of the resorts they owned or what employment in their resorts meant in personal terms to the mass of people who worked for them.

Owners also generally understood what mattered to local union leaders, whom they also knew personally and with whom they maintained good business-like relations. Every year or two, union representatives met with individual property owners to hammer out details of labor agreements, which dealt in a straightforward fashion with wages, hiring, and workplace concerns. The parties typically began by resolving nonmoney issues, chiefly relating to the rules of work; then addressed fringe benefits, which as cost items were then still of secondary importance; and, finally, wages. At that point management calculated the costs of proposed changes in work rules, job benefits, and wage increases. When these items were agreed upon orally, the negotiations ended with a handshake, and the two sides wrote up and signed a written and official version of what they had agreed upon.

Negotiations between resort owners and Local 226 of the Hotel Employees and Restaurant Employees International Union (HERE), popularly known as "the Culinary" and hereafter referred to by that name in this study, typically set collective bargaining patterns in the industry. The Culinary was then and is now the largest organization of Las Vegas resort workers. Established in 1938, this local quickly became the area's most powerful union. In the 1960s it had more than ten thousand members and roughly twice that number ten years later.[4] Unlike unions of hotel and restaurant workers elsewhere, the Culinary included not only kitchen workers, narrowly defined, but housekeepers, bellmen, banquet servers, cocktail waitresses, and other "front-of-the-house" workers as well. It was, then, an industrial rather than a craft union, which accounts for its size. It organized and bargained for occupational groups that were relatively low skilled and low paid. The union had close ties with Local 165 of the Bartenders and Beverage Dispensers Union, a much smaller organization, including joint bargaining arrangements.[5]

A strike by the Culinary could shut down resorts. With workers in smaller unions, such as those of musicians or stagehands, owners might operate on a limited or temporary basis when they struck, but not without the people in the Culinary. Owners therefore tried to resolve issues with this union first and then finalized their agreements with the smaller organizations on the basis of guidelines agreed to by the Culinary. The Culinary always insisted that owners provide those organizations wage hikes and benefits comparable to those it agreed to for its own members, and the potential of a sympathy strike by the big union encouraged the owners to do so. Though Taft-Hartley prohibited unions themselves from calling sympathy strikes, language in union contracts often permitted individual members of unions to consult their conscience on whether to cross the picket lines of other workers. This "picket line clause" strengthened in vital ways the bargaining power of unions in Las Vegas, for it enabled union negotiators to threaten a general strike whenever bargaining broke down.[6]

The strength of the Culinary in the postwar period can be attributed not only to its size but also to the effectiveness of Elmer "Al" Bramlet, who headed the union from 1954 until his untimely death in 1977. Bramlet shared the working-class background of the men and women his union represented. Raised on a small farm in Arkansas, he worked first as a dishwasher in Joliet, Illinois, and then served in the navy during World War II. After his discharge, Bramlet settled in Los Angeles, where he bartended and then served as a business agent for the local bartenders union. In 1946 the union sent him to Las Vegas to help the Culinary. Over the following decade, he worked tirelessly to increase that union's membership. He even made recruiting trips through southern and southwestern towns, recruiting hundreds of workers into diners, restaurants, and other eateries in Las Vegas, where they found jobs that paid more than they had ever earned. Bramlet drove many of them to Las Vegas himself, directly to the Culinary's hiring hall. For such dedication, in 1954 he became secretary-treasurer of the union, a post he held until his death.[7]

Bramlet was less committed to a political agenda than, say, Cesar Chavez or Walter Reuther, other prominent labor leaders of the time; nonetheless, for more than two decades, he furthered the careers of labor-friendly politicians in Nevada. He served as an adviser to key figures in the state's Democratic Party, including Governor Mike O'Callaghan, who held office from 1971 to 1978. His union's endorsement could influence electoral results and thus further the interests of workers and unions. In the words of Berkeley Bunker, a congressman and then senator from Nevada, Bramlet was one of the most powerful people in the state. "If you have his backing, you have a lot of votes, because Al Bramlet is a very, very formidable political figure."[8] As Bunker recognized, political relationships were especially important in the state's gaming industry because so many public officials had a say-so in its oversight. Bramlet could and often did use political connections to strengthen his union's hand at the bargaining table.

In 1956 owners of nearly a dozen Strip properties formed the Nevada Industrial Council to bargain with Bramlet and other union leaders. The council hired Roy B. Flippin, a retired army colonel, to head the council and lead its bargaining team. Flippin had little experience in bargaining or indeed in labor relations. He was a "cowboy" who bred Arabian horses and ran a riding stable outside Las Vegas. He had, however, been chief negotiator since 1948 for the Southern Nevada Employers Association, a diverse group of proprietors in such tourist-related businesses as restaurants, commercial cleaners, and food and beverage distributors. Despite the potential for confrontation in his new position, Flippin conducted his office and his duties in such a way that labor leaders in the Las Vegas tourist industry soon came to respect him for his conduct in bargaining sessions. He was "straight-talking" and "very laid back," one of them recalled.[9]

The 1957 contract between the council and the Culinary illustrated the continued straightforwardness of bargaining after Flippin's appointment. The contract was five pages in length. In it, the resorts recognized the participating unions as the "sole collective bargaining agency" for their members and pledged to hire workers through union hiring halls. Employers could hire "outside of the Union" only when the latter failed to provide "satisfactory" job applicants within a fixed period of time. The contract specified wages and working conditions for more than forty occupational groups, from dishwashers and chefs to cocktail waitresses and powder room maids. It also spelled out disciplinary and grievance procedures and stipulated that eight hours constituted a day's work, and six eight-hour shifts a week's work. Employees working such shifts were entitled to three meals a day at the employer's expense, the last meal coming at the end of the shift. The contract also required employers to contribute $5.10 a month per employee to the union's health and welfare funds, and gave nonstriking workers the right to honor picket lines sanctioned by the Clark County Central Labor Council.[10]

Union leaders later recalled the ease and straightforwardness of contractual negotiations in the years of Flippin's service. They recalled casual negotiating sessions with Flippin and other members of his Industrial Council, in which bargaining parties settled differences in informal conversations of give-and-take.

Mark Massagli of the musicians' union, which had been chartered by the American Federation of Musicians in 1931, described this bargaining process as "very easy." "We sat down with the guys who could make a deal," he remembered, "guys" typically anxious to make a deal. "In two hours you'd have an agreement," he recalled.[11] Dick Thomas of the Teamsters had similar recollections. "When I first got into the hotel business," Thomas explained, "our contract was six pages . . . with maybe five or six articles." "There were only a handful of people to do business with in those days, and you knew them all." Thomas typically met informally with Roy Flippin three or four times before signing a contract on behalf of the Teamsters but never had serious problems resolving differences with the group Flippin represented. "There was nothing you couldn't figure out a way to solve," he later explained. Thomas attributed this straightforwardness and success to employers' acceptance of trade unions and of the legitimacy of the workers' concerns that the unions voiced in negotiations. "They didn't have an argument with the union being there," he said of the employers' representatives in negotiations.

Las Vegas was no capitalist paradise, however. Resort owners were less effectively organized than many of the workers they employed in those years, which made it difficult to resist union demands. Moreover, some of them feared that work stoppages would draw attention to their gambling operations, which many Americans still wanted to outlaw. As long as profits were rising, they saw no need to confront the unions. Little versed in the economic or social rationales for collective bargaining, they knew that pay raises and job benefits ensured labor peace as well as a steady influx of new workers to Las Vegas, still a relatively isolated desert community. The Teamsters Central States Pension Fund may have been a factor in this relative tranquillity. The Teamsters made loans to entrepreneurs who provided jobs for its members, not to groups that resisted unions. Dick Thomas later acknowledged this stabilizing role of the fund in labor relations in Las Vegas. "It didn't hurt," he said.[12]

The owners took collective bargaining more seriously than the foregoing account may imply. The 1961 negotiations between the Industrial Council and the Culinary illustrate that point. Before those negotiations began, Roy Flippin called a meeting of the council. There, owners agreed that pay raises should be considerably less than the unions were asking and rejected union proposals on fringe benefits as too costly. Two days after the meeting, Flippin assembled his four-member negotiating team to discuss management's bargaining strategy, and at the ensuing negotiations he rejected most union proposals. Unions ultimately received about half of what they asked for. Neither the substance, processes, nor outcome of the 1961 negotiations can be explained or documented, but union leaders who attended the negotiations suggested a power balance between bargaining parties as well as a willingness to compromise accounted for their own concessions.[13]

Perhaps some of these things have to do with the activities of one of the shadowy figures in Las Vegas history, Sidney Korshak, depicted in FBI records as a labor relations specialist who helped the parties in collective bargaining processes that involved underworld figures and interests to reach mutually satisfactory agreements on the issues at stake in their bargaining. Korshak's involvement in the world of gambling dated back to the 1930s, when he fronted in Chicago for notorious underworld figures in their dealings with the public or the police. After the war, he worked as a labor relations consultant for the Chicago Hotel Association, which included several of the nation's largest hotel chains, and helped several clients obtain loans from the Teamster's pension fund to invest in gambling enterprises in Las Vegas. The FBI kept Korshak under surveillance in those years and believed him to be the "man behind the scenes" in resort development as well as labor negotiations insofar as those things involved or related to organized crime. The agency suggested he negotiated "sweetheart contracts" with unions representing workers in businesses controlled by organized crime and that those contracts involved illegal payoffs to labor leaders and Korshak's mob-connected clients in Chicago. This "kickback scheme" may have discouraged unions from organizing occupational groups that management wanted to remain unorganized.[14]

None of this was ever proved in a court of law or elsewhere to be true—or false. Korshak did indeed make trips to Las Vegas to meet with owners of the Desert Inn, the Sands, and other resorts with known or suspected connections to organized crime. He brought together investors with such connections to make business deals involving gambling properties in the city, and he represented these investors in negotiations with unions there. But Korshak remained a member of the American Bar Association in good standing throughout the years under study, and several attorneys and business leaders who knew him said he had high ethical standards.[15] In statements to New Jersey gaming authorities in the 1980s, for example, an attorney working for Hilton properties called Korshak "one of the finest human beings I've ever met, with a fine reputation in the legal community." Barron Hilton himself spoke well of the man and suggested he should be "commended rather than chastised for his highly successful career."[16] Union leaders attributed Korshak's success as a negotiator to his respect for trade unions and to his casual, informal approach to bargaining. "He's a hard adversary," one of them explained, "[but] he doesn't believe in breaking unions."[17] To the FBI, Korshak's presence in Las Vegas hinted of illegal bargaining tactics, but to labor leaders it spoke to the sense of reciprocity that characterized labor relations in the city.

The wages and benefits of union workers in Las Vegas were signs of organized labor's clout in the city. In the late 1960s, these were as good as or much better than those of their counterparts in the nation's largest metropolitan areas, where unions tended to be strong and the cost of living high. Housekeepers' earnings illustrate this point. In 1969 union housekeepers in New York, Chicago, and Los Angeles earned $12 to $16 a day, while all those in Las Vegas earned $16. Union bartenders in the three larger cities took home $17 to $21 a day in wages while those in Las Vegas made $27. Butchers, fry cooks, sauciers, and other kitchen workers enjoyed similar differentials, as did workers in dining room classifications.[18] The differential was not enough to make low-skilled workers in Las Vegas part of the American middle class, but it did help them own cars, lawn mowers, and home appliances characteristic of at least a lower-middle-class lifestyle. It also enabled some of them to enjoy the outdoor activities associated with camping, travel, and sporting activities.[19]

If somewhat exceptional, the economic gains of Las Vegas workers in these years were part of national trends. For more than two decades after World War II, the American economy expanded at an unprecedented pace. Labor shared in this expanding prosperity, and management learned to deal with unions in ways that encouraged industrial peace. Multiyear contracts negotiated through collective bargaining provided pay raises and increasing benefits, which nourished the growth of the unionized workforce. From 1955 to 1968, the real wages of union workers rose by almost 50 percent, by the end of which more union workers than ever had pensions and health insurance, as well as paid vacations, sick leave, and survivor benefits. More workers also belonged to unions. Between 1950 and 1968, the number of union workers in the nation rose by 35 percent, from 14 million to 19 million.[20]

In the late 1960s, this era of economic growth and industrial peace stalled. Inflation, declining productivity, and rising unemployment became growing problems. Increased foreign competition, rising oil prices, and other troubling developments encouraged employers to rethink labor relations.

These problems had little effect in Las Vegas, the nation's fastest-growing metropolitan area. In the 1960s its population more than doubled, from 130,000 to 275,000, and all sectors of the economy grew accordingly.[21] The year 1969 was record shattering for the gaming industry. The number of people arriving at McCarran International Airport rose by 15 percent, to more than four million. Gross taxable gaming revenue jumped more than 20 percent; the number of hotel and casino workers increased by more than 10 percent, to about thirty thousand.[22]

Yet there were signs by the turn of the decade that this remarkable growth might end. Relevant statewide trends in Nevada were troubling. In the early postwar years, the average earnings of Nevada's workers rose faster than the national average, and work stoppages were few and short-lived. By the mid-1960s the growth rates of both employment and income were declining, and stoppages became longer and more frequent and involved more workers. The number of workdays lost to strikes reached an all-time high in 1965, when there were thirty-seven strikes in Nevada, most of them involving disputes over wages and benefits.[23]

A yearlong strike against cab companies that year exposed the deepening rift between capital and labor in Las Vegas. The Teamsters, which represented the cab drivers, called the strike, charging cab companies with violating contract provisions regulating the number of cabs they could put on the street during holidays. In response, the companies began replacing striking employees, who in turn began harassing strikebreakers. In one unusual incident, strikers pulled a driver out of his cab at knifepoint, drove his vehicle into the desert, and burned it. Las Vegas police arrested a number of strikers involved in physical altercations with strikebreakers.[24] As a result of such incidents, a judge banned taxis from certain resorts, which prompted the resorts to organize their own fleet of taxis to shuttle their guests around town. Sidney Korshak tried to pressure both sides to end the strike, but the conflict dragged on. Governor Grant Sawyer eventually intervened in the conflict, but not before one of the struck employers, Checker Cab, declared itself nonunion. There had never been such a long and bitter strike in the city, or one that created such havoc for resorts.[25]

The election of Republican governor Paul Laxalt in 1966 was another sign of changing times. Laxalt, who defeated the incumbent Governor Grant Sawyer, was no friend of organized labor. As lieutenant governor, he had opposed union efforts to repeal Nevada's right-to-work law, and in his election campaign made it clear that he favored a "hands off" approach in industrial conflicts. "Government must take care *not* to involve itself in collective bargaining except in those cases— clear cut cases—when such a dispute is damaging the public interest," he told an audience of Las Vegas business people during the campaign; "and I don't mean by that using the term 'in the public interest' as an excuse for governmental interference when and where it wants." He added, "Once the government starts poking its nose like the camel under the tent, no one has immunity."[26] Laxalt was particularly critical of the National Labor Relations Board (NLRB), the agency that oversaw enforcement of the nation's labor laws. Like most employers, he believed the board had a "built-in bias" against management. "From the very day it was established in the 1930s," Laxalt said, "the NLRB has been criticized for its pro-union, anti-business, and anti-public bias. Its failures to do its job in an even-handed, impartial manner have been documented repeatedly in various congressional investigations."[27]

As governor, Laxalt was an ally of corporate resort owners like Howard Hughes and Barron Hilton. Shortly after taking office, he had signed the legislation that made possible large-scale corporate investment in gaming. Hughes and Hilton, who had already shown an interest in gaming, then began their move into Las Vegas. To his supporters, Laxalt cleaned up the city's image by altering the system of ownership in the industry. To his labor critics, he was a pawn of corporate leaders bent on changing a system of labor-management relations that unions had found responsive to their concerns and to the needs of their members. The old ownership structure in the resort industry had never been a problem for unions. Indeed, it functioned to promote their well-being and the well-being of their members.[28]

The first big strike in the resort industry occurred soon after Laxalt took office. In March 1967, after concluding negotiations with major Strip properties, the Culinary and Bartenders turned their attention to twelve downtown gambling establishments which bargained through the Downtown Casino Association (DCA). Though these properties were smaller and less profitable than their counterparts on the Strip, they nonetheless agreed to match the terms and conditions of the new agreements governing Strip resorts, which provided annual wage increases of 6 percent, boosted employer contributions to union health and welfare funds, provided guaranteed workweeks, and improved holiday and vacation benefits. Bramlet, however, insisted the properties pay food servers higher wages than those paid on the Strip because their recent reductions in the prices of meals and drinks had reduced their employees' tips. The "crux" of the problem, as Bramlet put it, was the recent introduction of "49-cent breakfasts, give-away drinks, and cut-rate meal prices."[29]

The DCA rejected Bramlet's proposal. Members of the association insisted that they could not afford to pay higher wages than their competitors on the Strip.

Whoever heard of companies establishing wage rates based on the tips that employees at other companies received, they asked. "If you work for any of the four auto companies," Frank Mooney of the Fremont Hotel explained to the press, "you get the same wages; tips have nothing to do with it."[30]

The Culinary and Bartenders remained firm, however, and called for a strike to accomplish their goals. On the evening of April 18, when their contracts with the properties expired, eight hundred members of the unions at the offending properties walked off their jobs. Another twelve hundred failed to report for work when their shifts began the next day. Employers responded by closing their dining facilities and staffing bars and hotel operations with supervisory employees. They also announced they would discharge dealers and other nonunion employees who honored picket lines. "We are prepared to withstand this strike if it takes all summer," DCA president Don Ashworth said.[31]

The work stoppage transformed the downtown area into a cavalcade of activities. Picketers marched around the properties day and night, singing songs of protest and chanting slogans like: "One, two, three, four, don't go near that open door!" Scores of workers from other unions refused to cross union picket lines and roamed the downtown area just to see and hear the pickets. Police officers were everywhere, as were news reporters and television camera crews. To get something to eat in the area, people stood in long lines outside coffee shops and restaurants like Denny's and Mon Woo's Café. As an employee at one of those places explained, people ordered food "faster than we can get the stuff off the griddle."[32]

The strike lasted six days. As soon it began, some DCA members expressed a willingness to meet union demands. A few showed genuine concern for the plight of their striking employees. Benny Binion, who owned the Horseshoe, provided meals to picketers outside his property. Italo Ghelfi of the Golden Nugget offered picketers cold drinks and cigarettes. The lack of unity within the DCA combined with labor solidarity to undermine management's bargaining position. The downtown employers ultimately agreed to pay their food and beverage servers about 4 percent more than they could earn on the Strip. They tried to downplay their concessions in the press. "It wasn't as bad as we thought," Frank Mooney of the Fremont said of the strike. "We could have survived the strike had it lasted longer." Billy Parker of the California Club agreed. "I think all the publicity we got in the Los Angeles newspapers actually helped; a lot of people came up out of curiosity." Culinary leader Al Bramlet offered a more candid assessment of the strike. The settlement that ended it, he said, "includes all the provisions of the Strip contract signed last month, including all adjustments of wage inequities."[33]

♠ ♣ ♥ ♦

The 1967 work stoppage was neither particularly bitter nor costly, but it warned employers that traditional ways of dealing with resort workers and their unions were now problematical. Times had changed. The prospect of publicly traded corporations investing in gaming promised to transform the industry. Tourism as an industry had grown and was becoming more competitive. Neither the personalized practices and customs of a Roy Flippin nor the subterranean services of syndicate "fixers" like Sidney Korshak could survive in the new circumstances. Industrial relations must be rationalized, subject to calculations of profitability, cost effectiveness, and efficiency. In terms of the workplace, this likely meant growing impersonalization and increased reliance on written rules and regulations—in a word, bureaucratization. The challenge this presented to unions was to humanize the transformation as best they could and to see after the material interests and social well-being of their members.

Corporate executives who worked for Howard Hughes in Las Vegas understood the nature of the transformation taking place. When Hughes purchased the Desert Inn in 1967, his chief aids expressed dismay at the absence of personnel offices in the resorts they were buying and the absence of such elementary management tools as usable personnel records. They wondered why no one was designated to oversee such basic areas of management as restaurant and food operations. They were equally surprised at the casual way in which the Nevada Industrial Council dealt with unions. To make Hughes's properties competitive and profitable, they set about enlisting other industrial leaders in an effort to create a new, stronger organization to deal with unions.[34]

The organization they would use for their purposes, the Nevada Resort Association (NRA), already existed. The brainchild of George Ullom, a onetime member of the Gaming Control Board, the NRA was the result of Ullom's effort to get resort owners to work together to understand how they could use Nevada's gaming laws and tax policies for their own advantage, and how they could work together to improve the images of the city and of its gaming industry. In 1961, at Ullom's initiative, representatives from nine resorts created the association, paid membership dues based on the number of hotel rooms in their properties, and solicited membership from other resort owners and managers. The original organizers appointed Ullom executive director, in which role he helped NRA members understand their interests and how to protect and expand them. Among other things, he helped members identify political candidates who might advance their interests politically.[35] But the association did not initially concern itself with matters involving collective bargaining or unions. "I would not handle any labor relations," Ullom explained. "That would be outside of the sphere of the [association's] activities."[36]

The NRA remained a relatively loose-knit organization adhering to its original purposes until 1966, when Robbins Cahill became its managing director. The appointment of Cahill, a respected former state assemblyman, state tax commissioner, and state Gaming Control Board chairman, no doubt improved public perceptions of the association and of the gaming industry it fronted for.[37] Cahill had been public spokesman for the association since the early 1960s and in that role helped keep industry leaders abreast of legislation and political trends affecting gaming. In these years, the organization increased the scope of its lobbying and public relations activities but steered clear of labor-management relations. Cahill spent much of his first year as director understanding the implications of the proposed corporate gaming act and helping resort managers prepare for its implementation. Working through Cahill and their attorneys, NRA members also sought to shape the language of the act to protect their interests.[38]

In 1968 management representatives from sixteen major Strip resorts joined together to transform the NRA by making it responsible for negotiating their labor contracts. This changed the basic nature and purpose of the association. Unlike the Industrial Council, which fell by the wayside, the NRA required the agreement of two-thirds of its members on the positions it took in industry-wide bargaining, and members agreed to pay fines to the association of up to $500,000 for breaking rank in negotiating contracts. The NRA executive board set the management agenda for collective bargaining and hired William Campbell as chief negotiator. Campbell was skilled, experienced, and widely respected by both resort owners and union leaders. He had previously represented the Federation Employers' Association, a sizable group of restaurateurs, launderette owners, and other local employers in labor negotiations, and knew many of the city's business, labor, and civic leaders. He had the confidence of Robbins Cahill, who thought hiring Campbell "the smartest thing" the NRA ever did. "The man is tremendously capable," Cahill remarked. "He knows the business backward and forwards."[39]

Campbell approached collective bargaining professionally. He collected detailed information on wages, working conditions, and job benefits in other tourist destinations and asked members to identify their problems, concerns, and expectations. He helped them prepare for work stoppages and taught them how to calculate their losses at any point in a strike. He also had them prepare plans to help individual resorts that became targets of "selective" strikes aimed at undermining the association through isolate-and-conquer techniques, which unions used on occasion to win concessions from multiemployer bargaining groups. When unions struck one or more but not all NRA properties, he reminded the group, the others had the option to lockout members of those unions while the strike lasted. Hiring so skilled and resourceful a strategist as Campbell changed the milieu of collective bargaining. The unions now faced a more united employer association ready to resist whatever it considered as excessive union demands.[40]

This transformation brought employers in Las Vegas in line with employers in other industries across the nation. That is, resort owners had come to believe that the unions they confronted had become strong enough to jeopardize the profitability and growth—that is, the future—of the industry. Cahill himself shared this view, which was no doubt one reason the NRA made him managing director. "To put it very boldly," he said in the early 1970s, "I think that labor has the hotels of Las Vegas by the throat. I think [union leaders] have got them by the jugular vein, and they know it." "That may sound like an anti-labor argument," he added, "but basically . . . it's an analysis of conditions as they are."[41] These words signaled a new era in collective bargaining in the industry Cahill represented.

That era dawned in 1969, when the contracts of "front-end" members of the Teamsters and Operating Engineers unions expired in Strip resorts. These unions were small, and one of them was a newcomer to the industry. The Teamsters had only recently chartered Local 995 to represent its resort workers, which included desk and registration clerks and switchboard operators as well as warehousemen, window cleaners, and receiving and dispatching clerks, who together in 1969 totaled more than 1,200 members. The Operating Engineers, a much smaller organization of mechanics and engineers, had gained a foothold in the resort industry in the 1950s, after a merger of engineers' unions in California and Nevada. Its 350 members installed and maintained power equipment in the resorts.[42]

In negotiations with the NRA, the unions proposed new three-year agreements boosting wages about 10 percent annually and creating new employer-funded retirement plans. These proposals they presented as justified by recent and still-rising increases in the cost of living. The U.S. Bureau of Labor Statistics had recently reported that the price of meat, poultry, and fish had jumped nearly 5 percent in the month of May alone and that food prices generally had risen nearly 2 percent. A dollar in 1969 bought what seventy-eight cents had a decade

earlier. The Las Vegas Convention and Visitors Authority had recently acknowledged the impact of inflation by approving sizable pay hikes for its employees.
The NRA nonetheless rejected the proposed wage increases as "excessive" and
"unreasonable," and the union contracts expired.[43]

In response, the two unions pulled telephone operators, desk clerks, and engineers off the job at the Dunes Hotel, one of the Howard Hughes properties represented by the NRA. This selective strike, union leaders hoped, would encourage
the Dunes to accept their wage and benefit proposals, thus giving the other properties little choice but to follow suit. Almost immediately, however, the resorts
represented by the NRA locked out members of the Teamsters and the Operating
Engineers, vowing to keep their properties open by staffing desks and switchboards with nonunion supervisors and managers. When the Central Labor Council sanctioned the strike, however, hundreds of employees from other unions refused to cross picket lines set up by teamsters and engineers at the Dunes. This
prompted employers to agree the next day to the union demands to raise wages by
nearly 30 percent over three years and to increase substantially retirement and
fringe benefits. Not surprisingly, union leaders saw the strike as a clear victory for
labor.[44]

The strike, however, revealed a heightened sense of animosity and distrust in
the bargaining environment. Union leaders insisted that Howard Hughes controlled the NRA and was out "to break" the unions in the resorts. Hughes and
other entrepreneurs were unconcerned about the well-being of their employees,
they charged. In response, employers painted union leaders as selfish schemers
with little interest in the future of tourism. "It is painfully obvious that the Teamsters and Operating Engineers, working with the Central Labor Council, are
making a concerted effort to wring an extravagant settlement out of the resort
industry," William Campbell told reporters when the strike began. "This is being attempted without regard to the serious impact on the area's economy [and]
the continued well-being of an industry which provides 20,000 jobs for union
members in Southern Nevada."[45] Such hyperbole reflected the growing divide
between labor and management.

This acrimonious state of affairs became more obvious the following year, when
the contracts of the 15,000 members of the Culinary and Bartenders unions expired. In an effort to avoid another costly defeat, the NRA members, in the words
of Robbins Cahill, approached negotiations in 1970 "in a different way than they
ever had before." The association's members formed a "protective agreement," as

Cahill later recalled. "They agreed that they'd all stick together, and that they wouldn't let [the unions] strike in one or two or three places and the rest stay open and take advantage of it, that it was a common cause, and that it was a life or death struggle."[46] The employers formed their negotiating committee "on a professional basis." That is, the committee consisted of salaried managers and experts rather than owners, and it had full power to negotiate on the association's behalf. Committee members were "not the bosses," as Cahill put it, but "working supervisors who knew the problems."[47] Campbell alone spoke for the NRA at the bargaining table. Committee members who wanted to shape the bargaining process did so before the bargaining began, or between bargaining sessions.

As soon as the negotiations began, the NRA rejected the unions' wage and benefit proposals. Union leaders no doubt expected that. Their proposals would not only boost wages more than 35 percent over three years but increase benefits, which, with the wage increases, would raise labor costs nearly 45 percent. They justified the demands on the grounds of inflation, which in their calculations had raised the cost of living 16 percent since 1967, wiping out gains workers had made in earlier contracts. And prices were still rising. The NRA did not deny those calculations but insisted that the resort industry had grown too competitive and profit margins too small to meet the unions' demands. Employers could no longer pass ever-increasing labor costs to consumers and continue to grow the industry. Market conditions had changed; new conditions demanded that employers control labor as well as other costs. Campbell offered to boost wages 18 percent over three years for tipped employees and 21 to 27 percent for others. The issue of benefits, he said, would have to wait until the parties agreed on wages.[48]

More important for the future of the unions than the specifics of wage increases was Campbell's insistence on eliminating one of the unions' most powerful weapons—the right of members to honor picket lines of other unions. That right had determined the outcome of the Teamsters and Operating Engineers strike a year earlier. It was also a major weapon in efforts to organize still unorganized workers, such as dealers and security guards. When any group professing to represent unorganized workers threw up informational picket lines at resorts, union workers could refuse to cross them without fear of being discharged or otherwise disciplined. In other words, contracts had traditionally given union workers the freedom to withhold their services in a variety of circumstances, including disputes involving employers and any of their employees. Employers now insisted on eliminating that language.[49]

Union leaders looked upon that insistence as an attack on a basic pillar of union strength and rejected it. "We will not change a provision that has been in

COMPLETE call number

_____
Author's last name

_____
Title

_____
Date due

_____
PRINT your name, student p.o.
number or address

JOP (46) 1984
288-99

E		HN
185.61		80
K3.538B		B9
		H83

JS	JS	JS	
1240	341	323	768
W37	P65		595
K37			

563 799 960|

the contract for twenty years," Culinary leader Al Bramlet told the press. "This is strictly a move by employers, not just to weaken, but to completely destroy the Southern Nevada labor movement. We will not be a party to it." "They are asking us to sell out every other labor organization in Nevada," Bramlet added, "which we won't do."[50]

On March 9, the day before contracts expired, Bramlet brought management's "final" offer before members of his own union and the Bartenders. The offer included wage and benefit increases that boosted labor costs by 25 percent over three years but eliminated the right to wage sympathy strikes. Addressing union members at a jammed convention center, Bramlet recommended rejecting the offer and authorizing a strike. A strike, he warned, could be long and difficult. "Don't any of you get the impression that this is a lark and that we're going out on strike for a few hours," Bramlet told the crowd.[51] The rank and file followed Bramlet's advice, voting overwhelmingly to reject management's offer and give union leaders authority to call a strike.

Though Bramlet promised to "hit them all at once," he targeted three NRA establishments—the Desert Inn, the International, and Caesars Palace. His choice was calculated. Each of the three was part of a corporate structure easy to vilify. The Desert Inn was one of the properties of Hughes, who had recently left Las Vegas to reside in the Bahamas. Kirk Kerkorian, who controlled the International, was more visible to workers than Hughes, but he too seemed like a distant overlord. Caesars Palace had recently been purchased by a Florida-based company chiefly involved in owning and/or operating large restaurant and retail chains nationwide. Workers perceived a growing gap between themselves and their employers in such distant places.[52]

The NRA responded to the selective strike by locking out culinary workers and bartenders and shutting down all of its properties. The association had little choice in the latter action, because almost all union workers refused to cross picket lines. Cab drivers supported the strike by refusing to drive passengers onto struck properties. Construction workers shut down expansion and renovation projects. Campbell acknowledged this massive show of solidarity. "Employees represented by all other unions," Campbell told officials, "respected the picket lines and did not report for work."[53] This unity impressed even union leaders. "For the first time many of us can remember," Bramlet told the press, "organized labor in southern Nevada is really working as a team." The solidarity showed to him the importance of workers' rights to honor picket lines. "We think basic unionism is at stake." The NRA disagreed. What was at stake, its spokesmen told the press, were the rights of management to the services of the workers it hired.[54]

The strike and lockout disrupted tourism, catching tourists by surprise. Many of those at closed resorts found rooms at motels on or near the Strip or downtown, or at one of the independent resorts still open, such as the Riviera and Circus Circus. Others left Las Vegas as soon as they could in the chaos caused by the absence of workers at checkout counters, parking lots, transport facilities, and the like. Though some tourists took the chaos in stride, others were angry or disappointed. "We are disgusted," one of them said.[55]

The strike and lockout also disrupted business in and around Las Vegas, soon forcing layoffs or wage cuts at places directly dependent on tourism. Companies that provided goods and services to resorts were immediately hard hit. The Nevada Dice Company, to illustrate, which made casino dice, lost 90 percent of its business as soon as the strike and lockout began, about $500 a day, a major loss for a small enterprise. If the strike lasted more than a week, the company manager told the press, he would close down his operation. New York Bagel Boys, a small firm that supplied Strip properties with kosher-style bakery goods, saw its orders decline 50 percent. And so it went with similar enterprises.[56]

When the strike began, Governor Laxalt, who had vowed to stay out of labor disputes, warned the public to prepare for a long and costly work stoppage. "We are in the midst of what could be the most severe economic strike in Nevada's history," he said, urging both parties to settle their differences for the sake of the community and the industry, as well as themselves. "I hope that both sides address themselves to the merits of this controversy with a firm resolve to settle as quickly as possible. If this does not occur the effects of this strike may be felt in southern Nevada for many years to come."[57] The governor could intervene in the strike only if one or both of the parties asked him to do so.

Continuation of the strike soon prompted elected officials to call for its end. Senator Howard Cannon, for example, urged parties to reach an agreement "without delay." "The present stalemate in negotiations serves no one," the senator said. "It brings hardship and privation to thousands of working men and women and their families."[58] Clark County district attorney George Franklin wrote personal letters to both Bramlet and Campbell reminding them that continuing the strike could result in the cancellation of upcoming conventions. "We are now the number one convention city in the world," Franklin pointed out. "If a number of long-committed conventions are cancelled or not serviced, it could have long range effects on our convention business many years after the current negotiations are mutually concluded."[59]

Political pressure soon combined with plunging profits to produce a breakthrough. On March 13, three days after the strike began, nine resorts agreed to drop their demands for language prohibiting employees from honoring picket lines of other union employees if the unions accepted contract language that required workers to cross lines set up for informational or organizational purposes. Such language would make it difficult for unions to organize dealers and security guards and was something the unions had always adamantly opposed.[60]

The following day, in the office of Hank Greenspun, editor and publisher of the *Las Vegas Sun*, the parties hammered out an agreement that gave the unions most of what they wanted in terms of pay and benefits. These amounted to about a 32 percent increase over the life of the contract and included generous increases in benefits. But, in return, Bramlet agreed that members of the Culinary and Bartenders no longer had the right to honor picket lines set up for informational or organizational purposes. Because Bramlet now viewed dealers as beyond the reach of his union, he conceded this point in return for a generous economic settlement. That would prove to be a momentous concession.[61]

After this bargaining session ended, both parties expressed satisfaction with the settlement. "It was a good settlement for both sides," Alex Shoofey of the International said. "We think a satisfactory agreement has been reached."[62] Al Benedict of the Hughes properties agreed. "I think an equitable settlement was worked out for both labor and management," he said. "I think we can live in harmony for the remainder of the three-year contract."[63] Bramlet was publicly silent about his compromise on crossing picket lines but said culinary workers and bartenders should be pleased with the new contract. "Both unions are happy with the contract in its final form," he said. "We believe it is a realistic increase in both wages and conditions in light of today's cost of living." Bramlet added, "We express our deepest thanks to all the other unions who gave their full support. . . . Their actions demonstrated the unity of the labor movement in southern Nevada."[64] The balance of power between management and labor had shifted, as the new contract language on crossing organizational and informational picket lines presaged, but had not yet shifted as significantly as the NRA was determined that it would.

The first strikes against the Las Vegas resort industry reflected the fact that a relatively relaxed world of labor relations was giving way to one of confrontation. By the 1970s this transition was well underway. The new corporate owners tended to be distant figures who delegated management tasks to little-known executives, who in turn assigned the job of dealing with unions to professional staffers, who, in streamlining and rationalizing it, diminished the human element it once boasted. Dick Thomas of the Teamsters complained that the corporate change made the process "much more difficult," and "much more time consuming." Instead of dealing with the owners, Thomas and other bargainers now dealt with what they called "labor relations persons" and "bean counters." "Their whole concept of negotiations was entirely different." "They were looking and wanting to make a profit out of every piece of the hotel business."[65]

The postwar consensus that had stabilized Las Vegas labor relations had begun to unravel, though there had been no mass arrests or violence during the first strikes. Indeed, when the 1970 conflict ended, both labor and management praised the "cooperative and courteous" handling of the incident by law-enforcement officials. "We appreciate the cooperation of the sheriff's office in the strike," Bramlet told reporters after the conflict. "Their officers certainly demonstrated absolute impartiality and in some instances were helpful in controlling traffic in and out of the hotels so union members would not be injured." Al Benedict similarly praised picketing workers for their orderliness. "We're proud of the way the pickets conducted themselves," the resort manager told the press. "We don't like to see picket lines, but we feel they were handled in a discreet manner in the recent strike."[66] Industrial relations had become adversarial, and employers had won some small restrictions on the right of workers to join sympathy strikes. But they had not yet demanded cuts in wages or benefits, or the elimination of work rules valued by workers. Those things were yet to come.

The Westside, 1943. In the age of segregation, African Americans lived in the "colored section" of Las Vegas, where homes generally lacked electricity and indoor plumbing. Courtesy UNLV Library Special Collections.

Downtown Las Vegas, circa 1950s. At midcentury, most hotels and gambling establishments were downtown, along Fremont Street. Courtesy UNLV Library Special Collections.

The Strip's first resort, circa 1950. Strip resorts like El Rancho offered more amenities than did their downtown counterparts. Like downtown establishments, however, they were owned by single proprietors or small groups of business partners. Courtesy UNLV Library Special Collections.

Opposite, top. Customers playing slot machines at the Sands, circa 1952. Many gamblers and hotel guests on the Strip were relatively well off and expected a wider range of services than downtown properties offered. Courtesy UNLV Library Special Collections.

Opposite, bottom. Freddie Bell and the Bell Boys at the Silver Queen Bar and Cocktail Lounge at the Sands, 1952. Resorts hired many small musical groups as entertainers in casino lounges. Courtesy UNLV Library Special Collections.

Dealers and gamblers at a craps table at El Morocco, 1954. In the early postwar years, Las Vegas gambling establishments generally refused to accept black guests. African Americans owned and operated several small casinos in the Westside. Courtesy UNLV Library Special Collections.

Waiting tables in the Hickory Room at the Riviera Hotel, 1955. At a time when custom and law segmented the labor market, waiters in fine-dining restaurants were typically male and their counterparts in coffee shops, female. Courtesy UNLV Library Special Collections.

Waiter in half-swim attire serves a guest in the Dunes swimming pool, 1955. Resorts offered a wide variety of services, even at poolside. Courtesy UNLV Library Special Collections.

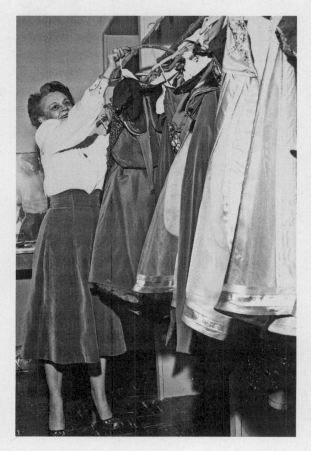

"A Beautiful Girl's Best Friend," a wardrobe mistress backstage at the Sands, circa 1960s. Resorts employed skilled seamstresses to repair and handle costumes used in production shows. Courtesy UNLV Library Special Collections.

Dealing blackjack at the Sands, circa 1960. Dealers constituted one of the largest occupational groups in the resort industry. Unlike most resort workers, they were not unionized. Courtesy UNLV Library Special Collections.

Opposite, bottom. The "Rat Pack" at the Sands Copa Room, 1961. Standing *left* to *right* are Dean Martin, Frank Sinatra, Sammy Davis Jr., and Joey Bishop, four of the Strip's most popular entertainers. Courtesy UNLV Library Special Collections.

The "Eye in the Sky" at the Mint Casino, circa 1960. To prevent theft in casinos, resorts scrutinized the habits and routines of employees as well as gamblers. Courtesy UNLV Library Special Collections.

Switchboard operators at the Sands, circa 1960s. Female employees operated telephone switchboards around the clock. The standing operator is verifying the names and room numbers of hotel guests for switchboard workers. Courtesy UNLV Library Special Collections.

Slot mechanics repair machines at the Mint, circa 1960s. Resorts employed skilled workers to install and repair slot machines. Courtesy UNLV Library Special Collections.

Looking north above the Strip, circa 1968. This aerial view offers a look at the Strip on the eve of the corporate revolution. The Dunes and Caesars Palace are visible in the foreground; the Sands is seen on the right. Courtesy UNLV Library Special Collections.

Chef Maurice Cau preparing dinner at the Sands, circa 1969. Feeding hundreds of guests each day required skill, organization, attention to detail, and a variety of special equipment. Courtesy UNLV Library Special Collections.

W. Davis dealing cards at the Sands, 1972. Davis was one of the first African American dealers on the Strip. The cocktail server is Toni Bright. Courtesy UNLV Library Special Collections.

Showgirls in the "Folies Bergere" at the Tropicana, circa 1977. Walking down long staircases wearing high heels and cumbersome headdresses, with arms extended and eyes on the audience, was more difficult than it appeared to be. Courtesy UNLV Library Special Collections.

Opposite, bottom. The Las Vegas Hilton, circa 1975. The rise of this giant Y-shaped resort in the late 1960s was a sign of the emerging era of corporate ownership in the resort industry in Las Vegas. Courtesy UNLV Library Special Collections.

Metropolitan police wrestle a striking protestor to the ground, March 23, 1976. Violent clashes between police and picketers exposed the growing ideological divide between workers and employers which characterized the new era of corporate ownership and management. Courtesy *Las Vegas Review-Journal.*

Dancers in "Casino de Paris" at the Dunes, circa 1978. Male and female dancers alike worked in major production shows. Their performances required skills as well as talent. Courtesy UNLV Library Special Collections.

Striking workers defending picket lines against tourists and strikebreakers, 1984. The widespread crossing of picket lines was another sign of the tenuous position of unions in the industry by the 1980s. Courtesy *Las Vegas Review-Journal*.

Picketers along the Strip, April 12, 1984. The massed picketing led to traffic jams, mass arrests, and flaring tempers, while showing the dedication of strikers to the union cause. Courtesy *Las Vegas Sun*.

Virginia Devine, a five-year employee of the Four Queens, drinks water on the picket line, 1984. The Four Queens and several other Las Vegas resorts broke the unions of their employees in the 1984–85 strike, leaving many employees disheartened as well as unemployed. Courtesy *Las Vegas Review-Journal*.

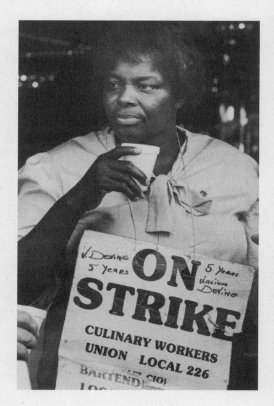

The Struggle for the Casinos

Through the 1960s and early 1970s, a number of unions and individuals made what amounted to a sustained effort to unionize casino dealers, the largest and most important group of nonunionized workers in Las Vegas resorts. Employers successfully resisted that effort but not before granting dealers many of the benefits union organizers promised them, including higher wages, improved work rules, and grievance machinery. The attempt to organize dealers failed because of the adroitness of management in making these concessions, the shortcomings of the union leaders behind the effort, and the indifference or resistance of many dealers to unionization.

The story of this effort, including its failure, reveals a good deal about the labor history of Las Vegas during the period of this study. It helps to illuminate how and why most resort workers joined and supported unions, and how and why employers dealt with unions as they did. Unions, employers, and nonunion workers were all primary players, and each group performed in accordance with its own imperatives. The National Labor Relations Board (NLRB) oversaw organizing drives, and its broad sympathy for labor within the constraints of the law encouraged organizers and many dealers in the 1960s and 1970s to believe they had a realistic chance to unionize the casinos.

The organizing effort demonstrates some of the limits to labor-management harmony in those years. The unwritten understandings that had stabilized labor relations in postwar Las Vegas had more effect on resort managers and union leaders than on workers and their immediate bosses. The social contract did not apply to nonunion employees, though it did bring them indirect benefits. From

1960 to 1976, the relationship between nonunion workers and their supervisors seems to have been testy and stressful, though there are no objective measures of such conflict. Union strength encouraged resort managers to codify and standardize personnel policies. As the age of corporate ownership unfolded, employers drew up ever more detailed and sophisticated strategies to limit union interference in management prerogatives. The Nevada Resort Association (NRA) contoured dealer organizing drives with the use of such strategies.

♠ ♣ ♥ ♦

Nonunion employees were always a significant minority of resort workforces. In the 1960s and 1970s, as many as a third of the wage earners at resorts were unorganized, the vast majority of them dealers. Of the 1,250 employees at the Tropicana and Sahara in 1970, for example, about 350 to 400 at each place were nonunion, approximately two-thirds of whom were dealers. Most of the other nonunion employees worked in security forces as guards or in casino cage and credit departments handling exchanges of money and credit, or counting and wrapping coins.[1]

Like their union counterparts, nonunion employees typically worked eight-hour shifts, five or six days a week. They had the same breaks during work shifts as union employees, and the same access to meals at resort cafeterias. They also worked in similarly structured settings with similar lines of authority and job responsibilities. Nonunion workers generally earned lower wages than union employees, had fewer fringe benefits, and had no guaranteed grievance procedures. Security guards, for example, typically earned less than $30 a day in 1970, had no medical and retirement programs, no dental and vision programs, and no grievance machinery in place that prohibited or even discouraged employers from firing or suspending them without "just cause."[2]

By 1970 nearly five thousand dealers ran games in greater Las Vegas, most of them in large casinos along the Strip. Though skills needed for the games they dealt varied widely, most knew the intricacies of several games. Dealing crap games demanded perhaps the most intricate skills, because craps was an exceptionally fast-paced game with its own esoteric vocabulary. The language of the game included such terms as "pass," "pass and odds," "come," and "don't come," all of which dealers had to understand readily; and they instinctively had to know how to issue playing chips, to move dice and gambling chips from place to place without hesitation, and how to handle proposition bets placed at the center of the table. They similarly had to know how to collect chips from losing players and pay off bets to winners.

Even such games as poker and twenty-one required specialized knowledge and sustained concentration on the part of dealers. After shuffling and dealing cards in twenty-one, dealers had to run the games according to established rules and procedures, compare their own "hand" to the "hands" of the players, and collect debts and pay off winners. At times, they had to explain the game to players, not just quickly but patiently and politely. Baccarat was perhaps the most complex card game. Three dealers usually worked a single baccarat game, two of them as money handlers while the other spelled out the rules, dealt cards, and determined winners. The least skilled dealers often ran games of "big six" wheel of fortune, bingo, or roulette, each of which was so simple to operate that experienced dealers resented being assigned to them. Nearly all dealers performed their tasks standing and under conditions that challenged their ability to concentrate. They worked in smoke-filled environments amid noise from nearby slot machines, lounges, gaming tables, and boisterous, intoxicated gamblers.[3]

Dealers had a wide range of attitudes toward their work. Some genuinely liked their jobs, seeing themselves as pivotal figures amid the noise of casinos and the excitement of customers winning and losing sometimes-substantial sums of money. "I've enjoyed it quite a bit," one of them recalled. "I've dealt to guys that I've seen win a quarter of a million dollars in one night, and I've seen guys lose a quarter million in one evening."[4] They occasionally dealt to celebrities, which boosted their self-esteem and their identification with their jobs. "We used to get a lot of movie stars come in, the Gabor sisters and oh, Natalie Wood, Elizabeth Taylor, several of the big name stars in those days," one of them reflected. "As a matter of fact, I dealt to Howard Hughes." This vivid memory of Hughes showed how much a celebrity might impress a dealer. "He was in his sneakers and this pair of old white duck pants and came over and bet a dollar back and forth on the '21' game." "He just bet his dollar back and forth, and everybody said, 'That's Howard Hughes, that's Howard Hughes!'"[5]

Other dealers described their job as a "good livelihood," yet stopped short of enthusiasm in remembering it. "It's all I know," one of them said. "I can't go do anything else. . . . I'm just hanging in there day-to-day."[6] Still others were entirely negative in their recollections. "It's really like working in a factory in Detroit," one of them observed. "The difference is that a casino is a type of factory where the customers come in to be waited on."[7] Interviewers who talked to dealers in the early 1970s found widespread dissatisfaction. Several dealers complained that rigid work rules made them feel like "machines" programmed to collect money from customers. "I think dealers, and that includes me, are always acting big and important," one of them said, "but deep down they know how boring the job is and how much crap they have to take from people."[8]

Casino managers monitored dealers more closely than any other group of workers and disciplined them for mistakes or misconduct swiftly and on the spot, which explains much of their dissatisfaction. In addition to the human "catwalks" and surveillance cameras hovering above dealers, "pit bosses" and "box men" watched their every move. Supervisors assigned dealers individually and perhaps arbitrarily to stations and games and constantly judged their performance, including the handling of customers. Dealers who struggled with the technicalities of games or failed in the niceties of customer relations might be admonished, shunted to tables with fewer customers (and thus fewer tips), or even dismissed. The rules for dealers and dealing were numerous and restrictive, and casinos enforced them rigidly.

Dealers might be disciplined for slack work, dress infractions, or overfriendliness with individual customers, or for more serious misconduct. "It's like this," one of them explained, "say you break the rules, just by a hair because, say you're tired. There's a boss behind you. He may not want to holler, but there's a boss behind him and he says, 'Either you take care of him, or I take care of you.'"[9] Supervisors were particularly hard on dealers who lost the house money. "The bosses behind the dealers would get very upset when the game blew up," one of them explained. "They would cuss at you and it was a tough situation."[10] Some dealers believed supervisors looked for reasons to discipline or dismiss them, especially older dealers. "Nobody wants a dealer who is growing old," one of them lamented.[11]

Unlike unionized workers, dealers had no institutionally or procedurally neutral way to challenge disciplinary action. Supervisors could fire them at will, or at least without having to justify their actions to a neutral third party. Fired or otherwise disciplined dealers could appeal to shift bosses or casino managers, but that seldom seemed to have helped. Casino and resort executives typically supported supervisors in personnel disputes, especially with nonunion employees and especially in cases involving workers charged with violating house rules.[12] Dealers also expected termination notices when new owners or managers took over the casinos in which they worked. "It's a common procedure," one of them explained, "when a new operation takes over everybody will be losing their job, at least the majority of the people."[13] Rather than fight these practices, dealers moved on to other jobs. In a rapidly expanding industry, it was not difficult for experienced, competent dealers to find jobs.

The absence of grievance procedures was one incentive for dealers to unionize. There were others. Dealers' wages were low relative to other skilled resort workers, averaging $15 to $25 a day in the 1960s. They thus relied heavily on tips, which generally equaled or exceeded their wages. Unlike union employees, however, dealers had no right to keep their tips. Casinos generally let dealers divide gratuities among themselves according to their own formulas, but they could and sometimes did make unilateral changes in tip-pooling policies to the detriment of individual dealers. A few casinos applied tips toward the minimum hourly wages of dealers, for example, and others made it difficult to collect gratuities on a daily basis. Most required dealers to share gratuities with credit clerks and other casino employees with no opportunities to earn their own tips. Tip-pooling policies were sources of friction in casinos, not only between dealers and supervisors but between groups of dealers working different games.[14]

Other workplace policies fueled grievances among dealers. Casinos might promote employees arbitrarily, that is, with little regard for qualifications or experience. In fact, they often filled managerial positions with friends of owners or managers, showing little regard for merit or qualifications. "Every time a promotion came up," one dealer explained, "it was always a friend of somebody's or something else." As a result of such favoritism, "I stayed a '21' dealer for a long, long time."[15] In downtown casinos, job-training programs often functioned to exploit experienced workers. In such programs, casinos hired trainees at half the wages of regular dealers, and when regular dealers had trained the trainees, the casinos might replace the regular dealers with the newly graduated trainees or replace the latter with newer and less costly trainees. "The working conditions in most of the downtown casinos are deplorable," one dealer claimed, referring to such problems as these. "Do you know dealers are working in these casinos for $10.00 a shift, holding down a dealer's job though classified as an apprentice?" Many such dealers, he said, were "living on false promises."[16] Dealers received none of the benefits of union workers, whether paid holidays and vacations or employer-supported health care.[17]

Some dealers publicly voiced their frustrations over these conditions. "Every day we read the papers," one of them wrote to the *Sun*, "we find some organization on strike for more pay or better working conditions. As the years go by only one group is still at the same poor wage—the dealers."[18] Another wrote the *Sun* accusing the resorts of "exploiting" dealers. "Are you now so rich," he asked resort managers and owners, "so secure, so free of worry and fear that you have forgotten what it is like to struggle to make a living? Have you forgotten whose sweat and whose labor put you in such an enviable position?" this letter writer continued. "Give us a pension plan, a retirement fund that we, as dealers, would financially contribute in part to. Give us a hospital and sickness plan comparable to that of the culinary union."[19] Letters to Governor Grant Sawyer voiced similar concerns. One letter described casino operators as "lily-white leeches [who] grow fat on the lifeblood of their employees." Only unionization would eliminate the dealers' problems, the letter-writer argued. "Mr. Governor, a union with no restrictions is the only solution that will protect dealers and other casino and hotel help from the exploitation, blackballing, and greed of the owner operators."[20]

Yet unionization held risks for dealers. Casino owners and managers vigorously and apparently unanimously opposed it. Their strongest argument was that union job protections and grievance machinery would make it impossible to rid themselves of dishonest dealers in the prompt manner necessary to protect themselves and their honest customers. "If we were held to the same levels of proof and have to provide the same quantum of evidence for termination as we are in a culinary case," a manager explained, "it would be extremely hard to get a termination." As he said of dishonest dealers, "You are dealing with sleight of hand. How the hell are you going to prove it beyond a reasonable doubt?"[21] Owners and managers worried that unionized dealers would work less rapidly or be more tempted to cheat than was currently the case. To keep gaming honest as well as profitable, they insisted, they must have complete control over dealers. This concern was real. Managers had in fact caught dealers stealing money and participating in scams involving customers and co-workers. How unionization would protect dishonest dealers, however, was not at all clear. How it would protect honest managers was equally puzzling.[22]

Dealers sympathetic to unionization worried that union activity on their or someone else's part would bring reprisals in the workplace and even threaten their employment. "When casinos hear talk of a union, they have been known to fire whoever's talking about it," a longtime dealer explained. "They've been known to fire an entire crew."[23] Management's response to an earlier effort to organize dealers in the 1950s reinforced these concerns. Within days after the fledgling Dealers Protective Association drew 200 dealers to its first public meeting in 1958, the resorts circulated the names of those dealers and promised to fire any of them who continued to support unionization. Only a dozen dealers showed up at the next meeting, and the association folded.[24] Dealers who complained to the press or public officials about such treatment withheld their names for fear of retaliation. "For obvious reasons, yes even physical violence," a dealer wrote to Governor Sawyer, "I must remain anonymous."[25]

While some dealers feared union activity, others saw no need for it. The latter regarded their relations with management as satisfactory and the prospect of unionization as potentially disruptive. They worried that union dues would be money poorly spent, and that union rules would be more burdensome than those they already confronted. Dealers also worried that unionization might require them to share their tips with a larger pool of workers than was already the case, or create a written record of their tip income, thus making that income more vulnerable to taxation. Some saw their jobs as temporary rather than as careers, which undercut their interest in long-range concerns. Others with personal connections to industry higher-ups—those who had "juice," as it was called—saw no advantage in union hiring halls or seniority systems. Then, too, some dealers saw themselves as individual entrepreneurs who "cut their own deals" with employers. These dealers, one might say, were libertarians who viewed unions as collectivized constraint on their freedom of movement, or "cowboys" in the western vernacular. Such dealers were likely to be antiunion. "Personally, I don't like unions," one such "cowboy" said. "There's no need for a union agent. We rely on 'juice.'" This attitude, or some variant of it, was sufficiently widespread to hinder unionization efforts.[26]

The effort to organize dealers began in the early 1960s, when the American Federation of Casino and Gaming Employees (AFCGE) first appeared in Las Vegas. This imposingly named organization was the handiwork of Thomas Hanley, who had earlier headed the Las Vegas local of the sheet metal workers' union. In 1963, with the help of labor activist Ragnald Fyhen, who had built one of the first trade unions at Boulder Dam, Hanley took control of an inactive local of the Operating Engineers as a vehicle for organizing casino dealers.[27]

Hanley's role in this effort was problematic from the start, at least from the standpoint of established unions. Hanley had been in Las Vegas since 1941. After the war, he had helped unionize sheet metal workers, who among other tasks installed air-conditioning units in hotels and casinos. While doing this earlier organizing, he had earned an unsavory reputation. Guns, narcotics, and violence seem to have been as much a part of his life as unions and labor relations. He was arrested several times in the 1950s and early 1960s on charges ranging from disorderly conduct to grand larceny, and he was a suspect in the unsolved murder of union agent James Hartley, who was shot in the head, his body thereafter dumped in the desert. Press accounts leave the impression that Hanley had arranged Hartley's murder as well as the brutal beating of another union business agent in order to consolidate his control over the sheet metal workers' union and its finances. Concerns about Hanley's character eventually resulted in his expulsion from the sheet metal workers' union for "bringing [the] union into disrepute."[28]

When Hanley's name resurfaced in the 1960s, the Las Vegas press described him as a "hoodlum" who had "crawled out from under the rocks." The *Sun* compared Hanley to Hitler and urged dealers to have nothing to do with him or his union. Casino managers charged that Hanley and some of his associates had bribery, larceny, and arson records and warned that the control of such men over gaming employees would destroy the integrity of casino gambling. Hanley's reputation thus compromised his drive to organize dealers, despite the fact that some dealers came to believe that only a man such as Hanley had the resourcefulness necessary to unionize the casinos. The din of adverse publicity Hanley generated drowned out his charges that management threatened to fire and blacklist dealers who had anything to do with any unionizing effort.[29]

Hanley was a master schemer. In 1964 he and his agents used multiple strategies to organize casino workers. They first approached slot machine mechanics, then numbering three or four hundred in and around Las Vegas, believing their special skills would make it difficult for management to replace them if they struck for union recognition. When the Operating Engineers claimed jurisdiction over the mechanics, Hanley switched to change girls and booth cashiers, promising them pay raises and increased benefits as well as training programs to improve their skills in return for joining his union. He also promised to "insist upon women receiving equal pay with men."[30] Originally targeting change girls and cashiers in major resorts, Hanley soon realized that those in small clubs, where tips were also small, were more interested in unionization. He therefore promised to negotiate wages according to the size and revenue of individual casinos, $25 a day for small ones and $30 a day for large ones. Throughout these maneuverings, Hanley turned to the National Labor Relations Board (NLRB) to legitimize his organizational effort and to prevent management from intimidating his organizers and sympathizers.[31]

Resort owners and the state officials beholden to them resisted Hanley's effort to involve the NLRB in his organizing effort, insisting that gaming was a local industry, distinct from interstate commerce, and thus beyond the reach of federal agencies. Nevada attorney general Harvey Dickerson went so far as to suggest that bringing casinos under the jurisdiction of federal agencies would compromise efforts already well underway to rid the Nevada gaming industry of organized crime. "If a guy's cheating, he's got to be fired today," Dickerson said of the generic dealer. "If you let him work two more weeks, he will be cheating for two more weeks."[32] Employers were responsible for curtailing illegal activity in their casinos, Dickerson reminded the NLRB, and must have the power to discharge employees caught in, or even suspected of, such activity "without delay" and without revealing how they discovered the illegal activity. He also noted that the Nevada Gaming Commission had the sole right to license dealers and that, in exercising that right, gave employers "flexibility" in matters relating to dealer honesty in the workplace. If either unions or the federal government prevented employers from hiring and firing dealers at will, Dickerson said, the state would likely establish a licensing system for dealers that would have the effect of strictly controlling the hiring and firing of all dealers and perhaps other casino employees as well.[33]

Hanley's insistence that the NLRB had jurisdiction over his efforts to organize dealers rested in part on an earlier NLRB ruling that the Thunderbird Hotel and the Clark County sheriff had violated the National Labor Relations Act by questioning employees about their union activities and by discharging a security guard for joining a union. In that case, the sheriff's office had revoked the guard's license for refusing to answer questions about his union activity. According to the sheriff, no one he deputized could join a union because to do so would conflict with his or her loyalties to his office. Sheriff's deputies, he argued, were employees of the state of Nevada and thus were not covered by the key provisions of the National Labor Relations Act. The Thunderbird supported the sheriff in this contention and dismissed the employee because he now lacked the proper security credentials. The NLRB rejected arguments that the sheriff's action was beyond its jurisdiction and ruled that, though licensed by the state, hotel security guards were resort employees with "self-organizational rights." The board then oversaw an election that resulted in the unionization of guards at the Thunderbird. That decision—as well as the outcome of that election—indicated that the NLRB would likely assert jurisdiction over disputes generated by Hanley's efforts to organize dealers.[34]

In the spring of 1964, Hanley's organizers began passing out registration cards, hoping to get 30 percent of the dealers in one or more casinos to pledge their intent to join his union; such a response could secure NLRB jurisdiction over a unionization vote. They promised to appeal to the NLRB on behalf of dealers fired for union sympathy or activity. When El Cortez and the Dunes did just that, Hanley charged them with unfair labor practices as defined by the federal Labor Relations Act and filed similar charges against the Tropicana when a slot mechanic there was allegedly fired for union activity.

In the summer of 1964, Hanley's union claimed that two thousand casino employees had signed membership applications. Though few of the signers had paid any union dues, the number emboldened Hanley. Claiming to have the necessary pledges of 30 percent of dealers at several resorts, including the Hacienda, the Showboat, and the Castaways, Hanley petitioned the NLRB to recognize his union as the bargaining agent for dealers in these properties. The board held hearings on the petition.[35] Pressing his case at the hearings, Hanley accused the casinos of refusing to negotiate with his union and of blacklisting his union's sympathizers. Overplaying his hand, Hanley called a strike at the Hacienda, the California Club, the New Frontier, and the Castaways. In response, a few dealers at these properties walked away from their jobs, and the resorts promptly fired them. Hanley then filed legal actions demanding reinstatement and compensation for lost wages for the fired employees.[36] At the same time, he urged Governor Sawyer to intervene in the dispute. Sawyer asked the resorts if they wanted his assistance or that of the state labor commissioner, but all declined the offer. Sawyer had no further authority. "The role of the governor in mediating labor disputes gives me no power to force mediation," he told Hanley concerning his authority under Nevada state law.[37]

Sawyer's earlier opposition to unionizing dealers probably undermined public support for the strike and the organizing drive. Unionization of dealers, Sawyer told state labor leaders in August, would infringe on the right of the state to regulate the employment of individuals engaged directly in gambling. Though the governor acknowledged the right of dealers to bargain collectively concerning wages, working conditions, and job benefits, he opposed any arrangement that gave unions—or any third party—control over the hiring and firing of dealers. If Hanley's union forced that on employers, Sawyer promised to implement a licensing system prohibiting the employment of dealers suspected of dishonesty or of ties to organized crime. "In order to properly control the industry," Sawyer said, "the state must not only be able to revoke a license granted to management, but as well the state must be in control of those who are engaged in the industry in [an] employee capacity."[38]

Hanley rejected the notion that unionization would result in the hiring of dishonest or mob-connected dealers or interfere with state oversight of employees engaged in gambling. In a strategic move to deflect Sawyer's opposition and to shore up support for his union, Hanley announced that the contracts of dealers he organized would include language assuring the right of resorts to discharge dealers quickly and easily. He was not seeking control over hiring and firing in casinos, he assured Sawyer and the Gaming Control Board, but over wages and working conditions there. These concessions did nothing to soften resistance to unionization, and a management spokesman dismissed them as a "desperation play." Moreover, the concessions removed a major incentive for unionizing. Hanley had agreed to leave matters of hiring and firing to management, a practice that currently blackballed job applicants for supporting union activity and terminated dealers for capricious or dubious reasons as well as for dishonesty or mob connections. "What good is a union that gave up the right to protect jobs?" union-leaning dealers now asked.[39]

♠ ♣ ♥ ♦

Buffeted by public criticism and uncertain leadership, Hanley's union had by 1965 lost many of its members. But his movement gained new life that year, when the NLRB completed investigating his appeals and ruled on the matters he raised. In a series of rulings known collectively as the El Dorado decision, the board gave the now largely discredited Hanley a major victory. The board found that resort owners in Nevada were engaged in interstate commerce and thus subject to NLRB jurisdiction; and that casino employees, including dealers, had the same right as other workers in interstate commerce to organize in accordance with relevant federal laws. In the words of the press, these rulings constituted a "poker-faced decision that jolted the Nevada gambling industry." In a bold stroke, the NLRB had dismissed management's interpretation of the law and had substituted for it a positive declaration that federal law encouraged collective bargaining, in gaming as in other industries, and that the resorts' fears of "undesirables" infiltrating the industry through a dealers' union were "unwarranted" by the facts of the case. The ruling had the potential for transforming labor relations in casinos.[40]

Hanley used the ruling to try to launch his organizing movement once again. He reiterated charges that the casinos had bargained in bad faith and had used "intimidation and coercion" against dealers favoring unionization. He petitioned the NLRB to approve representation elections at the Hacienda, the Sahara, the Thunderbird, and several smaller resorts, including the Silver Nugget in North Las Vegas and the Golden Gate and the California Club downtown. To husband his limited resources, he concentrated picketers at high-profile locations where he thought employers were most vulnerable to pressure. He thus made the most of his would-be union, which in late 1965 had perhaps 300 dues-paying members and a monthly income of no more than $1,500.[41]

Dealer unionization seemed to gain a foothold in January 1966, when an NLRB-ordered representation election occurred at the Golden Gate Hotel. In what the press called a "boss-wrenching victory," dealers there voted 72 to 38 to make Hanley's union their bargaining agent. A few weeks later, after another victory at another small casino in North Las Vegas, the Bonanza Club, Hanley signed the first union contract in history covering Las Vegas dealers. The contract gave the club's forty casino dealers wages of $25 a shift, health and welfare benefits, grievance procedures, paid vacations, and nondiscrimination guarantees.[42] It was a good contract for the dealers, giving them wages and benefits matching those of other equally skilled union employees in the industry.

Hanley and his union now savored the prospect of industry-wide success. His organization had tapped a reservoir of frustration among dealers and had won the right to represent a handful of them in and around Las Vegas. The NLRB had played a major role in this success, and the future of his union seemed bright. As this prospect dawned, the *Sun* blamed casino managers for "losing touch" with dealers and other workers, thereby inviting the unionization they and the *Sun* so dreaded. "Little by little, their faith, their confidence, their trust in you has eroded," the *Sun* said to the managers. "They feel you could not care less about their futures, their hopes, their ambitions."[43] Hanley and his union had turned anger and frustration into opportunity. In February 1966 the union threw an all-day party to celebrate its gains and prospects, inviting union members and sympathizers from across the city. Hanley was confident enough to use the occasion to criticize Governor Sawyer, who had begun to campaign for reelection. The governor, he charged, had done little to improve the livelihood of workers in Nevada.[44]

This confidence continued into the spring, when the NLRB ordered the Hacienda to reinstate forty-two dealers fired a year and a half earlier for sympathizing with union activity. Hanley hailed the ruling. "At no time have we ever asked for anything ridiculous," he told reporters, only that resort employees be "treated like human beings." The Hacienda ruling seemed, finally, to be the weapon Hanley needed to organize dealers.[45]

Suddenly, Hanley's hopes and expectations turned into disappointment. In May 1966, he lost a certification election at the Thunderbird, a major Strip casino, when dealers there voted 72 to 44 against his union. According to Thunderbird management, which spent more than $50,000 to fight the organizing campaign, most of their dealers realized that the unionization of dealers jeopardized the gaming industry and thus rejected it for their own well-being. Some dealers did in fact fear that union activity threatened their jobs. The Thunderbird had recently fired some of its security guards for trying to unionize. Hanley reacted to this major setback by accusing the Thunderbird of intimidating union sympathizers and bribing others to vote against the union, and by appealing to the NLRB. The NLRB found Hanley's charges justified and set aside the election results. Even so, in view of the lopsided vote against it, it seemed unlikely the union would win a new vote at the Thunderbird. The union's drive had stalled.[46]

The resulting stalemate continued through the summer of 1966, when the union suffered a series of setbacks. In June, Hanley's longtime associate and bodyguard Mike Marathon was brutally beaten by unidentified assailants outside a Las Vegas coffee shop. The reason for the attack was unclear, but it hospitalized Marathon and prompted the press to revive earlier charges of hooliganism or worse against Hanley and his associates. The *Sun* described Marathon as a "man of violence," a "five-cent punk," and suggested that the assault upon him was at Hanley's direction in retaliation for an act of betrayal. As these events unfolded, Ragnald Fyhen, the longtime labor activist who had helped Hanley's organizing effort, resigned as president of Hanley's union. Fyhen left the position, he said, because his declining health had kept him from involvement in union affairs for some time. The press rejected this explanation and instead described his resignation as a "revolt" against Hanley's "morals and ethics." Whether any or all of this was true is unclear, but the adverse publicity added to the mounting problems of Hanley and his effort to unionize dealers. In the aftermath, in July, his union lost NLRB-supervised elections at the Mint and Lucky Casino by wide margins. Hanley had significantly overestimated the appeal of his union, and these results fueled a sense of defeatism among his supporters and everyone else that supported dealer unionization.[47]

Hanley's unionization effort collapsed in November when Las Vegas police arrested Hanley and his chief organizer, Glen Herron, for assaulting an agent of the Internal Revenue Service. This untoward incident was a consequence of an IRS investigation of Hanley for income tax evasion. There is no hint in the available historical records of what prompted this investigation, though one may speculate on its relationship to his effort to unionize dealers. Be that as it may, in the course of the investigation, two IRS agents went to Hanley's office to serve a summons on Herron to testify in the case. When the agents arrived, Hanley and Herron were outside the office, where the agents served the summons. When Herron refused to accept the summons, Hanley allegedly became "abusive" and "pushed" one of the agents. The agents then decided to have Hanley arrested, for which purpose one of them called the police while the other followed Hanley into his office. There, Hanley allegedly hit the trailing agent in the face and stomach, whereupon the agent allegedly drew his gun and forced Hanley to back away. When the agent holstered his gun, Herron allegedly "attacked" him. At that point, the arrival of the police restored order and generated documentation for what happened thereafter. The injured IRS agent was taken to the hospital with "a bruise on the side of the face" and "a hurt tail bone," while Hanley and Herron were taken to the Clark County jail, where they spent eight hours before being released. A week later a federal grand jury indicted Hanley and Herron for interfering with the work of IRS agents.[48]

Hanley's union, along with its effort to organize dealers, faltered in the wake of this incident. It lost another certification election a few weeks later, at the New Pioneer. There, Hanley's organizers had been recruiting for more than two years, but the NLRB had repeatedly delayed a certification election to investigate charges of unfair labor practices by both management and the union. When the dealers finally voted, they rejected union representation by a margin of 31 to 17. Over the ensuing six months, the union lost representation elections at the California Club downtown, at Jerry's Nugget in North Las Vegas, and at the Silver Nugget on the Strip. In the last of these elections, only 4 of 72 dealers voted to make Hanley's union their bargaining agent. After this serialized debacle, Hanley promised to continue his organizing campaign, but he never did. His life deteriorated in the aftermath of these disappointments. In the late 1960s, he was arrested on four separate occasions for actions that generated charges of extortion, robbery, and even murder. He was convicted only of assaulting the IRS agent, however, for which he served a year in prison. When he was released in March 1970, his union had folded.[49]

While Hanley's union clung precariously to life, several other organizations surfaced in Las Vegas, each bent on unionizing casino dealers. The United Casino Employees Union (UCEU), headed by Truman Scott, an erstwhile Hanley lieutenant, emerged in 1967. Scott and others in his union had broken with Hanley that year and moved to Reno, where they endeavored to unionize dealers and other casino workers. Their effort had the backing of the International Seafarer's Union of the AFL-CIO, which had an eclectic membership of nearly 40,000 when it chartered Scott's union. Scott's efforts in Reno were no more successful than Hanley's in Las Vegas. When Hanley exited the labor scene in Las Vegas, Scott entered, only to see his union lose representation elections at the Dunes and the Desert Inn. The Seafarer's Union and then Scott himself abandoned the organizing campaign. A spokesman blamed the failure on the "tremendous element of fear" among casino workers.[50]

The fear was no doubt real. In the aftermath of Hanley's fall, hotel and casino managers continued their relentless opposition to the unionization of dealers, hiring spies to inform them of union activity. One of those spies, John McQueen, worked at the Castaways, which Scott tried to organize in 1968. Whenever Scott's organizers entered the Castaways, McQueen trailed them and made notes on what they did and said. "At approximately 1100 hours," McQueen wrote in January, "Frank Gill, an organizer for the seafarers union, arrived at the Castaways Casino. He was kept under close surveillance until his departure at 2300 hours." While there, Gill "was overheard on the telephone in the Castaways saying, 'They are not very friendly here. They won't let me solicit in the dealers' room.'"[51] In another confidential report, one of the Castaways dealers, Rick Sommers, told his supervisors that organizers had come to his home soliciting his support for the union drive. "They told me that organizing the dealers at the Castaways was the key to their organizing the other casinos," Sommers reported to his supervisors. "They told me again that I was a key man in their organizing the Castaways and if I signed other dealers would sign. I again refused to sign."[52] Such reports enabled employers to monitor union support and identify "loyal" as well as "disloyal" employees.

The Culinary also undertook a campaign to organize dealers. To do so, it created a new affiliate, Casino Employees Local 7, in April 1967. The head of the affiliate was M. R. "Mushy" Callahan, a longtime organizer from California who once worked on gambling ships off the coast of San Diego.[53] The Culinary evidently hoped that the impending end of its contract with downtown gambling establishments that year and the implicit threat of a work stoppage that it implied would provide the leverage necessary for Callahan to organize dealers. Events quickly proved otherwise. When culinary workers and bartenders struck downtown properties over wage-related issues on April 18, Callahan encouraged dealers at those properties to join the strike, promising that the Culinary would not settle the strike until employers recognized the casino workers' union and came to terms with it. But few dealers honored the Culinary's picket lines. On the contrary, some of them staffed struck positions. This response showed the limits of labor solidarity in Las Vegas and the lack of enthusiasm among dealers for unionism.[54]

Management developed new strategies against casino organizing after major Strip properties transformed the Nevada Resort Association into a management bargaining unit in the late 1960s. The association's chief negotiator, William Campbell, kept close track of the organizing campaigns and developed strategies to resist and ultimately defeat them. A centerpiece in those strategies was Campbell's insistence in 1970 that, in return for generous pay and benefit increases, the Culinary and Bartenders would give management the right to fire workers for honoring picket lines established for organizational purposes. That meant that unionized workers could not honor picket lines set up by or on behalf of unorganized dealers.

In 1971 the operating engineers' union challenged this management strategy in a well-publicized effort to organize dealers and slot machine mechanics at the Tropicana Hotel. The union hoped to capitalize on the Tropicana's pending sale, which generated uncertainty among employees about their jobs, and the union worked to turn this uncertainty into an advantage. Organizers collected enough pledge cards to warrant a representation election, which the NLRB scheduled for November 12, 1971.[55] Campbell promptly launched a "vigorous campaign" against the union effort. "The loss of control and the economic burdens that would flow from dealer's unionization," Campbell said, "dictate that the industry make whatever sacrifices as may be necessary to ensure the defeat of the union's efforts at the Tropicana." Should its dealers strike, Campbell advised, the Tropicana should hire replacements "as quickly as possible," without waiting for the response of the Culinary to the strike. The replacement workers, he pointed out, could then vote in the representation election, knowing that a union victory would cost them their jobs.[56]

Campbell's fears never materialized. The dealers and slot machine mechanics at the Tropicana rejected unionization by a vote of 97 to 48, most of them evidently preferring the uncertainties of the status quo to the risks of unionization in the face of management opposition. Wages and working conditions at the Tropicana were better than those in most casinos, a fact that reflected management strategies for dealing with unionization efforts. On the advice of Campbell, the Tropicana refused to allow organizers into the resort and prohibited its own employees from handing out union flyers or otherwise soliciting support for unionization. In communicating with the dealers and slot mechanics, managers emphasized the risks of unionization, including the loss of individuality when interacting with supervisors and the recurring periods of labor unrest, including strikes.[57]

As the struggle at the Tropicana unfolded, Nevada legislators passed laws eliminating some of the worst abuses in casinos. They made it a crime for employers to credit tips toward the payment of wages or to require employees to give them a share of their tips as a condition of employment. They also gave employees the right to agree among themselves on the division of tips. The new laws thus recognized that employees who received tips were entitled to them and that employers had no control over the tip income of their employees. Dealers welcomed these laws as devices that would meaningfully improve their income, and that may have been the legislative intent in enacting them: to undermine the trade-union movement by removing dealers' incentives to organize. Organizers had promised to address these issues and had hoped that such promises would encourage dealers to join the union cause.[58]

The legislature's action helped slow the unionization effort. It was not until 1974 that the next significant episodes occurred. In May of that year, dealers who worked the craps tables at the newly opened MGM Grand formed their own in-house union, the MGM Crap Dealers Association, and petitioned the NLRB for recognition. They evidently did so out of frustration with the MGM's tip-pooling procedures, which forced them to share tips with less experienced dealers who earned smaller tips or no tips at all. The association was unlike a union in that its members paid no dues and its leaders worked without compensation. Its president, Bob Jenkins, called unions "unruly monsters," and in bargaining with management promised to consider "the stockholders and the vast amount of money" they had invested in their properties. The NLRB refused to recognize Jenkins's association as a union, however, on grounds that its membership was too limited.[59]

In the wake of that refusal, dealers at the Sahara formed a more inclusive in-house organization, which the NLRB did recognize. The Sahara Dealers Association (SDA), as it called itself, included card and dice dealers as well as keno runners, baccarat game starters, shills, and brush-men. Its purpose was "to advance the interest of Sahara Hotel casino employees in their relationship with management," and to that end the SDA pledged to work to improve wages, benefits, and job security and to establish arbitration machinery to deal with employee grievances.[60] Job security was the reason for the association's initial success. The Sahara had recently dismissed a number of employees for what organizers of the new union considered arbitrary reasons, including unacceptable hairstyles, facial blemishes, and foreign accents. By August, when the association petitioned the NLRB for a representation election, it claimed 250 members.[61]

The SDA represented a new industry-wide challenge to management. If casino workers at the Sahara could form their own union, employers worried, so could those at other resorts. When the NLRB scheduled a certification election for the SDA for October 1974, managers at all resorts were concerned.[62] The Sahara itself acted to derail the SDA. A month before the election, its casino manager wrote to "all supervisors" detailing "basic rules" for dealing with organizing activity. Pit and shift bosses were not to discriminate against employees sympathetic to the union, but they should question them about the integrity of the SDA. "Does the union really have any interest in the welfare of the employees of this company," supervisors should ask, "or [is] it really interested in creating some good paying jobs for some union officials?" They should also remind pro-union employees that "there are certain risks involved in being represented by a union, such as the possibility of strikes and loss of your earnings if the union calls a strike."[63] The Sahara also told its casino employees that "leaders of the so-called 'association' haven't levelled with you." "DON'T BE MISLEAD [sic], a union means confrontation, not cooperation."[64]

Whether such admonitions had any effect is unclear, but dealers rejected the SDA by a vote of 180 to 155.[65] Casino managers across Las Vegas breathed a sigh of relief, and those at the Sahara were especially pleased. "It is with a deep sense of gratitude," they wrote to dealers, "that we accept your expression of confidence in us."[66] The results of this election are best read as an expression of the divided minds of dealers on unionization. Nearly half of those at the Sahara had voted to unionize, and it is difficult to know what those who voted against unionization thought of management. One of the latter voiced what seemed to be a widespread feeling when he asked after the election, "Why should you have two bosses?"[67] Some dealers apparently viewed the traditional role of management vis-à-vis labor as part of the natural order of work, a view that made unions suspect among workers who, as Marxists might say, had not had their class consciousness raised. In other words, these dealers rejected the notion that labor relations were "objectively" exploitative, an idea that, where it existed, pushed workers toward unionization.

Press reports suggested that the Sahara defeat spelled the end of dealer unions. But a month later, dealers at the Desert Inn voted 88 to 80 to make another emergent union, the Casino Employees of Nevada, their bargaining agent. An affiliate of the Chicago-based Brotherhood of Railway, Airline and Steamship Clerks, Freight Handlers, Express and Station Employees (BRAC), the union gained support at the Desert Inn with promises of higher wages, increased benefits, and "the right to work with a little self-respect and dignity." It won there despite management opposition, though the vote, like that at the Sahara, reflected the divided outlook of dealers as a group.[68] During the organizing campaign, Howard Hughes's Summa Corporation, the Desert Inn's parent company, announced significant pay raises for dealers at all of its properties. The hikes, management announced, were "one of the many steps that are being taken to continually insure that our employees are properly compensated for the fine jobs they perform."[69] Nonetheless, the union prevailed, and the victory buoyed the hopes of union activists. It is "just a matter of time," a BRAC spokesman boasted about the prospects of success for organizing dealers. "There is no question about that." In fact, there was a question. The Desert Inn challenged the result of the election, charging that union organizers had violated the law governing representation elections by misrepresenting conditions of employment at recently unionized casinos in Puerto Rico. The NLRB agreed to investigate the charge.[70]

As the investigation proceeded, the Culinary, prompted by BRAC's success, resurrected its dealers' organization, Local 7. According to Al Bramlet, "scores" of dealers had recently asked him to help them form a union, and the revival of Local 7 was his response to their plea. "Prior to this past year," Bramlet said, "the dealers have not shown the enthusiasm they have put forth in the past few weeks toward getting together." The Culinary, he added logically, was the "best and most logical" home for organized dealers. The union had a long and successful record of negotiating in the resort industry and, with more than twenty thousand members, was in a position to pressure management to recognize a dealers' union.[71]

This assessment was more hopeful than realistic. In early 1975 BRAC lost representation elections at the Royal Inn and the Flamingo Hotel, in both instances by three-to-one margins. The union rebounded with a narrow victory at the Landmark, where dealers earned smaller tips and harbored more resentment toward management, only to have the NLRB set aside the result after management charged the union with misleading dealers during the election campaign. A more significant setback came in April, when dealers at the MGM rejected unionization by a three-to-two margin. This decisive loss may be partly explained by the fact that three unions—BRAC, the Culinary, and a new organization affiliated with the Teamsters—vied for the right to represent the dealers.[72]

In all these elections, management maneuvering bested that of union organizers. At the larger Strip casinos, executive officers worked closely with casino supervisors to undermine union appeal. MGM president Alvin Benedict, former head of hotel operations for Howard Hughes and president of the NRA, urged casino managers to remind dealers that unionization "will present serious problems to the operation of the casino, and to dealers and supervisors alike." At the same time, Benedict warned the managers that he would no longer tolerate "thoughtless" disciplinary action. "We realize that a few of the supervisors have been too abrupt and inconsiderate in their contacts with dealers," Benedict said. "This we will not tolerate. If a dealer has to be reprimanded for an infraction of the rules, he should be taken aside and told. He should not be degraded by being shouted at in front of others."[73] In addition, Benedict met with dealers and reminded them that wages and working conditions at the MGM were among the best in Las Vegas and that unionization would reduce these to industry averages. "Hiring halls, hotel-wide seniority, formal grievance procedures, arguments about tips, hassles over leaves of absence and the loss of personal contact between players and management trouble me greatly," Benedict told dealers, predicting the troublesome consequences of unionization. "I think they should trouble you too."[74]

Employers found other ways to blunt the lure of unionization. They made notable improvements in workplace rules and conditions, for example, and some even raised wages. Benedict himself asked dealers how to improve the workplace and implemented some of their suggestions. He installed drinking fountains in the casinos and lockers for dealers, had the parking lot for casino employees fenced for safety purposes, and modified gaming tables to make dealing easier. "We have adjusted some salaries in accordance with area surveys," he also noted, as if the increases were voluntary. Most important, he rationalized personnel policies. Dealers would thenceforth receive written warnings of unsatisfactory work, and two such notices would be necessary within six months for termination except in cases of dishonesty, drunkenness, or willful misconduct. Benedict also instituted a seniority system for promotions and, thus, for pay and layoffs.[75]

At the industry-wide level, in the summer of 1974, the NRA established a Salary Review Committee to study wages and benefits for dealers and to recommend uniform standards as well as procedures for handling grievances. The committee soon proffered a pay scale for dealers ranging from $25 to $36 a day, as well as industry-wide policies on holidays, meal privileges, vacations, and benefit programs. It also proposed new procedures for nonunion workers to file complaints against supervisors without fear of reprisal.[76]

These recommendations were clearly designed to diminish the appeal of unionization, which the NRA continued to call a "serious threat" to management control of casinos. "I am convinced," William Campbell said at the time in a memorandum to NRA members, "that unions will prevail unless management immediately develops a comprehensive, positive program that offers casino personnel a rational alternative to union representation." Cooperation in achieving that goal was imperative. "We can ill afford the luxury of going it alone or tolerating half-hearted or ineffective measures by member establishments," Campbell continued. "If we don't hang together, we shall surely all hang separately." To facilitate the cooperation he thought necessary, Campbell proposed the formation of a steering committee, culled "from top management ranks only" to develop strategies for an ongoing antiunion campaign; to create a centralized agency to provide industry executives with "expert advice" on matters of publicity, law, and "campaign tactics"; and to implement an industry-wide program of assistance to individual resorts targeted by union organizers.[77]

Accepting Campbell's approach, industry leaders formed a seven-man committee that included such major management figures as Jack Binion, Steve Wynn, and Jackie Gaughan to direct the campaign against dealer unionization.[78] The committee concerned itself especially with the Culinary's effort to organize dealers. Campbell seems to have considered this the greatest threat. To blunt it, he suggested that the hotels learn all they could about relationships between their dealers and culinary workers, including "whether any [of their] casino employees [were] related to culinary workers by blood or marriage."[79] He had "no accurate information on the amount of success the Culinary is having" in organizing dealers, he complained, giving the hotels the names of two organizers "on the culinary payroll," urging that they be barred from casinos under the "no solicitation" rule.[80]

The hotels followed Campbell's advice. They checked dealers' relatives in the industry and contacted previous employers about the union sympathies of individual dealers. "Information is that he is an agitator, who may very well be involved in union activity," read a memo on Frontier hotel stationery evidently written by a house detective about a dealer suspected of union sympathy. The detective thought another dealer trustworthy because his father had been a "casino executive" at the Flamingo.[81]

In mid-1975 the NLRB dealt a major blow to the movement to unionize dealers by overturning BRAC's 1974 victory in the Desert Inn representation election. Accepting the employer's charges, the board concluded that a union organizer had "grossly" misrepresented the wages and working conditions of casino workers in Puerto Rico, whom BRAC had recently organized. The organizer, from Puerto Rico, had claimed that five thousand unionized dealers in Puerto Rico earned $1,200 to $1,500 a month, when in fact there were fewer than seven hundred dealers in Puerto Rico and their pay ranged from $300 to $1,125 a month. The organizer had also misrepresented grievance procedures in Puerto Rico, claiming that employers there had to prove charges of thievery against dealers in court before discharging them. Because the Desert Inn had had insufficient time to investigate and refute these claims, the board ordered a new representation election.[82]

With that setback, the unions had almost nothing substantial to show for their long struggle to organize dealers. Not a single casino was now organized, in part because the organizing drives had forced casinos to raise dealers' wages meaningfully and to relax their supervisory prerogatives notably. In addition, the casinos had introduced what William Campbell called a "formalized system of communication between management and casino employees and [an] appeals procedure in discharge cases."[83] To be sure, these results lacked the force of similar guarantees for unionized workers. Nonetheless, they gave dealers significant new benefits and protections. "The agitation itself did improve working conditions," a former head of the Nevada Gaming Control Board later acknowledged.[84] Even the local press, which never supported the unionization of dealers, recognized these gains. "In fact," the Valley Times stated, "the threat of unionization has resulted in improved working conditions and better benefits for casino workers. It has forced management to treat the dealers better." As a result, "the lure of unionization is less appealing."[85]

Hotel managers understood this result, and their confidence in the rightness of their approach increased when dealers at the Desert Inn rejected unionization in December 1975 by a vote of 110 to 94. This defeat ended BRAC's effort to organize dealers. Union sympathizers, perhaps buoyed again by the split minds of dealers that this vote once again showed, pledged plaintively to "try again." "The right to organize does not end here," one of them reminded the press. Management was nevertheless exultant. "Justice has prevailed," an executive of the Desert Inn said after this latest election. "My heart is warm."[86] These words recalled those of Andrew Carnegie when he heard that striking employees had lost everything at his Homestead Steel Plant in 1892, all but destroying the trade-union movement in the steel industry.

♠ ♣ ♥ ♦

The failure to organize Las Vegas dealers is best understood as an example of what adamant and effectively organized employers can accomplish in opposing unions when circumstances break in their favor. The management of every resort resisted dealers' unions; there was no known exception. All of them used whatever instruments of power, persuasion, or influence at their disposal to break dealer-organizing campaigns. Their hired consultants offered expert advice on how to use NLRB rules and procedures to delay and appeal the results of representation elections regardless of what those results indicated about dealers' preferences. William Campbell of the NRA played a major role in this. Campbell's opposition to dealer unions went beyond what one might term the call of his duty to his employers. Like all management consultants, Campbell identified with the interests of the men who paid him, and he saw labor-organizing campaigns as threats to those interests. In 1971 Campbell warned the NRA that casino organizing was an "industry-wide problem." If dealers won the right to grievance procedures comparable to those of union employees, he cautioned, management "would, in the process, lose many of [its] rights to manage the operation and control [its] employees." To avoid this, Campbell urged resorts to improve the wages and working conditions of dealers and to make sure they were protected against "capricious or unjust disciplinary action."[87]

The opposition of management, however, was only one reason for the failure of dealer unionization. Unions, would-be-unions, and the leaders of both responded inadequately to the challenges of organizing dealers. Among other deficiencies, they failed adequately to address the fears and uncertainties of many dealers concerning unionization, including concerns about how a dealers' union would deal with a hostile management. They called dealers who opposed unions "bootlickers" and "traitors," which hardly inspired them to rally to union banners. It is not possible to know the attitudes of all dealers, or even most typical dealers, to unionization, but it is apparent that many of them did not think in the collective terms necessary for union success. Some had more in common with casino managers than with union officials and preferred to distance themselves from unionized employees. Union activists never understood that many dealers liked their jobs, their supervisors, and their economic prospects. They failed to assure dealers that unionization would not threaten their tips, their "juice" to find better jobs, or their traditional means for influencing workplace outcomes. All too often, organizers made unrealistic promises about the benefits of organizing, and when organizing campaigns collapsed, they disappeared. In short, the labor movement in Las Vegas and Nevada made an unrealistic assessment of not only the dealers' situation but also of its own ability to challenge employers determined to crush unionization through intimidation and temptation.[88]

Workplace Incidents

On July 14, 1970, the Frontier Hotel fired Herman Buskin, an experienced warehouse worker, for "willful misconduct" and making "rash and inflammatory" statements to his overseer, the warehouse manager. Buskin had objected to new workplace rules, and when his supervisor insisted on enforcing the new rules, Buskin called him a "dirty bastard" and a "son-of-a-bitch." More important, he told a co-worker he intended "to kill" the supervisor. What provoked Buskin was the fact that the new rules relegated him to a new workstation and to more onerous tasks and responsibilities. The hotel considered Buskin's reaction in this encounter with his supervisor to constitute "gross disrespect toward supervision" and an "attack [on] principles of authority." On this basis, it dismissed him summarily. Buskin appealed the dismissal through the grievance procedure provided in his union contract. When the Frontier refused a plea to reinstate Buskin, his union thought his appeal weighty enough to take it to arbitration, only to have the arbitrator rule against him. Buskin's conduct, the arbitrator found, "could only be considered as destructive of good labor management relations."[1]

The workings of this arbitration process reveal a good deal about workers and labor relations in the resort industry. To begin with, it shows something of the workplace experience, including the problems and pressures generated therein. Resort workers in Las Vegas shared the gamut of attitudes and perspectives that characterized American workplaces generally, with special concerns that grew out of the specific nature of their work. The records generated by the arbitration process shed light on their attitudes toward work and labor relations, and on how they justified their workplace behavior and understood their social being as workers. They show that resort workers were generally cooperative and earnest but had a strong sense of self-worth and even entitlement.[2]

The arbitration process also shows how resort managers exercised and maintained the "right to manage." Managers always resisted grievance processes, viewing them as intrusions into their control of the workplace. In the Las Vegas resort industry, however, a union-backed grievance system was well ensconced by 1955, and managers had learned to work through rather than against the system to maintain their prerogatives. To a meaningful degree, they were able to use arbitration to improve the efficiency and productivity of workers and to ensure that workers and unions abided by management decisions. This was especially true after corporate managers took control of the industry in the late 1960s and the 1970s.[3]

Moreover, arbitration cases show that workers and their supervisors confronted one another at different levels and in different ways. Some encounters between labor and management were much more confrontational than others. Many took place in full view of everyone in the workplace, often including customers, and most revolved around unspectacular infractions of house rules and regulations. Though employers viewed their workplace policies as essential to the orderly functioning of their business operations, their house rules were not so much rooted in the natural order of things as in their understandings of what constituted workplace orderliness. Probably most workers considered some number of those rules as variously unnecessary, arbitrary, or even demeaning and ignored or circumvented them as best they could.

The origins of labor arbitration lay in federal statutes and court rulings as well as collective bargaining agreements. The Wagner Act of 1935 created the National Labor Relations Board (NLRB) to oversee the execution of federal responsibility in workplace relations, which the act itself spelled out. The Taft-Hartley Act of 1948 modified and institutionalized the system thus created, and declared arbitration the "most desirable" method of settling bargaining and workplace disputes and enforcing labor contracts. It also empowered the federal government to arbitrate labor disputes that threatened to disrupt interstate commerce. In a series of rulings over the years, the Supreme Court found that arbitration had a therapeutic effect on labor relations, functioning to reduce tensions and conflict and to reward compromise and responsible behavior on both sides. The Court's findings rested in no small degree on the willingness of arbitrators to weigh evidence and rule impartially within the parameters of relevant law and bargaining agreements.[4]

The selection of arbitrators was therefore contested. The Federal Mediation and Conciliation Service, which Taft-Hartley created, helped unions and employers establish and maintain panels of mutually acceptable arbitrators. In the Las Vegas resort industry, both parties worked assiduously to find sympathetic arbitrators, that is, those they thought could be swayed by reasonable evidence supporting their side. They then agreed on a panel of about a dozen individuals from which the two sides agreed on an arbitrator for each grievance procedure that reached the stage of formal arbitration. The two sides retained the right to strike names from the slate annually. In the resulting modifications, each side sought to retain members sympathetic to its views and replace those it considered hostile.[5]

Arbitrators handled only a minuscule fraction of grievances filed in any given year and industry. Labor and management settled most grievances informally, often over the telephone. When this was impossible, they referred the grievance to their own representatives, and only if those representatives failed to achieve a mutually agreeable resolution of the dispute, or if both parties waived this step, did the grievance go to an arbitrator, whose decision was final and binding. Both sides had reason to settle disputes informally. Arbitration was slow and costly, attorneys and arbitrators had to be paid, and the outcome of arbitration cases was always uncertain.

In deciding cases, arbitrators applied criteria of "just cause" to the actions of employees and employers. Labor contracts recognized employers' rights to discipline or discharge employees for specified causes. Unions acknowledged that workers could be dismissed or disciplined for flouting or ignoring legitimate supervisory authority or breaking house rules about which they had been informed. Except in the most flagrant cases, unions insisted that employers provide "progressive discipline." They expected employers to give offending employees written warnings and verbal admonitions for first or even second offenses, thus creating a written record of employee misconduct. Contracts often made three written warnings within a few months or a year sufficient grounds for suspension or discharge, depending on the nature of the offenses and the circumstances of the incidents. They also stipulated that grievances be filed within a specified time, usually a week or two following the discipline.[6]

This system of grievance resolution was well established in the Las Vegas resort industry. The 1957 agreement between the Culinary and the Nevada Industrial Council, for example, set up a three-step process for handling disputes in the workplace and the meaning of contract language, and that process continued through the period of this study.[7] Using this process, workers filed several hundred written complaints each year in the 1960s alleging mistreatment in the workplace. The grievance rate and the number of grievances that went to arbitration rose notably in the late 1960s and early 1970s, which suggests that labor, management, or both thought that the informal working of collective bargaining processes was functioning less effectively than it had in the past or that workplace relations had become more contentious. Still, the number of grievances filed is not by itself an accurate barometer of labor relations. The resort industry and its workforce grew rapidly, as did the bureaucratization and hence the depersonalization of workplace relations, and perhaps also the stressfulness of work and of worker-supervisor relations at the lowest levels. Each and all of these things might explain the rise in grievances filed and the increasing difficulty unions had in getting managers to abide by union understandings of the language of their contracts.[8]

A study of grievances filed in the Culinary in the 1970s and 1980s details the general trend. In the 1970s, when the Culinary had more than twenty thousand members in the metropolitan area, its members filed 1,500 to 2,000 grievances annually. In the following decade, when the Culinary's membership grew to more than thirty thousand, its members filed 2,200 to 3,000 grievances a year. In the 1970s and 1980s inclusive, the number of their grievances totaled more than 40,000. Of those, fewer than 350—less than 1 percent— went to arbitration, and more than two-thirds of these involved suspension or discharge of the employee. The union won about 65 percent of the cases formally arbitrated, which not only suggested that most arbitrated grievances were reasonable and justified but that union expenditure on arbitration was a good investment.[9]

Women and minorities were as likely to file grievances as white male employees, but neither they nor union officials targeted problems of gender or racial discrimination for arbitration. Unions established grievance machinery to resolve violations of labor contracts, and not until the 1970s did those contracts include language to address the problem of discrimination other than provisions that insisted on equal pay for men and women. Even then, they prohibited parties from denying employment only on the basis of race, sex, or national origins. Resort workers thus found other ways of fighting discrimination. Beginning in 1964, some filed complaints with the newly established Equal Employment Opportunity Commission (EEOC), which investigated discriminatory practices in society and encouraged the U.S. Justice Department to enforce civil rights laws. Others took their problems to the Nevada Equal Rights Commission, which also investigated charges of workplace discrimination and pushed to enforce the law. Still others alerted the local branch of the National Association of Colored People

(NAACP) of workplace problems. When it came to breaking down patterns of discrimination in resorts (as illustrated in the next chapter), grass-roots movements led by civil rights activists proved far more effective than the union resolution procedures. The problem of race and gender discrimination was common to both unions and management, as well as the larger society.

A representative grievance that went to an arbitrator in the early years of this study involved the discharge of bartender John Filizzola by the Thunderbird Hotel. Like other resort bartenders, Filizzola took orders from customers and cocktail waitresses, received payments, and recorded sales according to specified procedures, including procedures for rectifying his own mistakes. At the end of his shift, he counted his receipts and reconciled them with the cash register tape. He placed the receipts and the tape in a "cash envelope," which he turned over to management.[10]

The hotel fired Filizzola in September 1966 for violating regulations governing the handling of receipts and money. An undercover detective reported that he saw Filizzola serve drinks without ringing up sales and stuffing money into his pocket. Confronted with the report, Filizzola, who had worked at the hotel for three months, denied the charges and contacted his union for help. The union investigated the case and filed a grievance on Filizzola's behalf. The union concluded that whether Filizzola had actually stolen money was unclear; what was clear was that the hotel had not shown just cause for discharging him. Informal discussion failed to resolve the grievance, and the two sides agreed to submit the case to arbitrator Howard Duram. Duram heard the evidence and arguments, including the detective's reports and Filizzola's denial of the charges, in January 1967, four months after Filizzola's dismissal. Cocktail waitresses, Filizzola explained, sometimes made mistakes serving drinks, which forced him to prepare new drinks without ringing up sales, and he sometimes received cash tips from hotel guests who charged drinks, and put the money either in a glass on the bar or in his pocket. The money the detective saw him pocket, he insisted, was his own.[11]

Two months later, Duram ruled against the hotel. Filizzola's discharge, he found, violated the hotel's collective bargaining agreement with the Bartenders Union, which like state and federal laws required the employer to support accusations of theft beyond a reasonable doubt. The hotel had not done that, Duram found, having made no effort to document the validity of the detective's report. Although the bartender had worked at the Thunderbird for only three months, he had an unblemished employment record elsewhere of ten years. The money Filizzola put in his pocket could have been his own. The arbitrator thus ordered the Thunderbird to reinstate Filizzola with back pay.[12]

The Filizzola case showed the assiduity with which management oversaw and disciplined employees who handled money. The hiring of detectives for surveillance purposes was common and was just one of several ways employers let employees know they monitored their behavior. The case also indicated the limits of managerial authority. Union contracts placed meaningful restrictions on the rights of employers to discharge employees, restrictions that were procedural as well as substantive and applied even to employees suspected of thievery or incompetence. Whether Filizzola was guilty or innocent is moot, but in dismissing him the hotel had been procedurally amiss. If contractual niceties sometimes allowed dishonest barkeepers to keep their jobs, the knowledge that management monitored their behavior no doubt made bartenders careful of their conduct. Contractual language provided protection to employees against arbitrary employers and supervisors, and emboldened workers like Filizzola to resist what they considered managerial arbitrariness. A system that might occasionally reward a thieving employee benefited other employees wrongfully accused of misconduct.

A 1968 grievance involving female switchboard operators at the Frontier Hotel further demonstrates the nature of workplace relations and the value of the arbitration system for workers. The case documents an instance of solidarity as well as impulsiveness not normally associated with service workers and says something about how workers dealt with the failure of their union to address their problems. In May of that year, six switchboard operators walked off their jobs without warning to protest their treatment by their supervisor, Chief Operator Irene Cooper. Cooper, they charged, frequently insulted and ridiculed them, engaged in favoritism in assigning work shifts, and meted out punishment unfairly and unevenly, and on the basis of personal likes and dislikes. "The abuse and mistreatment that I have seen the girls subjected to," one of the operators later explained, "is so upsetting that it affects everyone in the office."[13]

The women had tried to resolve their problems with Cooper. Two days before the walkout, one of them told a hotel assistant manager that the operators were "having trouble" with Cooper and thinking of walking off their jobs. The manager promised to "check into the situation" and "get back to" the complainant, but failed to do so. One of the women told her union, the Teamsters, on the morning of the walkout that operators were about to strike. A union spokesman advised her to "hold everything" and dispatched a representative to discuss the matter with the hotel's personnel director. As this occurred, fourteen operators signed a complaint against Cooper, and another sent a handwritten note to the union saying of Cooper: "We will not go for anything less than to have her *out*." By one o'clock, six of the operators concluded that neither management nor the union was doing anything to help them and walked off the job. The hotel responded by calling in off-duty operators and discharging the disgruntled operators on grounds that their actions violated contract language prohibiting "wildcat" strikes.[14]

The Teamsters never condoned such strikes but thought the discharges in this case precipitate and unwarranted. It therefore filed a grievance on behalf of the discharged operators, arguing that extenuating circumstances justified their walkout and asking for their reinstatement. The hotel refused, viewing the walkout as a calculated challenge to management prerogative. By mutual agreement, the two parties sent the case to arbitration.

Two months later arbitrator Oran Gragson, who was also mayor of Las Vegas, ruled that the walkout did indeed violate the collective bargaining agreement. The protesting operators, Gragson explained, should have used established procedures to address their grievances before walking out. To sanction the walkout, he said, "would create a condition that would be intolerable to the employer and would greatly diminish the effectiveness of grievance procedures established in the collective bargaining contract."[15] The dismissal of the operators was thus justified.

This grievance showed how workers demanded some degree of respect and fairness from their supervisors. In detailing this incident, the switchboard operators insisted that supervisors had a responsibility to cultivate a pleasant work environment and treat employees equitably. "It's up to the chief operator to determine the atmosphere in an office," one of the women explained. "When she's raving at a girl for nothing it's pretty hard to maintain a pleasant atmosphere." Employees could be disciplined, she acknowledged, but it should be done discreetly, and without embarrassing them. "[She] makes girls cry the way she talks to them," one operator said of Cooper. "She should have quietly done her reprimanding and not gloated about it," another explained. Such comments suggest that workers expected a good supervisor to acknowledge their value and care about their well-being as well as their work. "Mrs. Cooper hasn't appreciated me in any way," one of operators said. "[She] does not show any understanding or compassion for her girls." The women thus let management know that a supervisor like Cooper jeopardized the success of the hotel. Cooper had driven "loyal" employees off the job and made it difficult for those who remained to treat hotel guests hospitably. "We are salesmen for the Hotel," as one of the women put it, "and [we] have to *feel* what we are trying to transmit to the public."[16]

These cases involving the Thunderbird and the Frontier underscore the importance of unions and grievance procedures in resort workers' lives. They show that
the grievance process helped workers assert their contractual rights and protect
their jobs, thus giving them a voice in decisions that affected their lives. Yet they
also demonstrated how employers could use the process to exercise their own
prerogatives in the workplace. Like unions, resorts could insist on including new
management rights in collective bargaining agreements, and those rights helped
win arbitration cases. They could also delay the resolution of workplace disputes
and sap unions of energy and funds. Resort workers understood the problems and
uncertainties associated with grievance procedures, and that knowledge no doubt
discouraged some of them from filing grievances. In the late 1960s and 1970s,
however, for which there are substantial records, thousands of workers appealed
to their unions for help in resolving their problems.

Many grievances concerned small matters of employee insubordination, which
employers were generally unwilling to tolerate. Collective bargaining agreements in the resort industry recognized management's right to "direct, plan and
control" the workforce as long as doing so was consistent with specifications
written into the contracts. They also permitted the summary discharge of employees for "willful misconduct" but not for "insubordination." Unions made a
sharp distinction between these two forms of misbehavior, insisting that the
"just cause" doctrine required management to prove more than insubordination
to justify a summary discharge.

A representative instance of this involved the 1970 discharge of Noel Durant,
a waiter in the Copa Room at the Sands Hotel, the most famous showroom in Las
Vegas. One or more of the "Rat Pack"—Dean Martin, Frank Sinatra, Sammy
Davis Jr., Joey Bishop, and Peter Lawford—appeared there regularly, as did Milton
Berle, Nat "King" Cole, and Danny Thomas. The room often filled with celebri-
ties and well-known socialites, and working there was understandably stressful.
With two shows nightly, waiters like Durant had to work quickly and efficiently.

Durant's work routine began about 6:30 p.m., when the doors opened for the
8:00 p.m. dinner show. As guests entered, hosts or hostesses seated them, and,
in teams, waitresses took their orders and gave them to waiters at assigned stations. The waiters recorded the orders and carried them to the executive chef,
Maurice Cau, who used an intercom to call them in to assistant chefs and cooks.
Because showroom meals were partially prepared in advance, the chefs and
cooks filled orders rapidly. They placed the filled orders at the waiters' window,

from which the waiters took them to waitresses who served them. After the meal, waitresses cleared the tables. This process began again at 9:30 p.m., when guests for the second show began arriving.[17]

Durant, who had worked at the Copa for two years, had had no problems with his work. On August 7, however, he submitted a customer's order to the executive chef on the yellow slip of paper the hotel reserved for room service orders rather than on the white one used for showroom customers. The chef told Durant of his mistake and cautioned him not to repeat it. When Durant did just that, the chef threw the order back at him and refused to fill it. Durant protested, whereupon the chef in a loud voice called Durant, an Englishman, a "limey," at which Durant took offense. "Fuck you," Durant said in return. The chef then banished Durant from the kitchen, informing his supervisor, the maitre d', of the banishment.

At that point, the captain of the room interceded in the dispute, admonishing Durant not to "talk back" to the chef, to which the waiter replied loudly, "The chef can go fuck himself!" Everyone in the kitchen, including the chef, heard the reply, but Durant rewrote the order on white paper and finished his shift without further incident. When he returned to work the next day, he learned that the chef had banished him from the kitchen. The banishment did not prevent Durant from doing his work, and for the next two nights he worked his shift as usual. The director of food and beverage services at the hotel, who had by then concluded that the situation was intolerable, decided to fire the waiter. When Durant reported for work the next day, a security guard at the employee's entrance handed him a termination notice. He was discharged, the note said, for "willful misconduct."

The Culinary agreed to grieve Durant's dismissal because the hotel had given Durant no written warning that his job performance was unsatisfactory. At the arbitration hearing, the hotel insisted that it had no such responsibility in this case because Durant's behavior showed "gross disrespect for supervision" and "undermined the fundamental concept of the employment relationship." Reinstating Durant would therefore "completely undermine the chef's authority in the kitchen."[18] The union representative argued that Durant had acted in the heat of the moment when he and the chef were both under pressure generated by a rush in the workload. He also noted that Durant had yelled at the chef only after he had been insulted, that the hotel occasionally ran out of white receipt slips, and that when that happened the hotel instructed employees to substitute yellow slips for them. Given these extenuating circumstances, the union attorneys argued, Durant should be returned to his job with compensation for lost wages and tips, and without loss of seniority and other benefits.

Arbitrator Irving Bernstein settled the case a year after the incident by dividing responsibility for it as well as the cost of the arbitration. Durant's misbehavior, he ruled, had been "very serious" and, if left unpunished, would undermine the chef's legitimate authority in the kitchen. But in handling the incident, the Sand's management had "misread" it. Durant's behavior had not been "calculated or intentional" but the product of "a moment of anger," which under terms of the union contract amounted to insubordination rather than willful misconduct. Durant should not have been dismissed but given a warning and "an opportunity to repair the damage he had caused," or perhaps suspended without pay for a few days. Anything more than a thirty-day suspension was unreasonable, Bernstein concluded. He therefore directed the Sands to reinstate Durant without loss of seniority and benefits, but also without full compensation for lost wages and tips. To claim back wages for the time he was out of work, Durant had to subtract from the total thirty days pay plus money he had received from the state unemployment office.[19]

Another vivid example of insubordination occurred at the Sahara. In May 1970 the Sahara discharged Antonio Sarmiento, a waiter, after he openly challenged a supervisor's authority. According to the hotel, Sarmiento had "flatly refused" to perform certain setup duties in the restaurant in which he worked because it was "not his job." When a manager objected, the waiter reportedly "lost his temper" and started "screaming" at him in front of customers, who were "shocked" at his behavior. The Sahara called the incident "willful misconduct" and "a gross violation" of rules pertaining to an employee's conduct in the presence of customers.[20] The union rejected this interpretation of the incident and the hotel's handling of it, noting that when the encounter occurred, Sarmiento had already completed his own setup duties and was simply refusing to perform someone else's tasks when the manager called him a "son-of-a-bitch." The union insisted therefore that Sarmiento's reaction to the manager's order deserved no more than a "warning and counseling."[21]

Arbitrator Sanford Cohen concluded that Sarmiento's behavior constituted willful misconduct. Several witnesses testified that the waiter had "shouted or screamed" at his supervisor in a voice "audible throughout the restaurant." Two of the witnesses considered Sarmiento's behavior a "threat to the physical safety" of his supervisors, one of whom had stepped between the two men to prevent a fight. The fact that the waiter had previously been fired at the Desert Inn for striking a supervisor with a pepper mill in front of customers no doubt influenced the arbitrator's decision. "By engaging in an emotional avenue of protest," Cohen ruled, Sarmiento had "made himself liable to discharge without warning notice."[22]

♠ ♣ ♥ ♦

Confrontations between employers and supervisors occasionally resulted not just in violent language but in physical violence and injury. In 1971, for example, Ruth De Jarnette, a waitress in the Savoy Room at the Dunes Hotel, stabbed her supervisor, Frieda Carter, with a ballpoint pen. Carter had complained in front of other waitresses that De Jarnette's handwritten orders to the chef were illegible, and said, "Kid, you have got to write more distinctly so the chef would know what you are writing." "Get off my back," De Jarnette responded in a loud and angry voice, "you don't know what you are talking about."[23]

Carter prepared a written warning for this incident but waited until De Jarnette went on break to deliver it. Outraged at the notice, De Jarnette warned Carter, "I'll get even with you." As the two women returned to work, De Jarnette jammed a pen into Carter's thigh, penetrating her dress and undergarments. Carter was apparently too frightened or surprised to fire De Jarnette summarily. Instead, she wrote out a termination notice, accusing her of willful misconduct. "Mad at hostess over warning slip," the notice specified. "Jabbed hostess in leg with her pen." "I didn't do it," De Jarnette responded angrily. "I'm going to the Union about that."

The Culinary appealed the case to an arbitrator despite the fact that several co-workers supported the supervisor's account of what happened. The co-workers testified that De Jarnette, who had worked at the Dunes for two years, had a history of threatening behavior. "I'm going to kill that bitch if she don't leave me alone," she once said to a co-worker about a supervisor. She had also been involved in earlier altercations, having been reprimanded at the Dunes on one occasion for striking another waitress with a serving tray and on another for kicking a co-worker. She had also had arguments with cooks and busboys, and once called the head chef "a little shit." The arbitrator considered this background information only secondary to the incident itself, but with De Jarnette's past behavior in mind, he concluded the hotel had "just cause" for discharging her.[24]

Some arbitration cases grew out of violence between workers. Despite the exceptional nature of such episodes, two or more employees sometimes found themselves in heated confrontations with each other. In rare instances, these confrontations ended in fistfights and injury. The problem was serious enough for employers to post rules prohibiting fighting in the workplace and to fire employees who "willfully" violated those rules. Management sometimes acted hastily, however, and discharged workers without fully investigating the disturbance between them.

In 1974 the Desert Inn fired Gail Corrow, a pantry worker, for "beating up an employee on company premises and during working hours." The termination notice described Corrow as a brutish woman with a bad temper, as well as a bad employee. Corrow had, however, worked for the Desert Inn for ten years without a problem. On May 3, Corrow got into a fight with Eva Shock, a waitress. Earlier in the day, Corrow had been aggravated once when Shock haphazardly dumped a batch of freshly baked muffins into a drawer, smashing most of them, and again when Shock gave her an improper order for a sandwich. The sandwich, a "Chef's Special," was made on an oval porcelain plate and heated in the kitchen's "radar oven." Waitresses were supposed to give the pantry worker one of those plates when placing the order, but in this instance Shock gave Corrow a metal plate unfit for a microwave. Corrow refused to fill the order, and the result was an exchange of harsh words between the women. The waitress further provoked Corrow when she said, "You got a god-damn big mouth," and spat at her. "Don't fuck with me," Corrow responded, leaving her station and slapping Shock. Corrow's supervisor rushed to the scene, asking what happened. "I hit her," Corrow admitted. The supervisor fired Corrow summarily. "You have no right to do that," he said of Corrow's action. "With that type of attitude I don't want you in the hotel. Consider yourself terminated."[25]

The Culinary asked the hotel to reinstate Corrow. Union officials agreed that Corrow had acted inappropriately but pointed out that Corrow had worked at the hotel for a decade and was well liked by her co-workers. Shock, on the other hand, had worked at the Desert Inn for less than two years and had been in fights before. The hotel refused. Corrow's action, management insisted, was clearly an example of the "willful misconduct" the union contract prohibited.[26]

The case ended up in the hands of arbitrator William E. Rentfro, who sided with the union. The hotel should have investigated the circumstances surrounding the fight before dismissing the employee, Rentfro ruled. "A full investigation may have led the employer to impose a more reasonable penalty." Corrow's actions were the result of a "brief outburst of temper [that] resulted from at least some provocation" and did not constitute willful misconduct. He therefore reduced the discharge to a thirty-day suspension, and ordered the Desert Inn to reinstate Corrow with back pay and without loss of seniority.[27]

♠ ♣ ♥ ♦

Some grievances centered on what management thought of as the problem of idling employees. Employers objected to paying workers for doing nothing and did what they could to keep them busy. Employees who kept busy were called "dependable," "efficient," and "loyal." Those who did not were told to keep busy. Employees working eight-hour shifts normally received two ten-minute breaks on the employer's time, one prior to a thirty-minute meal period and one after it. Employees could not take breaks at their pleasure but according to supervisor-issued schedules. In most workplaces, employees had to "sign out" when they went on break and "sign in" when they returned.[28]

An incident at the Frontier Hotel in 1968 illustrates management's concern with these matters. In that year, a hotel supervisor posted standard rules for the resort's cocktail waitresses prohibiting among other things "goofing off." "Shirking a fair share of the workload during normal working hours is against the best interest of the hotel and will not be permitted," the rule read. "Do not visit with other cocktail girls or bartenders. Stay on your station and watch for your customer's wants."[29]

Elaine Hallusco, a waitress at the resort, occasionally ignored this rule. In October 1968 a supervisor found Hallusco polishing her boots in a back room when she was supposed to be on the casino floor. Two days later he spotted her sitting on the arm of a customer's chair about thirty feet from her workstation. On both occasions, Hallusco received written warnings that she could be terminated for such behavior. Only a day after the second warning, when a security guard reported that Hallusco spent most of an hour sitting on the arm of a customer's chair outside her work area, the hotel fired her for repeated violations of work rules.[30]

Hallusco contested the discharge. The termination, she insisted, was the result of a new manager's urge to fire a few employees to impress others with a show of authority. The union may have doubted Hallusco's story, but it concluded that the waitress, who had worked in the industry for seven years, had not been given a "reasonable opportunity" to conform to the new prohibition on "goofing off." Moreover, it thought the prohibition vague. The union thus supported Hallusco when the hotel refused a request to reinstate her. Arbitrator A. Langley Coffey agreed with management, however, ruling that Hallusco, whom he described as an "educated" and "articulate" "young lady," had "willfully ignored" company rules. He also ruled that the policy in question did not violate the hotel's union contract.[31]

A case involving Turner Moore, a utility porter at the MGM Grand, also involved "goldbricking." As a porter, Moore removed trash from bars at the MGM, stocked the bars with ice, and arranged bar glasses by size. He performed this work on the casino floor, near the entrance to the employees' cafeteria. In April 1975 one of his supervisors observed Moore repeatedly interrupting his work in order to talk to security guards and other employees. Despite an oral warning, Moore continued the behavior. On one occasion, he left his work area to accompany a group of maids through the casino, a violation of work rules. At that point, the hotel gave him a written warning that repetition of such an act could result in termination. Seven months later, when the same manager caught Moore "standing around" outside his work area and "conversing with other employees," the hotel fired him.[32]

In settling this case, arbitrator Howard Block concluded that the hotel's actions were "excessive," and "not consistent with widely accepted industrial principles of corrective discipline." Block ruled, however, that Moore's conduct warranted "stern disciplinary action." "Quite obviously, something more than a slap on the wrist is necessary to impress the Grievant that such conduct will not be tolerated," he said. He therefore reduced the discharge to a suspension and loss of pay of one month.[33]

The cases of Moore and other idlers suggest that at least some workers had views of the natural rhythms of work that conflicted with those of management. Even dependable workers might occasionally resist management's cult of efficiency. Such employees wanted to schmooze with co-workers and sometimes left their workstations to do so. Ten-minute breaks provided only a limited respite. Employees wanted an atmosphere of sociability in the workplace and occasions to loosen up on the job. Pausing to share stories or to joke around with co-workers was no act of resistance but a way to sustain friendships or otherwise cope with the monotony or drudgery of the workday.[34]

Entertainers too "lounged around" on the job. Especially in the early postwar decades, resorts employed dozens of lounge groups who played music ranging from "top forty" hits to jazz or country standards. Most of them played four or five "sets" each shift, lasting perhaps forty-five minutes each. The musicians in such groups had relatively more freedom than other resort employees did because casinos and hotels contracted with bandleaders, who in turn employed their own sidemen. Entertainment directors, who made these contracts, ultimately controlled entertainment programs, but bandleaders generally determined what their musicians wore, when they rehearsed, and when they took their breaks.[35]

In 1971 the Landmark hired the Chuck Kovacs Trio for eight weeks to back up hypnotist and singer Pat Collins in its casino lounge. The resort expected the trio to play set songs and themes while Collins hypnotized volunteers from the audience. After three weeks, however, the hotel fired the trio, contending that its performance was inadequate. In the arbitration hearing, the entertainment director testified that members of the trio often failed to coordinate the music with Collins's act, distracted Collins by talking and laughing among themselves during serious moments in her performance, and often played in the wrong key. Collins herself testified that the band's behavior was so bad one night that she fell into a "hysterical state" and was unable to perform. In addition, she said, the musicians were habitually late and sometimes drank too much between shows. The musicians in turn complained that Collins's performances were often "erratic," and Collins was sometimes "unreasonable in her demands." She also sang in undesignated keys and failed to give clear cues during performances.[36]

In grieving the musicians' dismissal, their union acknowledged that the trio's behavior was sometimes problematic but appealed for its reinstatement on grounds that the union contract prohibited summary dismissal of musicians except for failure to perform at acceptable levels and then only two weeks after receipt of written notice. Arbitrator Leo Kotkin agreed with the union. Though the trio's performance was "improper and unacceptable," he ruled, the hotel should have warned the musicians in writing that they were in danger of losing their jobs. Because Collins insisted she was unable to perform with the musicians, the arbitrator refused to order the Landmark to rehire them. He did, however, award the trio a week's pay.[37]

Other grievances involved less weighty issues. One of those at the Dunes Hotel in 1969 concerned whether cocktail waitresses had to buy their work boots. These waitresses served complimentary drinks to gamblers and sold them to others, sometimes charging the cost to the rooms of hotel guests. The contract of the Culinary, to which most of them belonged, had long required employers to furnish and launder uniforms they required their employees to wear and had recently extended this requirement to shoes if the shoes were of a style not normally part of an employee's wardrobe.[38] The case at the Dunes involved this issue. At a time when miniskirts and "go-go" boots were popular among women, the Dunes management introduced white miniskirt uniforms for cocktail waitresses, whereupon the waitresses agreed among themselves that white calf-length boots best matched the new uniforms. Expecting the hotel to reimburse them under terms of their union contract, the waitresses bought boots for themselves at $26.00 a pair. The hotel refused their request for reimbursement, explaining that it had not specified the footwear waitresses had to wear.[39]

The waitresses complained, arguing to the union that the new uniforms demanded the boots. The union agreed that the boots were integral to the new attire and that management should pay for them. When the union pressed the case, the Dunes banned boots in the workplace. "Starting immediately," a notice to employees read, "everybody will have to wear shoes instead of boots while working." Shortly thereafter, the hotel changed the attire required to pink miniskirts, which "clashed" with white boots. The waitresses continued, defiantly, to wear the boots, dying them pink to match the new costumes.[40]

The dispute eventually reached arbitrator John Gorsuch, who in a hearing on the matter had two cocktail waitresses model the miniskirts required by the Dunes and the calf-length boots. The "young ladies looked gorgeous in them," Gorsuch thought; their appearance was "what makes a cocktail in Las Vegas such a pleasant experience." Despite this preference, Gorsuch ruled according to the terms of the collective bargaining agreement and found in favor of management. The Dunes had not required cocktail waitresses to wear boots, he ruled, and had never paid for employees' footwear. "Even though the Arbitrator might think a girl in a pink mini-skirt with matching boots is a bargain at $26.00," he ruled, "he has no right to make the Dunes pay the price of the boots."[41]

Such episodes were part of labor-management relations. In this era, the language concerning uniforms in the contracts of culinary and bartending employees grew from two sentences to two pages. By 1973 contracts gave employers the right to require certain types of attire, such as black trousers, neckties, and tuxedoes, with the obligation to furnish the required items to employees. No doubt reflecting the dispute at the Dunes, they permitted employers to require cocktail waitresses to wear shoes or boots that matched the color and style of their uniforms, as long as management paid for them.[42]

Arbitrators sometimes found a middle ground in disputes, obligating the two sides to compromise. They turned terminations of employees into suspensions and reinstated discharged workers with or without back pay. In 1975, for example, after several waitresses tripped walking up and down a set of stairs in the workplace at the MGM Grand, the resort posted a rule limiting the approved footwear of those who used the stairway. "For safety reasons, the maximum sole thickness allowed will be one-half inch and the maximum heel height allowed will be two and one-half inches," the hotel announced, and it threatened to suspend employees who violated the maximum. "Any employee found in violation of the above will be required to change footwear, which may necessitate the employee clocking out, leaving the premises, changing footwear, and returning to work."[43]

The hotel had the right to establish and administer such rules as long as they were not inconsistent with union contracts. It also had to provide unions copies of rules before posting them and discuss the issues involved with union representatives.[44] The union believed the MGM's new policy on footwear violated its contract unless management paid for shoes that conformed to the new requirement. The opportunity to insist on this came in 1976, when Billie Jo Hamamura, a cocktail server, violated the new footwear policy on two separate occasions. On January 29, her supervisor noticed that Hamamura wore a pair of "wedgies," the heels of which were more than two-and-a-half inches high. Confronted, she said her "regulation shoes" were in the repair shop. The manager gave her a written warning for "failure to follow posted house rules," noting that "repetition will result in suspension." When the manager noticed Hamamura wearing the same "wedgies" three months later, he suspended her for five days. It was then that she filed a grievance.

When the hotel and the union failed to the resolve the dispute, they submitted it to arbitrator David E. Feller, who ruled that the new rules on footwear were a reasonable safety precaution and did not violate contract language governing employee footwear, which stated that management could require food servers to wear "low heel" shoes. But the arbitrator also ruled that Hamamura's five-day suspension was excessive. Suspension for a single four-hour work shift, he said, "would have been reasonable under the circumstances of this case." He therefore directed the hotel to reimburse the cocktail waitress for the remainder of her lost wages.[45]

The Hamamura case illustrates how arbitration patterns expressed workplace behavior. To secure the labor of its employees, management had to accept a certain level of individuality. Supervisors could not enforce every routine work rule all the time without regard for specific circumstances. To do so would not only be bothersome but also risk annoying individual workers. In a rapidly expanding industry in which jobs were plentiful, supervisors sometimes had to relax rules that mattered little. They may have insisted on the footwear rule in this case because Hamamura was an indifferent employee. She had received a warning for "excessive absenteeism" a few weeks before her suspension.[46]

A case concerning personal cleanliness also indicates how arbitration shaped the work world. In 1970 management discharged Margie Duca, a cashier at the Frontier Hotel, for "failure to practice reasonable personal hygiene." According to the termination notice, Duca exuded "extreme body odor" that, "up to five feet" away, was "foul and offensive." Other employees complained of the odor to a supervisor, who spoke to Duca about it on three occasions. He had also given her a written warning that she could lose her job for a further offense. On the day of Duca's dismissal, a hotel executive visited her workstation and decided Duca "had to go."[47]

Duca appealed to her union, the Teamsters, which concluded that the Frontier had not proved its accusation and should reinstate Duca with back pay. The issue for the union was whether employers could terminate workers unfairly by simply concluding that they had offensive body odor. The arbitrator, William White, ruled that the employer had acted "without just cause" because it failed to prove "beyond a reasonable doubt" that Duca exuded the purported odor. Some of Duca's co-workers had in fact testified to the contrary. Only one co-worker testified against Duca, and she had qualified her statements by saying that the "foul" smell was not always noticeable. Given the lack of evidence, the arbitrator ordered the Frontier to reinstate Duca but without back pay.[48]

Management took the issue involved in this case quite seriously. Employees who dealt directly with customers could easily destroy the image of grandeur and fantasy the resorts fostered, especially if they were slovenly or unclean. Resorts expected clerks like Duca to convey the image they wanted to create, not the image workers had of themselves. All of them posted "grooming rules" for the workplace and threatened to suspend or discharge workers who violated them.

Resorts paid particularly close attention to the appearance of parking lot attendants and security guards, who were often the first and last employees hotel guests encountered. The MGM Grand, for example, required parking attendants to keep their fingernails "neat and trimmed," and their hair "neat and well groomed." It permitted short mustaches but "no Fu Manchus, handle-bars or beards" and no sideburns "longer than a quarter of an inch below the earlobes."[49] Similarly, the Landmark Hotel required security guards to "maintain vigilance and alertness at all time," which meant keeping their hands out of their pockets and refraining from casual interaction with guests and other employees. Even guards' private affairs had to be conducted "in such a manner as to cause no derogatory reflection on the Landmark or its Security Department."[50]

Employees often resented grooming rules and other uniformities that impinged on their sense of individuality and independence. Rather than flagrantly violate such rules, however, they occasionally "forgot" them—"forgot" to trim their nails or mustaches, to make sure their shirts were "clean and neatly pressed," to polish their boots and accessories, or always to look vigilant and alert. The

outward appearance of employees could and often did reflect their own preferences as well as the policies of management.

♠ ♣ ♥ ♦

Still other grievances concerned customer relations. House rules required employees to treat hotel guests courteously and respectfully, even if guests themselves were rude. But employees violated these rules. Waiters and waitresses
occasionally insulted customers for not tipping, and switchboard operators
sometimes lost patience with guests and hung up on them. Supervisors typically
resolved these problems without much difficulty. They knew that customers often
misinterpreted the words and gestures of workers or exaggerated their meaning.
They also knew how demanding and unreasonable guests could be. Success nonetheless hinged on customer satisfaction, and management was prepared to dismiss workers who offended customers.

While their main task was to park and retrieve the vehicles of guests, parking
attendants were also expected to greet customers by opening car doors and di-
recting them to the hotel or casino. The fact that attendants' income depended
heavily on tips usually ensured their courteous treatment of customers, but
problems arose when attendants lost their patience with boorish guests. After an
incident during summer 1978, the Showboat fired an attendant, Stanley Laird,
for cursing at a customer. The customer had violated the hotel's parking procedures, and Laird lost his temper. Rather than drive into the proper lane and wait
his turn behind other drivers, the customer left his vehicle in a through lane and
told Laird it belonged to the casino manager. While Laird knew this was untrue,
he was accustomed to customers "dropping names" to get special treatment. He
told the customer that "it doesn't make any difference" who owns the vehicle, it
had to be in the proper lane to be parked. According to Laird, the customer then
told him to "park the fucking car!" According to the customer, who turned out to
be a friend of the casino manager, the attendant said "fuck you!" and sped off to
park another car. Whatever actually happened, the customer complained and the
hotel dismissed Laird.[51]

Laird took the case to the Teamsters, which urged the Showboat to reinstate
him. The union insisted that if Laird had in fact directed "extreme profanity at
a customer," as management claimed, he deserved a reprimand or suspension,
not dismissal. Laird had worked at the Showboat for five years without problems,
and the customer had ignored parking rules and provoked Laird's outburst.
Management refused to reconsider the case, however, saying it could not afford
to employ people who offended customers.[52]

The dispute went to arbitrator Richard Basile, who concluded that Laird's use of profanity in addressing a customer justified the dismissal. "It must be accepted with little or no question that the use of profanity towards a guest of the hotel is sufficient cause for termination," Basile ruled, "not only under the terms of the collective bargaining agreement, but also under the fundamental understanding of expected customer relations." Those relations, as Basile put it, "require an employee to be tolerant of a guest's shortcomings." Though the arbitrator upheld the termination, he agreed with the union that management had acted "very hastily." What the employer should have done, he suggested, was to "verbally chastise" Laird and suspend him from duty. "Such a solution would have been more than likely satisfactory to the grieved customer, and a meaningful object lesson to the employee."[53] Those words were of little comfort to Laird, whose response to the contemptible, high-and-mighty customer cost him a job.

The only recourse for parties who lost grievance cases was to appeal to the courts, but such appeals were so rare as to be an unimportant part of the history of grievance proceedings. However, a union could file a court action if the employer refused to submit grievances to arbitration or refused to abide by an arbitrator's decision. The grievant could file a court action if his or her union did not meet its duty of providing fair representation, such as by failing to pursue a meritorious grievance. Either the union or employer could appeal to courts if they believed an arbitrator overstepped his or her authority. In the 1970s the U.S. Supreme Court established its authority to overturn arbitrators' decisions if they violated an employee's civil rights, or if union officials showed "bad faith" during the arbitration process. The high court, however, did not undermine arbitration as a useful instrument for settling workplace disputes.[54]

A dispute involving an employee in the housekeeping department at the Aladdin Hotel confirms the limited role courts were willing to assume in the arbitration process. In January 1983 the Aladdin fired one of its porters, William Prentiss, for leaving the hotel during his shift, violating the union contract as well as the house rules. The Culinary filed a grievance on Prentiss's behalf, claiming that leaving the hotel was not per se sufficient cause for discharge, especially if a worker faced a personal emergency. The arbitrator in this case sided with the union, concluding that the proper discipline for Prentiss's action would have been a one-month suspension without pay. He ordered the hotel to reinstate the employee. Hotel management disagreed so strongly with this ruling that it filed a complaint in federal court, arguing that the arbitrator had misinterpreted the hotel's agreement with the union and overstepped his authority. The district court agreed with the hotel, but a federal appeals court reversed that ruling. The courts ruled that, in cases involving disputes over the meaning of contract language, "the court should not usurp the power of an arbitrator to make the final decision."[55]

♠ ♣ ♥ ♦

The arbitration process seems to have had a generally calming effect on labor relations in Las Vegas. It helped labor and management to confront disputes through third parties and resolve them with minimal difficulty. It often protected workers' rights as well as their sense of personal integrity. Yet the process also aided employers in protecting their prerogatives and in rationalizing the workplace. In the new age of corporate ownership, employers used it to make sure workers carried out their tasks properly and with aplomb. Simply having a grievance system in place may have encouraged some workers to contest disciplinary actions, but it no doubt reduced the number of serious disputes in the workplace. Managers hesitated to take arbitrary action against union employees because of the likelihood of having to justify their behavior not only to their own superiors but to a neutral arbitrator as well.

Workplace grievances and arbitration cases speak to two basic premises of this book: that resort workers and their employers had different priorities and interests, and that conflict between the parties was more pervasive than is commonly assumed. Management viewed workplace incidents in terms of their effects on the services promised guests and other customers. In its view, union efforts to overturn disciplinary action amounted to assaults on management prerogatives. Workers saw grievance and arbitration cases as proof of management's overreach and unreasonableness and as another reason for belonging to a union. If less important in the end than matters of wages and benefits, these differing outlooks help explain why labor and management were often at odds.

Fighting for Equal Rights

In 1954 the U.S. Supreme Court ruled that racial segregation in schooling denied African Americans equal protection of the laws. A few years later, the federal government committed itself to the promise implicit in that ruling, and federal law and policy soon followed suit. A series of civil rights laws enacted in the 1960s erased legal bases for racial and gender discrimination in public accommodations and voting, and, most notably for this study, in employment. The 1964 Civil Rights Act was the statutory centerpiece of the resulting efforts to achieve racial and gender equality in the latter area. The act not only prohibited discrimination on the basis of race, sex, and national origin in employment, but created the Equal Employment Opportunity Commission (EEOC) to fight such discrimination. Enforcement of the EEOC's mandate was assigned to the U.S. Justice Department.

In the aftermath, the racial and sexual composition of workforces almost everywhere in the nation changed dramatically. In the Las Vegas resort industry, the EEOC investigated charges of worksite discrimination and used its findings to enable the Justice Department to enforce the new laws vigorously. The resulting transformation was not immediate or easy. Grass-roots movements led variously by black activists, political liberals, and proponents of women's liberation as well as aggrieved workers pressured public officials to eliminate workplace discrimination throughout the 1960s and 1970s. With more insistency and verve than any government agency or bureaucrat, they also challenged employers and union leaders to end discriminatory practices. Exploring the resulting changes broadens and enriches our understanding of the social transformations these forces produced in Las Vegas resorts.

Federal policy and grass-roots activism worked together to recompose the workforce in no more than a decade and a half. Resort owners and unions had always agreed, without ever discussing it or considering it a problem, that women and minority men should be employed in certain jobs but not others in patterns that fit the presumed abilities of these groups as well as the unions' and the resorts' presumed interests. In the 1960s African Americans took the lead in challenging these attitudes and practices, and their accomplishments in Las Vegas tourism are integral parts of the history this study is endeavoring to recreate. Their struggles challenged the procedures, values, and expectations of unions and union leaders no less than those of resorts and their managers, and of workers themselves, whom those struggles sometimes pitted against each another. Ultimately, the reformers achieved what amounted to a fundamental social transformation in the industry and its workforce.[1]

To suggest that reformers simply imposed their will on Las Vegas and its unions, however, would be naive. Resort owners and union leaders always shaped employment practices in the city, even when they had to do things neither of them were eager to do. As the civil rights movement gained momentum and muscle, both parties found ways to accommodate its demands without disrupting their operations. Though both initially opposed federally mandated affirmative action programs, they never posed as defenders of racial or sexual discrimination, or schemed after the 1960s to prevent women or minorities from finding jobs. While resort workers and managers may have indulged their prejudices, the workers never walked off the job or closed a resort to protest integration, and management never considered extreme measures to thwart enforcement of civil rights statutes. This is not to say that labor or management embraced enlightened racial and gender policies eagerly or voluntarily, but that the struggle for equality in Las Vegas tourism was less of a challenge than it was in manufacturing centers or service industries where jobs were scarce or even disappearing, or in areas of the Deep South where racialist attitudes were more rigid than those in Las Vegas tourism.

African Americans first appeared in Nevada in the nineteenth century, though their numbers remained small until industrial developments in the twentieth century opened jobs for laborers of all races. The Union Pacific Railroad Company brought the first sizable group of African Americans to Southern Nevada after 1900 to work as strikebreakers on railroad construction crews. When the construction ended, some of these men joined railroad maintenance crews stationed in Las Vegas and lived in company housing near the downtown rail depot. In the early 1930s a wave of African American migrants joined a much larger wave of whites moving into Southern Nevada to build Boulder Dam, though employers restricted blacks to menial and backbreaking tasks, thereby limiting black immigration. In 1935, when the dam was completed, African Americans constituted about 1 percent of the population of Clark County, fewer than two hundred people.[2]

That number jumped notably during World War II with the growth of magnesium mining south of Las Vegas. In the tight wartime labor market, processing magnesium, used in the production of ammunition and other war matériel, drew hundreds of African Americans to Clark County, most of them from Arkansas, Louisiana, and Mississippi. By 1943 nearly three thousand blacks resided in the county, many of whom worked as "smutters" and "metalers" in the magnesium plants and lived in segregated company facilities nearby. Those in Las Vegas lived in the "colored section" across the railroad tracks from downtown.[3]

The Westside, as this area came to be known, was a shantytown inside a growing town. In the 1940s many residents there lived in tents or shacks, and even those in permanent dwellings generally lacked electricity, indoor plumbing, and running water. Westside had no fire hydrants, streetlights, or paved roads. "It was just a lot of sand and gravel," one of its residents later remembered.[4] Poverty and racial discrimination kept blacks as well as their community marginalized and stigmatized. Whites took the community's physical and social degradation as proof that blacks were an economically improvident and socially undesirable element in the community. Bankers dismissed them as credit risks, and employers regarded them as fit only for menial housekeeping chores or outdoor tasks requiring brawn rather than knowledge or skill.[5]

The Westside was nonetheless a community with its own social and cultural life. "It was a neighborhood," one resident recalled. "Everybody kind of knew everybody."[6] Its churches, civic associations, and grammar school provided opportunities for social identity and exchange. Black-owned businesses also operated in the Westside, including a few gaming establishments. Places like the Brown Derby, the Cotton Club, the Harlem Club, and El Morocco provided entertainment for Westsiders and black tourists, along with jobs for black bartenders, dealers, and others. The Westside also sported a wartime USO, which doubled as a hostelry for more than one thousand black soldiers a month who visited the city and no doubt patronized Westside businesses.[7]

As the war wound down, the Westside and its residents faced new challenges. In 1944, when victory in the war seemed certain, city officials launched a campaign to "clean up" the Westside, an early instance of the use of "urban renewal" to achieve "Negro removal." City work crews bulldozed more than three hundred residential structures that failed to conform to city building codes. This transformed the housing shortage in the Westside into a crisis. To add to this crisis, a few months after the war the magnesium plant closed, throwing black and white workers alike out of jobs, but disproportionately impacting blacks. Many displaced workers moved away; others who remained looked for jobs in the growing resort industry. By the mid-1940s, resorts in and around Las Vegas employed several hundred African Americans, more or less all of them in menial labor. By the time the "Fabulous Flamingo" opened on the Strip in 1948, workers, though not supervisors, in the housekeeping departments at El Rancho, the Golden Nugget, and other new resorts consisted almost entirely of blacks.[8]

The experiences of Viola Johnson, who moved to Southern Nevada from rural Arkansas in 1942 at age twenty-one, mirrored those of many Westsiders in these years of hope, disappointment, and change. Johnson's father and several other relatives were already working at the magnesium plant when she left Arkansas. Her mother washed dishes at El Rancho, one of the first resorts on the Strip. Newly arrived, Johnson moved into a Westside tent with six relatives, including her own child. The tent was perhaps ten by twelve feet, sufficient to cover a large bed and an oil-burning stove. Because the men in the family worked different shifts, they took turns sleeping in the bed. "When the swing shift go, then the day shift would go to bed," Johnson recalled, "and when the swing shift come in, graveyard would be up, getting ready to go."[9] Johnson and her child slept outside "under the trees" in the cool desert night. Tents in the Westside were perhaps fifteen feet apart, and living conditions combined the difficulties of crowding with those of physical deprivation. "Oh, my goodness, it was terrible," Johnson remembered. "When we first came out here, it was so hot. I'm telling you, it was so hot." And hot winds blew all over the place. "Sand, sand, sand, blow, oh the sand would blow everywhere."[10]

Johnson's situation soon improved. In 1943, she married, moved into a one-bedroom house, and found a job as a maid at the Flamingo, where she worked until she misplaced several room keys, for which she was fired. But housekeeping jobs were easy to find in the expanding industry, and Johnson was soon again employed. She worked "on and off" at the Sands for nearly a decade, years Johnson remembered fondly.[11] "I used to enjoy going to work," she said of those years, "really, I enjoyed work." Her standard of comparison was no doubt her earlier situation in rural Arkansas. Still, this positive perspective influenced her view of her circumstances. Johnson came to see her housekeeper's job as a respite from her growing family responsibilities at home. "It was like getting away, I guess, getting away from home because I had kids at that time."[12]

Though Johnson appreciated her job, she no doubt resented the racial discrimination that was integral to her circumstance. Resorts in the city hired blacks in low-paying jobs only and excluded them as guests, whatever their capacity to pay. Even well-known black entertainers who performed in premier resort showrooms had to find living accommodations in the Westside. Casinos in "white" establishments had no black dealers and admitted black gamblers only in designated areas, if at all. When admitted, blacks had to use segregated restrooms.[13] Dance clubs, restaurants, and many shops in the city banned blacks altogether, while landlords outside the Westside refused to rent or sell to them. Some doctors and dentists refused to treat them, and public officials licensed them to operate businesses only inside the Westside. In the 1940s, in fact, the city forced the few black-owned businesses that had managed to surface downtown to close or relocate to the Westside.[14]

It was a wretched existence, and African Americans in the 1960s and 1970s had vivid memories of it and of personal instances of discrimination and humiliation: of being "shoo-ed out" of white-owned businesses, for example, or told not to touch merchandise. Those working in the resort industry recalled disrespectful treatment by white hotel guests. Timothy Wagner, a janitor at the Union Plaza, recalled being insulted by whites as he walked through downtown on the way to and from his job. "The people were so damn prejudice," Wagner recalled. "I used to walk down the street and people would call me names."[15] Arlone Scott, a maid at the Last Frontier, recalled that employers, including her own, prohibited African Americans from entering casinos. "You wasn't allowed into those casinos," Scott said. "You could work in them, but you couldn't gamble or go in for a meal or anything like that."[16]

This exclusion reflected class as well as racial prejudice. Resorts like the Flamingo catered to high rollers and well-to-do tourists, not to slot machine players and penny-ante gamblers. In such resorts, where large sums of money changed hands regularly, managers viewed with suspicion anyone who looked hard-up, regardless of skin color. "They didn't want anybody to come in the clubs that was poor," a resident of the Westside remembered of these resorts, "and naturally most black people, they figured, was poor. . . . There wasn't enough room to have all the people."[17]

African Americans in Southern Nevada had always protested discrimination. During construction of the Hoover Dam, some of them formed the Colored Citizens' Labor and Protective Association to protest hiring practices there, and the association continued to fight discrimination during and after the war. Local leaders like David Hoggard, Woodrow Wilson, and Lubertha Johnson played key roles in that fight and in efforts to strengthen the local branch of the NAACP. They also helped organize the Nevada Voters League and other groups to pressure political candidates to support their goals and agendas.[18]

During the late 1940s and 1950s, the efforts of civil rights groups in Nevada still centered in the Westside of Las Vegas, where the vast majority of the state's African Americans lived. Community leaders supported a 1947 bill to outlaw racial discrimination in public accommodations. Assemblyman E. R. "Boots" Miller (White Pine County) introduced the bill, which died in committee. Black leaders continued to back similar legislation through the 1950s with the same result. The Las Vegas NAACP tried to pressure social and business groups to support civil rights by boycotting the resorts, but without success. Efforts to convince the city to ban racial discrimination similarly failed. Officials steadfastly rejected such efforts as interference in the practices of private businesses. Nevada did form an advisory committee to the national Civil Rights Commission created in 1957, but state officials remained apathetic if not hostile to state civil rights legislation, and the commission was ineffectual.[19]

Despite these failures, black community activists had laid the groundwork for the civil rights movement of the 1950s and 1960s. By that time, the Las Vegas NAACP became more aggressive in the fight against discrimination. The effort had the blessings of Westside religious leaders, who used their pulpits to encourage it. The NAACP began working with liberal groups like the Anti-Defamation League, the League of Women Voters, and the National Conference of Christians and Jews, whose voices strengthened the call for equality and justice. These awakenings created a stronger sense of racial consciousness and identity in the Westside and helped to galvanize the community and to pressure political and business leaders on behalf of civil rights legislation.

These efforts soon began to influence local and state politics. In 1958 Democrat Grant Sawyer upset Republican governor Charles Russell after embracing a liberal political agenda that included expressions of support for racial equality. According to Clarence Ray, an African American who worked for the Democratic Party at the time, civil rights leaders believed Sawyer would help break patterns of discrimination, and they campaigned on his behalf. "When Grant was elected," Ray later explained, "we gave him eighty percent of the black votes down here, and he got about sixty percent up in Reno."[20]

♠ ♣ ♥ ♦

After Sawyer's support for civil rights proved lukewarm, James McMillan, head of the Las Vegas chapter of the NAACP, threatened protest marches against resorts unless officials acted to end racial discrimination. McMillan, a widely respected figure, had moved to Las Vegas in 1955. After his childhood in small-town Mississippi, he earned a degree in dentistry from the University of Detroit and served as an officer in the U.S. Army. He spoke out against racism and segregation in Las Vegas, winning praise from blacks as well as some whites, including Hank Greenspun of the *Las Vegas Sun*. Because of white inertia or opposition to his early efforts, McMillan turned to tactics of direct confrontation.[21]

Resort owners had always insisted that admitting black gamblers into casinos and black guests into hotels would turn white gamblers and guests away and thus damage the city's resort industry. They used that argument to block state civil rights legislation. Yet the growing effectiveness of civil rights demonstrations across the country and McMillan's threatened march in 1960 led them to reconsider their position. They agreed among themselves to desegregate Strip hotels, announcing the decision at the Moulin Rouge, a new, desegregated resort on the Westside, where black and white workers and customers already mingled. Owners also agreed to support the newly created Nevada Equal Rights Commission, which promised to investigate discriminatory practices in employment and public accommodations in the state and keep the public informed of civil rights issues. The mayor promised to hire more African Americans in city government and to get local banks to make more credit available to them.[22]

These moves had modest results. In the early 1960s, while Martin Luther King Jr. and others protested racial discrimination in the South, Westside leaders protested Las Vegas discrimination. Reverend Prentiss Walker complained to the state's Equal Rights Commission that "unwritten laws" in the housing market kept him from buying a home in most city neighborhoods. Moreover, some resorts refused to desegregate their hotels and casinos, telling blacks they had no vacancies, while others admitted limited numbers of blacks but charged them higher prices than whites.[23]

Reverend Donald Clark was one of the Westside's most active advocates of desegregation. Having moved to Las Vegas from the South ten years earlier, in 1961 he became president of the local NAACP. Clark frequently wrote letters to newspapers calling attention to discrimination. "Don't you think it is strange," he asked, "that there isn't a Negro of any stature whatsoever in any employment in the City of Las Vegas? Don't you think it peculiar?"[24]

In 1962, when blacks were nearly 10 percent of the population of Clark County, Clark criticized Governor Sawyer and other state and local officials for ignoring discrimination in the resort industry. "Governor Sawyer is narrating a story and depicting Nevada as a mecca," Clark said. "He wants all the tourists and conventions that will come, he wants industry to come, but in the industries already here 17,000 of the citizens already living here are deprived of even the opportunity to apply for a job."[25] Clark also criticized legislators for not giving the Equal Rights Commission the resources necessary to accomplish its goals. The commission had only two of the authorized five members in 1962 and its budget was an inconsequential $2,500.[26]

Like civil rights leaders elsewhere, Clark framed his critiques in the language of democracy and Christianity, calling the NAACP cause "righteous." The association "has an obligation to bring to public officials the need for implementing democratic principles with democratic practice," he said, urging officials to "do the unpopular thing and try to bring democracy where none exists."[27] A year later Clark intensified his rhetoric, accusing the state gaming commissioner of doing "nothing" to end discrimination in casinos. "If you don't believe in the equality of all citizens under the Constitution which you swore to uphold," Clark told the commissioners, "then you shouldn't be a commissioner."[28]

Other activists used similar language, among them Charles Kellar, an especially important figure in the local struggle for civil rights. Kellar had come to Las Vegas vowing to battle racial discrimination, and his presence added momentum to the civil rights struggle. His background explained his commitment. His mother had been a servant in the home of a wealthy black planter in the West Indies. Although the planter fathered Kellar and his siblings out of wedlock, he never acknowledged his paternity. As a young man, Kellar worked as a probation officer in New York City, where he witnessed widespread discrimination in the court system. "I saw that blacks could not find persons to represent them, so I decided to do it," he later recalled. Kellar enrolled in a New York law school and worked for a firm that sued people for violating civil rights laws. His work drew the attention of Thurgood Marshall, who then headed the NAACP legal division. In the late 1950s Marshall asked Kellar and other black lawyers to establish residency in places where African Americans lacked adequate legal assistance. By 1960 Kellar was practicing law in Las Vegas.[29]

He was not welcomed by whites. When he tried to deposit a large check at a bank in the city shortly after his arrival, bank officials called the police. "They assumed a black man with that much money had to be an escaped felon," Kellar explained. A year later, in Reno to take the bar exam, the hotel at which he had reservations refused to admit him. Kellar took the exam, but examiners refused to publish the results, charging that he had cheated. It took four years and a ruling from the state supreme court for Kellar to gain admission to the Nevada bar. In the meantime, he worked as legal adviser to the Las Vegas NAACP, attacking discriminatory housing practices and a zoning system that confined African American students to schools in West Las Vegas. Kellar's experiences explain why he and other civil rights advocates considered Nevada "the Mississippi of the West."[30]

Kellar and other black leaders met with Governor Sawyer in 1962 to protest the slow pace of change. At the meeting, Sawyer found himself under sharp attack for failing to match his words with deeds. Black leaders urged the governor to intervene personally to improve job opportunities for African Americans in the resort industry, if necessary by revoking the gambling licenses of establishments that continued discriminatory hiring and admission practices. They also told Sawyer that the Equal Rights Commission, which the governor defended, was poorly funded and had no real power. Where it found evidence of discrimination, it could only ask district attorneys to do something about it. The commission, they insisted, should have the power to issue cease-and-desist orders with the force of law and the right to suspend or revoke business licenses if necessary. Kellar dismissed the governor's statement that the commission was a "vigorous" organization. "It's been so vigorous that it hasn't even met," Kellar told Sawyer.[31]

In 1963 the NAACP and a coalition of religious and political groups sought to rectify these problems through civil rights legislation patterned after bills then before the U.S. Congress. Governor Sawyer endorsed the legislation because he realized that the federal government would soon outlaw racial discrimination, including discriminatory practices in Nevada's gaming industry, if the state failed to act first. He urged lawmakers to pass a civil rights act tailored to Nevada's needs and circumstances in order to avoid federal intervention. But legislators, some of whom went out of their way to criticize the civil rights movement, voted down Sawyer's proposals. "I feel that the colored people in this state have never been so well off," said Senator James Slattery of Storey County, who headed the committee that killed the proposed legislation. Some "colored people" in Las Vegas, Slattery added, lived in better homes than he did and drove better cars.

Senator William Dial of Ormsby County suggested that the problems of blacks in Nevada were no greater than those of Irish Americans in the state. He even proposed abolishing the state's Equal Rights Commission.[32]

Such words galvanized civil rights leaders. Adopting militant tactics, in the summer of 1963 the Las Vegas NAACP announced plans for a mass demonstration to be held just before a prizefight to be nationally televised from the Strip. Organizers promised authorities a "quiet," "orderly" march along Las Vegas Boulevard, but warned that they were determined to have their demands addressed. Charles West, the first black physician in Las Vegas and an influential local leader, evoked images of Abraham Lincoln and the Emancipation Proclamation when demanding an end to discrimination. "For 100 years we have been promised freedom," he said, "now we want pay-day!"[33] Black leaders canceled the demonstration only after executives of Strip resorts agreed to discuss with them the hows and whys of ending discrimination in the resorts.

A 1963 report by the Nevada Tuberculosis and Health Association demonstrated the plight of the city's black community. The Westside, the report noted, had the characteristics of an urban ghetto. More than a third of its residents were children under fourteen, and a quarter of them lived in broken homes. Nearly two-thirds of girls and women between the ages of fifteen and twenty-four had one or more children, and adults had educational levels far below those in the rest of the city. Four in five had never graduated from high school, and one in five had attended school no more than four years. For these and other reasons, median family income in the Westside was only 63 percent of that of the city as a whole. Area real estate values underscored the economic gap. Fewer than 20 percent of Westside homes were worth more than $15,000, compared to about 75 percent of homes elsewhere in the city.[34]

The national Civil Rights Act of 1964 spurred the push to end racial discrimination in Las Vegas. Title VII of that act prohibited employers from discriminating on the basis of race, sex, or national origins and unions from maintaining hiring halls and seniority systems that disadvantaged female and minority workers. It mandated substantial penalties for violations of these provisions and encouraged states to enact their own civil rights laws furthering equality in the workplace and in public accommodations. The law prompted the Nevada legislature to pass its own civil rights bill, which banned discrimination on the basis of race and gender in public accommodations and in businesses employing more than fifteen people. Governor Sawyer signed the bill in front of fifty of the state's lead-

ing civil rights advocates, calling it "one of the greatest landmarks in all legislation in the history of Nevada."[35]

However, discrimination was so deeply entrenched in Las Vegas and its resort industry and unions that the new legislation had little initial effect. In 1965–
66, African Americans filed record numbers of complaints with the Nevada
Equal Rights Commission, charging officials at all levels, including those in the
public schools as well as in private businesses, with violating the laws. Many of
the complaints focused on unions and the job referral system that was central to
their relations with management in the resort industry. Referrals privileged applicants according to their skills and experience, which protected seniority but
denied opportunity to women and minority men. The system had to be over-
hauled to eliminate inequities in its operational results.

Initially, labor leaders disregarded these demands. Most of those leaders considered charges of discrimination against unions as unwarranted, even malicious;
in their view, African Americans held menial jobs because they lacked the training and skills essential for better positions. Robert Park of the electricians' union,
for example, told reporters that "very few" African Americans had applied to his
union's apprenticeship program, and those who did so were too deficient in math,
"the electrical trade's most important tool," to succeed in the program. "Let someone send us Negroes who are qualified," Park stated, "and there will be no problem
of admitting them."[36] Dave McGinty of the Plumbers and Pipefitters Union similarly dismissed charges of discrimination against his union as "hogwash." Like
other officials in the building trades, he viewed the requirements for entry into
apprenticeship programs as race neutral. His union's program, he insisted, was
not only "fair" but its fairness was "well proven." "We are turning out the best ap-
prentices in Nevada, and we feel it is due in large measure to our method of
selection."[37]

Until the federal government enforced the civil rights act, the Culinary was
the only racially diverse union in Las Vegas. Yet almost all of the union's black
members had "back-of-the-house" jobs and subordinate positions in terms of
labor organization and leadership. Most worked under the direction of white
supervisors and were generally indifferent to their union. African Americans
were expected to stay in their "place" in the work environment and act deferen-
tially to white co-workers. The recollections of Alma Whitney, who worked as
a maid at the Desert Inn in the 1950s, spoke pointedly to these patterns. "When
I went there," she said of the Desert Inn, "they had one black supervisor and the
rest was white." There were no black waiters or waitresses in the resort, and no
black bartenders, dealers, or front desk workers. The resort's black workers had

their own "space" in the employee cafeteria. "The blacks would be sitting like in the back and the whites was in the front," Whitney recalled. Whitney was not particularly proud of her union and seldom attended union meetings. "I just kept my dues up," she said.[38]

In the early 1960s, however, black resort workers, including Alma Whitney, began to feel differently about the Culinary. By then, most resorts had hired African Americans to fill jobs previously held by whites, and the union had placed several of its black members in leadership positions. Black shop stewards helped monitor and enforce provisions of the collective bargaining agreements and disseminate union policies and directives. Whitney said the stewards, who were typically elected by co-workers, convinced her to attend union meetings and express her opinions about workplace problems. One of the stewards, Sarah Hughes, went from resort to resort to discuss the problems and challenges black workers faced in the new workplace environment. Whitney credited Hughes for breaking down customs and traditions that separated blacks and whites in dining and other areas at work. "I tell you, she was a black woman [who] was on the ball."[39] Indeed, Hughes was one of the many unsung heroes of the Las Vegas civil rights movement. In addition to her role as union steward, she was an early member of the Nevada Equal Rights Commission and used that role to identify discriminatory employment practices in resorts and to pressure public officials to end them.[40]

For Essie Shelton Jacobs, who moved to Las Vegas from Fordyce, Arkansas, in 1963, the elevation of African Americans in the Culinary gave black workers a new sense of pride and respect. Jacobs worked in the Aladdin's housekeeping department for twenty-three years, during which time she became a supervisor as well as a union steward. The Culinary, she recalled, had several black stewards and business agents in the 1960s, and she credited them with breaking down on-the-job forms of segregation and unease over desegregation. "All those peoples was good agents," she explained. "They was there for you. They was there."[41] When Jacobs herself became a steward, she too worked to advance the interests of black workers, "to keep our peoples from being dogged around," as she put it. She attended union meetings regularly and learned all she could about union affairs. She developed a new respect for union leaders at those meetings. "They kept educating me," she explained. "They said this is your union, give us your opinion, let us know what you want us to do. Let us know what you want us to put in the contract. When we go to the table, we'll negotiate, so that's the way they done it." Jacobs was especially fond of Al Bramlet, whom she called "one of the [most] gracious man I know."[42]

Overhauling hiring practices and training programs was difficult, however, even for well-intentioned people. If union policies had to meet legal requirements, union leaders also wanted policies acceptable to union members, whose attitudes about race and gender, though malleable, varied widely. Women and minorities sought increased employment opportunities and supported affirmative action programs. Implementation of those programs was often at the expense of union practices that favored skill and experience over race and gender equity, and thus favored skilled, experienced white males over minorities. Many who acquiesced in the need to eliminate discrimination had what they considered legitimate concerns about methods used to achieve that goal. Should applicants with little training and work experience have priority in the job market in order to compensate for past and present inequities? Should they be promoted over more skilled and experienced workers for the same purpose?

Union leaders confronted these discomforting questions as they faced the problem of negotiating new hiring policies with employers, whose attitudes on civil rights issues also varied. Some employers were willing to integrate their workforces and willing to cooperate with unions in order to do so. Others believed unions already had too much control of the hiring process and might use civil rights issues to enhance that control. Still others supported segregation and shared common values with employees in the workplace who harbored racial and gender prejudices. These views on both sides of the bargaining table made the task of dismantling racial and gender barriers difficult, but as things turned out, the controlling force proved to be relentless federal pressure on both unions and management to produce something approaching equality of results in hiring minorities and women.

In 1967 civil rights leaders urged newly elected Republican Governor Paul Laxalt to call a conference in Las Vegas to find "lasting solutions" to discrimination. As lieutenant governor, Laxalt had shown only limited support for civil rights and questioned the need for additional legislation or enforcement mechanisms. "I have constantly felt that legislation should be a last resort only when moral persuasion has failed to do the job," he told civil rights leaders in 1965.[43] As governor, however, Laxalt arranged the proposed conference and delivered the opening address. In November, before an audience that included the mayor and representatives from a broad base of Las Vegas business, union, and civic groups, Laxalt acknowledged the difficulties African Americans faced in employment and other areas and pledged himself and his administration to work with employers and others to rectify the situation. Recognizing the need for action, Laxalt had already increased funding for the Equal Employment Commission and directed the agency to work with business leaders to achieve equitable results.[44]

The "Solutions Conference," as it was called, gave civil rights leaders a public forum, which they used effectively. Charles Kellar, who now headed the Las Vegas NAACP, and Woodrow Wilson, the first black assemblyman in Nevada, gave rousing speeches, reminding Laxalt and other officials that previous efforts to integrate Las Vegas workplaces had failed in the face of long-standing discrimination and official indifference. Less than 2 percent of Nevada's five thousand state employees were African Americans, they noted, and those few held mostly menial jobs. Discriminatory practices in housing, public education, and law enforcement were equally pressing issues that had to be confronted.[45]

Conference working sessions gave special attention to the problem of employment discrimination. They identified practices that kept African Americans out of many areas of employment in the resort industry. Employers typically used word-of-mouth to fill supervisory and other high-paying positions, for example, and often evaluated candidates for such positions on the basis of criteria unrelated to the jobs themselves. Blacks necessarily lacked training and experience in jobs traditionally closed to them, making it impossible for them to break into "all-white occupations" without some form of special assistance. The conference recommended creating new employment agencies and job training programs specializing in helping minorities overcome problems relating to past discrimination. The conference insisted that the Nevada Gaming Commission require compliance with nondiscrimination policies as a condition for approving and renewing gaming licenses. It also urged resort leaders to make greater effort to inform African Americans of job openings and provide them opportunities for work experience through on-the-job training programs.[46]

The Solutions Conference had a significant impact on the city generally and on the resort industry specifically. It raised white consciousness about black problems and about policies and practices that caused or perpetuated those problems. In the aftermath, resorts, especially those on the Strip, hired African Americans in positions never before open to them. The Stardust, for example, hired black dealers, security guards, and wait people; other resorts did likewise.[47]

Progress, however, was still slow. In May 1968 the NAACP filed a complaint with the Equal Rights Commission accusing a dozen resorts and two unions of denying equal employment opportunity to African Americans. The accused parties, declared Charles Kellar, had done little or nothing to bring about racial equity in their hiring practices. As a result, the vast majority of black workers in the industry remained in menial jobs. "Almost all the Negroes employed are porters or maids. Any other kind of employment is just token," Kellar declared. "The Culinary Workers Union does nothing to improve this picture, [and] the Teamsters Union absolutely precludes it." Kellar asked the commission for redress: "Only governmental agencies [can] cure these situations."[48]

The commission investigated and upheld Kellar's complaints and found that the resorts and the unions did indeed limit blacks to low-paying, low-status jobs. Their hiring practices were thus not only illegal but intolerable and dangerous. "If this unequal treatment is allowed to continue," the commission concluded, "the respondent hotels, by their neglect and lack of affirmative action, will create an area of racial tension so severe as to endanger the entire economy of our state."[49]

♠ ♣ ♥ ♦

In fact, race relations were strained already. Since the riot in Los Angeles's Watts district in 1965, the racial situation was explosive everywhere. In early 1969 police broke up fights between white and black youths at three high schools in Las Vegas. At one, whites reportedly threw a black student through a trophy case, and a "wild melee" at another involved a thousand students, prompting officials to close the school temporarily.[50] The situation grew worse on October 6, when gang-related assaults in the Westside hospitalized nearly two dozen people. On the following day, black youths looted several stores, and police fired tear gas to stop them. By then, Governor Laxalt had imposed a 7:00 p.m. curfew in the community and placed the Nevada National Guard on alert; police sharpshooters stood atop several buildings, including a major shopping center.[51]

The resorts and the unions cooperated to diffuse these mounting tensions. They asked the Equal Rights Commission to dismiss Kellar's complaint because the underrepresentation of blacks in certain job categories was not in itself evidence of discrimination. African Americans constituted 10 percent of the local population and held 19 percent of hotel jobs. The problem, the lack of qualified black applicants for skilled and high-paying positions, would take time to solve, and to privilege unqualified or underqualified blacks over better-qualified whites would create a new set of problems.[52]

Robbins Cahill of the Nevada Resort Association (NRA) had already made similar arguments. After the Westside riots, however, he told the governor that the NRA understood the "urgency" of opening job opportunities for blacks, though the state should not assume resorts were discriminating "simply because an imbalance exists in certain categories of employment." The hotels had "worked earnestly to assist all minority groups to find better employment opportunities," he insisted, noting that two of the five members of the Equal Rights Commission agreed that there was "no evidence of unlawful discrimination" in the resort industry in Las Vegas.[53]

While Cahill made these points publicly, he privately urged the resorts to increase minority employment in underrepresented areas. "To do less," he told the hotels, "is to invite even more criticism of the industry no matter how unjustified and baseless we know it to be. To disarm our detractors we must be equipped with the ammunition of a plan."[54] Resort managers and owners now understood this and had in fact already begun to remedy the situation. In January 1970 the NRA announced an eight-point plan to place blacks in better jobs, pledging among other things financial support for an NAACP-sponsored program to train workers for jobs in the industry and for a scholarship program for minority students in the College of Hotel Administration at the University of Nevada, Las Vegas.[55]

Industry leaders considered these actions generous and progressive; civil rights advocates called them insufficient. "The sum of $75,000," Kellar said of money pledged for the job-training program, "is altogether too small to do the job. The Las Vegas Branch believes that a budget of $200,000 for each of three years is more feasible." Kellar also insisted that the hotels do what was necessary to dispel the perception that the money pledged was "a palliative to keep the Branch quiet."[56]

The situation reached a turning point in 1970, when the U.S. Justice Department made an investigation of industry hiring practices and promptly concluded that all members of the NRA were engaged in racially discriminatory and therefore illegal practices. So, too, were four unions to which workers within those resorts belonged—the Bartenders, the Culinary, the Stagehands, and the Teamsters. As evidence, department investigators pointed to the skewed distribution of employees in the industry. Assistant Attorney General Jerris Leonard, who headed the investigation, found that the concentration of minorities in menial jobs in the industry indicated "hiring, referral and assignment based on race" that worked to the disadvantage of minorities. Part of the problem was the provision in collective bargaining agreements that said union referrals gave priority to work experience. Those provisions are illegal, Leonard stated, because they had the effect of excluding minority applicants from well-paying and otherwise attractive jobs. In addition, some of the qualifications and requirements the unions used to judge members qualified for job referrals were legally suspect because the skills, knowledge, and/or experience specified had no relationship to the jobs themselves.[57]

Leonard threatened to sue both the hotels and the unions but agreed to with-hold the suit if the parties promptly established compliance programs that ended the discriminatory practices and meaningfully increased minority employment at nonmenial levels of work and pay. To meet Leonard's requirements, compliance programs would have to target specific job categories in which minorities were underrepresented, establish a central personnel office committed to increasing minority employment in these categories, and track improvements in minority employment. To facilitate realizing these goals, he advised the industry to establish recruitment programs in the black community.[58]

The industry and the unions alike took the threatened lawsuit seriously. Both wanted to limit federal "interference" in what each regarded as its own affairs. If outward displays of cooperation masked private intentions to contain as much as possible the changes demanded, both nonetheless took definite steps toward desegregating the workplace. In the first six months of 1971, they conferred jointly with the Justice Department and civil rights leaders to define, develop, and implement acceptable programs. By June they had hammered out a "Black Consent Decree," which the Justice Department filed with the federal court, giving the court authority to enforce its provisions. At the same time, the department filed suit against the signatories of the decree charging them with violations of the 1964 Civil Rights Act and threatening to press the suit unless they complied with the decree.

In the Consent Decree, the resorts and the unions promised to hire, promote, transfer, and train employees without regard to race. In nearly two dozen job categories, they pledged to post public notices of all vacancies for all employees to see and to hire at least one African American in every four new hires until blacks represented at least 12.5 percent of the workforce in each category. The unions pledged to cooperate in minority training programs and to track progress in minority employment in areas within their respective jurisdictions and in the movement of minorities into supervisory positions. Together, labor and management could ask the court to dissolve the decree after three years, which presumably the court would do if the patterns of discrimination had been eliminated.[59]

The NRA led the joint effort to comply with the decree, preparing compliance manuals, offering legal advice, and working with the unions to set up training programs and equalize job referrals. It also disseminated information about job opportunities in minority communities, making widespread use of newspapers and radio stations and working with the NAACP and the Nevada State Employment Security Department for this and related purposes.[60]

The effort soon drew praise from the Nixon administration's Justice Department. After reviewing the first compliance report, filed in late 1971, Assistant Attorney General Stuart Herman concluded that the industry had made "substantial progress" in implementing the decree, pointing to recent hiring of African Americans as dealers, cocktail waitresses, switchboard operators, and cashiers. Less progress had been made in hiring black bartenders, front desk workers, and restaurant servers. The unions, Herman thought, were referring adequate numbers of qualified black applicants in these and other categories, but some resorts—the Aladdin, the Riviera, the Stardust, and the Tropicana—had made too little progress in equalizing their workforces.[61]

Achieving these results meant rewriting collective bargaining agreements. In April 1972, for example, the Teamsters agreed to the hiring of qualified African Americans from outside its referral system. The "memorandum of understanding" that acknowledged this agreement permitted resorts to hire one African American "outsider" for each African American hired through union referral. The concession, which the union would never have agreed to under other circumstances, encouraged hiring blacks in such areas as parking attendants, gardeners, and warehousemen, as well as switchboard operators and room and reservation clerks.[62]

By summer 1972 the Consent Decree had reshaped personnel and hiring policies through unprecedented labor-management cooperation, which both agreed to with misgivings. Working with civil rights advocates was easier said than done, and the progress made was often disappointing to everyone. Nonetheless, by late 1972 the number of black bellmen at the hotels, for example, had risen from 10 to 15 percent of the total, and the number of black switchboard operators from none to nearly 10 percent. By then, African Americans had many jobs in casinos, too, their proportion of keno writers, for example, having increased from 2 percent to 16, and of dealers from 2 to 7 percent.[63]

Gains elsewhere were less impressive. African Americans held 5 percent of secretary-receptionists and parking lot attendants jobs, though their numbers in these categories had doubled; and they constituted just 6 percent of food and beverage servers. The latter figures could be attributed in part to problems in the job-training program. Sixty African Americans entered the training program for wait staff by late 1972, but only fifteen completed it. The reasons for this were multiple. Some trainees worked at other jobs and complained of being too tired to attend classes, while others lost interest after learning more about wait work.[64]

The Justice Department pressured laggard hotels and unions to match the progress others had made. After reviewing the situation in late 1972, for example, the department chided the Hilton Flamingo for "lack of progress," accusing it of "complete disregard for the goals and timetables to which the hotel obligated itself in the Consent Decree." Assistant Attorney General J. Stanley Pottinger, who made this accusation, was especially critical of the Flamingo's failure to hire more African American card and dice dealers. "This sort of progress," Pottinger said of the fact that the number of blacks dealing at the Flamingo had increased by only one, "is not tolerable." He noted too that in the preceding quarter, twelve of fourteen African Americans had failed auditions as dealers, compared to two of fifteen whites. "Such results," Pottinger thought, "raise serious questions as to the audition procedure and the Flamingo's intent to comply with the Decree."[65]

Despite such foot dragging, by early 1973 the industry had met thresholds for compliance in fourteen of twenty-three job categories, in some of which blacks were well over 12.5 percent of the workforce. Half of all warehousemen in the industry were now blacks, as were a third of all gardeners, doormen, and bar assistants, a quarter of all typists, and a fifth of front office cashiers and keno writers. In addition, black bartenders, cocktail waitresses, and bellmen had reached levels only slightly below the goal of 12.5 percent. Both management and labor expected such figures to justify dissolution of the decree within a year.[66]

In June 1974 the Teamsters petitioned the court to relieve it of obligations under the decree. Attorneys for the union argued that the union had fulfilled its responsibilities, citing levels of African American employment in job categories over which it had jurisdiction. But the EEOC, the plaintiff in the case, countered that the petition was premature because not all resorts had yet met the 12.5 percent hiring goal in some of the targeted areas under Teamster control. It also urged the court to keep the decree in place to facilitate elimination of beneath-the-surface practices that still favored whites over minority employees and men over women. Compliance with the decree, it insisted, was not equally vigorous or successful in all resorts or all areas of employment.[67]

EEOC attorneys offered testimony from African American employees to substantiate these charges. Harold Harkness, a timekeeper at the MGM Grand, claimed that MGM posted notices of openings in supervisory positions only after the openings were filled. "Only one notice was ever posted, and that was after the job had been filled," Harkness testified. "I was aware of this because of my employment in timekeeping." This practice had kept Harkness from applying for a job in public relations. "The Assistant Publicity Manager resigned on a Thursday in the latter part of April 1974," Harkness recalled. "I saw the resignation before it was even posted and called Mr. Burke [head of personnel], and he told me he was glad to accept my inquiry but the position had been filled Tuesday." Harkness had previously worked at the Las Vegas Hilton, which he said had also violated the decree. He told the EEOC that the hotel had filled at least three supervisory positions in the comptroller's office without advertising them.[68]

Clemmie Woodward also experienced racial discrimination in the industry. In 1973 the Mint Hotel promoted Woodward, one of its few black casino workers, from a change girl to cashier, only to fire her a few weeks later after she was involved in a fight with a white co-worker. According to Woodward, the experienced co-worker knew that the novice Woodward needed to ask job-related questions but refused to speak to her and provoked the incident that got her fired. The Culinary had investigated Woodward's dismissal but concluded that it had been justified, at which point Woodward charged the union as well as the Mint with discrimination. The Culinary had not taken her grievance seriously, she said, noting that the union had recently helped reinstate a white cashier dismissed by the Mint for stealing. "She made a complaint to the Union," Woodward said of the cashier, "and they took her case all the way up and got her job back for her."[69]

Aggrieved workers like Woodward not only thwarted efforts to dissolve the Consent Decree but brought to light problems of white women and Hispanics as well as those of African Americans. Employment practices in the industry had traditionally hurt all of these groups significantly. In 1970, when women accounted for a third of the Clark County workforce and about the same portion of employees in hotels and gaming, the resorts employed no female dealers or bartenders, and none as parking lot attendants, gardeners, or similar blue-collar workers. Women represented about three-quarters of the office and clerical workers, and the vast majority of maids, cashiers, and switchboard operators. Wages were low in these unskilled or semiskilled jobs.[70] Hispanics, who accounted for about 5 percent of the Clark County workforce, also found themselves disproportionately in unrewarding jobs. During the early 1970s, Hispanics had filed their own complaints with the EEOC accusing employers of discrimination.[71]

The struggle for employment rights in Las Vegas thus broadened significantly. After the courts refused to dissolve the Consent Decree, the EEOC asked major resorts and unions for permission to examine their personnel records for purposes of determining employment patterns among women and Hispanics. When both tried to limit access to their records, EEOC commissioner Raymond Telles charged them with discrimination, insisting that processes already well advanced in dealing with discrimination against African Americans be expanded to help females and Hispanics. To avoid litigation and bad publicity, the parties agreed to meet regularly with civic leaders and community groups in order to improve job opportunities for women and Hispanics and to submit regular reports to the commission detailing the status of their employment for the next five years. They agreed to set up new job training programs and to recompense women who could show that they had been denied equal job opportunities in the industry.[72]

Women and minority men continued to find new opportunities in resorts through the 1970s. By 1978, about a quarter of the Strip's 2,600 roulette, blackjack, and baccarat dealers were women, and Hispanics accounted for 7 percent of the Strip's dealers, 9 percent of its blue-collar workers, and 10 percent of housekeeping supervisors.[73] Meanwhile, job opportunities for African Americans improved. The EEOC concluded in 1978 that Strip properties had met their affirmative action goals in all but a handful of job categories targeted by the Consent Decree. The Flamingo, to cite one example, had met employment goals in nineteen of twenty-two targeted categories.[74] However, the commission concluded that the parties had not yet met their "ultimate goals" and should not yet be relieved of their obligations under the decree. Therefore, the decree remained in effect.[75]

By the late 1970s the civil rights movement in Las Vegas had largely succeeded in eliminating employment discrimination in the resort industry. Though discrimination in the industry persisted, the movement had reshaped the racial and sexual composition of resort workforces. That improvement owed much to the vigilance of the Justice Department and EEOC in enforcing the 1964 Civil Rights Act, but it also reflected the commitment and hard work of civil rights leaders and aggrieved workers, especially African Americans.[76] With the powerful language of "rights," African Americans had repudiated gradualist approaches to integration and won a real measure of equality in the workplace in Las Vegas resorts. "We want all of our rights, here and now," Reverend Donald Clark said at the time. "Even if the opportunity for the Negro in Las Vegas was ninety-nine percent better, we would still not be satisfied." Like civil rights advocates across the country, Clark measured "equality" and "progress" mainly by the number of black workers in jobs traditionally held strictly by whites.[77]

The role of the Nevada Resort Association and organized labor loomed large in this story. Like most employer associations, the NRA searched for ways to lower labor costs and increase worker efficiency without regard to such "nonmaterial" things as race, gender, or ethnicity. Personal prejudices no less than government dictates could be accommodated to market forces. Once it grasped the imperatives of the situation, the NRA approached workplace discrimination as it approached other labor problems, pragmatically, methodically, and with an eye on the bottom line of profitability. To be sure, trade unions in Las Vegas posed problems in the fight for employment rights, but those organizations were never as bent on restricting opportunities for African Americans as their counterparts in manufacturing centers that faced the problem of deindustrialization, or institutions in the Deep South that refused to take even a tokenistic approach to integration. By the time the Civil Rights Act passed into law, the Las Vegas Culinary was already a multiracial institution, with black stewards and business agents that helped women and minority men gain greater control of their labor power. With grass-roots activism and public policy leading the way, resort owners and organized labor played a constructive role in ushering in a new workplace regime in Las Vegas.

The Spirit of '76

In 1976, as the nation observed its bicentennial, thirteen thousand Las Vegas workers struck fifteen major resorts. The strikers were from four unions whose contracts with the Nevada Resort Association (NRA) had expired simultaneously. Employees from other unions refused to cross the picket lines, which helped force a dozen of the struck resorts to shut down, throwing ten thousand non-union employees out of work. The strike lasted sixteen days and took a sharp, temporary toll on the local economy as well as the striking workers. It affected almost all commercial enterprises in Las Vegas, and tax collections in the city and county. As it dragged on, striking employees grew increasingly militant and law enforcement officials increasingly resistant to breaches of the peace.

The strike was a major episode in the city's history, as well as that of its tourist industry and its labor relations. It grew out of a clash of wills between management and labor less over wages and working conditions than over more fundamental matters relating to control of the workplace and the right of union workers to honor picket lines of unions other than their own. The strike's timing and intensity show that, after national corporations took control of the resort industry, labor relations in Las Vegas became structurally adversarial. The growing size and centrality of the industry to the city and state economy meant that any serious disruption in it represented a grave concern to the region itself. As a result, public officials eventually intervened in the dispute and helped resolve it, something that had never before happened.

♠ ♣ ♥ ♦

The strike took place against ongoing changes in the national economy that were eclipsing the strength of organized labor. This national picture applied chiefly to heavy manufacturing and extractive industries, which had begun secular stages of decline that little affected a service industry like Las Vegas tourism. That industry was strong in the mid-1970s. Between 1970 and 1976, annual visitor counts for the area had risen by more than a third, to nearly ten million, and tourist spending more than doubled, to $2.5 billion. Yet industry managers worried about the future. The nation's first "oil shock" had increased the cost of travel and put downward pressure on major barometers of the industry's well-being, including projections of growth in revenue and visitor expenditure. The oil shock fueled inflation and economic uncertainties in an industry dependent on discretionary spending. Moreover, the leisure and recreation business had grown more competitive. Urban renewal was rejuvenating cities, making them again attractive to tourists, while new amusement parks, ocean cruises, and outdoor and sports-related tourism, as well as foreign travel, challenged Las Vegas for the tourist dollar. Even in Southern Nevada, alternatives to gambling and the glitz of Las Vegas were now widely available.[1]

The threat of competition from Atlantic City, New Jersey, was particularly worrisome. In the mid-1970s, Nevada was still the only place in the nation for legal gambling, but several states and localities were exploring gambling as a possible tourist attraction and cure for economic problems and thus a source of revenue. In 1974 New Jersey voters narrowly rejected a ballot initiative to legalize gambling in Atlantic City, an aging seaside community once known for its appeal to vacationers from New York, Philadelphia, and Baltimore. A coalition of influential business and civic leaders promised to put the measure before the voters again, and insiders in the gaming business in and out of Las Vegas expected it to pass. Casino gambling in the middle of the heavily populated East Coast would obviously have implications for Las Vegas. Atlantic City already rivaled Las Vegas as a convention site, and gambling there would no doubt siphon off high-spending conventioneers from Las Vegas. That possibility had prompted the Las Vegas Convention and Visitors Authority to launch an aggressive marketing campaign aimed at the convention market. "We must dismiss thoughts of complacency," the authority said of its marketing strategies. "Our job is to stay number one."[2]

Resort managers on the Strip needed no such incentives to get tough with their unionized employees. Executives at the six Summa properties, which Howard Hughes still owned, as well as Caesars Palace, the MGM Grand, the Hilton properties, and other major resorts were already committed for reasons of their own to bringing what they considered order, efficiency, and proper management control of the workforce in the resort industry. Like corporate managers everywhere, they believed in the supremacy of capital over labor, of managers over workers, and saw unions as obstacles to the achievement of their goals. For them, dealing with unions was a problem to be managed and constrained, not a cooperative economic and social endeavor to be addressed equitably.[3]

Correspondence between executives within these companies shed light on this outlook. In 1973 Henri Lewin of the Hilton Corporation complained to corporate headquarters that his employees acted too independently and that union work rules prevented him from improving services and holding down labor costs. "Labor problems occur on a daily basis," Lewin groused. "In some areas you can't even tell a man to cut his hair." To solve such "problems," Lewin asked for a "capable man" to handle "union negotiations, union grievances, and other day-to-day personnel matters." "I recommend that one of the strongest labor men be put in Las Vegas on a full-time basis." He added, "This would save money as well as give us the respect we should have."[4] Law and the realities of union strength in Las Vegas discouraged Lewin from calling for straightforward confrontation with workers and unions, and thus he embraced a strategy of calculation and maneuver, which required two or three cycles of contract negotiations—six to nine years—to achieve most of what he wanted.

Despite this evolution in management thinking, industrial relations remained peaceful in early 1976, when negotiations commenced to renew the three-year contracts signed in 1973. Those contracts had been signed without a work stoppage and with relatively general increases in wages and benefits for union employees. As a result, those employees were earning 30 to 40 percent more than they had earned in 1970, and they had comparable improvements in benefits and job security, along with employee-friendly grievance procedures.[5]

The situation among housekeepers illustrated these improvements. From 1970 to 1976, their wages increased more than 50 percent (from $16.90 to $25.80 per shift), and employer contributions to their health and welfare funds rose nearly 90 percent. Like other union employees, they were guaranteed full-time employment, paid vacations, and seven paid holidays a year, as well as two full meals each workday. Pregnant women and new mothers could take leaves of absence as long as doctors certified their inability to return to work, and they had the right to return to their job classifications and shifts.[6] These improvements, however, did little more than keep up with inflation. From 1970 to 1975, consumer prices in the nation as a whole increased 40 percent, nearly quadrupling the inflationary rate of the early 1960s. Energy and food prices rose dramatically in these years, as did the cost of health care, home ownership, and consumer goods.[7]

The resorts like their employees felt the resulting economic squeeze. The costs of doing business, including the cost of labor, rose as did inflation rates, and some resorts saw their profit margins decline or even disappear. The Summa Corporation, for example, lost a reported $100 million between 1971 and 1976, including $30 million in 1975 alone. Its smallest Las Vegas property, the Silver Slipper, had not shown a profit for several years, and the Castaways and the Landmark had barely broken even. Even the Desert Inn and the Sands, the most luxurious and profitable of the Summa properties, needed major refurbishments to remain competitive.[8]

These economic pressures weighed heavily on collective bargaining in 1976, influencing what unions could reasonably demand in wage and benefit increases, and what management felt it could afford in the face of the necessity to limit cost increases. Combined with management's new determination to gain greater control over the workplace as well as hiring procedures, these circumstances pointed to a difficult round of negotiations on the part of both sides. In addition, management was now more than ever determined to limit workers' right to honor picket lines of other workers and unions and to deny union employees the right to strike for the purpose of forcing employers to recognize new unions, especially unions of dealers and security guards.[9]

This last issue was especially urgent for both sides. In 1975 members of the Teamsters had honored picket lines at the Tropicana of sixteen striking security guards who belonged to a recently formed affiliate of the International Union of Police and Protection Employees. The union had won representation elections at several Strip resorts in the early 1970s, but a few of those properties, including the Tropicana, had refused to renew their contracts, which prompted the strike. The sympathetic action by "back-end" Teamster employees cut off not only food and beverage deliveries to the resort but also garbage collection, and it forced management to negotiate with the guards and increase their pay and benefits.[10]

The NRA, which represented the Summa properties and other major Strip resorts, was especially determined to outlaw sympathy strikes in the next contract with the Culinary and Bartenders. The existing contracts, set to expire on March 10, required employees to cross picket lines only when the picketing was for "organizational purposes" or the result of a dispute between another employer and employees. They specifically ensured workers the right to respect the picket lines of established unions provided the Southern Nevada Central Labor Council sanctioned the strike of the picketing workers.[11]

♠ ♣ ♥ ♦

When bargaining talks opened in February, the NRA's chief negotiator, William Campbell, began by insisting on prohibiting unionized employees from engaging in any "concerted economic activity" against the resorts that employed them during the life of the contract. Should any union employee violate the prohibition, he demanded, management must have the right "to lock out all members of the offending employee's union."[12] This would, of course, impose a major new restriction on the rights of unions and their members to protect their perceived interests, specifically the right to participate in sympathy strikes.

Campbell said the language he insisted on would do no more than prevent abuses of union power, especially by members of the Culinary or by the Culinary itself. Whenever another union calls a strike, one resort manager said at this point, the Culinary "threatens to pull all its people out of a single hotel in respect for the picket line and bring that one hotel to its knees."[13] That result was intolerable. Unless management had the power to lock out workers for refusing to cross picket lines, the Culinary would one day strike over the discharge of a single incompetent employee. "We need some leverage against every little union beef," another management spokesman explained. "Why, the way things are, every union can go out on strike if management tries to fire a bartender who may be drunk three times in a row on the job."[14]

Such statements trivialized the meaning of sympathy strikes and exaggerated the threat they posed. Sympathy strikes typically involved efforts to unionize unorganized workers—that is, workers in would-be or emergent unions opposed by management—not to reverse the firing of individual employees, for whatever reason.[15] Union negotiators at once recognized the significance of the lockout proposal, their chief, Al Bramlet, calling it "totally unacceptable" and a "union-breaking scheme."[16] Bramlet's assistant Jeff McColl told the press that to accept Campbell's proposal would make the Culinary the "leper of southern Nevada labor." "There's no way we can talk about money," McColl said adamantly, "when that clause is there."[17] Jack Stafford, head of the Bartenders agreed. His union would strike "as long as necessary" to protect the right to engage in sympathy strikes.[18]

Union negotiators were also unhappy with other NRA proposals. Rather than offering the customary three-year contracts with guaranteed annual pay raises, Campbell proposed a five-year contract that offered pay raises of 20 percent over the next three years plus additional wage increases determined by the behavior of the federal government's Consumer Price Index. From management's perspective, lengthening the terms of labor contracts promised to bring greater stability to the work environment and, by definition, reduce the likelihood of a work stoppage. "[The five-year contract] fortifies the industry with stability," a representative of the Hilton properties explained. "We think that it guarantees uninterrupted work."[19] The justification for incorporating cost-of-living adjustments in the latter years of the proposed contract was that wages should rise—or fall—automatically with fluctuations in the cost of living. By the 1970s, many companies and unions in the manufacturing sector of the economy had negotiated such arrangements, including parties in the aircraft, automotive, railroad, and textile industries.

Far more alarming to union leaders were management's proposals to reduce the guaranteed workweek for some workers from five to four days, to lengthen the list of reasons for which workers might be summarily discharged, and to subcontract or "outsource" to other firms some of the work currently done by kitchen workers, such as carving meat and preparing sauces. Moreover, they wanted more control of the job referral process, heretofore the exclusive prerogative of the unions. That process, employers claimed, prevented them from building up the labor reservoirs they needed to fill jobs quickly and often from hiring the best-qualified job candidates.[20]

Union leaders instantly rejected these various proposals. The proposals, they recognized, rolled back major gains their unions had made in earlier years and failed to offset the effects of recent inflation on the real income of union members. Consumer prices had risen 11 percent in the past year alone, yet the wages of many union employees only 5 to 6 percent. If management wanted to lengthen the terms of labor contracts, it had to offer more hefty pay raises than those proposed and to increase its contributions to the unions' retirement and health care programs. It also had to withdraw proposals to eliminate union jobs and work rules and to interfere in union hiring hall practices, which operated in ways that protected the rights and well-being of workers and their unions. Moreover, they needed to improve conditions of employment by offering new job perquisites, such as additional paid holidays, the extension of work breaks from ten to fifteen minutes, and more paid sick leave. Employers dismissed these suggestions as "unreasonable." "We might as well close our doors," NRA president Frank Scott said of them.[21]

Members of the musicians' union, whose contracts with the NRA also expired on March 10, felt especially vulnerable in the 1976 negotiations. For three years the resorts and the musicians had disagreed over who actually employed lounge musicians.[22] Unlike their counterparts in showrooms, who were on hotel payrolls, lounge musicians were hired by bandleaders who contracted with resorts for the services of their groups. Back in 1973, the NRA had tried to change this arrangement by making lounge musicians hotel employees like showroom musicians. Lounge musicians rejected the proposal because they thought it made them liable to the kind of treatment the resorts gave their other wageworkers, who had less control over their work routines. At issue were such things as rehearsal and work-break schedules and the right to enter the hotels through the front door rather than employees' entrances. Bandleaders also disliked the proposed change because they preferred to make their own deals with sidemen concerning such things as what to wear and how to perform in given circumstances. Rebuffed in 1973, the NRA in 1976 refused to negotiate the terms and conditions of the employment of lounge musicians, insisting that that was the responsibility of bandleaders as independent contractors.[23]

This NRA stance encouraged some bandleaders to consider forming their own collective bargaining unit. A group of bandleaders led by Charlie Peterson questioned whether the musicians' union had the right to bargain on their behalf. They insisted that it was bandleaders who employed their musicians and that they should therefore bargain for themselves and their musicians. The NRA found this position encouraging because it promised to give musicians the status of employees of private contractors and thus remove the resorts from labor negotiations with the musicians' union. "There would be no labor dispute between the hotels and the Musicians, but rather between the leader of an orchestra and the Union," as NRA negotiator William Campbell recognized.[24] The result of this dispute was that the musicians' union faced an internal revolt on the eve of the 1976 bargaining sessions. "Our own bandleaders were chewing us up and down," as Mark Massagli of the union later recalled. "When the hotels heard about this, all they did is sit back and say 'we don't even know if we should be here with you.'"[25]

The musicians' union faced other problems, too. The recent conversion of a few casino lounges into gaming areas promised to eliminate many of the jobs bandleaders now fought to control. To remedy the situation, the musicians' chief negotiator, Renny Ashleman, suggested that the union modify its wage proposals if resorts guaranteed more jobs for lounge musicians. Campbell rejected such a guarantee as "impractical." Employers, he insisted, must have the "flexibility" to meet changing consumer demands.[26] Meanwhile, the use of taped music in resorts threatened the careers of orchestra musicians. The hotels now, in 1976, insisted on the right to use taped music during show rehearsals, thus eliminating the cost of musicians for that purpose. Dancers, NRA negotiators insisted, did not need an orchestra to practice their acts. This argument made sense to management, but to musicians it was a formula for reduced employment and income. That was threatening enough in itself, but it also tapped into long-standing fears that "mechanical" music threatened live musicians with obsolescence. Union leaders therefore rejected the proposal, insisting that "any deviation" from current agreements regarding taped music would be viewed as an effort to "diminish our work opportunities."[27] Wages were another concern of the musicians. Ashleman insisted that musicians as well as stagehands get an immediate 20 percent wage hike as well as annual cost-of-living adjustments during the life of the new contract, a proposal that management saw as unjustified, unrealistic, and unnecessarily burdensome.[28]

Despite the magnitude of these differences, the NRA and the unions negotiated in the customary fashion in 1976. As usual, the center of attention was negotiations with the Culinary and Bartenders, which in early February extended into lengthy daily sessions. Discussions with the lesser unions occurred irregularly, because both sides understood that the terms of the contracts with these unions depended upon the terms reached with the Culinary. Throughout the process, management negotiators stressed the need to remain competitive, the threat from legalized gambling in Atlantic City, and the costs of marketing Las Vegas and refurbishing its aging resorts. Union leaders, on the other hand, emphasized the financial problems of workers and vowed to protect their rights in the workplace and to honor picket lines.

By March negotiators had resolved a range of secondary issues but remained, as a union spokesperson put it, "miles apart on money," on the length of the contract, on the subcontracting issue, and on management's insistence on prohibiting union workers from honoring picket lines of unorganized workers.[29] There had also been no agreement on the special concerns of musicians and stagehands, whose union leaders told them to prepare to strike.[30]

As the negotiations deadlocked, the local press called on both sides to reach an agreement "satisfactory to all," reminding them that a strike would hurt employees and employers alike and "shatter" Las Vegas tourism. "The tourist industry is not one which can be shut down instantly and then cranked up again overnight," the *Review-Journal* editorialized. "Conventions are scheduled in advance which cannot be cancelled because of labor disputes. Tourists who call off vacation plans when a strike is reported are not likely to reschedule their trip as soon as the workers are back on the job. Instead, they will take their business elsewhere." A strike would thus "seriously tarnish the image of Las Vegas as an ideal vacation spot."[31]

A flurry of last-minute efforts failed to break the deadlock. On the night of March 10, only hours before their contract expired, culinary workers met at the Las Vegas Convention Center to hear Bramlet denounce management's final offers as "unacceptable." By a three-to-one margin, the workers then gave Bramlet the authorization he requested to call a strike after twenty-four hours during which negotiators could make a "final attempt" to reach an agreement.[32]

That night, the twelve hundred members of the musicians' union went on strike, forcing the cancellation of all shows and musical entertainment in NRA properties, including performances of such entertainers as Sammy Davis Jr., Ann Margret, and Wayne Newton. Union representatives notified bandleaders around five o'clock that the strike was on, and the leaders informed their sidemen. A few lounge musicians began performances that evening but stopped when union representatives reminded them they could be fined and expelled from the union for scabbing. The union "slipped a few choice words in their ears, told them to finish the set and leave." And they left.[33] Stagehands and wardrobe attendants immediately joined the striking musicians, and management announced the cancellation of showroom performances "until further notice."[34]

The two small unions had acted aggressively, but the fate of the impending strike was in the hands of the Culinary and Bartenders. Would these unions join the strike after the twenty-four-hour delay Al Bramlet had asked for? The answer was certainly yes once members of the Culinary had voted, for the two sides remained far apart not only on cost items but on sympathy strikes and the length of contracts. Most independent hotels, including the Riviera, the Aladdin, the Stardust, the Fremont, and the Hacienda, had already accepted the Culinary's demands on cost items, which strengthened Bramlet's unwillingness to settle for less with the NRA. There, the impasse remained when the Culinary's twenty-four-hour wait-and-see period expired.[35]

About eight o'clock on the evening of March 11, thousands of housekeepers, wait people, and kitchen and barroom workers began forming picket lines around the fifteen resorts represented by the NRA. In a show of solidarity, other union employees, including members of the Teamsters and the building trades, honored the picket lines. Yellow Cab Company drivers did likewise. With the help of supervisors and volunteer workers, the struck resorts remained open overnight to accommodate hotel guests, but the next day most of them shut down, putting about ten thousand nonunion employees, among them dealers, out of work. In all, the strike idled perhaps twenty-three thousand workers.[36]

The tent-shaped Circus Circus, which Jay Sarno had turned over to William Bennett and William Pennington in 1974, vowed to remain open, as did Caesars Palace and the Dunes.[37] But they had to slash prices and curtail services to do so. They eliminated room service, closed their showrooms and restaurants, and used nonunion administrative personnel to check guests in and out. Guests had to carry their own luggage, make their own beds, and pick up fresh towels and otherwise fend for themselves. Charles and Peggy Balliro of Boston, who stayed at Caesars Palace during the strike, cleaned their own rooms, secured fresh towels and bed linen from nonunion pit bosses acting as bellhops, and did without phone service. When Peggy Balliro returned from a shopping trip by cab, the driver left her a hundred yards from the hotel because he refused to cross the picket line. "But what the hell?" her husband told a reporter, "The gambling and the sun are the same, and three times a day we get a free buffet, serviced by a hotel vice president!" Balliro's wife demurred. "You owe me another vacation," she told her husband.[38]

The strike exasperated tourists, whose numbers declined swiftly. With a dozen major resorts closed, newly arriving tourists had trouble finding accommodations. Those who did so had to settle for whatever they could find, and had to do without the services, entertainment, and the like they had been expecting.[39] When reporters asked tourists how they felt about all this, most expressed disappointment. "It spoiled my whole vacation," a Pennsylvania woman told reporters. "Everything is dead," another tourist agreed; "all of our reservations were cancelled."[40] A youth from Lovelock, Nevada, in Las Vegas with his high school basketball team, had the same reaction. "So far, it's really disappointing. You only get here once a year and want to have all the fun you can."[41] A woman from Ft. Wayne, Indiana, was even more let down. "We had planned this trip a long time," she told the press. "I'm disappointed we couldn't see Wayne Newton."[42]

The strike also frustrated idled dealers, most of whom were paid during the strike but received no tips. Some of them grew angry. "I won't be tipping these strikers when it's over," one dealer said, "at least not until I make back all this strike has cost me. I've always been a real George tipper, too." Others expressed support for the strike, but worried that the dispute harmed them financially. One dealer's wife was concerned that she would have difficulty putting food on the table if the strike lasted another week. "If it goes on, I'm going to file for food stamps," she told a reporter. "If our family qualified, why not?"[43]

The strike was much more burdensome to strikers than to idled dealers or disappointed tourists. Without incomes, they worried about the personal cost of what they were doing. "We can't afford to strike," a picketer at the Thunderbird told a reporter when the strike began. "I need to eat and so does my family." Others made similar statements to the press. "It's bad," one of them said of her situation. "I live check to check and have nothing saved." Walking the picket lines, strikers quickly discovered, was tedious and exhausting despite whatever degree of commitment one had to the strike and to the causes behind it. They had to walk in lockstep circles at hotel and parking lot entrances, in front of automobiles whose drivers were impatient and annoyed at the delays they experienced, if not opposed to the strike altogether. "It ain't fun," one picketer said of the experience. "Any knot-head who says we're singing and having fun is crazy." Though it was March rather than August, desert wind and scorching sun added to the discomforts of the long hours of midday, as did the chills of the hours of midnight. Southerly winds gusting at twenty-five to thirty miles an hour buffeted strikers almost daily. The winds reached sixty miles an hour on the worst day, when it was almost impossible even to hold onto picket signs much less impress onlookers with one's commitment to the strike. Indeed, many strikers found the weather the worst part of picketing. "It wouldn't be too bad if the weather was better," one of them complained.[44]

Long hours of picketing, however, created new social bonds and friendships, which helped ease the pressures of picketing as well as striking. When shifts ended, picketers often gathered at coffee shops or bars or in their own kitchens to share refreshments and experiences and discuss news and rumors about the strike. Many also met at union headquarters, which became centers of social activity as well as sources of information and assurance. The offices of the musicians' union, on East Tropicana Boulevard at the south end of the Strip, had long been a place where members rendezvoused and relaxed, and it continued so during the strike. There, musicians "jammed" after picketing, or played dominoes, poker, or other games. Another similar center was the "strike kitchen" in the culinary union parking lot, where volunteers made and served sandwiches, coffee, and other refreshments for picketers.[45]

This culture of solidarity had many components. It included the sense of belonging generated by doing whatever was necessary to help the strike along, including working not only in the strike kitchen but in makeshift child-care facilities, first-aid stations, and information centers. Strikers made their own picket signs, printed and distributed informational leaflets, attended rallies to hear their leaders denounce the "greed" of employers, pledged to "stick together" and to "stay out as long as it takes," and sang "We Shall Overcome" and "When the Saints Go Marching In." "Flying squadrons" of picketers rushed to wherever they were needed in whatever emergency situation developed, while picket "captains" dealt with reporters, police officers, and taunting tourists. The strike had its dramatic moments, when, for example, former heavyweight boxing champion Joe Louis served coffee to striking workers outside Caesars Palace.[46]

The strike culture fed on its demons. Union leaders boosted morale by denouncing resort owners as coldhearted capitalists out to break the labor movement. They heaped special scorn on Howard Hughes as a deranged billionaire oblivious to the damage he or his minions were doing to the Las Vegas economy and the well-being of workers. "This is a trap by one of the richest men in the world who pictures his Las Vegas hotels as pawns and playthings," Al Bramlet told striking workers in a typical pep rally speech. "He can afford to do this." "Howard Hughes and the other big hotel owners are trying to bust the unions here," Jeff McColl, Bramlet's assistant, told the press. "All they're going to do is kill the goose that's been laying golden eggs for all of us."[47]

As the strike continued and tempers rose along the picket lines, confrontations between picketers and police officers deployed to keep order inevitably arose. Increasingly, picketers came to view police officers as agents of management and to regard their tactics as "brutal." Confrontations between strikers and police officers thus became frequent and often violent, which resulted in arrests of picketers.[48]

Worker militancy was evident from the onset and not easily contained. At the three NRA resorts that remained open, picketers taunted and harassed nonunion workers and hotel guests as they entered and left the properties, sometimes threatening them with bodily harm. Security guards at those properties reported that striking workers hit cars with picket signs, and shouted such threats as "We know where you live," "I've got a gun," and "We're going to get you!" They also reportedly made "threatening gestures," as if to assault people crossing their picket lines. Reports of intimidation brought increased police surveillance, which fed the flames of protest. Picketers shouted profanities at police officers and refused their orders to back away from hotel entrances. In one notable incident, a female protestor "slugged" an officer, "breaking his glasses and cutting his face." That prompted police to arrest a handful of people at the site of the incident. The arrests restored order, but not for long. During the strike, police officers returned repeatedly to Circus Circus, one of the still-open resorts. Once, when they arrived with shotguns and guard dogs, someone threw a "Molotov Cocktail" at them. Though the "cocktail" exploded harmlessly on the ground, it prompted officers to form skirmish lines and push picketers from hotel entrances.[49]

Other resorts experienced similar disturbances. At Caesars Palace, picketers blocked cars from parking lots, backing up traffic along the Strip and damaging several automobiles. One hotel guest later testified that, as she and a female companion drove onto the property, picketers kicked her car, beat it with signs, and climbed on top of it, while repeatedly threatening the women. "Pickets called us, among other things a 'rich bitch,' 'motherfucker,' and 'cunt,'" while "two pickets, one male and one female, jumped onto the hood of [our] car," scratching it in several places. "One scratch was approximately three feet in length, and one about two feet in length."[50] The offending picketers had ignored the orders of hotel security guards during this incident, and ceased their intimidation only when the police arrived. When the police left, they resumed the intimidation, and the hotel called them back.[51]

There were bomb threats too. On the day the Culinary struck, callers impersonating police officers warned Caesars Palace of an impending explosion. "If you don't close your hotel tonight," one caller warned, "there will be a bomb." A few minutes later, another warned, "You have one hour to close the building or it will be bombed." Someone posing as a hotel security guard also called the police urging that Caesars Palace be evacuated immediately because of a bomb on its premises. Other resorts received similar threats. "You have thirteen minutes to honor the picket [line] or a bomb is going off," the Las Vegas Hilton was warned by telephone. "The showroom is going in fifteen minutes," the same voice telephoned a few minutes later. Searchers found no bombs at either of the resorts, both of which remained open, with no doubt a rattled management and guests.[52]

This chaos combined with the fall off in tourism to pressure management at least to settle the strike. At the request of Governor Mike O'Callaghan, both sides held separate meetings with the state labor commissioner, Stanley P. Jones, on March 18, before beginning marathon bargaining sessions. By then, the unions had made a counterproposal on the thorny problem of outsourcing, agreeing that employers could subcontract jobs customarily performed by union workers provided that the unions had veto power over any or all of the subcontracting; that subcontractors abide by terms of the unions' agreements governing wages, hours, and other conditions of employment; and that any dispute arising over the issue be resolved by arbitration. The NRA viewed this counterproposal as irrational. The philosophy behind subcontracting was to lower labor costs and reduce problems associated with collective bargaining. The unions' offer did nothing to cut costs and only complicated the bargaining process, and thus management rejected it.[53]

On the no-strike–lockout issue, management now proposed that new contract language prohibit union employees from honoring picket lines of any union other than their own until picketing had continued for sixty days. Because the practical effect of such language would be to ban sympathy strikes, the unions saw it as evidence of "bad faith bargaining." Labor Commissioner Jones considered the no-strike issue so volatile that he suggested outside arbitrators should be called in to resolve it by binding arbitration.[54]

Governor O'Callaghan endorsed that suggestion, but management quickly rejected it. "We refuse to think that we and the Unions are so lacking in ability or so callous to the needs of our employees and their members that we cannot bridge these gaps and end the strikes," NRA president Scott wrote O'Callaghan. "We must, therefore, respectfully decline to participate in any third party determination of the remaining issues." Scott reminded the governor that management's primary responsibility was to its stockholders, not its employees. "There is simply no way the hotels can abdicate their responsibility to manage. We are responsible to our shareholders for increases in our labor costs."[55]

Though union leaders never opposed arbitration as a means of settling on the no-strike issue, they worried that a neutral third party might split the difference between the bargaining positions and decide, say, on a thirty-day no-strike–lockout clause. The unions now hoped the governor himself would intervene in the strike, and help resolve such thorny issues to labor's advantage. O'Callaghan was a popular Democrat elected in 1970 and again in 1974. Having worked for the Lyndon Johnson administration in the Job Corps and in the Office of Emergency Preparedness, he was a strong supporter of the civil rights movement and organized labor, which had endorsed O'Callaghan during his gubernatorial campaigns.[56]

The governor did in fact work to resolve the strike. After management rejected the state's proposal to arbitrate the length of time union members could not cross picket lines, at O'Callaghan's request the parties met with the labor commissioner in long daily sessions at the MGM Grand Hotel. Between March 19 and 22, Commissioner Jones persuaded each side to withdraw some of its lesser demands in favor of existing contract language. He developed the framework for a four-year contract that increased cost items to management by about 35 percent. To resolve the controversy over hiring procedures, he got the parties to agree that unions, if requested, could refer applicants to hotels for positions that were not yet open. The hotels would then interview the applicants and hire the person or persons they preferred by name when vacancies occurred. This would enable employers to build labor reservoirs from which to hire as needed and ensure unions that only union members were hired.[57]

Neither side, however, would compromise on the lockout and subcontracting issues. "Our feet are in cement on Articles 23 and 30," MGM chief Fred Benninger said in reference to these issues on March 21, "even if the union says it will take less money."[58] The labor commissioner, disappointed, implored both the employers and unions to be more flexible. Reminding the parties that the resort industry was the "economic lifeblood" of the state, he urged them to "go the extra mile" to resolve the conflict. What if the unions, the commissioner asked, allowed employers to subcontract a few specific forms of kitchen work and the two sides submitted the no-strike–lockout language to arbitration? Would the parties agree? "Absolutely not," Benninger replied. "We are not going to move on those two areas." The mediation talks had reached an impasse.[59]

Meanwhile, the Silver Slipper, one of the Summa properties, reopened on a limited basis. Unlike other struck properties, the Silver Slipper had no hotel accommodations, swimming pool, or shopping arcade. Essentially a casino and bar with two small showrooms for entertainment and a coffee shop, it thus employed far fewer union employees than most struck properties. It reopened by simply recalling its dealers and other nonunion personnel, with low-level managers tending bar and additional security workers protecting employees who crossed picket lines. As this transpired, picketers no doubt wondered whether other Summa properties would follow the Silver Slipper's lead and reopen their casinos and bars, thereby weakening the strike. Asked about that possibility, Clark Eaton, manager of the Silver Slipper, said only that his own gaming tables and bar would remain open around the clock with or without union employees.[60] Perry Lieber, public relations manager for Summa, said only that the corporation had no "immediate plans" to reopen other properties but that that might change. Howard Hughes, Lieber added, had not made the decision to reopen the Silver Slipper. "It was made by his lieutenants."[61]

As the position of the two sides hardened, union militancy augmented. Conflicts between picketers and police had declined after March 17, when a federal court issued a temporary restraining order limiting picketing on the Strip. The order, which the NRA had asked for, prevented strikers from blocking entrances to resorts by limiting to two the number of pickets at resort entrances. It also required picketers to stay at least fifteen feet from resort property and prohibited picketers from intimidating or threatening anyone "in any manner."[62] The order had a calming effect, though picketers were still visible and noisy, especially at the three NRA resorts that remained open.[63]

A few days later, several hundred striking workers gathered outside Caesars Palace and marched toward the hotel "shaking their fists and shouting, 'We

want to eat,' and 'No lock-out!' " They blocked hotel entrances and stopped traffic, while state and local police rushed to the scene. The law enforcement officials closed a half-mile stretch of the Strip to relieve traffic congestion and ordered protestors away from hotel entrances and off the street. When protestors
refused to obey, officers began arresting them. In most cases, those arrested
went quietly, singing "We Shall Overcome" or "Smile on Your Brother." Some,
however, had to be wrestled to the ground, handcuffed, and dragged away. Within
an hour, the police made more than fifty arrests.[64]

They made a score of additional arrests when several hundred protestors
blocked entrances to the Dunes. As this occurred, protestors threw beer bottles,
rocks, and even a board at police, while others ran along the Strip taunting them.
Protestors then formed "human stop signs" in front of police cars, and kicked
the cars as they inched their way through the crowd. A female protestor yelled,
"We took the Strip yesterday! We're going to take it again today!" The press
charged that strike leaders had orchestrated this civil disobedience, but union
spokesmen denied the charge. "Each of those people has a mind of his own," Jeff
McColl of the Culinary told reporters.[65]

As the mayhem mounted, both sides tried to influence public opinion through
the press. In "notices" to the public in Las Vegas newspapers, both appealed to the
reason and the emotions of readers. Both linked their cause to cherished American
values and freedoms. An "open letter" from the management of Caesars Palace to
its striking employees, which appeared in the *Sun* on March 21, characterized the
resort's contract proposals as a "square shake" and suggested its effort to limit
sympathy strikes would increase the job security of its employees. "Why should
our employees be out of work any time some other union strikes?" the letter asked.
The question appealed to workers as individuals while discounting the logic
and value of collective action. The letter also portrayed employers as guardians of
the public interest. "Let's keep Las Vegas growing," it read. "We have fine schools,
hospitals, and wonderful recreational centers. We don't have to take a back seat to
any other city." The unions' demands, this implied, threatened those things.[66]

By now, the newspapers were blaming labor leaders, especially Bramlet, for
prolonging the strike. Headlines and editorials described him as vainglorious
and power hungry and the striking workers as his robotic pawns. "He thrives on
power," the *Valley Times* said of Bramlet, "and the immense power he has had
apparently isn't enough."[67] The *Review-Journal* suggested on March 25 that most
striking workers no longer supported the strike but were afraid to tell Bramlet
so. "Strikers Scared to Voice Opinions with Officials of Culinary Union," the
paper headlined.[68] The story under this headline suggested that picketers were

picketing over issues that mattered only to Bramlet, who would end the conflict whenever his whim told him to do so. The fact that newspapers had lost advertising revenue as a result of the strike may explain some of this criticism. In normal times, the resorts were among the papers' largest advertisers.[69]

As the strike entered its third week, Edward T. Hanley, president of the national Hotel Employees and Restaurant Employees (HERE), entered the fray. Hanley (no kin to the Tom Hanley discussed earlier in this study) was a young, ambitious, and increasingly powerful national labor leader. His arrival in Las Vegas raised hopes of a quick strike settlement because he had earlier been instrumental in resolving several bitter labor disputes. Like Bramlet, he was "street-smart," having grown up in a working-class neighborhood in Chicago, where he tended bar in his father's tavern before he became active in union affairs. He served in the Air Force during the Korean War and then returned to Chicago, where he rose to the top of the local Bartender and Beverage Dispensers Union. In 1962 he became president of the executive board that negotiated labor agreements for culinary and bartending workers in Chicago, a position he held until he became president of HERE in 1973. The U.S. Justice Department suspected that Hanley climbed union ladders with help from Chicago crime figures, but he was never convicted of any wrongdoing.[70]

On March 22, at the MGM Grand, Hanley, on behalf of the striking unions, met with NRA members Frank Scott, Fred Benninger, and Al Benedict as well as their legal counsel Walter Loomis, who advised the NRA on labor contracts.[71] Though the local union leaders denied it, their absence at this pivotal meeting was a sign of an internal dispute within the Culinary. Unlike Bramlet, Hanley and other national officers of the Culinary and Bartenders were prepared to compromise on noncost issues in return for pay and benefit increases they could sell to striking workers. "He wanted to stop the strike," Lewin later said of Hanley. "So he called a meeting for the executive board of the resort association."[72] Evidently, Hanley had recently berated Bramlet in the presence of local union leaders for letting the strike drag on. "[He] blew his stack because the negotiations were going nowhere," one of Bramlet's aides said of Hanley's handling of the strike. "[He] was saying things like 'Al, end this goddamn thing.' "[73]

Whether or not this account is the whole truth of the Hanley-Bramlet encounter—and it has the ring of truth to it—local journalists interpreted Hanley's presence in Las Vegas as an effort to enhance his own position as a labor leader at Bramlet's expense. Hanley had national political aspirations, the journalists suggested, and saw the Las Vegas strike as a chance to cast himself as a powerful, moderating voice in the national labor movement.

Whatever the veracity of these speculations, Hanley's involvement in the strike was part of a larger bargaining strategy. Local unions wanted and needed help from their parent organization, especially during costly, difficult strikes. National officers brought calming voices to bargaining sessions in such strikes precisely because they were distant from the emotions and militancy of strikers and the personal investments or territoriality of local union leaders in the strike. They also brought a sense of power to such sessions, for it was they who approved or rejected agreements made by locals of the unions they controlled. Men like Hanley could and did make concessions to employers that local negotiators could never make and, in so doing, they could deflect or defy the insistence of local negotiators on sensitive issues. In this case, however, the division between national and local leaders was much less than press accounts suggested. Hanley could influence but not control the Las Vegas Culinary. "The membership is so dynamic," as Henri Lewin recognized at the time. "Hanley cannot come and promise you anything."[74]

On March 22 management offered new proposals on both cost and noncost issues. Hanley demurred, insisting that he had to talk the proposals over with Bramlet but intimated that the Culinary was prepared to compromise. He also indicated the union would sign a four-year contract with employers, something it had never done. More important, he suggested that the union would accept contract provisions prohibiting its members from supporting dealers' organizing efforts and honoring picket lines of other unions for ten days. He also suggested that management might outsource a limited number of jobs now held by union employees. These issues, he said, could be clarified in a codicil, or "side letter" to the contract.[75]

Two days later, after both parties caucused, Governor O'Callaghan presided over a negotiating session attended only by the chief labor and management figures, among them Barron Hilton, Kirk Kerkorian, and Edward T. Hanley. O'Callaghan insisted at once that the parties end their conflict then and there and offered proposals to help them do so.[76] He supported management's call for a strong no-strike guarantee and labor's need for significant pay and benefit increases. According to the state labor commissioner, who also attended the session, O'Callaghan alternately cajoled and bullied the parties into resolving their differences. "Governor O'Callaghan was tough when toughness was required," the commissioner later wrote. "He exhibited integrity, common sense, and [a] keen sense of humor and courage." Without the governor's "expert leadership," the commissioner believed, "the gaming industry and the labor movement in Nevada could have destroyed themselves."[77]

The commissioner no doubt exaggerated the governor's role, but by the time the meeting ended, the parties had reached a compromise agreement. The agreement included wage and benefit increases of 35 percent over four years, a clear victory for workers on cost items.[78] In exchange, the unions agreed to restrictions on the right to honor picket lines, specifically prohibiting their members from honoring lines of other groups for ten days and obligating them to cross lines set up for organizational or informational purposes. In addition, they agreed that the resorts could purchase a variety of prepared foods from outside sources, from pre-mixed salads to peeled vegetables, which promised to eliminate certain union jobs in the kitchen.[79]

Settlement with the Musicians and Stagehands soon followed. The NRA had already agreed to a financial package with these unions resembling that of the Culinary and Bartenders. The agreement with the Musicians, however, covered only instrumentalists in showrooms. Arbitrators would decide the status of lounge musicians and settle disagreements over "mechanical music."[80] (In the first instance, the arbitrators sided with the union, ruling that hotels had to negotiate the terms and conditions of employment in lounges with unions, not bandleaders.[81] In the second, they ruled that hotels could record the performances of house orchestras and use the recordings during "brush up" and "replacement" rehearsals but had to pay musicians "double scale" during recording sessions.)[82] Like the vast majority of culinary workers and bartenders, musicians and stagehands promptly ratified the agreements. The strike was over.[83]

♠ ♣ ♥ ♦

On March 27, seventeen days after the strike began, the NRA resorts reopened. Workers returned to their jobs; marquees along the Strip flashed the good news. In spaces normally reserved for the names of stellar performers, resorts proclaimed "Welcome, We're Open." Musicians and stagehands returned the next day. Lounge shows reopened immediately; main showrooms followed suit in a few days. Tourists trickled back more slowly. The casinos were "nearly empty" the first weekend, the press reported. "It's really dead in here," a tourist told a reporter at the Frontier. "I guess I ought to come back later. Maybe my luck would change." In fact, some returning tourists were lucky. As soon as the MGM Grand reopened, a visitor from California won $2,300 on a nickel slot machine.[84]

As the Las Vegas resort industry recovered, the strike's meaning became clear. According to the Convention and Visitors Authority, the strike cost the city about thirty conventions, more than 225,000 tourists, and financial losses of $20 million to $26 million. If, as an old adage had it, money coming into resorts turned over five times in the city, the cost to the community was perhaps $100 to $130 million. The NRA estimated that the strike cost $131 million in "tourist and related revenue."[85] Whatever the exact figures, everyone lost significantly. No conflict in the industry had ever been so costly or shown so clearly how dependent the local economy was on tourism.

Ironically, the aftermath also demonstrated the strength and resilience of that economy. During the first quarter of 1976, the total number of hotel rooms occupied in Clark County, which reflected visitor volume in the area, increased about 12 percent from the previous year. Though a dozen major resorts had closed for two and a half weeks, nearly 800,000 people visited Las Vegas in March, almost as many as had visited the city in March 1975. Despite the cancellation of conventions, there were more than thirty thousand conventioneers in Las Vegas during the month of the strike, many of them during the strike itself. In other words, the Las Vegas economy held up surprisingly well, and the city's drawing power seemed greater than ever after the conflict ended.[86]

The implications of the strike for labor-management relations in Las Vegas were less clear immediately. The strike was largely the result of a struggle between the Culinary and the Summa Corporation, whose executives played a key role in challenging traditional bargaining practices in the Las Vegas resort industry. "What it boiled down to," as one of those executives said later of the strike, "was a power play between Bramlet and us. We wouldn't cave in to his bullying like some of the other owners."[87] But other properties had also followed the hard line against the unions. This unity suggested that patterns of collective bargaining that had generally benefited labor in the past were just that—a thing of the past.

Management Digs In, 1982–1984

In 1980 Las Vegas was a thriving Sunbelt community. Nearly half a million people inhabited the metropolitan area, more than twice as many as a decade earlier. At a time when industrial development stalled in many other parts of the country, including some areas of California, the resort industry and attendant service industries thrived in and around Las Vegas, from financial services and transportation to warehousing and distribution. Gaming and tourism were booming. Between 1976 and 1980, the annual number of tourists in the area jumped from ten million to twelve million. Although no giant resorts opened during these years, several existing ones launched major construction projects, among them the Dunes, the Sands, and the Hilton properties.[1] The Ramada Corporation boosted the presence of nationally known hotel chains by purchasing the Tropicana, telling its stockholders that the future of the city had never been brighter. A number of new small resorts sprung up on or around the Strip, including Bourbon Street, the Barbary Coast, the Imperial Palace, and the Marina Hotel. The size of the industry workforce skyrocketed from fifty thousand to seventy thousand.[2]

A national recession, however, had recently put downward pressure on tourism. The tourist count stalled in 1980 and fell 2 percent in 1981; occupancy rates declined as much as 5 percent in a few places.[3] By 1982 some financial consulting firms began suggesting that Las Vegas tourism had peaked. "It might well be that the growth Las Vegas traditionally has experienced is over forever," one of them concluded. Others were cautiously optimistic. "Gaming company profitability should be noticeably increased by the second half of 1982," one predicted, "[but] it is not probable that operators will sustain above average [earnings]."[4]

Publicly, resort managers put the best face on this situation. "After a year like 1981, it may be difficult for executives to be optimistic about the future," one of them said, "[but] I am confident that as the recession recedes, the casino-hotel industry will once again emerge as a major area of growth in America's fabulous leisure time field."[5] Privately, management was much more concerned than this assessment indicated.

The contracting economy was one problem behind this assessment. Another was the "oil shock" that sent the price of consumer goods soaring, especially energy prices. Between 1976 and 1980, the Consumer Price Index rose a discomforting 6 to 13 percent annually and jumped an additional 10 percent in 1981. This rising inflation at a time of economic stagnation prompted economists to coin the word "stagflation." For management, this meant higher operating costs; for wage earners, it signaled slowing employment growth, declining real incomes, economic uncertainty, and diminished expectations. For both, it strained labor relations.[6] Employers across the nation began thinking in terms of wage cuts and other concessions from unions and adopted unprecedented bargaining strategies to achieve those ends. Between 1982 and 1985, perhaps one-third of all unionized workers in the nation were members of unions that felt obliged to make concessions to employers. Trade union membership therefore declined steadily. By the mid-1980s, less than 17 percent of American workers belonged to unions, as compared to 28 percent in the late 1960s.[7] The experience of workers and unions in Las Vegas paralleled these trends, though less grimly than those in some of the nation's heavy and extractive industries.

Despite the bitterness generated during the strike and the negotiations of 1976, the resort industry was relatively peaceful in the late 1970s. Though workplace grievances continued apace, as did charges of workplace discrimination, there were no sustained organizing drives or work stoppages. Workers seem to have reconciled themselves to the gains management made in the 1976 contract even as management seemed not to press its advantages.

The most consequential event in these years, one that had incalculable but entirely negative repercussions for workers and their unions, was the murder of the Culinary leader Al Bramlet in 1977. At a time when the resort industry was growing vigorously and corporate management was stronger than ever, the loss of Bramlet, with his clout and steadying influence at the bargaining table, was a major blow to all of labor in Las Vegas. It seems no exaggeration to say that Bramlet's murder signaled a sea change in the history of workers and unionism in Las Vegas tourism and helps account for the setbacks unions experienced there in the coming years.

The murder was and is steeped in mystery. The Culinary leader disappeared on February 28, 1977, after arriving at McCarran Airport from Reno. Not until two weeks later did hikers discover his partially buried body under a pile of rocks in the desert forty miles from the airport. Bramlet had been handcuffed, stripped naked, stabbed in the stomach, and shot six times, including once in each ear.[8] News of the grisly discovery shocked all of Las Vegas as well as labor circles across the nation. Bramlet had been the most important, powerful, and effective labor leader in Nevada, and something of a hero and source of security to members of his union. He had twice been named "Man of the Year" in Las Vegas, where he had championed the rights of workers in the union-friendly town since the 1940s.

Who shot him, and why? The FBI launched a full-scale investigation and soon concluded that the notorious Tom Hanley, who had tried to organize dealers in the 1960s, had kidnapped and killed Bramlet with the help of his son, Gramby Hanley, a local hooligan who himself had a record of criminal activity. After a massive manhunt, FBI agents apprehended the Hanleys in Phoenix, Arizona, where they had holed up in a small garage apartment. As evidence in the case against them mounted, Tom Hanley confessed to the murder and his son corroborated his confession. The two men and an accomplice, Clem Vaughn, they told authorities, accosted Bramlet at the airport and drove him into the high desert, where the older Hanley killed him. "I didn't see the shooting," the younger Hanley insisted, "I was in the van." Vaughn, who played a minor role in the crime, provided evidence that helped authorities convict the Hanleys of murder and sentence them to life imprisonment.[9]

The motive for the murder remains unclear. Tom Hanley originally said he shot Bramlet in a dispute over pay for work he had done on air-conditioners at the Culinary offices. He later changed that story to say he killed the union leader on a contract for which he was paid several thousand dollars, only to undercut that version of the crime by failing to say who hired him for the job or why. Hanley's son offered a different motive, claiming Bramlet had contracted him to vandalize several restaurants embroiled in labor disputes with Bramlet's union, but then held back on the promised payment. "He was always trying to talk the price down once a job was done," Gramby complained.[10] Tom Hanley eventually backed up that story, saying he murdered Bramlet to keep him from identifying individuals involved in vandalizing the restaurants. "He was getting weak and going to finger everybody," Hanley said.[11] None of these explanations was ever corroborated independently, but authorities ultimately concluded that the Hanleys killed Bramlet over an unpaid debt.

Not surprisingly, the murder spawned other speculations. When Bramlet disappeared, friends and relatives told FBI agents he might have died in a power struggle over control of his union's multimillion-dollar health and pension funds. Bramlet had recently opposed plans to consolidate those funds into a single account to be controlled by the Culinary's parent organization, the Chicago-based Hotel Employees and Restaurant Employees International Union (HERE). This opposition had evidently angered leaders of this organization, who categorically denied any connection to the murder.[12] They speculated instead that employers in Reno might have had Bramlet killed. For more than a year, Bramlet had been involved in a contentious organizing campaign in Reno, where labor organizers had been murdered in the past. "He's been intimidated and threatened up there in Reno," one leader of HERE explained.[13] The press offered still another version of what happened, suggesting that the murder may have been the handiwork of Tony "the Ant" Spilotro, a well-known thug associated with other brutal crimes. Spilotro had previously set up illegal bookmaking and moneylending operations in Las Vegas and had recently tried to establish a clinic and pharmacy for ailing union members. During that effort, he reportedly threatened to kill Bramlet, who opposed his endeavor.[14]

As if the story needed more elaboration, Wendy Hanley, Tom's common-law wife, later told a journalist that Tom and Gramby had killed people for money before, and not only in Las Vegas. "They worked the San Jose area, the L.A. areas, the Phoenix area," she said. "If you could get corroborating evidence, a lot of files would be closed." The men carried out such crimes, Wendy Hanley also suggested, to support their drug habits. She said Gramby was a "die-hard heroin addict," who had committed numerous armed robberies to support his heroin addiction. The "loot" from those robberies, she added, had littered her home. Authorities had long suspected the Hanleys of involvement in drug trafficking and thought Wendy herself was an addict.[15]

Whatever its motives and circumstances, Bramlet's murder seriously weakened the Las Vegas labor movement. Bramlet had worked for a quarter century strengthening that movement, during which time he helped transform the Culinary from a fledgling organization of fifteen hundred members to the second largest local in the HERE. His political connections gave the Culinary and other unions considerable leverage with employers. Politics always played a role in union affairs, and Bramlet's connections with prolabor politicos guarded his and other unions and their members against antiunion politicos and made the "labor vote" count in local and state elections. He also knew how to involve union members, including women and minorities, in union activities and policy development. Looking back on his legacy years later, resort workers expressed admiration for the man. "He was a genius," a former maid concluded. Bramlet's mere presence, this woman recalled, gave her a sense of security in the workplace and even a sense of social belonging. "We had a union and we had a place to go," she explained. "We did our work and we had no problem because if you did, you called Mr. Bramlet." Resort workers across the spectrum recalled their mourning of Bramlet's death. "When Mr. Bramlet left us," as a former maid put it, "look like the whole Strip lost somebody and that's the way it was."[16]

Bramlet's successor, Ben Schmoutey, had spent ample time in the union—he had worked for Bramlet since 1956—but he had earned little respect. In the aftermath of the murder, Schmoutey was elected to fill Bramlet's unexpired term as secretary-treasurer, and reelected a year later to a three-year term. But by 1980, when this term expired, most culinary members had concluded that he was ineffective as a union leader. Some thought him too friendly with resort managers, perhaps even corrupt. "They bought him out," one member of the union later speculated.[17] Federal investigations of the Culinary in the late 1970s fueled such speculations. On the basis of allegations made by Gramby Hanley, federal officials suspected Schmoutey of ordering the "bombings" of nonunion restaurants in Las Vegas and of embezzling union funds. The federal government never proved any of these allegations. It did, however, charge Schmoutey with attempting to bribe Clark County district attorney George Holt, for which he was eventually acquitted.[18]

Schmoutey's support within the Culinary declined precipitously as a result of his conduct during the 1980 collective bargaining negotiations with the Nevada Resort Association (NRA). Union members rejected the first agreement that Schmoutey made because it granted too many concessions to employers, including a freeze on employer contributions to union health and welfare funds and new limitations on workers' right to honor picket lines. In 1976 Culinary members had agreed to a ten-day waiting period before honoring picket lines of other unions, but Schmoutey now agreed to prohibit sympathy strikes altogether.[19] Teamsters' leader Dick Thomas denounced that as a "total sellout of the other unions." "We might as well throw away our union cards if the Culinary accepts the contract," Thomas said, "because with the no-strike clause our union isn't worth a damn."[20] Shortly before Schmoutey had made his four-year agreement with the NRA, the Teamsters and Operating Engineers had signed three-year contracts. This meant among other things that if Schmoutey's agreement were ratified, the Teamsters and Operating Engineers would have to negotiate with the association in 1983 while culinary workers were still under contract and prohibited from honoring the picket lines of other unions for ten days. That would clearly work to management's advantage.[21]

Once members of the Culinary rejected Schmoutey's contract, it took the intervention of the regional director of the Federal Mediation and Conciliation Services to avert a strike. As a result of this intervention, culinary workers and bartenders agreed to a four-year contract that hiked wages more than 8 percent annually and protected their right to honor other union picket lines after ten days, but froze employer contributions to welfare funds. This agreement—to reiterate a crucial point—staggered the expiration dates of union contracts in the resort industry, which promised to undermine labor solidarity. The staggered expiration dates would permit the NRA to deal aggressively with individual trade unions in future bargaining. The association's long-term strategies were evidently of less concern to culinary workers than were generous pay raises for the next four years.[22]

The final blow to Schmoutey's position in the Culinary came in late 1980, when HERE assumed control of its Las Vegas affiliate's health and welfare fund. There were several reasons that justified merging local and national union health care funds into a single entity, one of which was the fact that Schmoutey and other local trustees of the fund had made questionable loans to real estate investors and developers, which prompted Lloyd's of London to cancel the fund's fiduciary liability insurance. To the rank and file, relinquishing control of the fund to HERE was a sign of weakness and incompetence.[23]

Culinary workers ousted Schmoutey from office in 1981, replacing him with Jeff McColl. McColl was a smoother, gentler labor leader than either of his immediate predecessors. He had moved to Las Vegas from Southern California with his parents in the 1930s, and worked in public relations until Bramlet brought him into the Culinary in 1960. He held several positions in the union while serving as a member of Bramlet's bargaining team but resigned in the late 1970s over disagreements with Schmoutey. "Ben and I were not real close," he later explained. "I was not happy at all."[24] McColl was competent and honest, but whether he could successfully lead the Culinary through troubled times ahead was unclear. When he took office, the national economy was in a recession and the prospects for labor peace in Las Vegas were problematic.

The NRA was also changing. William Campbell, who headed the association for a decade, became ill in 1981 and died the following year. Resort managers had valued his leadership, and labor leaders recognized him as a formidable but straightforward negotiator. "He was certainly respected by all the union officers,"

McColl later said of Campbell, whom he had faced in negotiation sessions. "He was absolutely a man of his word." Mark Massagli of the musicians' union agreed. "Even though we had labor disputes," Massagli recalled, "I was able to talk to the man. . . . He was honest, he could be trusted."[25]

Campbell's death came at a time of transition in the NRA. In 1982 the association represented nineteen Las Vegas resorts, which had major differences in their business operations and, thus, in their interests in collective bargaining. Most were now owned by publicly traded corporations that were themselves varied in size and business activity. Several small resorts had recently joined the association, including family-held properties downtown, which could ill afford the wages and benefits paid by large corporate-owned resorts. Because their entertainment expenses were low, the small resorts were less concerned about contractual relations with musicians and stagehands. They wanted to join larger resorts in bargaining with their employees "for convenience," but they also wanted their contracts with unions to be individualized to fit their circumstances. That represented a new departure in industry patterns and promised to complicate collective bargaining.[26]

By 1982 disappointing financial reports were prompting management executives in many sectors of the national economy to turn to aggressive new cost-cutting strategies in dealing with employees. In all such sectors, labor always was a major, often the largest, cost of doing business, and it had risen dramatically in recent years. Between 1976 and 1982, wages in the Nevada resort industry, for example, rose by more than 10 percent annually, and the cost of fringe benefits increased even more than that.[27] Resort managers had proposed various ways of controlling labor costs, but all of them agreed that the labor contracts under which they operated were too costly and too constrictive of management's prerogatives. Through the NRA, they would thenceforth aggressively resist union demands in collective bargaining.[28]

With this end in mind, the NRA divided the responsibilities William Campbell had exercised in two. Campbell's duties as chief administrator and public relations director devolved upon Vincent M. Helm, his deputy, a well-mannered, persuasive attorney experienced in labor relations. Helm had moved to Las Vegas from Kansas City in 1965 to serve as labor counsel for Reynolds Electrical and Engineering Company (REECO), a major contractor at the Nevada Test Site. There, about sixty-five miles northeast of Las Vegas, a consortium of private companies worked on the nation's nuclear testing program. At REECO, Helm's principal responsibility had been negotiating contracts with the company's five thousand unionized employees, represented by thirteen trade unions. He had also handled arbitration cases as well as cases involving the Justice Department and the Equal Employment Opportunity Commission. More recently, from 1978 to 1981, he had worked as a labor counsel in Idaho and Oregon and had occasionally handled arbitration cases involving members of the NRA. As Campbell's health had deteriorated, Helm had assumed many of his administrative responsibilities, including matters dealing with union contracts.[29]

The NRA hired another experienced attorney, Kevin Efroymson, to assume Campbell's duties as chief labor negotiator. Like Helm, the Chicago-born Efroymson had also represented employers at the Nevada Test Site, where he quickly gained a reputation as a conscientious, hard-nosed bargainer. In 1965 he negotiated a no-strike clause at the Test Site, which made it especially difficult for members of one union to honor another union's picket lines, as a result of which the incidence of work stoppage dropped markedly. Before 1980, Efroymson had also worked as a labor consultant for a number of Las Vegas resorts, including the new nonunion Imperial Palace.[30] In that year, he helped break a strike at the Showboat Hotel by demonstrating that striking workers were violating the language of their union contract. In that incident, culinary workers and bartenders had launched a sympathy strike before striking teamsters and operating engineers had maintained picket lines "continuously" for ten days. The strikers had shut down their lines during late night hours, Efroymson pointed out, which made the sympathy strike illegal. This ended the dispute in management's favor, an accomplishment that impressed the NRA.[31]

Efroymson was thus well suited to lead the association in an era of confrontational labor relations. Union leaders saw him as a "hired gun," in the words of one of them, who also conceded that Efroymson was a very good "gun."[32] When approached about representing the NRA in collective bargaining, Efroymson hesitated, questioning whether anyone could effectively represent so diverse and divided a group. He doubted that NRA members would stand together during the push and pull of a drawn-out bargaining process. If unions threatened to strike, or went on what promised to be an extended strike, he asked, would not some members pull out of the association and reach their own agreements with labor, as happened in 1976, to the detriment of the association? All of the members gave Efroymson the assurances he wanted on these points and made him their exclusive spokesmen during bargaining processes. "You're our man," they told him.[33]

♠ ♣ ♥ ♦

The significance of these developments became clear in early 1983, when the Teamsters and the Operating Engineers opened negotiations to renew their contracts with the NRA, which would expire on April 1. From the outset, Efroymson told the unions that the employers had to reduce their contributions to benefit funds, freeze wages for a year, and strengthen the prohibition against sympathy strikes. Before honoring picket lines of other unions, he insisted, unionized employees would have to wait not the ten days provided in current contracts but six months.[34]

The unions adamantly rejected these proposals. Dick Thomas of the Teamsters denounced Efroymson's performance in bargaining sessions as a "charade," part of a calculated effort to "bust" the unions. Bob Fox of the Operating Engineers agreed. His members would never accept a wage freeze or reduced benefits, he told Efroymson. To avoid a strike, both union leaders added, the NRA would have to improve the real income and benefits of union employees and accept current language in the contracts on sympathy strikes. A six-month prohibition would all but eliminate sympathy strikes, which had helped workers everywhere advance their interests. Any extension of the no-strike clause, they insisted, "will never be acceptable to us."[35]

Both the NRA and the unions refused to compromise on any of these issues, and the two union contracts expired. At that point, members of the unions continued to work under terms of their expired contract, promising to give management seventy-two hours' notice before its members went on strike. In late April, after bargaining talks failed to produce a settlement, the unions agreed to accept a wage freeze of three months and annual raises of only 3 percent for the years of the proposed contract, but the NRA rejected these counteroffers.[36]

The resulting standoff continued until May 4, more than a month after the expiration of the old contracts, when the unions launched a selective strike against the Golden Nugget, ordering all "back-end" members of the Teamsters— maintenance workers, gardeners, parking attendants, switchboard operators, warehousemen, and the like—off the job. The unions targeted the Golden Nugget because its chief executive and principal owner, Steve Wynn, was a leading critic of unions and a frequent disrupter of bargaining sessions. "He would come into the meeting and then would proceed to tear it apart," Dick Thomas recalled of bargaining sessions Wynn attended. "He was the loudest one in rejecting the things that we wanted, and was creating the strike and was trying to rally other employers to his position. And we thought that he was the best shot for us to take on. So we hit him first."[37]

Wynn was a formidable opponent, however. Like other employers who found themselves special targets of strikers, he denounced union officials as "irresponsible leaders who don't give a damn about the employees." He also threatened to give the jobs of striking workers to "permanent" replacements. "If they work at the Golden Nugget," he said of strikers, "it's time to come back or face that risk."[38]

The use of permanent replacements as strikebreakers was a new tactic in collective bargaining in Las Vegas, and one that had the potential of shifting bargaining strength in management's favor. The Supreme Court had ruled back in the late 1930s that striking workers had no legal recourse against the hiring of permanent replacements if the hiring of those replacements had been necessary to keep struck businesses open, and if the employer was not guilty of any unfair labor practice. Subsequent labor laws said nothing definitive on this issue, and courts had gradually given employers more freedom to replace striking employees. Yet employers had rarely discharged employees for participating in legal work stoppages. Such actions could provoke violent responses and turn public opinion against employers. Hiring permanent replacements for striking workers meant the loss of jobs, benefits, and seniority for displaced workers. It thus represented the ultimate breakdown of industrial harmony, the absolute loss of trust. Wherever it occurred, it promised to extend work stoppages, encourage violence, and even break unions or bankrupt employers.[39]

Yet, in the economic turbulence of the early 1980s, growing numbers of employers mulled the idea of hiring replacements to win labor disputes, and some of them succumbed to it. The precedents were not lost on labor leaders. Public sympathy for strikers had waned noticeably since the prosperous times of the postwar years, and business profits had been squeezed. Management consultants now advised uneasy employers to think of remaining open as one of their options during labor disputes and even offered guidebooks on how to hire and retain replacement workers. President Ronald Reagan's dismissal of several thousand striking air-traffic controllers in 1980 emboldened employers considering this course of action, even though the controllers were federal employees prohibited by law from striking. The 1983 strike against the Phelps Dodge Corporation, a copper mining firm in Arizona, provided a model of how private firms could use "scab" labor to crush unions and protect managerial prerogatives. When that strike ended, the company had destroyed thirty union locals by hiring more than two thousand nonunion workers to replace unionized strikers. If the story of this unhappy episode was a cautionary tale for all union leaders, it might be an inviting one for managers made desperate by shrinking profits or exasperated by bothersome union demands.[40]

By the time Wynn threatened to hire permanent replacements at the Golden Nugget, Nevada labor commissioner Frank MacDonald had at the direction of Governor Robert List become involved in the dispute between the NRA and the Teamsters and Operating Engineers. After separate meetings with both sides,

MacDonald concluded that the strike would likely become industry-wide. "Each side is highly antagonistic toward the other," MacDonald told List, "each indicating they are progressing in the war." The Dunes, he noted, had stopped contributing to union benefit funds, and the unions had set up "work and walk lines" at the Dunes: "People are still working, and when they get off the shift, they walk the line." MacDonald believed culinary workers and bartenders would honor union picket lines as soon as their contracts allowed them to do so.[41]

The strike at the Golden Nugget was peaceful until May 9, when hundreds of angry protestors descended on the resort following a rally at the Convention Center and a march along the Strip that snarled traffic for nearly two hours. Police officers in riot gear confronted the marchers, while police helicopters circled overhead. The demonstration went as planned but failed to impress Steve Wynn. "If the unions were looking to strike a blow at the Golden Nugget," Wynn said of the protest, "they missed the mark."[42]

The conflict became industry-wide on May 15, when the NRA locked out six hundred members of the Operating Engineers and "back-end" members of the Teamsters at thirteen properties. Vincent Helm defended the move. "You can't let things remain the way they are," he told the press. "You've got to apply pressure and get the contract issues resolved."[43] The lockout was not immediately disruptive. "Full hotel service will be maintained," Helm announced. "Some hotels will use people already in other capacities to fill the jobs and other hotels will hire temporary replacements."[44] If necessary, he warned, the resorts would keep the replacements on a permanent basis.[45]

The pressure worked both ways. As the confrontation spread, the two Hilton resorts and Circus Circus pulled out of the NRA, as Efroymson had feared, and offered the Teamsters and Operating Engineers four-year contracts with substantial wage and benefit hikes in return for ten-day no-strike agreements. The contracts included bothersome caveats, however: if the unions signed contracts giving other resorts more favorable terms on wages, benefits, and/or no-strike language, those terms would automatically apply to the three resorts. This "me-too" language was already commonplace in the industry. Independent resorts had long insisted on it, in effect, making the terms of their contracts contingent on terms negotiated by unions with the NRA.

The remaining members of the NRA stood firm. Faced with an imminent sympathy strike by members of the Culinary and Bartenders, Helm warned those unions that employers would discharge members who honored picket lines. He

had already told the leaders of those unions that the no-strike clauses in their contracts permitted their members to honor the picket lines only of workers who had
contracts "with the association." Since 1980, he pointed out, Teamsters and Operating Engineers had had contracts with individual resorts, not the association. Leaders of the Culinary and Bartenders ridiculed this interpretation, insisting the striking unions would never have agreed to contracts that prohibited sympathy strikes
and suggesting in response that Helm had violated their contracts by threatening
to discipline workers for exercising their contractual rights. The unions announced
they would wait and see if the courts allowed them to picket after ten days, which
was perhaps what employers wanted to know all along.[46]

This turn to the courts over the meaning of the no-strike language evidenced
the deteriorated state of labor-management relations in the industry. Correspondence between NRA and union leaders on this issue was caustic and threatening,
mirroring the depth of the ideological divide between the two sides. Vincent Helm
told Jeff McColl, for example, that McColl's interpretation of the picket line clause
had "no rational meaning" and "absolutely no basis" in contractual language, and
he accused McColl of making "shocking" and "blatant" efforts to "twist the plain
and clear meaning" of contract language. The NRA, he added, "will avail itself of
all available legal means to remedy the situation."[47]

Subsequent events deepened this division. On May 18 several NRA members,
including the Golden Nugget, announced they would keep their replacement
workers after the strike-lockout ended and would hire employees on full- or part-
time bases as their needs demanded and without regard to union wishes. At this
point, the Teamsters and Operating Engineers offered to accept a fifteen-day no-
strike clause and an eleven-month wage freeze, only to have the NRA respond
that its members insisted on a six-month clause and a twelve-month wage freeze.
"No way," Efroymson told Frank MacDonald of the unions' compromise proposals. Two days later, Helm told MacDonald that the Golden Nugget's next wage
proposal would be less generous than its previous one.[48]

At the same time, however, MacDonald told Governor List that other NRA
properties were in a compromising mood. "I read that the other hotels are not
willing to be as hard-nosed at this point and might be getting a little itchy for
early settlement," he told List.[49] The strike had not only generated bad publicity
for the resorts but also prompted canceled reservations. Tourists were crossing
picket lines in large numbers, but inside the resort they encountered unexpected
problems. They were concerned about the availability of services, even anxious
about their personal safety. When they expressed these concerns to on-duty
union employees who sympathized with picketers and locked-out employees,

the responses were not what they expected. Hotel managers tried to reassure guests, but worried privately about the effects the dispute had on guests.

Meanwhile, the Teamsters and Operating Engineers feared that their members' picket lines might collapse. In response to a warning from management that striking workers could be fired, nine of twenty-two parking attendants returned to work at the Golden Nugget, and elsewhere strikers were insisting on their need to return to work. Striking employees received $75 a week from the strike fund, hardly enough make ends meet. Locked-out employees, receiving nothing from their unions, were even harder pressed and suggested that they too might return to work. Members pressured union leaders into calling special meetings to explain the logic of their strike strategy and to assess the prospects of its success.

Dick Thomas and Bob Fox acknowledged the legitimacy of these concerns, which expressed the limits of labor solidarity. Their relations with the leaders of the Culinary and Bartenders had been strained since 1980, when those unions agreed to the staggered expiration dates of labor contracts. They were now unsure whether culinary workers and bartenders would honor their picket lines, even if the courts allowed them to.[50] Rather than take the risks, both made new concessions to management. In return for four-year contracts that boosted wages about 12 percent and maintained employer contributions to benefit funds at current levels, the unions accepted a six-month wage freeze and a thirty-day no-strike clause. They also agreed to new limitations on the amount of overtime pay workers could earn and gave management more control of holiday scheduling. These concessions negated the more favorable terms in contracts unions had earlier signed with Hilton and Circus Circus and with independent properties like the Hacienda, the Riviera, and the Sahara. Moreover, the agreement failed to ensure the return of striking workers the Golden Nugget had replaced.[51]

Vincent Helm welcomed the new agreements as "a framework for the continued viability of the resort industry," protecting as they did the future of Las Vegas and its resort industry. But Dick Thomas saw the contracts as setbacks for workers and their unions. "It doesn't do a thing for anyone except the association," he said after accepting the agreements with the Teamsters and Engineers. Still, Thomas's union was unwilling or unable to hold out for better terms. In fact, two-thirds of those who voted on the new contract voted to accept it, no doubt because that was the option that enabled them to return to work immediately.[52]

NRA contracts with the Culinary and Bartenders as well as the Musicians and Stagehands were to expire a year later, on April 1, 1984. Because of the problematic results of the 1983 stoppages, leaders of those unions braced for the upcoming bargaining with misgivings. They hoped that the improving economy would work to their advantage. The number of visitors to Las Vegas jumped 6 percent in 1983, to nearly 12.5 million, and casino revenues rose by more than 10 percent, to $4.5 billion. On the basis of such figures, financial consultants were predicting rising profits for hotels and casinos. "We project continued strong growth for the Las Vegas industry, in the area of ten to twelve percent through 1985," one of them said.[53] Executives in the resort industry also expressed hope for better times. "We enter 1984 with confidence," Barron Hilton told his stockholders. "Our books are up and signs abound that business and leisure travel are once again forming a strong upward momentum."[54]

A look at the state's resort industry, however, showed that the recovery from the recession was uneven and incomplete. Growth rates in gaming revenue remained well below those figures of the 1970s. Though most publicly traded corporations in the industry saw their revenues rise in 1983, some did not, including the parent company of Caesars Palace. A fire had damaged large parts of the MGM Grand in 1980, killing 86 people (including nine employees), and that resort was still reporting financial losses in 1984. The recession had forced some resorts to postpone renovation projects and curtail advertising. Financial analysts who predicted continued growth for the industry in 1984 noted that some resorts were having far more difficulty than others in recovering from the recession. Over the next few years, one of them predicted, a few highly capitalized corporations would likely increase their share of the tourist market significantly. "It may prove to be a period where the rich get richer and the poor fall further behind," he said.[55]

Rapid development in Atlantic City, New Jersey, which had legalized casino gambling in 1976, raised the question of whether the "poor" would even survive. By 1984 Atlantic City had changed from a seaside resort with a few aging hotels to a bustling tourist destination with nearly a dozen new casinos. At least some gaming industry analysts were then predicting that the East Coast city would overtake Las Vegas as the center of the nation's gaming industry. "What has happened in Atlantic City during the past five years is remarkable," one of them explained. "The competition from Atlantic City is a real and continuing factor that could cut Las Vegas's long-term growth rate in half." Other analysts thought easterners were "thirsting" for local casinos, and predicted that other northeastern states, including New York and Pennsylvania, would soon legalize gaming.[56]

By 1984 the owners of perhaps a third of Las Vegas's corporately owned resorts had similar properties in Atlantic City, including Caesars World, Del E.

Webb, Golden Nugget, Hilton Hotels, Holiday Inns, and Ramada Inns. Such diversification helped companies capitalize on new opportunities in the East, and perhaps neutralize the effects of competition there, but it also increased their operating costs and the costs of servicing their debt. It also created problems of its own. Establishing or acquiring casinos in New Jersey proved to be complicated and costly. The standards and requirements for licensing there were different from those of Nevada, and raising the investment capital needed to enter that market was often problematic. As a result, some ventures became overextended and failed.[57]

These uncertainties, both local and national, convinced NRA members that 1984 was not a propitious time to raise their labor costs. Resort managers like Joe Buckley of the Summa Corporation, which still controlled six resorts in Las Vegas, told Vincent Helm that the increasingly competitive nature of the resort business demanded a new approach to dealing with unions. Al Benedict of the MGM Grand, Tom Pilkington of Caesars Palace, and other representatives of large Strip resorts agreed. So, too, did spokesmen for three downtown properties whose management had joined the NRA—the California, the Four Queens, and the Las Vegas Club. All of these men pointed out that their employees earned higher wages than their counterparts did in other tourist destinations, where the cost of living was often higher than it was in Las Vegas. Union wages in Las Vegas had increased steadily for years, by more than 10 percent annually for some occupational groups. Corporate taxes and the cost of benefits had risen too, and at faster rates than profits. Instead of agreeing again to raise their labor costs, NRA members should aim to freeze wages for two years and keep contributions to union benefit funds at current levels for perhaps the same period of time.[58]

NRA members must also have greater control over the workplace than current contracts permitted. Work rules previously negotiated with unions were too costly and restrictive. Rules that guaranteed forty-hour workweeks for all workers, which precluded part-time hiring, for example, must be eliminated. There were also too many paid holidays and too many minute job classifications that must be broadened in order to increase flexibility in the assignment of tasks to workers and thereby increase productivity. Workers saying "that's not my job" when asked to take on new responsibilities must become a thing of the past. Workers must accept new tasks without challenge. Such changes were dictated by changing times, Helm was told in 1984. Hotel occupancy rates had dropped substantially during the recession and had yet to return to prerecession levels. How could Las Vegas compete with Atlantic City with higher labor costs and lower worker productivity?[59]

Resort workers and their unions were aware that such reasoning was afoot among management in 1984 and girded themselves to resist it. Like manufacturing workers elsewhere at the time, however, they found themselves in weaker bargaining positions than their predecessors had been in the 1960s and 1970s. The sluggish national economy was still slowing hotel and casino development in Las Vegas and pressuring union membership downward in privately owned enterprises in the city. Since 1977, the size of some local unions had shrunk noticeably, paralleling what was happening to their parent organizations nationally, many of which struggled with indifferent success to cope with industrial contraction. Membership in the Culinary held steady in these years, at twenty-six thousand, but membership in its national parent, HERE, fell by nearly 20 percent.[60]

The Las Vegas culinary union had had stable, effective leadership since Jeff McColl became its head in 1981. Whether McColl and his leadership team could protect its members' interest in the 1984 bargaining, however, was far from clear. The problem was circumstances—not McColl's integrity or negotiating skill, but his union's loss of clout, of leverage in bargaining with management in a strong, confident position. Employers saw McColl as an inexperienced labor leader who lacked the charisma necessary to sway the public to the union cause. His union was, moreover, already in retreat. Employers had staggered the expiration dates of union contracts and strengthened "no-strike" clauses in those contracts, which compromised the ability of unions to support one another during strikes. Teamsters and operating engineers, who once helped culinary workers shut down resorts, had now agreed to contracts that prohibited them from crossing the picket lines of those workers until the lines had been maintained for thirty days. This enormously increased management's bargaining power. McColl's predecessors had never had to negotiate at such disadvantage. They had always been able to use the threat of immediate sympathy strikes to leverage their position.

In addition to the standard concerns about increasing pay and benefits and protecting work rules, individual unions in 1984 had special concerns. Culinary workers and bartenders wanted larger-than-usual increases in management contributions to employee health and welfare funds because their 1980 contracts had frozen such contributions for four years. (They also wanted their union leaders to return contributions to health and welfare funds to local union administration, which their national union opposed.) Musicians and stagehands were concerned about the threat of job displacement. Some resorts had turned their casino lounges into gaming areas, where customers rather than entertainers filled space. They were also still exploring the use of new technologies to reduce the size of house orchestras and stage crews.[61]

In January, the Culinary and Bartenders opened negotiations with twenty-one independent resorts, including the Dunes, the Hacienda, the Riviera, the Stardust, and other properties on the Strip. The "Indies," as they were called, typically negotiated their contracts ahead of the NRA, including, in those agreements they reached, provisions that gave them whatever concessions on noncost items the unions later made to the NRA. These "me too" clauses helped the unions set general patterns in each round of bargaining, but the practice also put pressure on union negotiators to protect the terms of those agreements.

As the bargaining began in 1984, the Golden Nugget unexpectedly pulled out of the NRA and reached its own settlement with the unions. In January, Steve Wynn of the Nugget told union leaders Jeff McColl and Jack Stafford he would sign a four-year contract doubling his contributions to benefit funds and boosting hourly wages about 8 percent each year of the contract. He insisted, however, on the usual "me too" language that made his offer contingent on the unions exacting similar costs from his competitors. The union leaders welcomed this offer, but it also caught them by surprise. The outspoken Wynn had never been a friend of the unions. Only a year earlier, in 1983, about fifty Golden Nugget employees had lost their jobs as a result of that year's strike, and the Teamsters and Operating Engineers still had pickets outside Wynn's downtown resort.[62]

Wynn's motivation became clear a few days later, when the NRA opened bargaining talks with the unions. At those talks, between January 16 and 19, NRA negotiator Kevin Efroymson made what union negotiators immediately recognized as the most regressive contract proposals ever made in contract negotiations in the Las Vegas resort industry. Each of his clients, Efroymson announced, would sign individual contracts with the unions rather than the traditional "master" agreement that bound all of them to the same terms. Each of them also wanted a five-year agreement that froze wages for two years; eliminated work rules that "hurt efficiency," including those that made unionized jobs full-time and prevented management from combining job classifications for purposes of increasing productivity; instituted a new two-tiered wage scale that paid new hires less than continuing employees; and extended the prohibition on sympathy strikes from the current ten days of picketing to six months, which would effectively eliminate the right to wage sympathy strikes. Union leaders expressed astonishment at these proposals and promised to "fight like hell" against them.[63]

Philip Bowe, chief negotiator for the Culinary and Bartenders, led this fight. Like Efroymson, Bowe was an experienced bargainer. After graduating from

Harvard Law School in the early 1960s, Bowe had moved to San Francisco to work first for the National Labor Relations Board and then for the law firm headed by Roland Davis, which represented the Culinary and Bartenders. In the latter capacity, Bowe handled arbitration cases for the two Las Vegas locals of those unions and advised them on collective bargaining. He had helped Davis and the unions in the 1976 strike and by 1980 had taken over as chief negotiator for the unions.[64]

Bowe was frank and assertive at the bargaining table. When bargaining resumed in February, he called Efroymson's proposals "totally unrealistic" and "totally unacceptable." The plan to "individualize" contracts was a "sham" to complicate and prolong bargaining. How could his unions tailor contracts to meet endlessly extending lists of specific demands by each NRA member? he asked. And why should workers in one resort accept different terms for essentially the same work under the same circumstances from those in another? Efroymson defended the proposals as reasonable responses to current conditions. "The last couple of years have been hard on the hotels," he told union leaders. Bowe accused Efroymson of "lying" about the financial state of his clients.[65]

Bowe countered Efroymson's proposals with a pitch for a four-year contract that included annual wage increases of 8 percent and similar increases in benefits and preserved current work rules and provisions regarding sympathy strikes. The unions would strike, he vowed, to protect what they already had. His clients were on the verge of signing new contracts with several independent properties, he added, and once they had done so he would have less flexibility in dealing with the NRA. "Quit fooling around [and] give us your bottom line," Bowe then admonished Efroymson, only to have Efroymson quickly reject Bowe's offer. "We won't bargain with a gun at our heads," Efroymson replied. The impasse seemed to be total; another strike loomed.[66]

Alarmed by this prospect, the Culinary and Bartenders launched an "informational campaign" to inspire their members and influence public opinion. Toward these ends, McColl made several "reports" to his members describing Efroymson's proposals and detailing their devastating consequences for the union and its members should they be agreed to. If the NRA insisted on those proposals, McColl warned, there would be a strike. "The 1984 contract campaign may be the greatest challenge our Union has ever faced," he warned, vowing to use every resource at his disposal to resist the NRA: "Our entire membership and staff, our allies in the Labor Movement and our friends in the community will join together to fight these bosses and the corporations that control them until they treat Las Vegas workers with the dignity and respect they deserve."[67]

The Culinary and Bartenders leafleted media outlets, tourist agencies, and everywhere else in Las Vegas and Clark County with pleas for sympathy that called NRA proposals "takeaways" and "givebacks," and with a warning that a "long and bitter" strike was sure to result unless the association withdrew its proposals. The leafleting even called for a boycott of NRA properties, reminding sympathetic readers that there were plenty of other resorts in the area not out to "degrade" or otherwise exploit their employees. In fact, those "other" resorts had not renewed their contracts with the unions but had only indicated a willingness to raise wages and benefits as NRA properties did.[68]

The informational campaign pushed the parties further apart. Efroymson accused union leaders of distorting his proposals and trying to manipulate public opinion for their own selfish purposes and to the detriment of the industry and the community. When the Nevada labor commissioner asked him about the bargaining negotiations, Efroymson depicted the unions as self-serving and unreasonable and a threat to harmonious industrial relations in Las Vegas. They were boxing his clients into a corner, he insisted. McColl was a string-puppet manipulated by higher-ups in his union, who had recently sent a member of its executive board, Vincent Sirabella, to Las Vegas to oversee the bargaining process. The press and NRA representatives suggested that Sirabella was in Las Vegas to ensure national control of local union benefit funds, implying that national officials benefited personally from control of those funds. Union leaders countered that it was irrational to expect national officials to stay out of the affairs of a local in troublesome negotiations with a recalcitrant management association. After all, the Las Vegas local was one of HERE's largest affiliates. As such, its contracts influenced wages and working conditions in hotels and restaurants across the country.[69]

Amid such developments, bargaining sessions resumed in March. Unproductive, they sometimes degenerated into shouting matches. On March 16, for example, when Efroymson showed up an hour late for a scheduled session, Bowe accused him of waging "psychological warfare" and of "bad faith bargaining." Jack Stafford of the Bartenders was outraged. "When are you going to start bargaining you asshole?" he asked Efroymson. Efroymson ignored the insults and asked Bowe and Stafford if they had studied his recent proposal on holiday pay. "We looked at your proposal and laughed at it," Bowe retorted.[70] Negotiations had given way to belligerency and mulishness. The unions and their members were clearly on the defensive, yet their leaders were not cowed. On the contrary, given their situation they seemed confident and unafraid.

In late March, while this impasse with the NRA dragged on, the Culinary and Bartenders reached "me too" agreements with more than a dozen independent resorts, a few days before their contracts expired. Circus Circus, the Dunes, the Fremont, the Stardust, and several smaller establishments signed four-year agreements with the unions that increased wages about 5 percent annually, restored health and welfare benefits to 1980 levels, and protected existing work rules. Because these agreements were contingent on union contracts with the NRA, however, they were almost meaningless. Jeff McColl hoped they would revive the stalemated talks with the NRA, but Vincent Helm still insisted that agreements with independent resorts would not influence NRA negotiations. These "sweetheart deals" were "ludicrous," he said of those just mentioned, because they incorporated "inefficient" work rules and failed to reflect industry realities.[71]

Helm made it clear NRA properties would do what was necessary to remain open if the unions called a strike. As soon as workers walked off their jobs, managers would hire substitutes to fill their positions. Some NRA executives threatened to import workers if necessary and to turn temporary jobs into permanent ones. "A lot of people are willing to work to protect the property," a Hilton executive told the press.[72] Helm advised NRA members preparing for a strike to augment their security forces and collect "intelligence" that might be useful in breaking a strike. "Even unsupported rumors and hearsay" might prove helpful, Helm advised, as might "picket line observation teams" equipped with binoculars, cameras, and walkie-talkies. Such teams might detect striking workers violating court orders or laws regulating picket line activity.[73]

Meanwhile, unions assessed the situation and planned contingent strategies. Their parent organizations began collecting strike funds and making those funds available to striking workers in Las Vegas.[74] They also sent activists to Las Vegas to help unions prepare for a strike. Workers themselves began making picket signs, scheduling picket duty, and learning anew how to conduct themselves on picket lines.[75] They set up child-care and financial counseling centers for striking workers. They also erected a "kitchen" in the Culinary parking lot capable of making twenty-five thousand sandwiches a day and delivering food and beverages to picketers every four hours.[76] In the meantime, the unions staged rallies to disseminate information and engender support for the looming strike. "Are you ready? Are you ready?" Jeff McColl yelled at one of the rallies. "We're ready!" the audience roared back. Pumping up the crowd, Jack Stafford yelled, "We're not going to quit until we win!"[77]

Amid this commotion at the proverbial eleventh hour, the NRA offered increased contributions to health and welfare programs if the unions accepted the proposed wage freeze and no-strike language as well as the elimination of work rules management found objectionable. Union leaders rejected these proposed modifications and walked out of bargaining talks. Governor Richard Bryan, a Democrat who had tried to remain neutral in the dispute, struggled unsuccessfully to keep the parties bargaining, as did state and federal mediators. Efroymson suggested that HERE president Edward T. Hanley would now enter negotiations wearing a "white hat" and "save the day," but that did not happen. Thus, in April 1984, when their contracts with employers expired, approximately twenty thousand workers struck the Las Vegas tourist industry.[78]

The inability to avoid this strike reveals what had happened to labor relations in the Las Vegas resort industry. Management had come to see organized labor as a threat to its interests and was now fully committed to containing that threat. The NRA strategy embodied that commitment. Rather than trying to "bust" unions summarily, which promised to be counterproductive and even impossible, the association sought to weaken unions by corroding their support among their members no less than the general public. This represented a radical break from past practices, and union leaders resisted it as best they could. They had no more fondness for work stoppages than did management, but what could they do when backed into a corner with no other honorable way out?[79]

Nº 9

The Strike of 1984–1985

On April 2, 1984, the look and feel of Las Vegas changed dramatically when more than twenty thousand workers from four trade unions struck the area's resort industry. By six o'clock that morning, the striking workers had picket lines at thirty-two hotels and casinos, including a handful of small, nonunion properties. The lines stretched from Fremont Street downtown to the Tropicana at the end of the Strip. They wrapped around giant properties like the Las Vegas Hilton and the MGM Grand, and out to Sam's Town and the Showboat on the Boulder Highway. Sounds of the city changed, too. Motorists honked and shouted encouragement to picketers, who shouted back appreciatively. Picketers sang songs of rebellion and protest and yelled at whoever tried to cross their lines: "You're a fucking scab!" "We'll get you!"[1]

The strike was a defining moment in industrial relations in the city, the crisis in which employers finally established their "right to manage" and thus notably reduced the role of unions in the workplace.[2] The strike was bigger, longer, and more costly than any in Las Vegas history, and more embittering. Police arrested nearly a thousand picketers during the conflict, "billy-clubbing" and dragging some of them away. Veteran gamer Jackie Gaughan rightly labeled it "the saddest thing that ever happened to Las Vegas."[3] In the wake of previous work stoppages, it constituted the final erosion of the postwar consensus in labor-management relations and confirmed for the first time that strategically and for the foreseeable future labor was now on the defensive and management on the offensive.

♠ ♣ ♥ ♦

The show of labor solidarity on the first day of the strike obscured this ultimate result. In fact, it had an immediate, opposite impact: it prompted several independent properties, including the Hacienda and the Sahara, to agree to the terms of contracts that other "Indies" had signed a few days earlier, thus enabling their striking employees to return to work. But twenty NRA properties, which employed about seventeen thousand of the striking workers, remained without contracts with their employees. Rather than settling on terms agreeable to the unions, these properties announced their intention to remain open during the strike. To do so, they slashed room rates, curtailed services to whatever level they could provide, and shut their showrooms, lounges, and dining facilities as necessary.

More ominously, they also hired temporary workers and used supervisors and nonunion employees, including showgirls and dealers, to do the duties of striking workers. In effect, they sacrificed short-term profits for what they confidently expected would be long-term gains. The fact that their contracts prohibited members of the Teamsters and Operating Engineers from honoring picket lines for thirty days made this course of action easier. Desk clerks, switchboard operators, slot mechanics, and other members of those unions found themselves obligated to continue working, whatever their attitude toward the strike or toward management actions in response to it.[4]

There were problems on the picket lines from the beginning. Picketers permitted teamsters and operating engineers to cross their lines without difficulty but harassed and tried to intimidate everyone else, especially those they knew to be strikebreakers. Picketers believed tourists, especially those staying at, or trying to enter, one of the struck resorts, were insensitive to their problems, and they tried to deny them entry to those resorts or frighten them away with shouted tales that the resort's food was poisoned or bombs were planted in its casinos.[5] On the first day of the strike, a woman driving into the Flamingo Hilton had the windshield of her car smashed, and others had their cars variously damaged by infuriated sign-wielding picketers. Fights between picketers and guests trying to enter the resorts broke out, a few of which resulted in serious injuries. At Caesars Palace, the Flamingo Hilton, and several other places, strikers abandoned their own cars at resort entrances, triggering traffic jams.[6]

An altercation at the MGM showed how hotel guests could get caught up in these confrontations. The incident began when a van from Bauer Helicopter Rides arrived to pick up guests for an excursion to the Grand Canyon. The driver of the van passed through the bus entrance of the property with no problem, but when he tried to leave, picketers formed a double line in front of his vehicle and refused to move. "You shouldn't come here," one of them yelled at the driver. When the driver edged forward, one of the picketers jammed the end of his picket sign though the window of the van, striking the driver in the face. After a flurry of harsh words to the driver, the picketer opened the van door and punched the driver several times, leaving him bruised and bleeding. The driver backed up his van and reported the incident to security guards, who contacted the police. Meanwhile, the passengers left the van and withdrew from the excursion.[7]

The first major confrontation between picketers and resort security forces took place in midafternoon on the second day of the strike, at the entrance to the Las Vegas Hilton. According to police, about fifty picketers pushed their way past barricades near the front of the Hilton and started "fistfights" with uniformed security guards. The aggressive picketers ignored police warnings to turn back and instead broke through barriers and assaulted police. In reporting this incident, the *Valley Times* described "hand-to-hand combat" between picketers and police and fights between picketers and hotel guests. Police arrested more than forty people involved in this melee, including union leaders Jeff McColl, Mark Massagli, and Dennis Kist, and charged them with "inciting a riot."[8] The strike grew uglier later in the day, when perhaps three hundred picketers clashed with security guards at the MGM. The press called this clash a "wild melee." "Fists began to fly," the *Sun* reported, as striking workers "pushed" guards to get to the main entrance of the resort, where they wanted to picket. Police broke up the push by arresting more than a dozen picketers, including some of those arrested earlier in the day.[9]

These incidents encouraged strikers to conclude that the police were siding with management. Some of those strikers, who may have developed a similar distrust of law enforcement during the 1976 strike, now viewed the police as enemies of the strike. Union spokesmen insisted that the police had started the MGM "riot" by attacking picketers with clubs. "They were beating anybody that looked like they might be associated with the union," Jeff McColl told the press of the police in the incident. Dennis Kist, a lawyer who had headed the Stagehands for three years, said security guards at the Hilton put him in a chokehold with a billyclub while handcuffing him to a pole. "I didn't break any law," Kist insisted to reporters. McColl self-servingly compared the confrontations to murderous civil rights conflicts in the South in the 1960s. "I never thought living in Las Vegas that I would see anything that would approach what we saw in Selma, Alabama," he said. Such words reflected more than the growing sense of outrage among strikers; they also voiced the desire of union leaders to equate their struggle for more pay and benefits, more control of the workplace, and the right to stage sympathy strikes with the objectives of the heroic foot soldiers of the most dangerous and compelling episode in the struggle for black equality.[10]

Labor leaders considered the roles of the police and resort security forces in these incidents parts of a "naked effort" to destroy unions in Las Vegas. AFL-CIO president Lane Kirkland told Attorney General William French Smith that the police actions in Las Vegas were "brutal" and "unwarranted" violations of the right to strike and picket peacefully. "These violations of the rights of the striking workers are clearly intended to intimidate these workers and interfere with the exercise of their federally protected rights," Kirkland charged. "In such a hostile environment where local police have been proven unable or unwilling to maintain order and protect workers' rights, it is incumbent upon you and the Justice Department to take all steps necessary to protect these rights, including the dispatch of marshals."[11] Kirkland wrote an equally charged letter to leaders of the Las Vegas resort industry insisting that they or their underlings had deliberately used security guards to intimidate strikers. "Your immediate intervention to assert control over these private guards to prevent further assaults on pickets is required under any standard of decent conduct," he wrote.[12] Employers tried similarly to use these incidents to advantage, insisting that picketers had provoked violence by ignoring lawful police orders and that those arrested were "troublemakers" or "strike agitators." Armed with testimony from their own security guards who witnessed the incidents, NRA attorneys filed a motion in federal court asking for restrictions on picket line activity to prevent a recurrence of violence.

In response to this motion, Judge J. Charles Thompson on April 5 issued a restraining order prohibiting picketers from trespassing on resort property, restricting the number of picketers at resort entrances, and forbidding picketers from "harassing and intimidating" anyone crossing their lines.[13] Striking workers saw this as further evidence of the one-sidedness of the law and initially ignored the order.[14] Thus, at some resorts, they continued to block entrances completely, threatening everyone who sought to cross their picket lines. Over the next two days, police arrested more than 150 picketers for violating the court order, many of whom had to be handcuffed and forced into police vehicles because they refused to submit peacefully to legal police orders. One of the men arrested was carrying light bulbs filled with flammable liquid, which he apparently planned to screw into light sockets in a hotel hoping to cause an explosion and fire. In the wake of these developments, resorts increased their security forces and their precautions against security threats. At the two Hilton properties, for example, security forces began stopping and questioning everyone entering the hotels.[15]

Employers also continued to hire replacement workers, which intensified problems on picket lines. Strikers distributed flyers defining strikebreakers in vile, disgusting terms. "After God had finished the rattlesnake, the toad, and the vampire, he had some awful substance left with which he made a scab," a typical flyer read. "A scab is a two-legged animal with a corkscrew soul, a water-logged brain, and a combination backbone made of jelly and glue," read another. "Where others have hearts, [a scab] carries a tumor of rotten principles." Still others compared strikebreakers to Judas, Benedict Arnold, and other "traitors": "A strikebreaker is a traitor to his God, his Country, his family, and his class!"[16]

Picket lines remained volatile, and the worries of hotel guests intense. On the evening of April 12, a device exploded in the swimming pool at the MGM, resulting in minor damage but no injuries. The police had by this time investigated bomb threats at several resorts and discovered a small explosive at the Tropicana tucked between two slot machines.[17] There was another major confrontation between picketers and police at the MGM on April 14, following a two-hour march by striking protestors along the Strip. The strikers, who had just heard a rousing speech endorsing their strike by the charismatic Cesar Chavez of the United Farmworkers Union, sat down on a sidewalk outside the resort, linked arms, and refused to move, claiming the sidewalks as public property. The police promptly arrested more than seventy of them, almost all of whom they had to drag into police buses. Those not arrested "cheered and raised clenched fists as the busses pulled away." Hundreds of tourists witnessed this confrontation.[18]

Hotel occupancy rates declined markedly as a result of the strike and the picketing, by more than 50 percent in some properties; but publicly employers remained united and resolute. "It was not as bad as we expected," an executive at Caesars Palace said.[19] This reaction confirmed the fact that resorts were better prepared for this strike than they had been for the one in 1976. In addition to augmented security forces and new picket line "observation teams," they also had plans in place for dealing with such matters as garbage collectors and with the untoward consequences of the absence of other essential service workers who refused to cross picket lines. The resorts had stockpiled a two-month supply of nonperishables and fresh foods in storage facilities, and arranged for management personnel to deliver them. "Contingency plans were made long ago to take care of these things," Vincent Helm told the press.[20]

The fact that the resorts were functioning a week into the strike reflected more than management foresight and preparation. It also reflected public indifference to the cause of striking workers. The negative publicity the strike generated discouraged many tourists from coming to Las Vegas, but many of those who did come seemed generally unfazed by the inconveniences and disappointments the strike caused them. Some of them crossed picket lines with no evident anxiety unless danger seemed to loom, even chiding or ridiculing picketers as they did so. Closed restaurants and showrooms were disappointments, but the city had too many alternatives to make this sufficient cause to go home. Many tourists gambled and slept at struck properties but dined and found entertainment at resorts that had settled with the unions. They saw "Lido de Paris" at the Stardust, for example, and country music performer Mickey Gilley at the Riviera. They also appreciated the discounted room prices that resulted from the strike, and no doubt felt secure in the presence of so many police and security officers on the streets and in the resorts.[21]

The sight of tourists braving picket lines hardened employers' resolve and encouraged them to restore services as they were able to do so. Caesars Palace and the Four Queens reopened lounges with nonunion musicians, for example, and the MGM resumed its stage show "Jubilee" with nonunion employees. Such developments triggered new fears of the loss of unionized jobs and no doubt increased the hostility of strikers toward employers. The resumption of "Jubilee" at the MGM particularly irked union musicians and stagehands, who demonstrated for several nights outside the showroom. The demonstrations led to new confrontations between police and protestors and to the arrests of more than a hundred people, including, again, several union leaders.[22]

By mid-April, a fortnight into the strike, labor relations in Las Vegas had reached their nadir. Seventeen thousand workers remained on strike in a bitter confrontation that showed no signs of resolution and in which a sense of fury and desperation pervaded picket lines. Police officers worked overtime to contain violence, which often required physical force on their part. A television reporter lamented that the situation seemed insolvable. "We've never seen a combination of history, politics, labor issues and personalities come together so that things conceivable may never be worked out," he said in a televised editorial.[23]

Amid this evident desperation, the situation changed suddenly and unexpectedly. Representatives of the Hilton properties informed the Culinary of their willingness to settle the conflict, thus breaking the management unity that had sustained the conflict. At a secret meeting with union representatives, they negotiated an agreement with terms much like those the unions had recently negotiated with independent properties. After making this agreement, Hilton management asked the NRA's chief negotiator, Kevin Efroymson, to schedule negotiating sessions with the two unions. "We had an agreement which was illegal as hell," McColl later explained of the arrangement. "So then we had to have a meeting with Kevin present. We went through the charade of negotiating this contract."[24]

The sequence of events frustrated Efroymson, who realized at once what had happened. NRA members had assured him they would stick together during the strike. "I had told them I was unwilling to work for a group that cuts deals on the side," Efroymson later mused.[25] Hilton had not only broken rank in this ostensibly ironclad arrangement but had done so in a secretive, manipulative way. This not only jeopardized the bargaining position of all NRA members but offended Efroymson, who threatened publicly to resign from his job.[26] Union leaders were understandably elated, viewing the "breakthrough" as evidence of a successful endeavor to pressure management into settling the strike on terms favorable to labor. "We're winning the battle," McColl told the press, suggesting that Barron Hilton himself was unhappy with the way Efroymson was handling negotiations and had ordered his executives in Las Vegas to make their own proposals to the unions. "Mr. Hilton himself directed this to happen," McColl stated. "This is a proposition Mr. Hilton wanted on the table so the Nevada Resort Association had no choice but to put it on the table.[27]

A national anti-Hilton campaign had much to do with this turn of events. To make Hilton's intransigence in Las Vegas costly, the unions had put picketers outside Hilton properties across the country, even outside banks that financed Hilton. The unions encouraged investors to sell their stock in Hilton hotels. After the strike, Barron Hilton acknowledged that this "corporate campaign" affected his actions. "I couldn't believe the organization efforts, particularly putting four hundred pickets or so out in front of my bank in New York, the Manufacturers Hanover Bank, criticizing them for making loans to me."[28]

Other factors also help explain Hilton's actions. Hilton was more capable of meeting union demands than most NRA members. Indeed, his was one of the most profitable corporations in the gaming industry. Hilton's casino revenue, which accounted for about 40 percent of the corporation's operating income, had jumped by 11 percent the previous year. Occupancy rates in his Nevada properties (including the Hilton Reno) had risen 8 percent in 1983, reversing a 9 percent decline in 1982. Hilton himself had recently bragged about his corporation's bright future. "The Company has emerged from this recent economic downturn in a strong financial position, poised to take advantage of the improved economic environment," he told stockholders.[29] Then, too, Hilton's offer to the unions was an easy, self-serving way out of the strike. It stipulated that his company would get whatever advantages other resorts received in their final settlement with the unions.

The NRA downplayed the significance of the Hilton offer. Vincent Helm told the press that the Hilton resorts were simply offering "separate proposals tailored to their special needs," which would have "no impact" on the bargaining process. But soon after Helm said that, Caesars Palace agreed to negotiate separately on terms consistent with those of Hilton, as did Jackie Gaughan's two downtown properties, El Cortez and the Western Hotel. These developments elated striking workers and union negotiators.[30]

Talks involving the Hilton group, however, soon bogged down. The disagreement involved all of the fundamental matters at stake in the strike—cost items, length of the contract, and language governing sympathy strikes—but also the divisive issues involving musicians and stagehands, whose special concerns the large unions had hardly considered.[31] Employers were insisting that the unions agree to work rules that would eliminate many jobs musicians now held. Specifically, they wanted musicians to accept new work rules that permitted the use of synthesizers in showrooms. These voltage-controlled, keyboard-operated instruments could mimic the sounds of acoustic instruments. One or two "synthesists" could replace several orchestra musicians with little sacrifice in the quality of the sound of orchestral performances. Employers also again wanted to use recorded music during show rehearsals, which would reduce the work available to musicians.[32]

As negotiators wrestled with these matters, tempers continued to flare along picket lines. Strikers defied the restraining order restricting the number of picketers at resort entrances and the harassing of hotel guests. They clashed again with police on April 27, during a "sit-in" at the Las Vegas Convention Center to protest a new city advertising campaign that said nothing of the industry-wide strike. Police arrested nearly a hundred people at the center for disorderly conduct, many of whom were confined for hours in large cages in the recreation yard of the Clark County Jail.[33] When they were finally released, many complained of having been "kicked," "billy-clubbed," or "beaten" by the police. Some filed affidavits in federal court describing their experiences. "It was like they were attacking [us]," one person said of the police.[34] A few days after the arrests, about fifteen hundred people marched through downtown protesting police brutality. At a rally following the march, union leaders denounced the police for their handling of protestors at the center.[35]

Union leaders' were now also berating elected officials for not supporting the strike. Claude "Blackie" Evans, who headed the Nevada Central Labor Council, criticized Governor Bryan and others for not helping the striking workers, accusing them of ignoring their campaign promises. "They wanted our money, they wanted our votes, they kissed our asses," Evans fumed. "Where are they now?"[36] Dennis Kist, who had emerged as one of the most charismatic of the union leaders, described Bryan as a "hired gun" "in the pocket" of management. At stake in the strike, he said, were the basic rights and well-being of striking workers.[37]

Such words reflected the unions' beleaguered position. The Easter season had been good for employers and thus bad for the unions. Hotel occupancy jumped 8 percent over the previous Easter at some of the struck properties, and most of the people who stayed at those properties seemed generally unfazed by the strike. In responses to hotel questionnaires about their experiences, several tourists at the Four Queens reported enjoying their stays. "My husband and I, in spite of the strike, found everything very accommodating," one of them said. "We enjoyed our visit." "Disspite the strike," another wrote, "you still have managed to provide excelent service."[38] Such responses encouraged resorts to believe they no longer needed to bargain with the unions.

The Boyd Group, which owned the California Hotel and Sam's Town, had already reached that conclusion. Only three days into the strike, the company threatened to replace striking workers at the California permanently if they refused to return to work within the week. Bill Boyd, who had recently become head of the company, wrote his striking employees, predicting the strike would last "a long time" and saying he therefore had a "difficult decision to make." "As you are aware," he told the strikers, "we have hired and are still hiring replacements in order to continue operating. We will have to decide whether their employment will be permanent." Boyd acknowledged that many of the strikers had worked for him and his group for years, but their actions now threatened the jobs of other employees as well as the future of the group's two properties. "Many of you have worked for the California Hotel for a long time and have been part of the California Hotel 'family,'" he continued. "[But] we have to protect the jobs of our employees who want to work, our customers, and our business." "If you do not return to work by 5:00 p.m. Tuesday, April 10, 1984," he concluded, "we cannot guarantee that your job will still be available. In other words, you may be permanently replaced."[39]

Other resorts waited three weeks to threaten that their striking employees would be permanently replaced. Bill Bray of the MGM announced on April 23 that he would begin doing "whatever is necessary" to restore lost services. "We do have contingency plans which are to recruit, develop, train and secure the man-power to bring us back to one hundred percent," he told the press. In fact, the MGM had already hired a thousand temporary workers. A week later, Robert Brooke of the Marina Hotel and Casino, a small independent property at the south end of the Strip, made a similar announcement. The Marina had no inten-tion of discharging recently hired employees when the strike ended, Brooke said. "We won't fire somebody who went to work for us under strike conditions just to bring somebody [else] back."[40] By then, the Four Queens and the Union Plaza had taken similar steps. These actions, it deserves repeating, represented radical innovation in labor-management relations in Las Vegas. In all previous strikes, when managers hired substitute workers, they hired them as temporar-ies and discharged them when the strike ended. Permanent replacement hiring meant that nonunion employees had priority over unionized strikers for the jobs they filled. As the press put it, this was a "stunning blow" to strikers, who had hoped the renewed negotiations with Hilton would end the strike largely on their terms.[41]

It also raised the stakes for both sides in the strike, altering as it did the cli-mate of labor-management relations. It ratified the abandonment of traditional bargaining tactics on the part of management, something for which striking workers had not prepared. Strikebreakers were now a serious threat to the future of striking workers, jeopardizing their employment, and thus their economic well-being. Resort workers reacted to the threat in various ways. Some, evidently dismissing it as an empty bluff on the part of management, scoffed at it. "If they were trying to scare me, they did not scare me at all," one picketer at the Califor-nia said. New union contracts, the picketer was confident, would return strikers to their jobs, rights, and privileges.[42] Others, made fearful perhaps by the threat, became ever more aggressive on picket lines, insulting alike "scabs," police of-ficers, and everyone else who sought to cross their lines or regulate their behav-ior. Still others, accepting the threat as a promise, returned to their jobs. About 10 percent of the unionized culinary workers at the Union Plaza were back at work by the third week of the strike. Many of these "defectors," as union leaders labeled them, probably never really supported the strike, while others no doubt acted out of financial desperation present or looming.[43]

A "defector" who returned to her job as a coffee shop waitress at the MGM spoke of her decision to return to work in a way that revealed some of this group's sentiments. The waitress had agonized for days before giving up the strike but surrendered to financial need. "I tried to make the most intelligent decision, and definitely financial reasons were the number one reason," she said. But other factors influenced her choice, including a disdain for labor activism and activists. "I felt so degraded walking on that picket line," she said. "I didn't want to walk with people who insult customers. . . . They got mad at me because I wouldn't hit cars with my sign or yell obscenities at customers going into the hotel." A letter from the MGM also influenced her decision. The letter explained her options as a striking employee and implied that she might lose her job if she continued to strike. She soon found that returning to work created new problems. She began receiving harassing telephone calls and became the object of personal insults as she drove past picket lines fronting the resort.[44]

Such defections plus the threat of permanent replacement that lay behind many of them prompted the unions to make significant concessions. In the last week of April, the Culinary and Bartenders reached four-year agreements with the Hilton properties that gave workers smaller economic gains than those accepted by some independent properties. They also instituted a two-tiered wage system with lowered wages for new employees, allowed management to combine job classifications and assign workers new tasks, and bound unions to no-sympathy-strike pledges of thirty days. These provisions, which under the "me too" rule were incorporated into the earlier agreements signed with independent resorts, had the effect of reducing the income and benefit gains the workers had hoped to receive from the strike as well the degree of workplace independence to which they had been accustomed.[45]

Strikers tended to emphasize the positive side of the new agreement, especially those who worked for Hilton. The contract promised them their jobs, as well as wage and benefit increases. When union leaders announced the agreement on May 3, Hilton employees held "victory toasts" to celebrate. "It's wonderful," gleamed a showroom waitress sipping whisky from a Styrofoam cup. "Now we can pay the rent!" "No more bologna sandwiches," another cheered. The consensus seemed to be, at least for the moment, that the agreement was a union victory. "Our work week is secure, our seniority is intact, the insurance is up, the things we wanted and needed we pretty much got," as one celebrator put it.[46] These words mirrored the union leaders' gloss on the settlement. Jeff McColl thought it a decent and acceptable settlement under difficult circumstances. "It does preserve those basic working conditions which constitute the heart and soul of our traditional Las Vegas collective bargaining agreement," he said.[47]

The recollections of Sam Savalli, a food server at the Las Vegas Hilton in these years, help explain why workers celebrated a settlement that fell short of their hopes. Savalli had been employed at the Hilton for fourteen years and was the sole supporter of his family. His monthly bills included $750 for his mortgage and $125 for his car. When he and his fellow employees went on strike, he suddenly found himself walking a picket line for $50 a week. To cope with this impossible situation, Savalli took a variety of odd jobs, such as washing and waxing cars, hanging wall paper, and mowing lawns. These things helped a bit, but he faced a financial squeeze in early May, when he learned of the Hilton settlement. He remembered the moment vividly: "Jeff McColl and Phil Bowe came out and gathered picketers around, and they let us know the union had reached an agreement. It was very exciting, a big relief." Union leaders did not immediately detail the terms of the agreement, and neither Savalli nor other relieved strikers asked about them: "We were just glad it was over."[48]

The unions and their members hoped the Hilton pact would have a domino effect, and it did lead to settlements with Caesars Palace and the Gaughan resorts in early May, which ended the strike for about six thousand employees.[49] But other NRA properties rejected the terms those resorts accepted. Spokesmen for the MGM, the Tropicana, and others denounced the pact as too "costly" and "burdensome"; if the unions wanted an agreement, they would have to make a more "reasonable" offer. One of the holdouts, Mel Exber of the Las Vegas Club, told reporters that small properties like his were at a disadvantage in the marketplace dominated by large, corporate enterprises and could not afford "Hilton wages." "There's such a great disparity in what the Hilton gets for room, food and beverage than what the Las Vegas Club gets," Exber lamented. "How could I accept a Hilton contract?"[50] But Exber and other employers like him wanted more than cost items suited to their circumstances; they too wanted more control of the workplace. That meant broadening job classifications and adjusting work schedules and assignments to management's convenience. It also meant the right to discipline workers with much less regard than had previously been the case.

The threat of a sympathy strike by operating engineers and teamsters had seemed a distant prospect when the Culinary and Bartenders went on strike in early April. But in early May that threat encouraged a flurry of new settlements. On May 3, when the thirty-day no-strike clauses of the two nonstriking unions expired, the Engineers sanctioned a sympathy strike against the five Summa properties as well as the MGM and the Tropicana, all members of the NRA.[51] More than two hundred engineers honored the sanction. "We sympathize with them and what they're trying to do," one engineer said of the strikers.[52] But almost no teamsters joined the walkout. This disappointed striking workers, who hoped that a united front with members of the Teamsters and Operating Engineers would force employers to settle on their terms.

The failure of Teamsters members to join the strikers was partly a strategy to keep pressure on management while minimizing the strike's effect on individual teamsters and engineers. It gave the unions the flexibility to ramp up the strike at any time. "Just because the Teamsters don't go out on Wednesday doesn't mean they couldn't go out the day after," one of their leaders explained.[53] Yet some individual teamsters saw no need for a sympathy strike, hoping, as their union leaders did, that the Hilton pact would lead to a general settlement of the strike regardless of their own actions. Others recalled that the Culinary had not always supported them in their disputes with management and doubted whether they would do so in the future. Employer resistance to sympathy strikes also helps explain why individual teamsters refused to join the work stoppage. The Summa properties had already promised to replace unionized workers who honored picket lines. If the engineers walked off the job, Efroymson told the Governor's Office, his clients would replace them "permanently."[54] Whatever its causes, the teamsters' refusal to stage sympathy strikes reflected the declining fortunes of organized labor and encouraged unsigned properties to keep resisting union demands.

Negotiations with more than a dozen NRA properties were still at a standstill in the second week of May, more than a month into the strike. By then, most of these and the other resorts whose workers were still on strike were hiring permanent replacements for striking workers, including replacements for their engineers who refused to cross union picket lines. Managers were encouraging temporary hires to apply for permanent positions before they advertised them. A memo from Sam's Town to "all temporary workers" illustrates how resorts created an alternative workforce to the strikers. "Please be advised that beginning Monday, May 7, 1984," read the memo, "adds [sic] will appear in all three local newspapers advertising the fact that Sam's Town is now accepting applications for permanent employment in ALL Culinary and Bartenders classifications. Please understand that you are also eligible for any of these aforementioned classifications (if qualified), including the one you currently hold." At the same time, a Sam's Town manager, Robert Kenneth told the press: "We've gone as far as we can. We've got to hire permanently and get on with our business."[55]

The advertisements aggravated problems on the street. Strikers defended picket lines with a new sense of desperation. Police officers were now arresting dozens of strikers each week, including nearly sixty in one week at the MGM, for violating their orders governing picketing. Tempers flared on May 8 when federal judge J. Charles Thompson turned his earlier temporary order regulating picketing into a permanent one. Strikers staged a noisy rally at the federal building downtown protesting this action, at which police made fourteen arrests. These events further exasperated union leaders, who seemed to be unable to do anything about them. Jeff McColl told reporters at this point that he had never been so "frustrated, angry and disgusted." Resort managers, he said, had a "callous, don't give a damn attitude about employees and the community."[56] His words well expressed the frustrations of striking workers at the impasse they faced with no obvious way out.

On May 15 members of the Culinary reelected McColl secretary-treasurer, effective head of the union. This no doubt disappointed employers in Las Vegas resorts, but it may have similarly disappointed officers of the parent union of the Culinary. McColl's adversary in his reelection, the ubiquitous Ben Schmoutey, waged an impressive campaign to recapture his lost office, criticizing the strike as unnecessary and poorly conducted, blaming its onset and the failures of its conduct on McColl, and promising to end it quickly if elected. In a move that underscored the relevance of racial identity in the resort industry, Schmoutey also went door-to-door in the black community soliciting the support of housekeeping workers. Despite this effort, McColl won by a landslide, a result that amounted to an endorsement of his conduct of the strike as well as an expression of a willingness to carry on the fight. Evidently disappointed with these results, which pointed to a continuation of the strike, the national leadership of the Culinary promptly took a more active role in the strike, dispatching its highest-ranking officers, Edward T. Hanley and Herman Leavitt, to break the deadlock with Kevin Efroymson and his NRA supporters.[57]

Hanley and Leavitt's entry into the negotiations had an immediate effect. On May 22, after a weekend of marathon talks, the Culinary and Bartenders reached an agreement with eleven NRA members, including the MGM, the Tropicana, the Union Plaza, the Sands, the Showboat, and the five Summa properties. A few days later, they reached a similar settlement with the downtown Las Vegas Club. These agreements differed from those reached earlier with the Hilton properties in two significant provisions. They were for five years, not four, and the prohibition on sympathy strikes was for ninety days, not thirty. Both provisions would now apply to all other labor contracts in the Las Vegas industry. The agreement postponed wage hikes for a year, and then boosted wages by about 26 percent over the ensuing four years, which was about what employers were prepared to pay when the strike began. Moreover, the agreement permitted employers to combine certain job classifications for three hours a day, which meant additional tasks for many workers. They also enabled employers to request workers from union hiring halls by name, which allowed them to staff their workforces with cooperative—or pliable—people. The agreement was a major setback for workers in the Las Vegas resorts.[58]

This transformative development suggested local concerns had given way to national interests on the part of the unions. McColl had said repeatedly he would never accept a stronger no-strike clause, yet now backed down on that and other issues. Efroymson had predicted that HERE would intervene in negotiations and make the kinds of concessions on which the NRA was insisting.[59] The pressure to make the concessions came from Efroymson, under whose leadership the NRA took an uncharacteristically insistent approach in the negotiations. According to McColl, national officers of the Culinary never interfered in the bargaining process, but Edward Hanley played a major role in resolving key issues. "Hanley, I guess, mediated, if you will," he later mused. "He just brought the issues to the sides and said, 'what's your position, what's your position.' He never tried to tell me, and I'm the one he would have had to tell, that this is what you have to do, never."[60] McColl swallowed the concessions to get what he could from management—significant increases in wages and contributions to benefit funds.

McColl thus called the settlement a "victory for the unions." Local and national leaders had worked together to prevent the NRA from "busting" the unions. "I think there was absolute effort, if not to break the unions to really weaken them," he later reflected. "And they didn't do it." The concessions were necessary but tolerable, not "bread and butter issues." "We didn't lose any guaranteed work weeks, we didn't lose any seniority, we didn't lose any holidays. . . . Sure there were some changes, but they didn't emasculate anything."[61] "Blackie" Evans of the Nevada Central Labor Council had a similar perspective. "I guess if someone is out to kill you and you survive," as Evans said at the time, "you've won."[62]

The settlement was calamitous for the Musicians and Stagehands, however. The small unions had settled with the Hilton properties and Caesars Palace but not with the Desert Inn, the Frontier, the MGM, and the Tropicana. These four properties continued to insist on the right to use recorded music and self-contained traveling groups in shows; to reduce the size of orchestras and stagehand crews; and, in return for increased health and welfare benefits, to freeze musicians' and stagehands' wages for five years. McColl and Stafford had pledged to keep members of their unions off the job until the Musicians and Stagehands had new contracts, but many of those members ignored that pledge. "Why should a few hundred musicians and stagehands keep thousands of others out of work?" returning strikers asked. By late May, when temperatures on the street occasionally topped 100 degrees, about twenty-five hundred culinary workers and bartenders, a quarter of those still on strike, had returned to work while the Musicians and Stagehands were still bargaining. The small unions thus saw their leverage at the bargaining table rapidly drain away.

As the small unions struggled, the remaining picketers became more desperate. Strikers still on picket lines taunted former picketers as well as tourists and replacement workers. Police arrested scores of picketers in late May for blocking hotel entrances and otherwise disrupting business operations. A rash of bomb threats again frightened tourists and kept bomb squads and police officers busy. An incendiary device exploded in the parking lot of the Tropicana, damaging several cars. Another detonated outside the Frontier, also damaging vehicles. At the MGM on May 25, firefighters defused a bomb they said was powerful enough to kill. A few days later, security guards discovered a purse filled with live bees in the resort's casino. Protestors also set off a "smoke bomb" near the Desert Inn and threw "stink bombs" at downtown properties. Press reports suggested that striking stagehands were responsible for these acts. Union leader Dennis Kist denied the suggestions, though he admitted that stagehands were angry enough to break the law. "I can sure understand how some people can resort to that kind of thing," he said of a bomb threat. "If I were a tourist, I'd be scared shitless."[63]

The violence subsided when the strike of the small unions collapsed. On June 16, the musicians and stagehands both went back to work after agreeing to sharp reductions in guaranteed work and the five-year freeze on wages.[64] Their unions had already removed their last picket lines to allow culinary workers and bartenders to return to their jobs, an act of despair they called a "gesture of good faith." Jeff McColl insisted that culinary workers supported the small unions but conceded that most of them were unwilling to continue the strike on their behalf. The unions scheduled rallies to draw attention to the plight of musicians and stagehands, but they were poorly attended and ineffective. The first rally, near the Desert Inn, drew perhaps two hundred people; a subsequent one at the Tropicana even fewer.[65]

The June agreements ended the strike for everyone except nearly two thousand bartenders and culinary workers at six small properties whose managements had had little if any role in the bargaining process. None of the properties had showrooms or contractual relations with musicians and stagehands, and all hired permanent replacements during the strike. They continued to resist the demands of striking unions, including the demand that their striking union employees be returned to their jobs. Bill Boyd explained this adamancy: "We did not want, nor did we call this strike. We will not turn our backs on those employees who kept our operation going when others were trying to destroy us."[66]

Such comments infuriated Boyd's striking employees, some of whom had worked for him for years. "The fact is," one of them said of Boyd, "he's hired people to take our place after some of us have been here nine years." "They say the permanent replacements they hired have more loyalty toward them than we did," a longtime employee of the Four Queens added. "What the hell do they call thirteen years?" A striking coffee shop hostess at the Four Queens echoed that sentiment: "After being called family for ten years, now they don't want us back." Other veteran employees referred to Four Queens manager Jeanne Hood as a "witch" and vowed never to return to work without a union contract. "I don't care if my baby needs food," another said, "I'm not going back."[67]

The Culinary and Bartenders pressured the holdouts in various ways. In late May, for example, the unions launched a publicity campaign against the Hyatt Corporation, which owned the parent of the Four Queens, accusing it of "assaulting" American workers with "union-busting tactics."[68] Vincent Sirabella of HERE, who had recently come to Las Vegas to help with negotiations, told strikers that the media campaign would pressure the corporations out to "break the city's labor movement."[69] Activists also distributed leaflets in the Las Vegas neighborhoods in which executives of the holdout properties lived, calling attention to their role in trying to break the strike. "Chuck Ruthe is leading the NRA attack against thousands of honest, hard-working members of our community," read leaflets distributed near the home of the administrative head of the Boyd Group. About twenty picketers paraded in front of Ruthe's residence one morning in early June as he left for work and showed up again to greet him when he returned. "He's been a leader in the permanent replacement movement," one of the picketers charged.[70]

Meanwhile, AFL-CIO president Lane Kirkland flew to Las Vegas to spotlight this final round of the lingering strike. Joining picket lines at the California, the Four Queens, and other properties, Kirkland flashed V for victory, chanted strike slogans, and tried otherwise to boost the morale of striking workers. "Your struggle is being watched with sympathy, support, and great pride," he told one group of picketers. "You're fighting the same fight your brothers and sisters in other industries are fighting. Your fight is our fight!" Kirkland later attended Wayne

Newton's concert on behalf of the striking workers at the Aladdin Hotel, at which he made another pep talk.[71] According to state labor leader "Blackie" Evans, who heard the talk, Kirkland emphasized "the commitment of American labor to the Las Vegas struggle by thousands of workers forced to defend their rights and security against unmitigated corporate greed."[72]

As this wearying fight dragged on, scores of strikers gave up. Some, including a third of those at the Boyd properties, withdrew from their union and returned to work. Others found jobs in other resorts. The few who remained committed blamed their union leaders as well as their former employers for their plight. Their unions had mishandled the strike, they charged, and left strikers at the mercy of market forces. Employers agreed. Robert Maxey of the Four Queens insisted that union leaders had long ago rejected his reasonable proposals to end the conflict, and he thus had no sympathy for holdout strikers. Like Boyd, Maxey was satisfied to "bust" the unions.[73]

The management of these small holdouts succeeded in this feat of union busting with tactics devised by corporate professionals. They hired nonunion replacements until their workforces were complete. At the same time, they set up modest health and welfare programs for the replacements, as well as new rules concerning work and personnel policy. They then turned "temporary positions" into "permanent" ones and invited their "temporary" employees to apply for them. Because the employees stood to lose their jobs if the unions ever "won" the strike, they petitioned the National Labor Relations Board for decertification elections. Employers campaigned vigorously to win those elections, even turning to labor relations consultants for help. Because striking workers had the right to vote in decertification elections for a year, some of the unsigned properties used legal tactics to delay voting until that year was past.[74]

McColl and other union officers worked diligently to defeat the decertification efforts. They maintained picket lines at the properties, often walking the lines themselves; made house calls on the striking workers, including workers who had found temporary jobs elsewhere; and urged striking workers to vote no in the decertification elections. They held meetings to explain the voting process and the meaning and significance of the elections. "There is nothing more important than winning [these elections]," Jeff McColl said at one of the meetings. Decertification at any of the properties would threaten the labor movement in Las Vegas. "What makes you think other employers won't try the same thing?" he asked his audiences.[75] Meanwhile, Vincent Sirabella wrote letters to labor leaders across the country, asking for contributions to help save the unions by warding off decertification. "We must not forget that the strike continues for 1,800 workers," he pleaded. "The workers are walking every day in the hot, 110-plus Las Vegas weather. They still need your help."[76]

By July 1985, five of the six properties had rid themselves of unions, and the sixth had closed down for reasons having little to do with the strike. Union strategies had failed, leaving union leaders embittered. Walt Elliot of the Bartenders suggested the "lost" properties had been planning decertification for more than a year and perhaps since 1980, when they signed their last collective bargaining agreement with the unions. Joe Hays of the Culinary agreed. "I'm sure they were thinking of this all along. I'm sure enough to bet my life on it." Whether or not those statements were literally true, the circumstances of the 1985 strike presented these properties the opportunity to "bust" the unions, and they took full advantage of it. They began hiring replacement workers early in the strike, promised those workers permanent jobs, refused to discharge those workers in favor of returning union members, and encouraged them to decertify the unions.[77] As the strike dragged on and on, union leaders came to see what the results of these efforts would be. "I don't care how you cut it," Jeff McColl said later, "you're going to lose. . . . If you can let the strikebreakers vote, you've got a full staff in house and they're going to vote one-hundred percent against the union. On the outside you've got the strikers or the former employees; you're lucky if you can get 50 or 60 percent of them to the vote." "It's sad but it's true," he lamented.[78]

For unionized strikers, decertification added insult to injury. Though most workers who struck the holdout properties returned to work or found jobs elsewhere, the impact of the strike loomed large in their lives. Many had piled up debts while they picketed and saw their families face hardships. They also endured the gut-wrenching experiences of watching "scabs" take their jobs, parking spots, customers, and work stations. The result was an unsettling sense of loss and longing. Even workers who for whatever reason survived the strike relatively intact economically and psychologically felt something had been taken from them callously and unfairly. Decertification shook their confidence; solidarity failed them, and their unions lost the strike. What had happened, and why?[79]

The strike of 1984–85 was the most important setback for organized labor in the history of Las Vegas. At the end of its difficult and still imperfectly documented course, employers in the resort industry had more managerial independence vis-à-vis their unionized employees than they had ever had, had greater control of the cost of the labor they employed, and had a workforce chastened by the experience of a long strike in which they lost more than they won. But the employers lost too, especially in the short run. They lost perhaps $100 million in revenue and generated unknowable amounts of mistrust and perhaps even hostility on the part of a workforce among which hospitality mattered. The city and the state similarly lost their millions in taxes, while tourist-related small businesses may have suffered relatively more than any of these.[80] Jackie Gaughan, whose properties lost about $2 million in the strike, made a characteristic assessment. "This was a loss to everybody," Gaughan lamented. "The unions lost, the operators lost, and the people got killed."[81]

Afterword

Strikers walking picket lines in the 1984–85 strike often waxed nostalgically about their work and circumstances in earlier times. "I liked it better in the old days, before Howard Hughes and the other corporations came in," one of them said. "This used to be a fun town," another complained, "but the fun is gone. So is the family atmosphere."[1] Union leaders agreed. "This used to be a proud industry," Jeff McColl later reminisced of the times before 1985, "and that's all gone."[2] Mark Massagli, whose musicians were the strike's biggest losers, thought large corporations had drained the "warmth" out of Las Vegas. He described their managers as "cold granite," "masters," and "machines."[3] Such words reflected more than the usual separation and discord of labor-management relations. They suggested that management had effectively contained the role of organized labor and tilted the balance of power to its advantage.

The steady expansion and labor-intensive nature of the resort industry helped workers and their unions escape the fate of many of their counterparts in manufacturing and extractive industries. Employers in declining industries like steel and machine-tools could point to their shrinking share of domestic and world markets to justify assaults on trade union power. They could also threaten to shift production to low-wage areas overseas if unions resisted their contract demands. Belligerence toward labor was harder to explain in booming enterprises like the Las Vegas resorts. In the period here reviewed, employers could not easily export, subcontract, or mechanize resort jobs. Not until the recession of the early 1980s, when the tourist count in the area dipped for the first time, did belt-tightening policies look necessary to anyone but resort managers.[4]

Although management gained major concessions from Las Vegas unions in the 1984–85 strike, its efforts to smash the unions were generally unsuccessful. Trade unions were too entrenched to be eliminated. Corporate leaders understood this, even those among them who were viscerally opposed to unions. In the strike's aftermath, most sought labor peace within the latitudinarian limits they had imposed on the unions.[5] As a result, Las Vegas resort workers continued to earn decent wages and enjoy job security, which were their most immediate concerns. The events recounted in these final pages offer an opportunity to reflect more fully on general patterns in the resort industry and its workforce in the years after 1985. Las Vegas, it needs to be emphasized, remains a city in the making, and organized labor's future there is unclear.

Through the late twentieth century, Las Vegas continued to be the nation's fastest-growing metropolitan area. Between 1985 and 2000, its population more than doubled, to 1.3 million people. The growth rate was not just rapid but dizzying and disorienting. It strained all facets of community life and sustained an unprecedented construction boom. New homes went up "as fast as stucco could dry," a journalist noted, yet people still scrambled to buy them.[6] The growth overwhelmed public agencies and institutions and was no doubt all the more impressive to the people who had long lived and worked in the city.[7]

Newcomers to Las Vegas in those years generally resembled their predecessors. Most were working-class Americans who came to Las Vegas to work in a place of opportunity, perhaps mobility, and hopefully economic and social security. More than a third arrived from California, another third from elsewhere in the Southwest, including Texas. More surprising, about a quarter of them had migrated from east of the Mississippi River. Although retirees made up 10 percent of the new population, they were greatly outnumbered by the largest demographic group, those between the ages of twenty-five and forty-five. Most of these had no children, were relatively uneducated, and had limited skills.[8] Latinos composed the largest ethnic minority among the new arrivals and constituted the fastest-growing ethnic group in the metropolitan area. People with Spanish surnames represented less than 10 percent of the Clark County population in 1985 but nearly 15 percent in 2000. Perhaps more unexpectedly, the percentage of Asians and Pacific Islanders jumped too, to more than 5 percent of the population.[9]

Asked why they moved to Las Vegas, newcomers often spoke of the climate, and the low cost of housing, taxes, and living, but the city's growing economy and its abundance of low- and semiskilled jobs were the principal magnet. While industrial employment and economic development stalled in many parts of the country, the Las Vegas economy not only grew rapidly but also diversified in fields from financial services and manufacturing to warehousing and distribution services, as well as tourism and the proliferating economic enterprises related to it. As always, gaming and tourism remained the primary engine of growth. The annual visitor count in Clark County nearly doubled in the 1990s, to thirty-two million people. By the beginning of the new millennium, tourists were pumping more than $30 billion a year into the local economy, more than four times the total for 1985.[10]

Such figures reflected the most spectacular wave of resort construction in the history of Las Vegas. A dozen major resorts sprang up along the Strip in the late 1980s and 1990s, most of them financed by corporations already heavily invested in the area. The Mirage, Treasure Island, Excalibur, the Luxor, and a new MGM Grand opened between 1989 and 1994. The Stratosphere Tower, the Monte Carlo, and New York–New York opened in the mid-1990s. The Bellagio, the Mandalay Bay, the Paris, and the Venetian soon followed. These new "mega-resorts" had larger casinos and more hotel rooms than their predecessors did and many more nongaming amenities, which enhanced the Las Vegas experience, whatever one's interests and expectations.

The new MGM Grand and the Bellagio illustrated these points. The former, which radiated a Hollywood theme, had four gaming areas, more than 3,500 slot machines, and 170 gaming tables. It also had two large showrooms, twenty restaurants and eating places, a thirty-three-acre theme park, and a 15,200 seat special events center. The Bellagio was even more impressive. The eleven-acre replica of Lombardy's Lake Como that fronted the resort had within it 1,300 lights that illuminated fountains that burst forth every fifteen minutes and "danced" to recorded music piped into a surrounding high-tech sound system. Inside the resort were more than $300 million worth of art treasures, as well as Italian marble floors, lush gardens, and a walkway of shops resembling New York's Fifth Avenue.[11]

Other spectacular changes altered the visible landscape. Several older Strip properties, including the Flamingo Hilton, the Frontier, the Riviera, the Sahara, and the Stardust, built new hotel towers. City officials and developers turned Fremont Street into a pedestrian mall covered by a ninety-foot high canopy that stretched from Main Street to Las Vegas Boulevard. The canopy contained two million colored lights, and functioned as a backdrop for nightly light-and-sound shows. Developers also built several new "neighborhood" resorts in these years. The Gold Coast and the Palms opened a mile west of the Strip, and the Fiesta, the

Santa Fe, and the Texas further north. Like large Strip resorts, these properties had impressive themed architecture and interiors designed to appeal to customers' dreams and imaginations. They, too, added to the idea of Las Vegas as the "stuff of fantasy."[12]

Behind the fantasy and hidden from tourists, however, were continuing signs of the ongoing struggle between workers and employers. Organizers still tried to unionize dealers; arbitrators still heard testimony about "willful misconduct" and "insubordination" on the part of employees; and aggrieved workers as well as civil rights advocates still fought discriminatory employment practices. The range of these activities showed that many resort managers continued the confrontational tactics that had won them concessions from unions and workers in the 1970s and 1980s. These tactics connected the story of workers in Las Vegas resorts to the parallel decay of organized labor nationwide except in the public-sector unions. It also showed that workers in all sectors of the economy except government faced problems unprecedented since the 1930s.[13]

There were three major work stoppages in the resort industry after 1985. The first signaled the dismal end of an era for musicians. In 1989, when the musicians' union contract with major resorts expired, the Tropicana, the Hilton properties, and other Strip properties took this occasion to demand the right to use taped music and keyboard-operated synthesizers in place of showroom orchestras in order to lower labor costs. The union resisted and struck the properties to protect showroom jobs. The strike, which lasted for eight months, won little support from the Culinary and other unions, and the musicians lost utterly. The once proud orchestra musicians all but vanished, and other equally skilled musicians left the city or sought other work. The mechanization of showroom music was a near fatal blow to the union. Between 1989 and 1995, its membership fell from fourteen hundred to fewer than nine hundred members. Four years later, the union still had contracts with nine Strip resorts, but only a few musicians worked in those properties.[14]

The other strikes pitted unions against family-owned resorts, which had continued to lose economic ground to corporate properties. In 1989 the Culinary and other unions struck the Horseshoe after its owner, Jack Binion, who recently had inherited the property from his father, refused to accept the same provisions of the labor agreements that Strip properties had signed. In his rejection, Binion pointed to the difficulties his small property had competing against nearby operations that had decertified their unions in the mid-1980s as well as increasingly large Strip resorts. Developments in the resort industry, in other words, threatened to overwhelm places like his. Labor leaders dismissed this rationale, arguing that the Horseshoe was one of the city's most profitable businesses. Striking workers maintained picket lines outside the property for nine months, until Binion finally agreed to a four-year contract that hiked wages and benefits in return for work-rule changes that enhanced his control over hiring and firing.[15]

The third strike began in 1991, after the Frontier's new owners unilaterally slashed wages, imposed new work rules, and reduced benefits over the protests of their unionized employees. The owners, Margaret Elardi and her two sons, were resolutely antiunion. They refused to bargain with union leaders, ignored state efforts to mediate the dispute, and even defied NLRB rulings. Despite those efforts, the Elardis were unable to break the unions. In a remarkable demonstration of solidarity, the Culinary and three other unions kept picketers outside the Frontier for nearly seven years, until the Elardis sold the property and the new owner reached an agreement with the striking unions. No union worker crossed the picket line during this protracted strike.[16]

These conflicts exemplified the patterns of collective bargaining after 1985. The Nevada Resort Association withdrew from labor negotiations and reverted to its original role of lobbying and public relations for the industry. Resorts resumed bargaining in small, loosely knit groups that reflected the size, circumstances, and purposes of their members. Large corporate resorts like Caesars Palace and the Hilton properties aligned themselves in one cluster. Smaller corporate-owned resorts like the Stardust and the Sahara formed another bargaining group, as did still-smaller downtown properties such as the Fremont, El Cortez, and the Horseshoe. Yet other resorts, including some large properties on the Strip, insisted on negotiating individually with the unions. Typically, and generally successfully, these properties demanded wage and benefit packages that cost them less than those agreed to by large industry leaders. This complicated the bargaining process.[17]

Under these arrangements, collective bargaining became less volatile, essentially because the labor market in Las Vegas tightened. The new resorts that opened on the Strip in the late 1980s and early 1990s employed more than twenty-five thousand workers, largely depleting the pool of available employees. The new MGM Grand alone employed seventy-five hundred, more than six times as many people as resorts like the Desert Inn and the Sahara had on staff in the early 1970s. The resulting labor shortage became acute when the Bellagio began recruiting its workforce of more than eight thousand. By the time the Mandalay Bay, the Venetian, and the Paris opened, personnel officers were desperate for workers in all categories. "The number of talented employees out there looking for work is very dry," one resort manager said in 1998. "There's good people but they're far and few between."[18] To build workforces, resorts sent job recruiters throughout the area. Others "raided" competitors' workforces, which sometimes resulted in workplace confrontations. "We've been thrown out of some of the best places in town," one "raider" admitted.[19]

The tightening labor market helped the Culinary organize most of the new resorts while boosting its members' wages. From 1988 to 1998, as trade union membership in the private sector declined across the nation, membership in the Culinary more than doubled to forty thousand, and in 2008 topped sixty thousand. The wages of the union's members might have risen as fast or faster in these years than those of any private-sector union in the nation. In the first decade of the twenty-first century, many culinary workers in Las Vegas earned more than twice the wages of their counterparts in other tourist destinations. The base wage of union waiters, for example, topped $10 an hour in 2004, nearly three times that of average waiters in New York.[20]

There was nothing automatic about the Culinary's success. It came as a result of effective leadership and strategizing. In the aftermath of the 1984–85 strike, Culinary leaders came to realize that their approach to collective bargaining had been more or less ad hoc; that is, they had dealt with industrial developments not by intense calculation, planning, and organizing but simply as they came up. They had made no detailed studies of their own situation or that of their industry, gathered no systematic data on industry profits and income, and developed no long-term strategies for each and every level of their organization. In other words, it was not only the professionalization, organization, and rationalization that management went through that accounted for Culinary losses in the 1984–85 strike but also the absence of a similar transformation on the part of the union. Under the leadership of Jim Arnold, who replaced Jeff McColl as secretary-treasurer in 1987, the Culinary brought in seasoned organizers and professional researchers to deal with the increasingly complex businesses that had replaced the simpler enterprises of earlier times.[21]

In traditional trade-union terms, the Culinary's success after 1985 carried a high price. Beginning with the staffing of the workforce at the Mirage in 1988, the union asked for recognition as bargaining agent for the resort's culinary workers as soon as 51 percent of the workers hired for Culinary jobs signed cards asking to join the union. This innovative "card check" strategy, which Canadian unions had pioneered, allowed unions to circumvent the costly and lengthy process of holding representation elections, which the union believed functioned in management's favor. As badly as the Mirage and other employers needed workers

by the late 1980s, they agreed to the card-check system only in return for the right
to reclassify and lay-off employees as workplace demands dictated. Some of them
also demanded and got contract language prohibiting their employees from engaging in sympathy strikes "or any other form of economic action" for the dura-
tion of their labor contracts.[22]

This concession largely ended the struggle over workers' right to honor picket
lines other than their own and eclipsed the power of small unions. Once resorts
like the Mirage, the Monte Carlo, the Stratosphere, and Treasure Island reached
agreements with the Culinary prohibiting sympathy strikes, they often refused
to negotiate with other unions. By the late 1990s, when more than forty resorts
in the area had contracts with the Culinary, fewer than thirty had contracts with
the Operating Engineers and only twenty with the Teamsters.[23] The inability of
those unions to organize new resorts because of the Culinary's organizing tactics
drove a new wedge between the unions. In 1994 John Wilhelm of the International Culinary (and a future president of the national AFL-CIO) acknowledged
this division and called for new "joint organizing strategies" to eliminate it. He
and other national labor leaders, Wilhelm told the Operating Engineers that year,
intended to "restore the solidarity which had once existed among the casino
unions in Las Vegas." "Each union will get its traditional casino jurisdiction when
we are successful."[24]

The Culinary orchestrated public protests to pressure some of the new resorts
to recognize the union as the bargaining agent for its workers. Thus, on May 26,
1993, the union put five thousand picketers outside the new MGM Grand, whose
corporate executives refused to bargain. For three hours, the protesters waved
American flags, chanted union slogans, and blasted Bruce Springsteen's "Born
in the USA" through loudspeakers. The police arrested more than five hundred
of the protestors, the largest mass arrest in Nevada history.[25] Four years later, on
July 29, 1997, the union put twice that many picketers outside New York–New
York to protest that resort's subcontracting of its restaurants to nonunion firms.
The latter demonstration coincided with a meeting of the national conference of
governors at the nearby Mirage, and visiting journalists witnessed and reported
the event across the national media.[26] Such tactics were not always successful, but
they no doubt encouraged employers to acknowledge the union's power.

Las Vegas today remains a place where wage earners partake of the American
dream. Trade unions in the area still win contracts providing decent wages and
benefits, and job security. This does not make the city a workers' paradise, as one

journalist has recently suggested.[27] Resort workers are not immune to forces of automation, global competition, or economic recession, or to the effects of terrorism or oil shortages that limit the free movement of people and goods and services to an isolated desert metropolis. Their unions hold their own rather than march triumphantly over rich and powerful employers. In other words, labor relations in Las Vegas today are contentious without being oppressive, relatively peaceful without much harmony. The differing realities of the social being of laborers and capitalists still govern their functioning. The result is very far from the overwhelming degradation of workers that Marx foresaw as the inevitable outcome of capitalism. But it is also somewhat removed from the efficiencies implied in Adam Smith's account of the workings of capitalism's "invisible hand."

Notes

ABBREVIATIONS

FBI Records	Federal Bureau of Investigation, Washington, D.C.
Federation Papers, NSHS	Nevada State Federation of Labor Papers, Nevada State Historical Society, Reno
Herald-Examiner	*Los Angeles Herald-Examiner*
IRC, Honolulu	Industrial Relations Center, Sinclair Library, University of Hawaii at Manoa.
Kefauver Committee Hearings	*Third Interim Report of the Special Committee to Investigate Organized Crime in Interstate Commerce: A Resolution to Investigate Gambling and Racketeering Activities*, 82nd Congress, Part 10 (Washington, D.C.: U.S. Government Printing Office, 1951).
Local 226 Papers	Papers of Culinary Local 226, Las Vegas, Nevada, at the local's headquarters in Las Vegas
NRA Papers	Papers of Nevada Resort Association, at the law firm of Armstrong Teasdale LLP, 317 South 6th Street, Las Vegas
NSHS, Reno	Nevada State Historical Society, Reno
NSMA Special Collections	Nevada State Museum and Archives, Special Collections, Carson City
Review-Journal	*Las Vegas Review-Journal*
Senate Report, 98th Cong.	Summaries of Hearing Testimony, U.S. Congress, Senate Committee on Governmental Affairs, *Hotel Employees and Restaurant Employees International Unions*, 98th Cong., 2nd sess., 1984
Sun	*Las Vegas Sun*
Testimony before CRNPTG	*Summaries of Hearing Testimony before the Commission on the Review of the National Policy toward Gambling* (Washington, D.C.: Government Printing Office, 1976)
UNLV Special Collections	Special Collections Department, Lied Library, University of Nevada, Las Vegas

UNOHP, Reno   University of Nevada Oral History Program, at the
                               University of Nevada, Reno

INTRODUCTION

1. For an overview of the scholarly and popular studies of Las Vegas, see the Essay on Sources.

2. Films that perpetuate myths about Las Vegas include *Viva Las Vegas* (1964), *Diamonds Are Forever* (1971), *Starman* (1985), *Rain Man* (1988), *Honeymoon in Vegas* (1992), *Indecent Proposal* (1993), *Casino* (1995), *Leaving Las Vegas* (1995), *Showgirls* (1996), and *Vegas Vacation* (1996). Since the early 1980s, the motion picture division of the Nevada Commission on Economic Development has tried to control images of Las Vegas on film and generally kept moviemakers from portraying the city in an unflattering light. For a good overview of this subject, see Francisco Menendez, "Las Vegas of the Mind: Shooting Movies in and about Nevada," in *The Grit Beneath the Glitter: Tales from the Real Las Vegas*, ed. Hal K. Rothman and Mike Davis (Berkeley: University of California Press, 2002), 30–58.

3. *Honolulu Advertiser*, December 8, 2004. As the *Advertiser* noted, a television commercial that plays off the slogan features a respectable-looking young man asking a hotel desk clerk if wake-up calls can be made to cell phones, implying that he might wake up in a room other than his own. With an all-knowing look and smile, the clerk assures the man that calls can indeed be so made.

4. Frank Scott, president of the Nevada Resort Association, in *Review-Journal*, March 12, 1976.

5. "An Interview with Essie Shelton Jacobs: An Oral History Conducted by Claytee D. White," Las Vegas Women in Gaming and Entertainment Oral History Project, 1997, 54, UNLV Special Collections.

6. On Las Vegas as the epitome of postindustrial society, see Hal Rothman, *Neon Metropolis: How Las Vegas Started the Twenty-First Century* (New York: Routledge, 2002), xxvi–xxvii. Also Rothman, "The Future Belongs to Las Vegas," *Sun*, July 16, 2006.

CHAPTER 1: THE RISE OF CORPORATE RESORTS

1. "State of Nevada Business Trends during 1946–1950 and Future Outlook," box 0178, folder 7, Papers of Governor Charles Russell, NSMA Special Collections.

2. Untitled letter of Charles H. Russell, December 26, 1957, box 23, folder 0188, Papers of Governor Charles Russell.

3. On tourism in postwar Nevada, see Thomas Cox, "Before the Casino: James G. Scugham, State Parks, and Nevada's Quest for Tourism," *Western Historical Quarterly* 24 (August 1993): 333–50.

4. On visitation to Lake Mead and Hoover Dam, see *Las Vegas Report 1957: A Compendium of Statistical Commercial and Social Facets of Las Vegas*, an annual publication of the Las Vegas Chamber of Commerce, box 0178, folder 29, Papers of Governor Charles Russell. (Many of these Chamber of Commerce publications are in UNLV Special Collections.)

On Hoover Dam, see Joseph E. Stevens, *Hoover Dam: An American Adventure* (Norman: University of Oklahoma Press, 1988).

5. In 1951, 3 percent of gross gambling income amounted to $1.5 million. For a list of gross gambling revenue and fees paid to the state in the late 1940s and 1950s, see the Las Vegas Chamber of Commerce's *Las Vegas Report 1961*, 19, UNLV Special Collections. On the value of mineral production, see "State of Nevada Business Trends during 1946–1950 and Future Outlook," box 7, folder 0178, Papers of Governor Charles Russell.

6. On gambling establishments in prewar Nevada, see Jerome E. Edwards, "Nevada Gambling: Just Another Business Enterprise," *Nevada Historical Society Quarterly* 37, no. 2 (Summer 1994): 101–14. Also, Eric N. Moody, "Nevada's Legalization of Casino Gambling in 1931: Purely a Business Proposition," *Nevada Historical Society Quarterly* 37, no. 2 (Summer 1994): 79–100.

7. "A Brief History of Gambling," in Western States Historical Publishers, *Nevada: The Silver State* (Carson City: Western States Historical Publishers, 1970), 1:51–52.

8. On early Las Vegas, see Barbara Land and Myrick Land, *A Short History of Las Vegas* (Reno: University of Nevada Press, 1999).

9. Magnesium was used in the production of aircraft and incendiary bombs. On Basic Magnesium Incorporated, see *Las Vegas Report 1952–58*, 18, UNLV Special Collections. Also, James W. Hulse, *The Silver State: Nevada's Heritage Reinterpreted* (Las Vegas: University of Nevada Press, 1991), 213–14.

10. On population figures in Southern Nevada, see "Las Vegas and Clark County Nevada, an Economic and Industrial Analysis," box 1078, folder 28, Papers of Governor Charles Russell. See also U.S. Department of Commerce, *Census of the Population: 1960*, vol. 1, part 30 (Washington, D.C.: Government Printing Office, 1963), 15, 51. See also *Las Vegas Report: A Decade of Progress, 1956–1966*, 6–14, UNLV Special Collections; and Eugene P. Moehring, *Resort City in the Sunbelt: Las Vegas, 1930–1970* (Reno: University of Nevada Press, 1989), 269–70.

11. On manufacturing and construction, see *Las Vegas Report 1961*, 1–26. See also Eugene P. Moehring, "Las Vegas and the Second World War," *Nevada Historical Society Quarterly* 29, no. 1 (Spring 1986): 1–30.

12. Useful works on the rise of Strip resorts include Albert Woods Moe, *Nevada's Golden Age of Gambling* (Gig Harbor, Wash.: Puget Sound Books, 2001), 75–80, at NSHS, Reno; Robert D. McCracken, *Las Vegas: The Great American Playground* (Reno: University of Nevada Press, 1997), 53–68; and Moehring, *Resort City*, 44–52.

13. McCracken, *The Great America Playground*, 60–63; and Frank Wright, *World War II and the Emergence of Modern Las Vegas* (Las Vegas: Nevada State Museum and Historical Society, 1991), 28.

14. The Thunderbird also served Mexican dinners twice nightly in its main showroom, the Continental Theater. See "Thunderbird Cuisine," clipping, box 6, folder 3, Thunderbird Hotel Collection, UNLV Special Collections.

15. On the Desert Inn, see R. T. King, "An Interview with Morton Saiger," February 18, 1985, 41–44, UNOHP, Reno; also, McCracken, *The Great American Playground*, 69–86.

16. Michael J. Gaughn, August 21, 1975, *Testimony before the CRNPTG*, 364. See also McCracken, *The Great American Playground*, 64–65, 77–78. The sign at the Golden Nugget was erected three years after the resort opened.

17. *Las Vegas Report 1961*, 6–14.

18. On the expansion of McCarran Airport, see Moehring, *Resort City*, 132–33. On the tourist count and gaming revenue in the mid-1960s, see *Las Vegas Report 1967*, 1–10, UNLV Special Collections.

19. On Governor Sawyer's address, see "Remarks of Governor Grant Sawyer," in folder "Unionizing Casino Employees," located in "Union Organizing Files," Papers of Nevada Resort Association, Las Vegas, Nevada. See also *Review-Journal*, January 5, 1976.

20. U.S. Department of Commerce, *1970 Census of the Population*, vol. 1, part 30 (Washington, D.C.: Government Printing Office, 1972), 13. On water problems in Las Vegas, see Moehring, *Resort City*, 212–17.

21. *Las Vegas Report: A Decade of Progress, 1956–1966*, 11–13. In the summer of 1962, licensed gaming establishments in Nevada employed about thirty-five thousand people, more than half of whom worked in Clark County. On employment in gaming, see "A Brief History of Gambling," in *Nevada: The Silver State*, 57.

22. On the nature and structure of the Mafia, see "Mafia Monograph," section I: Sicily, July 1958, iii–xii, FBI Records, at http://foia.fbi.gov/foiaindex/mafiamon.htm.

23. Kefauver Committee Hearings, 80–94. The figures on Chicago gambling establishments are from FBI Records, at http://foia.fbi.gov/foiaindex/siege.htm. On gambling establishments in Chicago, see the FBI memorandum from the agency's Los Angeles office, dated August 13, 1963, at http://foia.fbi.gov/filelink.html?file=/sidneykorshak/sidneykorshak/sidneykorshak_part01.pdf. The same file offers insight into "mob" financing in Las Vegas. For more on that subject, see Hal Rothman, "Colony, Capital, and Casino: Money in the Real Las Vegas," 310–18, in *The Grit Beneath the Glitter: Tales from the Real Las Vegas*, ed. Hal K. Rothman and Mike Davis (Los Angeles: University of California Press, 2002); and Ronald A. Farrell and Carole Case, *The Black Book and the Mob: The Untold Story of the Control of Nevada's Casinos* (Madison: University of Wisconsin Press, 1995), 24–25.

24. Some casino owners reportedly paid off "hidden" investors by letting their representatives win at gambling tables. On skimming operations, see "Memo to Director," February 14, 1961, 10–11, in FBI Records on Morris B. Dalitz, file number 92-3068, section 2, part 3.

25. Testimony of Jerry W. Gordon to State of Nevada, County of Clark, October 18, 1971, 1–6, box: Various Skim/Mob Influence Files, folder: Downtown/4/Flamingo Skim, Local 226 Papers.

26. "Memo to Director," February 14, 1961, 10–11, FBI Records on Morris B. Dalitz, file number 92-3068, section 2, part 3.

27. "Organized Crime in Southern Nevada, 1984, Annual Report to Sheriff John Moran," 3, box: Various Skim/Mob Influence Files, folder: Organized Crime, Local 226 Papers.

28. "Memo to Director," February 14, 1961, 10–11, FBI Records on Morris B. Dalitz, file number 92-3068, section 2, part 3.

29. Kefauver Committee Hearings, 91. William Wilkerson, who owned the *Holly-wood Reporter*, sank about $600,000 into the Flamingo before selling most of his interests in the property to Siegel. See also FBI Records, at http://foia.fbi.gov/foiaindex/siege .htm. On Siegel's racing wire services, see report to FBI Director, July 22, 1946, at http://foia.fbi.gov/filelink.html?file=siegel/siegel1.a.pdf, 40. For more on Siegel, see Moehring, *Resort City*, 49–53; Hal Rothman, *Neon Metropolis: How Las Vegas Started the Twenty-First Century* (New York: Routledge, 2002), 10–16; and John L. Smith, "The Ghost of Ben Siegel," in *The Players: The Men Who Made Las Vegas*, ed. Jack Sheehan (Reno: University of Nevada Press, 1997), 81–91.

30. Kefauver Committee Hearings, 92. Clark also invested in two smaller casinos in Las Vegas, the Monte Carlo and Players Club. On Clark, Dalitz, and patterns of finance at the Desert Inn, see FBI Records on Morris B. Dalitz, especially file number 92-3068, section 2, parts 3 and 4 (of 12). On Clark, see also Lester Ben "Benny" Binion, in "Some Recollections of a Texas and Las Vegas Gaming Operator," 73–74, UNOHP, Reno; also Moehring, *Resort City*, 74–75.

31. *Wall Street Journal*, May 23, 1969. The FBI maintains extensive files on Meyer Lansky, which are available to researchers at its headquarters in Washington, D.C. On the Sands and organized crime, see also Farrell and Case, *The Black Book*, 24–25, 34–35; and Rothman, "Colony, Capital, and Casino," 310–15.

32. "Organized Crime in Southern Nevada, 1984, Annual Report to Sheriff John Moran," 2.

33. David G. Schwartz, *Suburban Xanadu: The Casino Resort on the Las Vegas Strip and Beyond* (New York: Routledge, 2003), 110; and Moehring, *Resort City*, 244–45. Thomas's respect for many of the investors in the Las Vegas resort industry is evident in personal letters he wrote to Barron Hilton in 1963 about men who purchased the Dunes from its original owners in the late 1950s. "I know nothing derogatory about any of them," he told Hilton. "I have met a considerable number of people who know them or know of them, and have yet to hear anybody speak against them" E. Parry Thomas to Barron Hilton, September 26, 1963, box: Hilton—N.J. Licensing Files (1984), folder: Hilton/N.J. License I, Local 226 Papers.

34. On the Central States Pension Fund, see "Like Old Man River: Central States Pension Fund," *International Teamster* 73, no. 8 (August 1976): 12–13, IRC, Honolulu. On the Fund and Las Vegas, see *Reno-Gazette-Journal*, July 20, 1985; and *Valley Times*, March 22, 1976. See also Steven Brill, *The Teamsters* (New York: Simon and Schuster, 1978), 202–10; Schwartz, *Suburban Xanadu*, 108–10; Sally Denton and Roger Morris, *The Money and the Power: The Making of Las Vegas and Its Hold on America, 1947–2000* (New York: Alfred A. Knopf (2001), 231–33; and Rothman, *Neon Metropolis*, 15–19.

35. Howard Hughes refused to tap the Teamster fund because he believed it would "downgrade the overall financial image of [Hughes Tool Company]." "Don't forget that the Teamsters' Fund money has financed practically every one of the entities in the state which have housed the multitude of underworld personalities who have drawn the mass of public censure," he told his trusted counsel Robert Maheu in the late 1960s. See Letter from Hughes to Maheu, n.d., Howard Robard Hughes Files, file number 95-211845, part 5b, 50, FBI Records.

36. On corruption and lending practices, see "The Central States Pension Fund Is Alive and Well," *International Teamster* 73, no. 8 (August 1976): 8–10, IRC, Honolulu; and "Thoughts of the General President," ibid., 18–19. See also *Los Angeles Times*, May 31, 1973; *Reno-Gazette-Journal*, July 20, 1985; and Brill, *The Teamsters*, 202–10. For a broader view, see James B. Jacobs, *Mobsters, Unions, and Feds: The Mafia and the American Labor Movement* (New York: New York University Press, 2006).

37. Kefauver Committee Hearings, 90–94. See also "A Brief History of Gambling," in *Nevada: The Silver State*, 51–59. The list of excluded persons initially included eleven men, but the list soon grew to thirty-eight. See also *Reno-Gazette-Journal*, September 2, 1979; July 14, 1985; July 28, 1985. Also, *Wall Street Journal*, September 2, 1966; "The Game Is 'Skimming,'" *Newsweek Magazine*, August 29, 1966; and Denton and Morris, *The Money and the Power*, 236–37.

38. Kefauver Committee Hearings, 92–93; Testimony of Peter Echeverria, Chairman of Nevada Gaming Commission, *Testimony before CRNPTG*, 310; Farrell and Case, *The Black Book*, 42–43.

39. Sam Giancana was associated with the 1960 presidential election of John Kennedy and with Kennedy's assassination in 1963. He was murdered "gangland style" in 1975, after being called to testify before a congressional committee investigating Kennedy's assassination. On both Sinatra and Giancana, see FBI Records, www.fbi.org. For more on this subject, see Farrell and Case, *The Black Book*, 44–45.

40. Testimony of Jack Keith, August 20, 1975, *Testimony before CRNPTG*, 353. Also, *Reno-Gazette-Journal*, September 2, 1979; and *Sun*, October 18, 1977.

41. Kefauver Committee Hearings, 93; Farrell and Case, *The Black Book*, 21–28, 43.

42. Robbins E. Cahill, "Recollections of Work in State Politics, Government, Taxation, Gaming Control, Clark County Administration and the Nevada Resort Association," 949, 1545, UNOHP, Reno.

43. *Wall Street Journal*, May 23, 1969. The Justice Department suspected Chicago-based mobsters of trying to control the Central States Pension Fund but ultimately rejected efforts to prosecute them. Brill, *The Teamsters*, 202–10; *Review-Journal*, June 10, 1990.

44. "Business Owes Big Debt to Sam Boyd," *Las Vegas Today*, July 9, 1975; and "Boyds Break Ground," ibid., September 19, 1978.

45. The Sahara was a Strip property largely financed by a businessman based in Portland, Oregon. On Boyd, see Jack Sheehan, "Sam Boyd's Quiet Legacy," in Sheehan, *The Players*, 104–19.

46. David Dearing, "Up, Up, Up: Veteran Mel Exber Sees Vegas Gambling Future as Bright," *Las Vegas Today*, January 23, 1979, 7–8. On Binion, see Lester Ben "Benny" Binion, "Some Recollections of a Texas and Las Vegas Gaming Operator," UNOHP, Reno.

47. On Gaughan, see Bill Moody, "Jackie Gaughan," *Nevadan*, September 17, 1989. In the game of "faro," players bet on cards as they were drawn from a box by dealers.

48. Wright, *World War II and the Emergence of Modern Las Vegas*, 28.

49. On the evolution of entertainment in Las Vegas, see Dave Palermo, "The Adult Playground Becomes a Heaven for Families," in Sheehan, *The Players*, 200–211.

50. The Sands employed a Beverly Hills publicity firm to write a short biography of Entratter. See "Biography—Jack Entratter," n.d., 1–8, box 4, folder 11, Sands Hotel Collection, UNLV Special Collections.

51. On the Copa Girls, see publicity releases in box 4, folder 1, Sands Hotel Collection. Also, Land and Land, *A Short History of Las Vegas*, 141–43.

52. On showgirls, see Joanne L. Goodwin, "She Works Hard for Her Money: A Reassessment of Las Vegas Women Workers, 1945–1985," 243–59, in Rothman and Davis, *The Grit Beneath the Glitter*.

53. On the Hacienda, see *Las Vegas Hacienda Hotel History*, a collection of news clippings compiled by Richard B. Taylor, 1986, in UNOHP, Reno.

54. Ibid. In this collection of clippings, see "Opening of Barstow Freeway to End Job of Pretty Miss."

55. On Caesars Palace, see Cherrie L. Guzman, "Caesars Palace, 1966–1996," master's thesis, UNLV Special Collections. See also Schwartz, *Suburban Xanadu*, 133.

56. On Sarno, see A. D. Hopkins, "Jay Sarno: He Came to Play," in Sheehan, *The Players*, 92–103; Moehring, *Resort City*, 116–19; and Hal K. Rothman, *Devil's Bargains: Tourism in the Twentieth-Century American West* (Lawrence: University Press of Kansas, 1998), 307–8.

57. On social values and popular amusement, see John F. Kasson, *Amusing the Million: Coney Island at the Turn of the Century* (New York: Hill & Wang, 1978).

58. In 1939, to illustrate the point more clearly, producers of *Gone With the Wind* had to pay a hefty $5,000 fine to a movie censorship board for Rhett Butler saying, "Frankly, my dear, I don't give a damn." On gambling and changing cultural values, see John M. Findlay, *People of Chance: Gambling in American Society from Jamestown to Las Vegas* (New York: Oxford University Press, 1986), 200–209.

59. On Hacienda ownership, see "The Editor Speaks," October 20, 1956, in Taylor, *Las Vegas Hacienda Hotel History*.

60. Albert Parvin, the primary owner of the Parvin-Dohrmann Company, had also invested in Las Vegas gaming. On Webb's entrance into gaming, see Tom Alexander, "What Del Webb Is Up To in Nevada," *Fortune*, May 1965, 130–33. See also Alan Balboni, *Beyond the Mafia: Italian Americans and the Development of Las Vegas* (Las Vegas: University of Nevada Press, 1996), 61–63; and A. D. Hopkins, "Man of the Years," *The First 100 Persons Who Shaped Southern Nevada*, at www.1st100.com/part2/webb.html.

61. Webb's associates included L. C. Jacobson, Milton Prell, and Alfred Winter, who owned the entity that operated the Sahara and the Mint. See Alexander, "What Del Webb Is Up To," 186. See also *Wall Street Journal*, May 23, 1969; and Schwartz, *Suburban Xanadu*, 105–6.

62. The new laws provided that the Gaming Control Board could investigate stockholders with 5–10 percent of the stock of a publicly traded corporation at its discretion. *Sun*, June 7, 1969. See also Sergio Lalli, "A Peculiar Institution," in Sheehan, *The Players*, 18. See also *Reno-Gazette-Journal*, September 2, 1979; and Edward A. Olsen, "My Careers as a Journalist in Oregon, Idaho, and Nevada; in Nevada Gaming Control; and at the University of Nevada," 463–65, UNOHP, Reno.

63. Hughes's entry into Las Vegas and its resort industry is documented in a memorandum from SAC, Las Vegas, to J. Edgar Hoover, December 14, 1967, Howard Robard Hughes Files, file number 46-7004, part 7b, 25- 29, FBI Records.

64. On Hughes, see Ovid Demaris, "You and I are very different from Howard Hughes—We don't own Las Vegas," *Esquire*, March 1969, 5–20. On the "secret" life of Hughes, see *Time*, December 13, 1976, 22–32. Also, *Christian Science Monitor*, October 1, 1970; *Review-Journal*, April 6, 1972. Other useful work includes Sergio Lalli, "Howard Hughes in Vegas," 133–58, in Sheehan, *The Players*, 133–58; Denton and Morris, *The Money and the Power*, 266–74; and Schwartz, *Suburban Xanadu*, 148–52. Hughes agreed, among other things, to finance construction of a medical school for the University of Nevada if granted a gaming license. For more on Hughes, see James Phelan, *Howard Hughes: The Hidden Years* (New York: Random House, 1976); Robert Maheu, *Next to Hughes* (New York: Harper Collins, 1992); and Michael Drosnin, *Citizen Hughes* (New York: Holt, Rinehart, Winston, 1985).

65. Hank Greenspun, publisher of the *Sun* and owner of KLAS-TV, also helped Hughes. See John L. Smith, "Moe Dalitz and the Desert," in Sheehan, *The Players*, 36–45. See also John L. Smith, "The Double Life of Moe Dalitz," *The First 100*, at www.1st100.com/part2/dalitz.html. For more on Hughes, see K. J. Evans, "Sky Was No Limit," *The First 100*, at www.1st100.com/part3/hughes.html. Also, Schwartz, *Suburban Xanadu*, 149.

66. Testimony of Barron Hilton to State of New Jersey Casino Control Commission, 44–54, in box labeled Hilton—N.J. Licensing Files (1984), from folder: Hilton N.J., in Local 226 Papers. Also, *Las Vegas Today*, August 10, 1976. Hilton acquired 50 percent of International Leisure Corporation in 1970, which Kirk Kerkorian formed to build the International and buy the Flamingo. Guzman, "Caesars Palace."

67. On the subject of business organization, see Naomi R. Lamoreaux, "Partnerships, Corporations, and Theory of the Firm," *American Economic Review* 88 (May 1988): 66–70.

68. On Wynn, see Mark Seal, "Steve Wynn: King of Wow!" in Sheehan, *The Players*, 174–78. On Hughes, Kerkorian, and Wynn, see also Rothman, *Devil's Bargains*, 297, 322–24, 329.

69. "The corporation doesn't consider the future the end of the current quarter and the long-term as being the quarter after that," Hilton added. Testimony of Barron Hilton to State of New Jersey Casino Control Commission, 57, 75, 82, in box: Hilton—N.J. Licensing Files (1984), from folder: Hilton N.J., Local 226 Papers.

70. Testimony of Barron Hilton and John Giovenco, in Findlay, *Gambling in America*, 367–70. On the administration of large business enterprise, see Alfred D. Chandler Jr., *Strategy and Structure: Chapters in the History of the Industrial Enterprise* (Cambridge: MIT Press, 1960), 7–17, 314–23.

71. Testimony of Jack K. Pieper, August 21, 1975, *Testimony before CRNPTG*, 372.

72. Lewin, a survivor of a World War II internment camp, had worked as a busboy and waiter in Shanghai hotels before moving to San Francisco in 1947. He worked at the city's Fairmount Hotel for eighteen years before taking a managerial position with the Hilton Hotel in San Francisco. See testimony of Henri Lewin before State of New Jersey Casino Control Commission, September 17, 1984, 667–71, in box: Hilton—N.J. Licensing Files (1984), in folder: Hilton N.J. Gaming Commission 1984, Local 226 Papers.

73. Colin Dangaard, "Henri Lewin: A Feisty Survivor Keeps Hiltons Humming," *Las Vegas Today*, July 13, 1976, 12–13.

74. Ibid.

75. On Hughes Tool Company statements to the Securities and Exchange Commission, see *Wall Street Journal*, October 17, 1972; *Newsweek*, October 30, 1972; and *Time*, October 30, 1972.

76. *A Personal Welcome from the President*, pamphlet given to author by Bill Champion, former MGM Personal Director. Also, Schwartz, *Suburban Xanadu*, 156, 163, 169–70. Also, McCracken, *Las Vegas*, 95.

77. A Personal Welcome from the President.

78. Ibid.

79. Ibid.

80. U.S. Department of Commerce, *1970 Census of Population*, vol. 1, part 30, 13; *Las Vegas Report 1972*, 2, UNLV Special Collections. The words are those of James Cashman Jr.

81. On the growth of the resort industry in the early 1970s, see "Quarterly and Fiscal Year Reports of the State Gaming Control Board," box 68, folder: Nevada Gaming Commission, Howard Hughes Collection, UNLV Special Collections. See also *Wall Street Journal*, September 27, 1972; *Las Vegas Report 1972*, 14; and *Las Vegas Report 1973*, 8, UNLV Special Collections.

CHAPTER 2: WORKING IN LAS VEGAS

1. *Las Vegas Report 1952–1958: A Compendium of Statistical Commercial and Social Facets of Las Vegas*, 1, 14, a compilation of annual publications of the Las Vegas Chamber of Commerce, UNLV Special Collections. See also, Testimony of Governor Mike O'Callaghan, August 18, 1975, *Testimony before CRNPTG*, 304.

2. *Las Vegas Report 1973*, 34–35, UNLV Special Collections. Also, M. Gottdiener, Claudia C. Collins, and David R. Dickens, *Las Vegas: The Social Production of an All-American City* (Malden, Mass.: Blackwell Publishers, 1999), 111–20; and Robert D. McCracken, *Las Vegas: The Great American Playground* (Reno: University of Nevada Press, 1997), 95.

3. David G. Schwartz, *Suburban Xanadu: The Casino Resort on the Las Vegas Strip and Beyond* (New York: Routledge, 2003), 152–54.

4. On general categories of employment in American industry, see Charles C. Heckscher, *The New Unionism: Employee Involvement in the Changing Corporation* (New York: Basic Books, 1988), 62–71, 264.

5. Howard Mark Levy, "A Comparative Study of Management's Perception of Front Desk Service Quality at Casino and Non-Casino Hotels" (master's thesis, University of Nevada, Las Vegas, 1993), 13–16.

6. Security Officers' Information Folders, August 1, 1976, folder: Security Guards vs. Landmark, 1980, in Miscellaneous Labor Files, NRA Papers.

7. U.S. Department of Commerce, *Census of the Population: 1960*, vol. 1, part 30 (Washington, D.C.: Government Printing Office, 1963), ii–v, 15, 51. Median family income in Las Vegas was about $7,000 in 1960.

8. On turnover, see Jamie McKee, "Jobs Program's 'Unrealistic Goal' Falls Short," *Las Vegas Business Press*, March 7, 1994, folder: Casinos' Employment, in Vertical Files, UNLV Special Collections. On turnover in security, see list of security employees at Four Queens, n.d., folder: Organizing of Security Guards (Four Queens), in Miscellaneous Labor Files, NRA Papers. In kitchen and housekeeping, see "Culinary Contract—Adjusted Costs by Property," folder: 1984 Bargaining Data, in 1984 Culinary/Bartender Negotiations Files, NRA Papers. Also *Sun*, June 2, 1975; July 13, 1975.

9. For an overview of discriminatory practices, see Russell R. Elliott, *History of Nevada*, 2nd ed. (Lincoln: University of Nebraska Press, 1993), 393–94; and James W. Hulse, *The Silver State: Nevada's Heritage Reinterpreted* (Reno: University of Nevada Press, 1991), 307–12.

10. *Collective Bargaining Agreement between Nevada Resort Association and Hotel & Restaurant Employees and Bartenders Internal Union, AFL-CIO, 1970–1973, 50–52; and Agreement between Las Vegas Resort Hotels and the International Brotherhood of Teamsters, Chauffeurs, and Warehousemen and Helpers of America, 1969–1972, 23*, in Expired Labor Contracts Files, NRA Papers.

11. Italian Americans accounted for about 10 percent of the population of Las Vegas in the 1960s and perhaps a third of the names on marquees along the Strip. See Alan Balboni, *Beyond the Mafia: Italian Americans and the Development of Las Vegas* (Las Vegas: University of Nevada Press, 1996), 30–43.

12. Interview with Mark Massagli, Las Vegas, June 12, 1997.

13. Ibid. Massagli had belonged to the Los Angeles local of the American Federation of Musicians. When he moved to Las Vegas, union rules prohibited him from accepting steady engagements for three months while he transferred his membership from one local to the other.

14. Denise Garon Miller, Oral History, conducted by Deborah Whicker, March 2, 1981, transcribed interview, UNLV Special Collections.

15. Ibid. In the course of her dance career, Miller worked with such luminaries as Cab Calaway, Peggy Lee, Kay Starr, and Andy Williams.

16. Joanne L. Goodwin, "She Works Hard for Her Money: A Reassessment of Las Vegas Women Workers, 1945–85," in *The Grit Beneath the Glitter: Tales from the Real Las Vegas*, ed. Hal K. Rothman and Mike Davis (Berkeley: University of California Press, 2002), 243–59. Also, "An Interview with Kim Krantz," conducted by Joyce Marshall, February 26, 1996, UNLV Special Collections, 9.

17. "An Interview with Julie Menard, an Oral History Conducted by Joyce Marshall," Las Vegas Women in Gaming and Entertainment Oral History Project, 1997, 1–3, 11, 17, UNLV Special Collections.

18. "Decision and Direction of Election," June 28, 1971, 1–3, folder: IATSE v. Tropicana Wardrobe Mistresses, Case No. 31-RC-1619, 1673, 1674, in NLRB Files, NRA Papers. In same folder, see "Decision and Direction of Election," June 30, 1971, 2–3; and "Decision and Direction of Election," July 12, 1971, 2–3. Also, interview with Dennis Kist, Las Vegas, October 17, 2003.

19. *Las Vegas Today*, August 13, 1975, 22. Like artisans in preindustrial times, wardrobe workers typically took their own tools to the workplace, including needles, scissors, and thread. See also "Decision and Direction of Order," June 28, 1971, 4–5.

20. Interview with former stagehand Dennis Kist, Las Vegas, October 17, 2003.

21. "Joe Moll: Not Bored Once in 24 Years," *Las Vegas Today*, June 22, 1976.

22. Interview with Dennis Kist, Las Vegas, October 17, 2003. Virgil Kist worked briefly in El Paso, Texas, as an insurance agent, before relocating to Las Vegas.

23. "Petition," Hacienda—Dealer Organizing by Local 711—1969, October 7, 1969, folder: Case No. 31-RC-1232, in NLRB Files, NRA Papers. See also "Petition," February 26, 1975, folder: Case No. 31-RC-3052 Landmark/BRAC, in NLRB Files, NRA Papers. In same folder, see John R. Frederick, memo to Al Sachs, March 2, 1971.

24. "Appeal," May 15, 1974, 1–5, folder: Case No. 31-RC-2768, MGM Grand, Dealer Organization Attempt, in NLRB Files, NRA Papers. See also "Petition," March 26, 1975, folder: Petition for Election—Casino Case No. 31-RC-3141, in NLRB Files, NRA Papers.

25. Marvin Vallone, Oral History, conducted by Eileen Jonas, March 2, 1980, transcribed interview, UNLV Special Collections.

26. Ibid.

27. Interview with Yvonne Mattes, Las Vegas, January 31, 2005.

28. Kit Miller, *Inside the Glitter: Lives of Casino Workers* (Carson City, Nev.: Great Basin Publishing, 2000), 44.

29. Jenny Mead, Oral History, conducted by Pastora Roldan, March 4, 1978, UNLV Special Collections.

30. *Sun*, September 14, 1969.

31. *Nevadan*, October 3, 1982.

32. "An Interview with Alma Whitney: An Oral History Conducted by Claytee D. White," Las Vegas Women in Gaming and Entertainment Oral History Project, 1997, 1–9, UNLV Special Collections.

33. When Whitney arrived in Las Vegas, she stayed with an older sister who had moved to the city several years earlier. Ibid., 13, 27, 40–44.

34. "Decision and Direction of Election," December 24, 1969, 8–16, folder: NLRB Case 31-RC-1251, Hacienda Hotel Re. Security Guards, in NLRB Files, NRA Papers.

35. On the conduct, duties, and uniform regulations of security guards, see C. W. Callaham, "Security Guards Information Folders," August 1, 1976, folder: Security Guards vs. Landmark, 1980, in Miscellaneous Labor Files, NRA Papers.

36. On background of guards, see folder: Organizing of Security Guards (Four Queens), in Miscellaneous Labor Files, NRA Papers. On income, see "Security Guards Wages," folder: Security Guards vs. Landmark, 1980, in Miscellaneous Labor Files, NRA Papers. Also, *Sun*, June 2, 1975; July 13, 1975.

37. *Las Vegas Today*, February 15, 1977.

38. On surveillance technology, see Margaret B. Parkinson, "How Sophisticated Can You Get?" *Gaming Business Magazine*, January 1981, 6–10, folder: Gambling-Surveillance, in Vertical Files, UNLV Special Collections. In same folder, see Howard J. Klein, "A Systems Strategy for Winning the Security War," *Gaming Business* 4, no. 1 (January 1984): 46–47; and clipping by Ron Turner, "Surveillance and Security: An Art in Itself," n.d.

39. Interview with Dick Thomas, June 15, 1998, Las Vegas. Thomas was head of Teamsters Local 995 from 1968 to 1991. Several unions in the state were formed in the late 1920s

and early 1930s, during the construction Hoover Dam. Joseph E. Stevens, *Hoover Dam: An American Adventure* (Norman: University of Oklahoma Press, 1988), 235.

40. These are the words of Dick Thomas, quoted in *Las Vegas Today*, January 1, 1976.

41. See "Right to Work," box 1029, folder 9, Papers of Governor Charles Russell, NSMA Special Collections. On the impact and significance of right-to-work laws, see Michael Goldfield, *The Decline of Organized Labor in the United States* (Chicago: University of Chicago Press, 1987), 185–87; and Albert Rees, *The Economics of Trade Unions*, 3rd ed. (Chicago: University of Chicago Press, 1989), 122–24.

42. For a union leader's comment on Nevada's right-to-work law, see Al Bramlet to Governor Robert Laxalt, January 10, 1967, box: Misc. 1-B, file: Paul D. Laxalt, Governor, Federation Papers, NSHS.

43. After 1958, an initiative petition required signatures from 10 percent of the voters in thirteen of the state's seventeen counties in order to qualify for the ballot. This provision was "democratic" in that it required petitioners to collect a significant number of signatures in most of Nevada's counties; it was undemocratic in that most Nevadans lived in just two of the state's counties. It was objectively antiunion because the vast majority of union members in the state resided in those two counties. See Mary Ellen Glass, "Nevada in the Fifties—A Glance at State Politics and Economics," *Nevada Historical Society Quarterly* 19, no. 2 (1976): 134–35. See also unpublished script for labor documentary, by Guy Louis Rocha, state archivist at the Nevada State Museum and Archives, Carson City, Nevada; and *Review-Journal*, April 8, 1984. The subject as it relates to Southern Nevada is discussed in Michael Andrew Nyre, "Union Jackpot: Culinary Workers Local 226, Las Vegas Nevada, 1970–2000" (master's thesis, California State University, Fullerton), 27–28.

44. On right-to-work laws and union hiring halls, see Archibald Cox, Derek Curtis Bok, and Robert A. Gorman, *Labor Law: Cases and Materials*, 9th ed. (Mineola, N.Y.: Foundation Press, 1981), 1076–1082; and Hal Rothman, *Neon Metropolis: How Las Vegas Started the Twenty-First Century* (New York: Routledge, 2002), 65–67. For more on the language of union shop arrangements after passage of right-to-work laws, see union security clauses and "check-off" agreements in labor contracts.

45. On the use of the strike, see Heckscher, *The New Unionism: Employee Involvement in the Changing Corporation*, 30–32.

46. The addresses and leaders of local labor unions in Las Vegas during the 1960s are identified in "List of Local Unions," box 6, folder 13, Oran K. Gragson Collection, UNLV Special Collections. The council also engaged in community service work, promoting the activities of organizations like the United Way and the Red Cross.

47. See "Executive Board Meeting, December 21, 1946," box: Executive Board Minutes [1944–1986], Quarterly Reports, folder: Executive Board Minutes, 1946, Federation Papers, NSHS.

48. "An Interview with Essie Shelton Jacobs: An Oral History Conducted by Claytee D. White," Las Vegas Women in Gaming and Entertainment Oral History Project, 1997, 25, UNLV Special Collections.

CHAPTER 3: THE FIRST WORK STOPPAGES

1. "An Interview with Alma Whitney: An Oral History Conducted by Claytee D. White," Las Vegas Women in Gaming and Entertainment Oral History Project, 1997, 39, UNLV Special Collections. On workplace relations in southern textile mills, see I. A. Newby, *Plain Folk in the New South: Social Change and Cultural Persistence, 1880–1915* (Baton Rouge: Louisiana State University Press, 1989).

2. Jenny Mead, Oral History, conducted by Pastora Roldan, March 4, 1978, UNLV Special Collections.

3. Ibid.

4. Senate Report, 98th Cong., 68.

5. HERE traces its origins to the 1890s. In 1970 HERE had 460,000 members nationally, when the Las Vegas Culinary had 17,000 members and was HERE's second largest affiliate. Local 165 of the Bartenders and Beverage Dispensers Union was the official name of the smaller organization mentioned. See Mel Sandler, "A Return to Fundamentals: Make a Choice," *Cornell Hotel and Restaurant Administration Quarterly*, May 1973, 4; *Sun*, March 8, 1970; March 15, 1970; and Hal Rothman, *Neon Metropolis: How Las Vegas Started the Twenty-First Century* (New York: Routledge, 2002), 66–67.

6. See Robbins E. Cahill, "Recollections of Work in State Politics, Government, Taxation, Gaming Control, Clark County Administration and the Nevada Resort Association," 1438–41, UNOHP, Reno. Mary Ellen Glass of the University of Nevada, Reno, interviewed Cahill sixteen times between November 1971 and August 1972, in Las Vegas. The conversations were recorded and later transcribed.

7. Senate Report, 98th Cong., 68; and A. D. Hopkins, "Al Bramlet: The Organizer," *The First 100 Persons Who Shaped Southern Nevada*, at www.1st100.com/part3bramlet.html, 1–3. See also, D. W. Everett, "Report of Mediation and Conciliation in Labor Dispute," box 0217, file 28, Papers of Governor Charles Russell, NSMA Special Collections. On Bramlet, see too Sally Denton and Roger Morris, *The Money and the Power: The Making of Las Vegas and Its Hold on America, 1947–2000* (New York: Alfred A. Knopf, 2001), 367. Also, Rothman, *Neon Metropolis*, 70–71.

8. Berkeley L. Bunker, "Life and Work of a Southern Nevada Pioneer: Businessman, Funeral Director, Mormon Church Leader, Legislator, U.S. Senator, and Congressman," UNOHP, Reno.

9. Interview with Mark Massagli, Las Vegas, June 12, 1998. Flippin was deputy commander of Stead Air Force Base in Reno during the war. For more on Flippin, see *Reno Evening Gazette*, November 10, 1952; and Western States Historical Publishers, *Nevada: The Silver State*, vol. 1 (Carson City: Western States Historical Publishers, 1970), 316. Obituaries appeared in *Review-Journal*, January 15, 1985; and *Sun*, January 15, 1985. See also D. W. Everett, "Report of Mediation and Conciliation in Labor Dispute," May 1951, box 0217, folder 32, Papers of Governor Charles Russell.

10. *Agreement between Local 226 and Nevada Industrial Council, 1957*, folder: Culinary Negotiations, 1957–1963, in Culinary Bartender Negotiations Files, NRA Papers. Labor and management occasionally amended contracts with "letters of understanding."

11. Interviews with Mark Massagli, Las Vegas, June 12, 1997, and June 12, 1998; and Dick Thomas, Las Vegas, June 15, 1998.

12. Interview with Dick Thomas, June 15, 1998.

13. "Meeting with Roy Flippin Regarding Culinary Workers and Bartenders Contract," June 10, 1961, folder: Culinary Negotiations, 1957–63, in Culinary Negotiations Files, NRA Papers. Interview with Mark Massagli, June 12, 1998, and interview with Dick Thomas, June 15, 1998.

14. FBI Records, see www.foia.fbi.gov/foiaindex/korshak_sidney.htm. The *New York Times* published a scathing four-part article on Korshak from June 27 to 30, 1976. Korshak maintained a home in Los Angeles from which he made frequent trips to Las Vegas to meet with owners of the Desert Inn, the Sands, and other properties.

15. Testimony of John Cullerton to State of New Jersey Casino Control Commission, July 24, 1984, 346–47, box: Hilton—N.J. Licensing Files (1984), folder: Hilton—Cullerton, Local 226 Papers. See also editorial by Rufus King in *American Bar Association Journal*, October 1976, 1224–25.

16. Deposition of Stanley R. Zax in the Matter of Hilton New Jersey Corporation Casino License Application, May 31, 1984, 23, box: Hilton—N.J. Licensing Files (1984), folder: Hilton N.J., Local 226 Papers; and Barron Hilton to Marshall Korshak, November 29, 1976, box: Hilton—N.J. Licensing Files (1984), folder: Hilton N.J., Local 226 Papers.

17. The words are those of Herman Leavitt of the International Culinary Union, *New York Times*, June 28, 1976. Korshak evidently brought no documents with him to labor negotiations and took few notes during the bargaining process. "I've never seen Sidney get involved in details," as one attorney said of his business methods. "He writes down important figures on the backs of envelopes or pieces of paper," one labor attorney said of him. To the FBI, such comments hinted of secretive and illegal bargaining tactics.

18. See lists of comparative wages rates in folder: Bargaining Data, Culinary Negotiations, 1970, in Culinary Bartender Negotiations Files, NRA Papers.

19. Barbara Land and Myrick Land, *A Short History of Las Vegas* (Reno: University of Nevada Press, 1999), 205.

20. *Handbook of Labor Statistics, 1980b* (Washington, D.C.: Government Printing Office, 1980), table 165, 412. Also, Michael Goldfield, *The Decline of Organized Labor in the United States* (Chicago: University of Chicago Press, 1987), 10–11.

21. U.S. Department of Commerce, *1970 Census of Population*, vol. 1, part 30 (Washington, D.C.: Government Printing Office, 1972), 13. See also statistics compiled by the Las Vegas Chamber of Commerce in *Las Vegas Report 1970*, 2–3, UNLV Special Collections.

22. U.S. Department of Commerce, *1970 Census of Population*, vol. 1, part 30, 4, 30–33. Also, *Quarterly and Fiscal Year Reports of State Gaming Control Board*, box 68, folder: Nevada Gaming Commission, Howard Hughes Collection, UNLV Special Collections.

23. "Report of the Commissioner of Labor," *26th Annual Report and Directory of Labor Unions*, July 1, 1964, to June 30, 1966, 26–27, NSMA Special Collections.

24. *Wall Street Journal*, March 1, 1966.

25. FBI Records, http://foia.fbi.gov/filelink.html?file=/sidneykorshak/sidneykorshak_part02.pdf, 5–8. On the Governor's role, see Grant Sawyer to Eugene Maday, September 29, 1965, box 0321, folder 8, Papers of Governor Grant Sawyer, NSMA Special Collections.

26. Address by Lt. Governor Paul Laxalt before the 12th Annual Dinner of the Federated Employers of Nevada, June 16, 1966, box 0518, folder 39, Papers of Governor Paul Laxalt, NSMA Special Collections. *Nevada State Journal*, October 6, 1975.

27. See speech of Senator Paul Laxalt to American Mining Congress, September 30, 1975, box: AFL—MISC 4A, folder: Paul Laxalt, AFL-CIO State Labor Council Papers, NSHS, Reno.

28. *Reno-Gazette-Journal*, September 2, 1979. Also, Russell R. Elliot, *History of Nevada*, 2nd ed. (Lincoln: University of Nebraska Press, 1987), 355–57.

29. Senate Report, 98th Cong., 68–70; and Al Bramlet to Grant Sawyer, December 20, 1966, box 0332, folder 7, Papers of Governor Grant Sawyer. Also, *Review-Journal*, March 28, and April 3, 12, 19, 20, 21, 1967; and *Nevada State Journal*, May 25, 1967. DCA members included such well-known places as El Cortez, the Golden Nugget, the Fremont, the Horseshoe, the Las Vegas Club, and the Pioneer, most of which were family-owned and family-operated properties with relatively few lodging facilities. One member, the Showboat, was actually located outside the downtown area, on the road to Hoover Dam.

30. *Sun*, April 19, 1967.

31. *Review-Journal*, April 22, 1967; and *Sun*, April 12, 19, 1967. Also Rothman, *Neon Metropolis*, 73.

32. *Review-Journal*, April 23, 1967.

33. *Review-Journal*, April 18, 21, 22, 23, 24, 1967; *Sun*, April 12, 19, 1967, and May 7, 1971. Also, interview with Jeff McColl, Las Vegas, June 23, 1998. Employers suggested business in the struck properties declined by only 10 to 15 percent during the strike, but the closing of dining facilities and hotel operations no doubt resulted in a much larger decline of business.

34. Cahill, "Recollections of Work in State Politics," 948–49.

35. Ibid., 1422–23. NRA headquarters were on Sahara Boulevard, just off the Strip.

36. George L. Ullom, "Politics and Development in Las Vegas, 1930s–1970s," 119–21, an oral history conducted by Jamie Coughtry, 1989, UNOHP, Reno.

37. Edward A. Olsen, "My Careers as a Journalist in Oregon, Idaho, and Nevada; in Nevada Gaming Control; and at the University of Nevada," 461, Oral History Project, UBOHP, Reno. Also, *Las Vegas Today*, December 17, 1975; and *Review-Journal, The First 100*, at www.1st100.com/part2/cahill.html, 1–6.

38. Alvin Benedict of the Stardust was president of the NRA in 1968. Benedict began his career in Las Vegas in 1952 with the Last Frontier Hotel and later worked at the Desert Inn. Joe Digles, former editor of the *Review-Journal*, wrote several stories for the NRA during these years. *Sun*, July 31, 1969. Also, Cahill, "Recollections of Work in State Politics," 1422–23.

39. Cahill, "Recollections of Work in State Politics," 1422–23.

40. See "Memorandum," 1970, folder: Miscellaneous Correspondence, in Culinary Bartender Negotiations Files, NRA Papers. Also Cahill, "Recollections of Work in State Politics," 1439.

41. Cahill, "Recollections of Work in State Politics," 1422–23.

42. Interview with Dick Thomas, Las Vegas, June 15, 1998. Local 631 was the original Teamsters in Las Vegas. There was also a Teamster Local 14 in the city that represented

general sales drivers. The union of operating engineers in Las Vegas sprang from a merger of locals in California and Nevada during the 1950s. *Review-Journal*, July 25, 1969.

43. Interview with Dick Thomas, Las Vegas, June 15, 1998. Plasters, sheet metal workers, and other groups of construction workers in Las Vegas won pay raises of more than 10 percent annually in 1969 by waging strikes against the Southern Nevada Contractors Association. See also *Sun*, July 11, 16, 18, and August 1, 1969. On the cost of living, see *Sun*, July 24, 1969.

44. The strike began on July 24. Interview with Dick Thomas, June 15, 1998; and Cahill, "Recollections of Work in State Politics," 1437. Also, *Review-Journal*, July 25, 1969; *Sun*, July 25–27, 1969. On terms of the contract, see *Sun*, July 29, 1969.

45. *Review-Journal*, July 25, 1969; *Sun*, July 25, 26, 1969.

46. Cahill, "Recollections of Work in State Politics," 1437–40.

47. Ibid.

48. The Culinary proposed across-the-board raises of 15 percent in the first year of a three-year contract, and 10 percent raises each of the following two years. *Review-Journal*, March 9, 1970; *Sun*, March 10, 1970. Cahill, "Recollections of Work in State Politics," 1440.

49. Cahill, "Recollections of Work in State Politics," 1438–40.

50. *Sun*, March 11, 13, 16, 1970. Details of the strike are discussed in Bureau of National Affairs, *Labor Arbitration Reports*, vol. 56 (Washington, D.C.: Government Printing Office, 1971), 1263–70, in an arbitration award involving musicians, stagehands, and variety artists.

51. *Review-Journal*, March 10, 1970.

52. Cahill, "Recollections of Work in State Politics," 949, 1443–49. Also, William Campbell to W. Byer, April 2, 1970, folder: Miscellaneous Correspondence, in Culinary Bartender Negotiations Files, NRA Papers. The Florida-based Lum's Corporation had purchased Caesars Palace.

53. William Campbell to W. Byer, April 2, 1970. Campbell noted that a few security personnel who belonged to members of Local 151 of the Independent Watchmen's Association did report for work.

54. *Sun*, March 12, 1970.

55. *Review-Journal*, March 12, 1970.

56. *Sun*, March 13, 1970; *Review-Journal*, March 14, 1970.

57. Statement by Governor Paul Laxalt, March 11, 1970, box 0445, folder 42, Papers of Governor Paul Laxalt. See also *Sun* March 11, 1970; and *Review-Journal*, 16, 1970.

58. *Sun*, March 13, 1970; *Review-Journal*, March 13, 15, 1970.

59. George E. Franklin Jr. to Al Bramlet and William Campbell, March 11, 1970, folder: Miscellaneous Correspondence, in Culinary Bartender Negotiations Files, NRA Papers.

60. *Sun*, March 14, 1970. The Hughes properties denied that they alone wanted to defend the picket line clause.

61. *Sun*, March 15, 17, 1970. In this final meeting, Alex Shoofey of the International, Robert Cannon of the Tropicana, and Al Benedict of the Hughes properties represented

management, and Bramlet alone represented labor. The new picket line clause also prohibited workers from honoring lines set up by members of other unions who were not actually employed by the resorts, such as construction workers who were working for private contractors.

62. *Sun*, March 16, 1970.

63. *Review-Journal*, March 17, 1970.

64. Ibid.

65. Interview with Dick Thomas, Las Vegas, June 15, 1998. Thomas moved to Las Vegas after graduating from high school in 1945. He became a member of the Teamsters the same year, when the union organized cab drivers. He was active in union affairs throughout the early 1960s, and became the first secretary-treasurer of Teamsters Local 881 in 1964. When the Teamsters created Local 995, he became its head.

66. *Review-Journal*, March 18, 1970.

CHAPTER 4: THE STRUGGLE FOR THE CASINOS

1. Insights into the size and nature of the nonunion workforce in the 1960s and 1970s can be gleaned from NRLB rulings. See, for example, "Decision and Order," July 26, 1971, 1–3, folder: Teamsters v. Sahara, Case No. 31-RC-1727, in NLRB Files, NRA Papers; and "Decision and Order," October 16, 1970, 1–4, folder: I.A.M. v. Caesars Palace, Case No. 31-RC-1508, in NLRB Files, NRA Papers. See also, "Vegas Casino Employees Reject Proposed Union in NLRB Election," *Wall Street Journal*, May 19, 1971.

2. Frank A. Modica to Security Guards, October 17, 1974, folder: Union Organizing Materials General, in Union Organizing Files, NRA Papers. Also, *Review-Journal*, June 2, 13, 17, 1975; September 14, 1975.

3. Peter G. Demos Jr., *Casino Supervision: A Basic Guide* (Atlantic City: CSI Press, n.d.), 61–62, UNLV Special Collections. On the skills of dealers, see also "Hotel, Gaming, and Related Occupations," a report prepared by the Employment Security Research Section of the Nevada Employment Security Department, September 1985, 18–22, NSHS, Reno.

4. Doug Charles, Oral History, conducted by Colleen Seifert, February 29, 1980, untranscribed interview, UNLV Special Collections.

5. Silvio Petricciani, "The Evolution of Gaming in Nevada: The Twenties to the Eighties," 224, UNOHP, Reno.

6. Tony Grasso, Oral History, conducted by Colleen Seifert, February 29, 1980, untranscribed interview, UNLV Special Collections.

7. As quoted in Terri Gilbert, "Divided We Fall: The Unionization of Casino Card Dealers," 7, unpublished manuscript, UNLV Special Collections. Also, James H. Frey, "Labor Issues in the Gaming Industry," *Nevada Public Affairs Review*, no. 2 (1986): 32–38.

8. Ronald W. Smith, Frederick Preston, and Harry L. Humphries, "Alienation from Work: A Study of Casino Card Dealers," in *Gambling and Society: Interdisciplinary Studies on the Subject of Gambling*, ed. William R. Eadington (Springfield, Ill.: Charles C. Thomas, 1976), 229–43.

9. *Review-Journal*, October 6, 1966.

10. Marvin Vallone, Oral History, conducted by Eileen Jonas, March 2, 1980, 4, transcribed interview, UNLV Special Collections.

11. *Sun*, February 17, 1966.

12. Danny Kaminski, Oral History, conducted by Brian Corcoran, March 14, 1978, untranscribed interview, UNLV Special Collections.

13. Grasso, Oral History.

14. On controversies generated by tip-pooling policies, see Charles E. Springer to Nevada State Gaming Control Board, May 2, 1972, box 0567, folder 2, Papers of Governor Mike O'Callahan, NSMA Special Collections. See also Charles E. Springer to Philip P. Hannifin, May 18, 1972, and Julian C. Smith Jr. to Stanley P. Jones, October 21, 1971, box 544, folder 19, Papers of Governor Mike O'Callaghan.

15. Silvio Petricciani, "The Evolution of Gaming in Nevada," 226, UNOHP, Reno.

16. "An Open Letter to Our Governor," August 7, 1964, box 0309, folder 29, Papers of Governor Grant Sawyer, NSMA Special Collections.

17. Vallone, Oral History, 3–4.

18. *Sun*, February 24, 1966.

19. *Sun*, February 17, 1966.

20. An Open Letter to Our Governor," August 7, 1964.

21. As quoted in Frey, "Labor Issues in the Gaming Industry," 33.

22. See Gilbert, "Divided We Fall," 14–16. Also, Frey, "Labor Issues in the Gaming Industry," 33.

23. Charles, Oral History.

24. *Herald-Examiner*, January 25, 1966.

25. "An Open Letter to Our Governor," August 7, 1964.

26. On dealers' attitudes toward unionization, see Smith et al., "Alienation from Work"; Frey, "Labor Issues in the Gaming Industry;" and Gilbert "Divided We Fall." Interview with Norman Domsky, February 8, 2005, Las Vegas. Also, Rick Wittway to Governor Paul Laxalt, February 24, 1969, box 0494, folder 16, Papers of Governor Paul Laxalt, NSMA Special Collections.

27. Fyhen was a retired machinist and a veteran organizer. He served as secretary-treasurer of the Central Labor Council from 1933 to 1947. On Fyhen's life in Clark County, see Ragnald Fyhen, "Labor Notes," in box 1, folder 1, Ragnald Fyhen Collection, UNLV Specials Collections.

28. On the business community's view of Hanley, see Pete Peterson to P. A. McCarran, June 1, 1950, Collection NC 430, folder 30, UNOHP, Reno. Also, *Sun*, December 1, 1965; August 10, 1966; and November 25, 1969. Hanley was also linked to the beating of Walter Vickers in Las Vegas in June 1956. Vickers was a business agent for a union opposed to Hanley and eventually played a role in Hanley's ouster. Hanley had moved to Las Vegas from Dallas, Texas.

29. *Sun*, November 29, 1965; December 1, 1965; and November 25, 1969. AFCGE officers included Truman Scott, James Miller, David Bates, Robert Murphy, and Don Emery. Hanley's son, Gramby Hanley, was then serving a fifteen-year sentence in the county jail.

30. "Memo: Gaming Union Status," May 24, 1967, folder: Unionizing of Casino Employees, in Union Organizing Files, NRA Papers. Also, *Herald-Examiner*, January 26, 1966; and *Sun*, November 25, 1969.

31. *Sun*, January 13, 1966. Albert Dreyer was Hanley's attorney.

32. *Nevada State Journal*, August 25, 1964.

33. Charles G. Munson to Governor Grant Sawyer, August 11, 1964, box 0309, folder 29, Papers of Governor Grant Sawyer.

34. *Labor Relations Reference Manual: The Law and Facts of Labor Relations*, vol. 59 (Washington D.C.: Bureau of National Affairs, 1965), 1313–16. Also, *Herald-Examiner*, January 25, 1966.

35. *Sun*, January 16, 1965.

36. Ibid. The union's lead attorney was Albert M. Dreyer.

37. Tom Hanley to Grant Sawyer, September 25, 1964, box 0309, folder 29; Warren Bayley to Grant Sawyer, October 20, 1964, box 0309, folder 29; and Grant Sawyer to Tom Hanley, October 30, 1964, box 0309, folder 20, all in Papers of Governor Grant Sawyer.

38. Grant Sawyer to Tom Hanley, September 4, 1964, box 0309, folder 29, Papers of Governor Grant Sawyer. Also, *Reno Evening Gazette*, July 31, 1964.

39. See Edward A. Olsen, "My Careers as a Journalist in Oregon, Idaho, and Nevada, in Nevada Gaming Control, and at the University of Nevada," 457, Oral History Project, UNOHP, Reno. See also *Sun* October 1, 2, 1964; and *Review-Journal*, October 19, 1964.

40. *Labor Relations Reference Manual: The Law and the Facts of Labor Relations*, vol. 58 (Washington D.C.: Bureau of National Affairs, 1965), 1455–59. The board asserted jurisdiction over properties whose gross annual revenue from gambling was in excess of $550,000. The board noted that eight planes a day flew into Las Vegas, while forty-eight reached Reno. It directed elections at the New Pioneer Club, which were held in late 1966. Also, *Herald-Examiner*, January 25, 1966; *Sun*, November 20, 1964.

41. "We Speak," October 1968, clipping, folder: Unionizing of Casino Employees, in Union Organizing Files, NRA Papers.

42. *Sun*, January 6, 13, 1966; February 16, 1966. A rival of Hanley, Bob Feldman, established the Hotel and Casino Employees Union before the election. The union received no votes in the Golden Gate election and merged with Hanley's organization after the election. Feldman became a business agent for Hanley.

43. *Sun*, February 17, 1966.

44. *Review-Journal*, May 12, 1966; *Sun*, March 29, 1966; *Herald-Examiner*, January 26, 1966.

45. *Review-Journal*, April 3, 1966.

46. *Review-Journal*, May 12, 1966.

47. *Sun*, June, 26, 1966; July 7, 8, 1966; September 22, 1966; *Review-Journal*, July 9, 1966. "I left the position," Fyhen said, "because I haven't been too close to the union's affairs."

48. *Review-Journal*, November 3, 1966; *Sun*, November 3, 1966. Hanley was arrested at his union headquarters at 111 N. Seventh Street. The day after the assault, federal agents

returned to AFCGE headquarters looking for a gun that IRS officers had seen. They never found it.

49. *Sun*, November 22, 1966; *Sun*, December 21, 1966. For more on Hanley's legal problems, see *Sun*, May 1, 1968; *Review-Journal*, May 27, 1968; and June 11, 1968. See also "Thomas Burke Hanley v. Casino Operations, Inc.," a complaint (Civil No. 1638) filed in U.S. District Court on May 26, 1971, 5–6, in Union Organizing Files, NRA Papers.

50. Gilbert, "Divided We Fall," 11. Also, *Review-Journal*, June 21, 22, 1967; September 6, 1967; and *Sun*, June 22, 1967.

51. John R. McQueen to General Nigro, January 1968, folder: Unionizing Casino Workers, in Union Organizing Files, NRA Papers.

52. Rick Sommers, "To Whom It May Concern," n.d., folder: Unionizing Casino Workers, in Union Organizing Files, NRA Papers.

53. Digles to Vogliotti, "Memo: Gaming Union State," May 24, 1967, folder: Unionizing Casino Workers, in Union Organizing Files, NRA Papers.

54. *Sun*, April 19, 1967; and *Review-Journal*, April 18, 24, 1967. A final blow for Callahan and Local 7 came later in the year, when dealers at a small casino in northern Las Vegas, Jerry's Nugget, handed Callahan's and all the other fledgling unions a crushing defeat. See *Sun*, June 22, 1967; September 6, 1967.

55. *Review-Journal*, October 22, 1971; November 9, 1971; and *Sun*, November 13, 1971.

56. William N. Campbell to Walter P. Loomis Jr., October 4, 1971, folder: Dealer Organizing, Tropicana, in Union Organizing Files, NRA Papers.

57. Seyfarth, Shaw, Fairweather and Geraldson, "Guide for Management and Supervisory Personnel in Event of Union Organization Activity," 1970, folder: Dealer Organizing, Tropicana, in Union Organizing Files, NRA Papers.

58. Julian C. Smith Jr. to Stanley P. Jones, October 21, 1971, box 544, folder 19, Papers of Governor Mike O'Callaghan. It ultimately took the United States District Court to settle the tip-pooling issue. In 1975 the court rejected a dealer's argument that tips handed to him were his personal property and ruled that employers could require employees to participate in tip-pooling systems. For more on the tip-sharing controversy, see Moen v. Las Vegas International Hotel, October 2, 1975, box 0822, folder 2, Papers of Governor Mike O'Callaghan. Also, *Review-Journal*, April 27, 1972.

59. *Sun*, May 15, 1974; June 12, 1974.

60. "Union Propaganda," n.d., clipping, folder: Sahara Dealers Organizing Drive 1974, in Union Organizing Files, NRA Papers.

61. Sahara Dealers Association to Employees, n.d., folder: Sahara Dealers Organizing Drive 1974, in Union Organizing Files, NRA Papers.

62. *Sun*, September 5, 1974.

63. Vernon Daniel and Chet Edwards to All Supervisors, September 7, 1974, folder: Sahara Dealers Organizing Drive 1974, in Union Organizing Files, NRA Papers.

64. Chet Edwards to Dealers, Baccarat Game Starters, Shills, Keno Runners, Keno Writers and Cardroom Brushmen, September 24, 1974, folder: Sahara Dealers Organizing Drive 1974, in Union Organizing Drives, NRA Papers.

65. *Sun*, October 3, 1974.

66. Vernon Daniel and Chet Edwards to Employees, October 2, 1974, folder, Sahara Dealers Organizing Drive 1974, in Union Organizing Files, NRA Papers.

67. *Review-Journal*, October 6, 1974.

68. *Sun*, November 13, 1974; December 28, 1974. Frank Modica was the general manager at the Desert Inn.

69. *Review-Journal*, November 8, 1974; and *Sun* November 26, 1974.

70. *Sun*, December 28, 1974.

71. *Review-Journal*, January 1, 1975.

72. *Sun*, April 13, 1975. Dealers at the Landmark voted 94 to 72 in favor of unionism. Shortly after the vote at the MGM, dealers at the Silver Slipper voted 3 to 1 against unionization.

73. Al Benedict to Supervision, April 3, 1975, folder: MGM Organizing Drive 1975, in Union Organizing Files, NRA Papers.

74. Al Benedict to Dealers, April 3, 1975, folder: MGM Organizing Drive 1975, in Union Organizing Files, NRA Papers.

75. Ibid.

76. William N. Campbell to Top Management of Member Establishments, December 16, 1974, folder: Campaign Material—Dealers Organization, in Union Organizing Files, NRA Papers.

77. Ibid.

78. W. N. Campbell to All Member Establishments, December 27, 1974, folder: Campaign Material—Dealers Organization, in Union Organizing Files, NRA Papers.

79. William N. Campbell to Top Management of Member Establishments, December 16, 1974, folder: Campaign Material—Dealers Organization, in Union Organizing Files, NRA Papers.

80. W. N. Campbell to All Chief Executives, January 24, 1975, 1, folder: Campaign Material—Dealers Organization, in Union Organizing Files, NRA Papers.

81. "Confidential Comments," n.d., folder: Dealer Organizing Campaigns, Frontier, in Union Organizing Files, NRA Papers. The Frontier faced an organizing drive in 1976.

82. See NLRB Case No. 31-RC-2960, folder: Desert Inn/Organization of Dealers, in NLRB Files, NRA Papers. Marco Vega was the labor organizer. The board also overturned the election at the Landmark Hotel, where BRAC had also scored a victory. See NLRB Case No. 31-RC-3052 Landmark/BRAC, in Union Organizing Files, NRA Papers.

83. Campbell to Top Management, December 16, 1974, 4−6, folder: Campaign Material, Dealers Organization, in Union Organizing Files, NRA Papers.

84. Edward A. Olsen, "My Careers as a Journalist in Oregon, Idaho, and Nevada; in Nevada Gaming Control; and at the University of Nevada," 456, UNOHP, Reno.

85. *Valley Times*, January 6, 1976.

86. *Sun*, January 1, 1976; January 6, 1976. Also, *Review-Journal*, January 1, 1976.

87. William N. Campbell to All Members of the Executive Committee, February 19, 1971, folder: Dealer Organizing, Tropicana, in Union Organizing Files, NRA Papers.

88. On attitudes of nonunion workers to labor organizers, see I. A. Newby, *Plain Folk in the New South: Social Change and Cultural Persistence, 1880–1915* (Baton Rouge: Louisiana State University Press, 1989), 519–46.

CHAPTER 5: WORKPLACE INCIDENTS

1. "Decision on Grievance," October 8, 1970, folder: Teamsters v. Frontier, (Herman Buskin), in Arbitration Files, NRA Papers.

2. On the modern union arbitration process, see David Lewin and Richard B. Peterson, *The Modern Grievance Procedure in the Unites States* (New York: Quorum Books, 1988). Useful articles on the process include Peter Feuille, "Changing Patterns in Dispute Resolution," in *Labor Economics and Industrial Relations: Markets and Institutions*, ed. Clark Kerr and Paul D. Staudohar (Cambridge, Mass.: Harvard University Press, 1994), 475–511; David E. Feller, "Arbitration: The Days of Its Glory Are Numbered," *Industrial Relations Law Journal* 2 (1977): 97–130; Michael E. Gordon and Sandra J. Miller, "Grievances: A Review of Research and Practice," *Personnel Psychology* 37 (1984): 117–46. Also, Paul Staudohar, *The Sports Industry and Collective Bargaining*, 2nd ed. (Ithaca, N.Y.: Industrial Labor Relations Press, 1989).

3. On matters of control and hierarchy see David Montgomery, *Workers' Control in America: Studies in the History of Work, Technology, and Labor Struggles* (Cambridge: Cambridge University Press, 1979); Richard Edwards, *Contested Terrain: The Transformation of the Workplace in the Twentieth Century* (New York: Basic Books, 1979); Dan Clawson, *Bureaucracy and the Labor Process: The Transformation of U.S. Industry, 1860–1920* (New York: Monthly Review Press, 1980). Also, Robert R. Locke, *The Collapse of the American Management Mystique* (Oxford: Oxford University Press, 1996). On work culture, see Rick Fantasia, *Cultures of Solidarity: Consciousness, Action, and Contemporary American Workers* (Berkeley: University of California Press, 1988).

4. Feuille, "Changing Patterns in Dispute Resolution," 495. In three cases involving steelworkers, the Court ruled that arbitration would be undermined if the courts had the final say on the merits of the awards; see *United Steelworkers of America v. Warrior & Gulf Navigation Co.*, 363 U.S. 574 (1960); *United Steelworkers of America v. American Manufacturing Co.*, 363 U.S. 564 (1960); *United Steelworkers of America v. Enterprise Wheel & Car Corp.*, 363 U.S. 593 1960 (collectively known as the "Steelworkers Trilogy" cases).

5. See "Appearances," October 3, 1985, 9–14, folder: 31-CB-5993, NRA Member Hotels v. Culinary Workers 226 RE: Decisions, in NLRB Files, NRA Papers.

6. The Culinary contract said employees could wait thirty days before filing grievances and made three written warnings within ninety days sufficient grounds for suspension or discharge. See "Time Limits Set for Grievances," *Topics*, October 1985, a Local 226 publication in UNLV Special Collections.

7. *Agreement between Culinary Union Local 226 and Nevada Industrial Council, 1957*, 3, folder: Culinary Negotiations 1957–63, in Culinary Bartender Negotiations Files, NRA Papers.

8. Interview with Greg Smith, former legal counsel for NRA, Las Vegas, April 14, 1998. Also, interview with Gary Moss, former legal counsel for NRA, Las Vegas, March 4, 2005; and interview with Alan Ware, former business agent at the Las Vegas Musicians Union, Las Vegas, March 8, 2005.

9. Some workers filed multiple grievances, even within the same year. On arbitration and the Culinary, see Vincent H. Eade, "Grievance and Arbitration Trends within the

Culinary Workers Union, Local 226," *Labor Studies Journal* 16 (Spring 1993): 17–31. The percentage of grievances resolved in labor's favor varied widely across unionized industries. On national patterns of arbitration, see Feuille, "Changing Patterns in Dispute Resolution," 494–95.

10. "Decision and Award," September 19, 1975, 3–9, folder: Circus Circus v. Culinary, Arbitration Award, Maldonado/Brough Discharges, in Arbitration Files, NRA Papers. See also "Opinion and Award," July 9, 1975, 1–8, folder: Bartenders v. MGM Grand, Award— Leo Kotin, Jack Brady Discharge, in Arbitration Files; in same folder, see "Post-Hearing Statement of the Company," n.d., 1–4.

11. "Opinion and Award," March 27, 1967, folder: Thunderbird-Fillizola, John-1976- Won, in Arbitration Awards, Local 226 Papers.

12. Ibid.

13. See grievance reports of switchboard operators, box 3, folder 13, Oran K. Gragson Collection, UNLV Special Collections.

14. See "Opinion and Award," June 24, 1968, box 3, folder 13, Oran K. Gragson Collection.

15. Ibid.

16. Grievance reports of switchboard operators, box 3, folder 13, Oran K. Gragson Collection.

17. "Award," July 29, 1971, 1–3, folder: Sands-Durant, Noel-1971-Won, in Arbitration Awards, Local 226 Papers.

18. "Post-Hearing Brief of the Hotel," July 6, 1971, 1–4, Culinary v. Sands, Brief and Award, Noel Durant—Discharge, in Arbitration Files, NRA Papers.

19. Ibid. Durant had received four months of unemployment compensation.

20. "Post-Hearing Brief of the Hotel," November 17, 1970, folder: Culinary v. Sahara, Briefs and Award, Anthony Sarmiento—Discharge, in Arbitration Files, NRA Papers.

21. "Union's Brief," November 17, 1970, folder: Culinary v. Sahara, Briefs and Award, Anthony Sarmiento—Discharge, in Arbitration Files, NRA Papers.

22. "Opinion and Award," December 3, 1970, folder: Sahara-Sarmiento, in Arbitration Awards, Local 226 Papers.

23. "Opinion and Award," June 20, 1972, folder: Dunes-DeJarnette, Ruth-1972-Lost, in Arbitration Awards, Local 226 Papers.

24. Ibid.

25. "Award of the Arbitrator," October 4, 1974, Desert Inn-Corrow, Gail-1974-Lost, in Arbitration Awards, Local 226 Papers.

26. Ibid.

27. Ibid.

28. *Collective Bargaining Agreement between NRA and Culinary and Bartenders Union, 1970–1973,* 29, in Expired Labor Contracts, NRA Papers.

29. "Post-Hearing Brief Statement of the Company," n.d., folder: Culinary v. Frontier Hotel—Elaine Hallusco, in Arbitration Files, NRA Papers.

30. Ibid.

31. "Memorandum Decision and Award," August 19, 1969, folder: Frontier-Hallusco, in Arbitration Awards, Local 226 Papers.

32. "Post-Hearing Statement of the Hotel," n.d., folder: Culinary v. MGM Grand—Discharge of Turner Moore, in Arbitration Files, NRA Papers.

33. "Arbitration Opinion and Award," February 26, 1977, folder: MGM-Moore, Turner-1977-Won, in Arbitration Awards, Local 226 Papers.

34. See Fantasia, *Cultures of Solidarity*, 78–81.

35. "Brief on Behalf of the Union," April 20, 1979, 41–43, 113, folder: Musicians v. NRA and Summa, Case No. 31-CB-2368 and 310CA-6306, in NLRB Files, NRA Papers.

36. "Opinion and Award," July 16, 1973, folder: Musicians v. Landmark, Opinion and Award, RE: Chuck Kovacs Trio, in Arbitration Files, NRA Papers.

37. Ibid.

38. "Agreement between Fremont Hotel and Culinary Union, 1967," 10–11, folder: Culinary Negotiations, 1967, in Culinary Bartender Negotiations Files, NRA Papers.

39. "Decision and Award," March 30, 1970, folder: Dunes-General-Cocktail Boots-Lost, in Arbitration Awards, Local 226 Papers.

40. Ibid.

41. Ibid.

42. *Collective Bargaining Agreement between the Culinary Workers Union and Resort Hotels, 1964–1967*, 7, Culinary Negotiations, 1967, in Culinary Bartender Negotiations Files, NRA Papers. See also, *Collective Bargaining Agreement between Nevada Resort Association and Culinary Union, 1970–1973*, 26–27, in Expired Labor Contracts, NRA Papers.

43. "Opinion and Award," October 26, 1976, folder: MGM-Hamamura, Billie Jo-1976-Won, in Arbitration Awards, Local 226 Papers.

44. See "Rules and Posting," in *Collective Bargaining Agreement between NRA and Culinary and Bartenders Union, 1970–1973*, 45.

45. "Opinion and Award," October 26, 1976, folder: MGM-Hamamura, Billie Joe-1976-Won, in Arbitration Awards, Local 226 Papers. See also "Uniforms and Facilities," in *Collective Bargaining Agreement Between NRA and Culinary and Bartenders Union, 1970–1973*, 39.

46. "Opinion and Award," October 26, 1976.

47. "Award and Opinion of the Arbitrator," October 9, 1970, folder: M. Duca v. Frontier, in Arbitration Files, NRA Papers.

48. Ibid. See also "Post-Hearing Brief of the Hotel, September 26, 1970," in same folder and file.

49. "Award," November 12, 1981, MGM Grand Hotel vs. Teamsters Union, Beards, in Arbitration Files, NRA Papers.

50. "Security Guards vs. Landmark, 1980," see "Uniform Regulations," August 1, 1980, 1–2, in Arbitration Files, NRA Papers.

51. "Opinion and Award," September 29, 1978, Teamsters v. Showboat, Award—Richard Basile, Stanley Laird Grievance, in Arbitration Files, NRA Papers.

52. "Post-Hearing Brief of the Hotel," n.d., folder: Teamsters v. Showboat, Award—Richard Basile, Stanley Laird Grievance, in Arbitration Files, NRA Papers.

53. "Opinion and Award," September 29, 1978.

54. On the courts and the arbitration process, see Arthur A. Sloane and Fred Witney, *Labor Relations*, 5th ed. (Englewood Cliffs, N.J., Prentice-Hall, 1985), 240–42.

55. "Order Denying Motion to Confirm Arbitrator's Award and Granting Motion for Summary Judgement," March 30, 1986, folder: Case No. CV-LV-83-853-LDG, Aladdin Hotel v. Culinary Union Local 226, in Court Cases Files, NRA Papers.

CHAPTER 6: FIGHTING FOR EQUAL RIGHTS

1. For an overview of the literature on struggles over discriminatory employment practices, see Essay on Sources.

2. On the history of African Americans in Southern Nevada during the postwar years, see Elizabeth Nelson Patrick, "The Black Experience in Southern Nevada," *Nevada Historical Society Quarterly* 22, no. 2 (Summer 1979): 128–40; Earnest Bracey, "The African Americans," in *The Peoples of Las Vegas: One City, Many Faces*, ed. Jerry Simich and Thomas Wright (Reno: University of Nevada Press, 2005), 78–97. On women in the resort industry, see Claytee D. White, "The Roles of African American Women in the Las Vegas Gaming Industry, 1940–1980," master's thesis, UNLV Special Collections. For a good general perspective, Eugene P. Moehring's *Resort City in the Sunbelt: Las Vegas, 1930–1970* (Las Vegas: University of Nevada Press, 1989), 173–202. On African Americans in the area in more recent times, M. Gottdiener, Claudia C. Collins, and David R. Dickens, *Las Vegas: The Social Production of an All-American City* (Malden, Mass.: Blackwell Publishers, 1999), 16, 103–4.

3. *Review-Journal*, August 24, 1980.

4. Arlone Scott, Oral Interview, conducted by Glen Ette Davis, June 3, 1975, transcribed interview, UNLV Special Collections.

5. On the significance of housing conditions in black communities, see Thomas J. Sugrue, *The Origins of the Urban Crisis: Race and Inequality in Postwar Detroit* (Princeton: Princeton University Press, 1996), 33–88.

6. "An Interview with Lucille Bryant: An Oral History Conducted by Claytee White," Las Vegas Women in Gaming and Entertainment Oral History Project, 1997, 20, UNLV Special Collections.

7. On descriptions of the Westside, see "An Interview with Sarann Preddy: An Oral History Conducted by Claytee D. White," Las Vegas Women in Gaming and Entertainment Oral History Project, 1998, 8, UNLV Special Collections. See also, "McWilliams Townsite, 1905–1980," folder: "Westside," in Vertical Files, UNLV Specials Collections; "Pioneers and Settlers," in *Nevada Black History Yesterday and Today*, clipping, box 1, folder 7, Alice Key Collection, UNLV Special Collections. In addition, Roosevelt Fitzgerald, "The Evolution of a Black Community in Las Vegas: 1905–1940," *Nevada Public Affairs Review*, no. 2 (1987): 23–28.

8. Moehring, *Resort City*, 178–79. See also, "Pioneers and Settlers," in *Nevada Black History Yesterday and Today*, 7.

9. "An Interview with Viola Johnson: An Oral History Conducted by Claytee D. White," Las Vegas Women in Gaming and Entertainment Oral History Project, 1997, 1–5, UNLV Special Collections.

10. Ibid., 6–9.

11. Ibid., 9–11. Johnson had six children at the time.

12. Ibid., 1–2, 18.

13. In the early 1960s, there were roughly two thousand black workers in Las Vegas hotels. See John Tofano, "Employment Discrimination in Strip Casinos: The Prima Facie Case," unpublished article, folder: Consent Decree—Employment Discrimination in Strip Casinos, in Black Consent Decree Files, NRA Papers. According to Tofano, there were thirty-six hundred black workers in resorts in 1971, when the industry's total workforce was around twenty thousand.

14. Perry Bruce Kaufman, "The Best City of Them All: A History of Las Vegas, 1930–1960" (Ph.D. diss., University of California, Santa Barbara, 1974), 350–55. Also, Lubertha Johnson, "Civil Rights Efforts in Las Vegas: 1940s-1960s," 31–32, UNOHP, Reno; Moehring, *Resort City*, 176.

15. Timothy Wagner, Oral Interview, conducted by Melvin Carter, February 23, 1980, transcribed interview, UNLV Special Collections.

16. Mrs. Arlone Scott, Oral Interview, conducted by Glen Ette Davis, June 3, 1975, transcribed interview, UNLV Special Collections.

17. "An Interview with Sarann Preddy," 8.

18. Moehring, *Resort City*, 173–75, 184.

19. Elmer R. Rusco, "The Civil Rights Movement in Nevada," *Nevada Public Affairs Review*, no. 2 (1987): 76.

20. Clarence Ray, *Black Politics and Gaming in Las Vegas, 1920s-1980s* (Reno: UNOHP, 1991), 90–91.

21. James McMillan, *Fighting Back: A Life in the Struggle for Civil Rights* (Reno: UNOHP, 1998), 92–94.

22. Hal Rothman, *Neon Metropolis: How Las Vegas Started the Twenty-First Century* (New York: Routledge, 2002), 130. *Review-Journal*, "James B. McMillan," *The First 100 Persons Who Shaped Southern Nevada*, at www.1st100.com/part2/mcmillan.html, 4–5.

23. "Report on First Hearing of Equal Rights Commission," July 15, 1961, box 1, folder 18, Donald Clark Collection, UNLV Special Collections. On incidents of discrimination, see Harold D. Burt to Donald M. Clark, September 21, 1961, box 1, folder 5, and Tom Juanarena to Southern Nevada Human Relations Commission, November 9, 1960, box 1, folder 4, both in Donald Clark Collection, UNLV Special Collections.

24. Donald Clark to Robert Brown, October 14, 1961, box 1, folder 5, Donald Clark Collection.

25. Donald Clark to Robert L. Brown, March 23, 1962, box 1, folder 5, Donald Clark Collection.

26. On the weaknesses of the state's Equal Rights Commission, see Elmer R. Rusco, "Racial Discrimination in Employment in Nevada: A Continuing Problem," *Government Research Newsletter* 11, no. 5 (February 1973), UNLV Special Collections. Neither of the Commission's two members was salaried in 1962.

27. Donald Clark to Robert L. Brown, October 14, 1962, box 1, folder 5, Donald Clark Collection.

28. Donald Clark to Norman Brown, March 23, 1962, box CR7C, folder: Donald Clark Collection, Elmer Rusco Collection, NSHS, Reno.

29. Interview with Charles Kellar, September 20, 1991, box CR9, folder: Charles Kellar, NSHS, Reno. *The First 100*, at www.1st100.com/part2/kellar.html, 1–4.

30. Reverend Donald Clark to Clarence Horton, January 11, 1962, box CR7C, folder: Donald Clark Collection, Elmer Rusco Collection. *The First 100*, 4–5.

31. Gottdiener et. al., *Las Vegas*, 95, 104. See also Moehring, *Resort City*, 184–90.

32. Rusco, "The Civil Rights Movement in Nevada," 75–80.

33. *Sun*, July 22, 1963.

34. See report by Nevada Tuberculosis and Health Association, "Operation Independence," June 1, 1963, box 2, folder 14, Donald Clark Collection. See also, "Survey for Operation Independence," February 1965, box NC 692, UNOHP, Reno.

35. *Sun*, April 6, 1965. Also, *Nevada State Journal*, March 31, 1965.

36. *Review-Journal*, July 27, 1967.

37. *Review-Journal*, November 16, 1969. Dave McGinty headed Local 525.

38. "An Interview with Alma Whitney: An Oral History Conducted by Claytee D. White," Las Vegas Women in Gaming and Entertainment Oral History Project, 1997, 31–33, UNLV Special Collections. Also, George W. Hardbeck, "Impact of the Nevada Consent Decree," *Cornell Hotel and Restaurant Administration Quarterly* 14, no. 3 (1973): 15–16.

39. "An Interview with Alma Whitney," 33.

40. Commission on Equal Rights of Citizens to Paul Laxalt, "Report to the Honorable Paul Laxalt," n.d., folder: Miscellaneous, in Black Consent Decree Files, NRA Papers. The report was likely written in November 1969; its authors attached a separate letter to the report dated November 14, 1969.

41. "An Interview with Essie Shelton Jacobs: An Oral History Conducted by Claytee D. White," Las Vegas Women in Gaming and Entertainment Oral History Project, 1997, 31–33, UNLV Special Collections.

42. Ibid., 17, 31–34, 48. Jacobs also liked Joe Hays, a white officer who oversaw matters relating to her own department. "When Joe was in there, everybody to me was treated equal," she said. She also recognized the contribution of stewards Sarah Hughes, Amos Knight, Rachel Coleman, and Addie Mackmoore.

43. Statement of Lt. Governor Paul Laxalt, March 18, 1965, box 024, folder 0321, Papers of Governor Paul Laxalt, NSMA Special Collections.

44. See "Solutions Conference, Report of Proceedings," 1–5, box 11, folder 3, Oran K. Gragson Collection, UNLV Special Collections.

45. Ibid. On Woodrow Wilson, see box 001, folder 0893, Papers of Governor Robert List, NSMA Special Collections.

46. Ibid., 17–21.

47. The Stardust, for example, hired African Americans in positions that had previously been closed to them. See "Information Report" by Sgt. John L. Conner, May 20, 1968, box 9, folder 2, Oran Gragson Collection.

48. Charles A. Kellar to Commission on Equal Rights of Citizens, State of Nevada, March 28, 1968, folder: National Association for the Advancement of Colored People

(NAACP) General Correspondence, in Black Consent Decree Files, NRA Papers. Kellar also filed a complaint with the National Labor Relations Board accusing parties of violating civil rights legislation; see Moehring, *Resort City*, 190.

49. Commission on Equal Rights of Citizens to Paul Laxalt, "Report to the Honorable Paul Laxalt," n.d.

50. *Sun*, February 1, 1969.

51. See *Herald-Examiner*, October 7, 1969; *Los Angeles Times*, October 8, 1969; and *Sun*, October 6 and 7, 1969. See also, Moehring, *Resort City*, 192–93.

52. Hardbeck, "Impact of the Nevada Consent Decree," 11–13.

53. Robbins Cahill to Paul Laxalt, November 19, 1969, folder: NAACP General Correspondence, in Black Consent Decree Files, NRA Papers. See also, *The First 100*, 3–4.

54. Robbins Cahill to Nevada Resort Association, December 10, 1969, folder: NAACP General Correspondence, in Black Consent Decree Files, NRA Papers.

55. Ibid. See also Alvin Benedict to Charles Kellar, January 30, 1970, folder: NAACP General Correspondence, in Black Consent Decree, NRA Papers; and Hardbeck, "Impact of the Nevada Consent Decree," 12; and Moehring, *Resort City*, 198.

56. Charles Kellar to Alvin Benedict, February 4, 1970, folder: NAACP General Correspondence, Black Consent Decree Files, NRA Papers.

57. Jerris Leonard to William Campbell et al., December 10, 1970, folder: Consent Decree Implementation—Correspondence, in Black Consent Decree Files, NRA Papers.

58. Ibid.

59. On the Consent Decree, see Jeffrey J. Sallaz, "Civil Rights and Employment Equity in Las Vegas Casinos: The Failed Enforcement of the Casino Consent Decree, 1971–1986," *Nevada Historical Society Quarterly* 47, no. 4 (2004): 283–99. Also, Nevada Advisory Committee to the U.S. Commission on Civil Rights, "The Impact of Two Consent Decrees on Employment at Major Hotel/Casinos in Nevada," NSHS, Reno; Hardbeck, "Impact of the Nevada Consent Decree," 11–16; and "Casino Consent Decree," box 1, folder 6, Elmer Rusco Collection, UNLV Special Collections.

60. William Campbell to Mike O'Callaghan, August 7, 1973, folder: Consent Decree Implementation—Correspondence, in Black Consent Decree Files, NRA Papers.

61. Stuart P. Herman to William Campbell, n.d., folder: Consent Decree Implementation—Correspondence, in Black Consent Decree Files, NRA Papers.

62. As explained in W. N. Campbell to R. S. Thomas, May 21, 1972, folder: Consent Decree Implementation—Correspondence, in Black Consent Decree Files, NRA Papers.

63. Hardbeck, "Impact of the Nevada Consent Decree," 14.

64. Ibid., 13–14.

65. J. Stanley Pottinger to E. Timothy Applegate, February 6, 1973, folder: Consent Decree Implementation—Correspondence, in Black Consent Decree Files, NRA Papers.

66. Hardbeck, "Impact of the Nevada Consent Decree," 15.

67. "Memorandum of EEOC In Opposition to Motion for Dissolution of Consent Decree," folder: U.S. v. Nevada Resort Association, et al., Civil Action No. LV 1645, in Black Consent Decree Files, NRA Papers.

68. See "Motion to Compel Answers to Plaintiff's Interrogatories and Response to Defendants' Motion for Protective Order," and "Affidavit of Howard Eugene Harkness,"

folder: Case No. CV-LV-1645 Black Consent Decree-Pleadings, in Black Consent Decree Files, NRA Papers.

69. "Affidavit of Clemmie Jewel Woodard," folder: Case No. CV-LV-1645 Black Consent Decree-Pleadings, in Black Consent Decree Files, NRA Papers. On the Woodward case, see also John C. Cooney to Jesse D. Scott, May 20, 1975, box 0658, folder 1, Papers of Governor Mike O'Callaghan, NSMA Special Collections.

70. "Memorandum for Nevada Resort Association," October 4, 1974, folder: EEOC— Possible Commissioners' Charge of Sex and National Origin Discrimination (1974–75), in Equal Employment Opportunity Commission/Nevada Equal Rights Commission Files, NRA Papers.

71. Records of the EEOC suggest that Hispanics accounted for about 5 percent of the Clark County workforce by the mid-1970s, or roughly three thousand to four thousand people. On charges of discrimination by Hispanics, see "Charges under Investigation by the Nevada Commission on the Equal Rights of Citizens," n.d., folder: EEOC Department of Labor Investigation, in Equal Employment Opportunity Commission/Nevada Equal Rights Commission Files, NRA Papers.

72. Walter Loomis to William Campbell, October 30, 1974, 4, folder: EEOC—Possible Commissioners Charge of Sex and National Origin Discrimination (1974–75), in Equal Employment Opportunity Commission/Nevada Equal Rights Commission Files, NRA Papers.

73. Moehring, *Resort City*, 201.

74. The resort had not reached its goals in the categories of dealer, secretary-receptionist, and switchboard operator. See Jennifer Gee to Virginia Pendleton, September 1978, Telles v. Flamingo Hotel, in Telles Charges Files, NRA Papers.

75. Barbara Lindemann Schlei to William Davis, July 21, 1986, folder: Case No. CV-LV-81, in Telles Charges Files, NRA Papers. See also "Order Dissolving Consent Decree," from same folder and file. The Black Consent Decree has never been dissolved. On efforts to enforce the decree in the 1980s, see Nevada Advisory Committee to the U.S. Commission on Civil Rights, "The Impact of Two Consent Decrees," and Sallaz, "Civil Rights and Employment Equity," 295–99.

76. Interview with Woodrow Wilson, September 18, 1997, box CR7, folder: Woodrow Wilson, NSHS, Reno.

77. *Sun*, July 22, 1963.

CHAPTER 7: THE SPIRIT OF '76

1. *Las Vegas Perspective, 1981*, 50–53, UNLV Special Collections.

2. The words are those of Paul Titus of the Las Vegas Convention and Visitors Authority, *Variety*, March 16, 1977. Also, *Hollywood Reporter*, April 12, 1977; *Los Angeles Times*, May 18, 1977. On Atlantic City, see David G. Schwartz, *Suburban Xanadu: The Casino Resort on the Las Vegas Strip and Beyond* (New York: Routledge, 2003), 173–82.

3. Robbins E. Cahill, "Recollections of Work in State Politics, Government, Taxation, Gaming Control, Clark County Administration and the Nevada Resort Association," 948–49, UNOHP, Reno.

4. Henri Lewin to William H. Edwards, March 27, 29, and 30, 1973, box: Hilton—N.J. Licensing Files (1984), folder: Hilton/N.J. License I, Local 226 Papers.

5. *Review-Journal,* March 11, 1971. Also, *Collective Bargaining Agreement between Nevada Resort Association and Culinary Workers and Bartenders Unions, 1973–1976,* in Expired Labor Contracts Files, NRA Papers. See also *Agreement between Las Vegas Resort Hotels and Teamsters, 1973–76,* in Expired Labor Contracts Files, NRA Papers. The Culinary agreed to a one-year wage freeze followed by a flat-rate raise of only $2.00 a day for employees for each of the next two years.

6. *Collective Bargaining Agreement between Nevada Resort Association and Culinary Workers and Bartenders Unions, 1970–73,* in Expired Labor Contracts Files, NRA Papers. Also, see the bargaining agreement of 1973–76. From 1970 to 1976, employer contributions to the unions' health and welfare fund rose from $19 to $36 a month, per employee, and contributions to the retirement fund rose from nothing to a rate of $.25 for each hour an employee worked.

7. According to the federal government, the price of consumer goods and services rose 67 percent between 1967 and 1976. On the rising cost of consumer goods in Las Vegas, see *Review-Journal,* March 19, 1976.

8. *Wall Street Journal,* October 17, 1972; *Sun,* May 4, 1977. See also "The Secret Life of Howard Hughes," *Time,* December 13, 1976, 22–24, 32.

9. In 1970, in *Boys Markets v. Retail Clerks* (398 U.S. 235), the Supreme Court reversed a decision made eight years earlier that said lower courts could not issue injunctions to stop strikes in violation of no-strike agreements because federal laws had not made such strikes illegal. See Arthur A. Sloan and Fred Witney, *Labor Relations,* 5th ed. (Englewood Cliffs: Prentice Hall, 1985), 416–17.

10. The guards belonged to Local 151 of the International Union of Police and Protection Employees. *Sun,* June 28, 1975; July 13, 1975.

11. "Management Committee Meeting," March 7, 1976, folder: Management Committee Meetings, in Culinary Bartender Negotiations Files, NRA Papers. Also, *Valley Times,* March 24, 1976; *Review-Journal,* February, 23, March 14, 1976.

12. "Minutes of Collective Bargaining Sessions," February 26, Minutes of Meetings, Culinary Negotiations, 1976, in Culinary Bartender Negotiations Files, NRA Papers; *Review-Journal,* March 14, 1976; March 18. Al Bramlet of the Culinary had recently talked of organizing casino personnel in the Reno-Tahoe area. Bramlet told the press that the International had given him "the green light" to expand the scope of organizing efforts.

13. *Carson City Appeal,* March 18, 1976.

14. *San Francisco Chronicle,* March 26, 1976.

15. The AFL urged members "not to tie themselves up with contracts so that they cannot help each other when able." On sympathy strikes, see David Montgomery, *Workers Control in America: Studies in the History of Work, Technology, and Labor Struggles* (Cambridge: Cambridge University Press, 1979), 21–27.

16. *Review-Journal,* March 11, 1976.

17. *San Diego Tribune,* March 15, 1976.

18. *San Francisco Chronicle,* March 26, 1976.

19. Testimony of John Cullerton before State of New Jersey Casino Control Commission, July 24, 1984, box: Hilton—N.J. Licensing Files (1984), folder: Hilton—Cullerton, Local 226 Papers.

20. "Minutes of Management Committee Meetings," December 29, 1975, February 9, and March 7, 1976, folder: Management Committee Meetings, in Culinary Bartender Negotiations Files, NRA Papers.

21. *San Francisco Chronicle*, March 28, 1976; and *Review-Journal*, March 2, 6, 10, 12, and 20, 1976. Frank Scott was also a top executive at the Union Plaza.

22. Jack Foy to Governor Mike O'Callaghan, April 20, 1976, box 0696, folder 16, Papers of Governor Mike O'Callaghan, NSMA Special Collections.

23. Interview with Mark Massagli, Riviera Hotel, June 23, 1997; and interview with Dennis Sabbath, Riviera Hotel, June 25, 1997. The Musicians contract expired on February 15.

24. William N. Campbell to Lee C. Shaw, December 17, 1975, folder: Miscellaneous, Musicians Negotiations 1976, in Musicians Negotiations Files, NRA Papers. In same folder and file, see also William N. Campbell to Jack Foy, March 18, 1976.

25. Interview with Mark Massagli, at Riviera Hotel, June 23, 1997.

26. *Variety*, March 10, 1976. Also, *Valley Times*, March 9, 1976.

27. James Koteas to Herb Tobman, Bill Champion, Alan Lee, and Pepper Davis, January 10, 1975, folder: Miscellaneous, Musicians Negotiations 1976, in Musicians Negotiations Files, NRA Papers. Also, Jack Foy to James Koteas, January 9, 1975, folder: Membership Correspondence, in Musicians Negotiations 1976 Files, in Musicians Negotiations Files, NRA Papers.

28. *Variety*, March 10, 1976. Also, *Valley Times*, March 9, 1976.

29. *Hollywood Reporter*, March 13, 1976; *Review-Journal*, March 6, 8, 10, 1976.

30. W. N. Campbell to Establishments Signatory to Musicians Labor Agreement, March 6, 1976, folder: Membership Correspondence, Musicians Negotiations, 1976, in Musicians Negotiations Files, NRA Papers.

31. *Review-Journal*, March 9, 1976.

32. *Hollywood Reporter*, March 13, 1976; *Review-Journal*, March 10, 11, 1976.

33. "Status of Musicians and Stagehands," March 11, 1976, folder: Miscellaneous, Musicians Negotiations, 1976, in Musicians Negotiations Files, NRA Papers.

34. *Daily Variety*, March 11, 1976.

35. *Review-Journal*, March 11, 12, 1976; *Sun*, March 11, 1976.

36. *San Francisco Chronicle*, March 28, 1976; *Review-Journal*, March 14, 1976. Also, *Daily Variety*, March 15, 1976; and *North Valley Times*, March 12, 1976.

37. William Bennett had been an executive at Del Webb, and William Pennington was a gaming equipment manufacturer. These men reversed the decline of Circus Circus by redesigning its casino to give gamblers more space and fewer distractions, and eliminated risqué entertainment in favor of more family-oriented attractions. As a result of such changes, Circus Circus became one of the most profitable resorts on the Strip. Robert D. McCracken, *Las Vegas: The Great American Playground* (Reno: University of Nevada Press, 1997), 92; and A. D. Hopkins, "Jay Sarno: He Came to Play," in *The Players: The*

Men Who Made Las Vegas, ed. Jack Sheehan (Las Vegas: University of Nevada Press, 1997), 97–98.

38. *San Francisco Chronicle*, March 13 and 26, 1976.

39. *Herald-Examiner*, March 15, 1976; *Review-Journal*, March 13, 1976.

40. *Sun*, March 12 and 13, 1976.

41. *Herald-Examiner*, March 15, 1976; *Review-Journal*, March 13, 1976.

42. *San Francisco Chronicle*, March 15, 1976.

43. *Sacramento Union*, March 14, 1976; *Atlanta Journal Constitution*, March 21, 1976.

44. *Valley Times*, March 11 and 25, 1976; *Hollywood Reporter*, March 26, 1976.

45. *Sun*, March 21 and 22, 1976. Some three hundred people volunteered to work in four-hour shifts at the kitchen. According to the press, the kitchen turned out about ten thousand sandwiches a day, along with fifteen thousand donuts and five hundred gallons of coffee.

46. See Rick Fantasia, *Cultures of Solidarity: Consciousness, Action, and Contemporary American Workers* (Berkeley: University of California Press, 1988), 192–93.

47. *Daily Variety*, March 11, 1976; *Review-Journal*, March 11, 1976.

48. *Review-Journal*, April 4, 1976.

49. "Affidavit of Kenneth L. Betts," March 17, 1976, 1–4, folder: Case No. A152518, Civil Docket B, Circus Circus v. Local Joint Executive Board et. al, in Court Cases Files, NRA Papers. See also the affidavits of Donald Richardson, John McElroy, Jules Pursley, and Delfino Alamo in the same folder and files. See, too, *Review-Journal*, March 17, 1976.

50. "Affidavit of Gretchen T. Gotchy," March 17, 1976, folder: Case No. A152517, Civil Dock B, Caesars Palace vs. Local Joint Executive Board, et al., in Court Cases Files, NRA Papers.

51. "Affidavit of Larry Mills," March 17, 1976, folder: Case No. A152517, Caesars Palace vs. Local Joint Executive Board, et al., in Court Cases Files, NRA Papers. *Review-Journal*, March 23, 1976.

52. *Review-Journal*, March 11, 12, 13, 1976.

53. "Minutes of Mediation Sessions," March 18, Culinary Negotiations, 1976, Miscellaneous, in Culinary Bartender Negotiations Files, NRA Papers. Also, *Collective Bargaining Agreement between Nevada Resort Association and Culinary Workers and Bartenders Unions, 1976–1980*, article 30, 87–88, in Expired Labor Contracts Files, NRA Papers.

54. Stanley P. Jones to William Campbell, February 26, 1976, folder: Culinary Negotiations, 1976, Miscellaneous, in Culinary Bartender Negotiations Files, NRA Papers. Also, *San Francisco Chronicle*, March 18, 1976; *Valley Times*, March 18, 1976.

55. Frank Scott to Mike O'Callaghan, March 18, 1976, box 0696, folder 16, Papers of Mike O'Callaghan NSMA Special Collections. Scott also criticized the union for taking "an inflexible position" on this issue. "We simply cannot believe that the Culinary Workers or any other striking union," he told the governor, "will continue to sacrifice the welfare of their members and the best interests of our community by slavish adherence to an unrealistic position that is unchanging."

56. A. D. Hopkins, "Mike O'Callaghan: The Popular Pugilist," *Review-Journal, The First 100 Persons Who Shaped Southern Nevada*, at www.1st100.com/part3/ocallaghan .html.

57. "Minutes of Mediation Sessions," March 19, 20, 21, 1976, folder: Culinary Negotiations, 1976, Miscellaneous, in Culinary Bartender Negotiations Files, NRA Papers.

58. Ibid., March 21. On Benninger's concerns about the right to strike, see also Fred Benninger to Mike O'Callaghan, April 13, 1976, box 0696, folder 16, Papers of Governor Mike O'Callaghan.

59. "Minutes of Mediation Sessions," March 21, 22.

60. *Daily Variety*, March 22, 1976.

61. *Reno State Journal*, March 21, 1976. Howard Hughes died on April 5, 1976, only two weeks after the Silver Slipper reopened. On Lieber, see also, Mike O'Callaghan to Perry Lieber, April 1, 1976, box 0696, folder 16, Papers of Governor Mike O'Callaghan.

62. "Temporary Restraining Order," folder: Case No. A152517, Civil Docket B, Caesars Palace vs. Local Joint Executive Board, et al., in Court Cases Files, NRA Papers.

63. *Sun*, March 21 and 22, 1976.

64. *Los Angeles Times*, March 24, 1976; *Review-Journal*, March 23, 1976; *Sun*, March 23, 1976.

65. *Review-Journal*, March 23 and 24, 1976; *Sun*, March 24 and 25, 1976; *Valley Times*, March 24 and 25, 1976.

66. *Sun*, March 21, 1976.

67. *Valley Times*, March 23 and 25, 1976.

68. *Review-Journal*, March 25, 1976.

69. *Review-Journal*, March 24, 1976. Once the strike ended, the *Review-Journal* expected to see "widespread promotional efforts to herald the end of the strike."

70. Ed Hanley died in a car accident in January 2000. See *Business Week*, May 18, 1998, 6; *New York Times*, January 16, 2000.

71. "Minutes of Mediation Sessions," March 22, 1976, folder: Culinary Negotiations, 1976, Miscellaneous, in Culinary Bartender Negotiations Files, NRA Papers. NRA president Frank Scott as well as Alvin Benedict and Fred Benninger attended the meeting, as did the state labor commissioner.

72. Testimony of Henri Lewin before State of New Jersey Department of Law and Public Safety Division of Gaming Enforcement, September 17, 1984, 138, box: Hilton—N.J. Licensing Files (1984), folder: Hilton—Lewin, Local 226 Papers.

73. Senate Report, 98th Cong., 69. Local journalists interpreted Hanley's presence in Las Vegas as an effort to enhance his own reputation at Bramlet's expense. They suggested he had national political aspirations and saw the strike as a chance to cast himself as a powerful yet moderate voice within the labor movement. See John Whitmarsh, "Las Vegas, Los Angeles, McDonald's, Marriott—Where will the union strike next?" box 0696, folder 15, Papers of Governor Mike O'Callaghan. Also, *Reno Gazette-Journal*, July 22, 1985.

74. Testimony of Henri Lewin before State of New Jersey Department of Law and Public Safety Division of Gaming Enforcement, September 17, 1984, 138, box: Hilton—N.J. Licensing Files (1984), folder: Hilton—Lewin, Local 226 Papers. On relations between local and national unions, see Fantasia, *Cultures of Solidarity*, 223–25; and Sloan and Witney, *Labor Relations*, 129, 157–58.

75. "Minutes of Mediation Sessions," March 22, 1976, folder: Culinary Negotiations, 1976, Miscellaneous, in Culinary Bartender Negotiations Files, NRA Papers. Hanley

rejected a management proposal for a thirty- to forty-five-day cooling-off period as unreasonable.

76. On the governor's position, see "Minutes of Mediation Sessions," March 22, 1976, folder: Culinary Negotiations, 1976, Miscellaneous, in Culinary Bartender Negotiations Files, NRA Papers. Also, "Minutes of Mediation Sessions," March 18, 1976, Culinary Negotiations, 1976, Miscellaneous, in Culinary Bartender Negotiations, NRA Papers.

77. O'Callaghan was not only a popular governor but a former boxer and a decorated Korean War veteran. On the governor's role in the dispute, see editorial by Stanley P. Jones, in *Southern Nevada Labor News*, April 1976, 2, box 0696, folder 15, Papers of Mike O'Callaghan. This editorial is attached to a letter from Jones to Callaghan, April 28, 1976, in same box and folder.

78. *San Francisco Chronicle*, March 28, 1976. Also, *Review-Journal*, April 9, 1976. The settlement translated into hourly wage increases of $1.55 over four years; the unions had demanded $1.35 over three years.

79. "Brief on Behalf of Showboat Hotel," March 29, 1982, 7, 33, from "The Matter of Arbitration between Showboat Hotel and the Las Vegas Joint Executive Board," folder: Culinary & Showboat Hotel: Violation of No-Strike Clause, Rentfo, in Arbitration Files, NRA Papers. Hanley met with Bramlet and Bowe the morning after his meeting with the Governor, at the Riviera Hotel. *Review-Journal*, March 24 and 28, 1976. Also, W. N. Campbell to Phil Arce, June 9, 1976, No Strike, No Lockout Provision Letter, in Miscellaneous Labor Files, NRA Papers.

80. *Sun*, March 27, 29, 31, 1976. Local 720 of the Stagehands was the last union to settle. Its leaders struggled unsuccessfully to reduce the workweek from six to five days. Several showrooms remained closed until stagehands ratified their contract in early April. See *Valley Times*, April 2, 1976.

81. The "lounge case" dragged on until 1979. Interview with Mark Massagli, June 21, 1997; and interview with Dennis Sabbath, June 23, 1997. See also *Review-Journal*, January 9, 1979.

82. "Minutes of Collective Bargaining Sessions," February 2, 4, and March 25, 1976, folder: Minutes of Meetings, Musicians Negotiations, 1976, in Musicians Negotiations Files, NRA Papers.

83. The Culinary and Bartenders negotiated new agreements with the downtown properties, who bargained through their own association, during the last week of March. The agreements resembled NRA contracts except that they offered waitresses a $.55 an hour higher wage because tips in the downtown area were lower. *Valley Times*, March 31, 1976; *Sun*, March 26, 1976; and *Review-Journal*, April 8, 1976. See also W. N. Campbell to Phil Arce, June 9, 1976, No Strike, No Lockout Provision Letter.

84. *Review-Journal*, March 27, 28, 1976.

85. *Review-Journal*, April 4, 1976. *Sun*, March 26, 29, 1976. See also "Backgrounder," 16, April 4, 1984, folder: Publicity File, 1984 Culinary/Bartender Negotiations Files, NRA Papers.

86. *Daily Variety*, June 4, 1976. Clark County's gaming revenue increased 10 percent for the first quarter of 1976.

87. Senate Report, 98th Cong., 69.

CHAPTER 8: MANAGEMENT DIGS IN, 1982–1984

1. *Las Vegas Perspective, 1981*, 3–26, UNLV Special Collections. The *Perspective* is a collection of facts and statistics compiled by the Nevada Development Authority, the First Interstate Bank of Nevada, the Center for Business and Economic Research at the University of Nevada, Las Vegas, and published with the help of the *Review-Journal*. See also Hal Rothman, "Colony, Capital, and Casino: Money in the Real Las Vegas," in *The Grit Beneath the Glitter: Tales of the Real Las Vegas*, ed. Hal K. Rothman and Mike Davis (Berkeley: University of California Press, 2002), 327.

2. Ramada Inns, Incorporated, *1979 Annual Report* (Phoenix: Ramada Inns, Incorporated, 1979), 12, Tropicana Promotional and Publicity files, UNLV Special Collections; *Las Vegas Perspective, 1981*, 42–45. Other properties that opened off the Strip include Alexis Park, the Bingo Palace (now Palace Station), the Maxim, and Vegas World.

3. Nevada Resort Association, "The Gaming Industry: Will It Remain a Positive Force in the Nevada Economy?" January 1983, 3–4, folder: Gambling—United States: Nevada: Economic, in Vertical Files, UNLV Special Collections. Nearly half of all gaming establishments in the state had suffered net operating losses the previous year, and about two dozen of those places went out of business in 1982, along with more than five hundred firms in other areas of the state's economy.

4. The first quotation is from a consultant at the company of Drexel, Burnham, and Lambert, the second from an analyst at Merrill Lynch. For similar statements, see "Study of Financial Results and Reporting Trends in the Gaming Industry," 1982, 6–9, folder: Gambling Management, in Vertical Files, UNLV Special Collections. The accounting firm of Laventhol and Horwath conducted this study, which focused on the health of fifteen corporations involved in the gaming business, and included financial reports and statements to stockholders.

5. Ibid., 7. The words are those of Joseph Amoroso, president of the Elsinore Corporation.

6. For a good overview of the national economy in the late 1970s and early 1980s, see Michael French, *US Economic History since 1945* (New York: Manchester University Press, 1997), 42–53.

7. On the decline of trade unionism, see Michael Goldfield, *The Decline of Organized Labor in the United States* (Chicago: University of Chicago Press, 1987). See too, Melvyn Dubofsky and Foster Rhea Dulles, *Labor in America: A History*, 7th ed. (Wheeling, Ill.: Harlan Davidson, 2004), 393–96. On the erosion of union membership in the building trades, see "Construction Workers Try to Shore Up a Crumbling Foundation," *Business Week*, February 4, 1985, 52–53, reprinted in Eileen Boris and Nelson Lichtenstein, *Major Problems in the History of American Workers* (Lexington, Mass.: D.C. Heath, 1991), 590–92.

8. On the autopsy of Bramlet's body, see *Report Made by Las Vegas Reporting Office*, March 30, 1977, part IX, 108, in FBI Records on Elmer Alton Bramlet.

9. Documentary by George Knapp, at KLAS Television Station, Las Vegas. Knapp provided a transcript of the documentary, which is in my possession. See also *Valley Times*, April 22, 1977; and *New York Times*, May 5, 1984. Authorities interviewed Clem Vaughn

repeatedly, using both polygraph tests and sodium pentothal; see SAC to Director, FBI, April 4, 1977, FBI Records on Elmer Alton Bramlet. On Vaughn's account of the crime, see *Review-Journal*, August 30, 1977. For an overview of the murder, see Michael Andrew Nyre, "Union Jackpot: Culinary Workers Local 226, Las Vegas Nevada, 1970–2000," (master's thesis, California State University, Fullerton, 2001), 45–48.

10. On the vandalism of restaurants, see SAC Las Vegas to Director, FBI, April 4, 1977, FBI Records on Elmer Alton Bramlet. On Gramby Hanley's version of the crime, see *Sun*, September 29, 1982.

11. Tom Hanley also admitted being drunk when he shot Bramlet. *Review-Journal*, November 2, 1979; *New York Times*, May 5, 1984; Senate Report, 98th Cong., 69–70. For more on motives, see *Carson City Appeal*, November 2, 1979; *Review-Journal*, March 22, 1977; November 9 and 24, 1979; and October 10, 1982; and *Sun*, March 24, 1977; November 2 and 24, 1979; September 29 and 30, 1982; and October 1, 1982.

12. *Report Made by Las Vegas Reporting Office*, March 30, 1977, part III, FBI Records on Elmer Al Bramlet. Also, *San Francisco Examiner*, March 6, 1977. U.S. senators probing allegations of union racketeering in western states suggested that the International had waged a ruthless campaign to consolidate the health and welfare funds of its affiliates, which was never proved. On the probe, see Senate Report, 98th Cong., 69–71; *Review-Journal*, September 29, 1982; *Sun*, September 28 and 30, 1982. On reactions of HERE to the probe, see *Review-Journal*, November 3, 1982.

13. The quotation is from the *Wall Street Journal*, March 9, 1977. On speculation that Reno employers orchestrated Bramlet's murder, see *Report Made by Las Vegas Reporting Office*, March 30, 1977, part IV, 38, FBI Records on Elmer Al Bramlet. Also, interview with Jeff McColl, May 8, 2008; *Review-Journal*, June 4, 1974; January 3, 1975; and *Sun*, August 22, 1974. Also, *Review-Journal*, November 3, 1982.

14. On Spilotro, see FBI files at www.fbi.org. See also, Senate Report, 98th Cong., 70–71; Hal Rothman, *Neon Metropolis: How Las Vegas Started the Twenty-First Century* (New York: Routledge, 2002), 75–76; John L. Smith, *Sharks in the Desert: The Founding Fathers and Current Kings of Las Vegas* (Fort Lee, N.J.: Barricade Books, 2005), 39–47; and Steve Fisher, *When the Mob Ran Las Vegas: Stories of Money, Mayhem, and Murder* (Omaha, Neb.: Berkline Press, 2006), 202–7, 218–24.

15. Wendy Hanley, who was forty years younger than Tom, said Tom was abusive as well as dangerous. "He threatened my life a couple of times," she told the journalist. See Documentary by George Knapp, at KLAS Television, Las Vegas. Also, *Nevada State Journal*, June 10, 1977; *Review-Journal*, May 11, 1977; and interview with unidentified individual, April 29, 1977, FBI Records on Elmer Alton Bramlet.

16. "An Interview with Essie Shelton Jacobs: An Oral History Conducted by Claytee D. White," Las Vegas Women in Gaming and Entertainment Oral History Project, 1997, 31–32, 46, UNLV Special Collections. On workers' attitudes toward Bramlet, see also "An Interview with Alma Whitney: An Oral History Conducted by Claytee D. White," *Las Vegas Women in Gaming and Entertainment Oral History Project*, 1997, 24.

17. "Interview with Essie Shelton Jacobs," 50.

18. Senate Report, 98th Cong., 70–71. Schmoutey had served as president of Local 226 for a decade before Bramlet's murder. Also, *Review-Journal*, March 22, 1987.

19. Robert Lanyon to Governor Richard Bryan, April 2, 1984, box 0696, file 008, Papers of Governor Richard Bryan, NSMA Special Collections. Also, Interview with Dick Thomas, Las Vegas, June 15, 1998; *Review-Journal*, November 25, 1979; and Nyre, "Union Jackpot," 48–55.

20. As quoted in Nyre, "Union Jackpot," 56. Also, *Review-Journal*, April 4, 1980.

21. Interview with Dick Thomas, Las Vegas, June 15, 1998. Also, "Press Release," folder: Publicity File, in Culinary Bartender Negotiation Files, NRA Papers. In same folder and file, see also "Las Vegas Joint Board Press Release." In the late 1970s, several restaurants in the area had vowed to turn their establishments into nonunion properties, including seven Denny's and two Bob's Big Boy restaurants. *Sun*, March 24, 1977.

22. The new picket line clause prohibited workers from honoring picket lines of groups who were not "currently party to a collective bargaining agreement with the NRA," which the union had construed to mean unorganized groups. See "Press Release," folder: Publicity File, in Culinary Bartender Negotiation Files, NRA Papers; and *Valley Times*, April 4, 18, 27, and 30, 1980.

23. An Appeal from the U.S. District Court District of Nevada, No. 87-2789, April 13, 1988, folder: Case CV-LV-81-555, Management Trustees/Culinary, in Court Cases Files, NRA Papers. Also, F. T. MacDonald to Tim Hay, February 13, 1984, box 1173, folder: 1984 Strike, Labor Commissioner Updates, Papers of Governor Richard Bryan.

24. Interview with Jeff McColl, Las Vegas, June 23, 1998.

25. *Review-Journal*, November 11, 1982; interview with Mark Massagli, June 12, 1998, Las Vegas.

26. Nevada Resort Association, "The Gaming Industry," UNLV Special Collections.

27. Ibid., 5.

28. "Study of Financial Results and Reporting Trends in the Gaming Industry," 1982, 9, folder: Gambling Management, in Vertical Files, UNLV Special Collections.

29. *Sun*, June 29, July 12, 1981; *Review-Journal*, July 12, 1981. Helm had also been field attorney for the National Labor Relations Board.

30. Interview with Kevin Efroymson, Las Vegas, June 16, 1998.

31. *Labor Arbitration Reports: Awards of Arbitrators; Reports of Fact Finding Boards*, vol. 79 (Washington D.C.: Bureau of National Affairs, 1983), 478–83. Also *Valley Times*, April 4, 1980; and April 6, 1984. Interview with Greg Smith, Las Vegas, April 14, 1998.

32. Interview with Dennis Kist, Las Vegas, September 8, 2003.

33. Interview with Kevin Efroymson, Las Vegas, June 16, 1998; interview with Dick Thomas, Las Vegas, June 15, 1998.

34. "Minutes, Contract Negotiations Committee," folder: Miscellaneous (1983), in Teamsters Backend Negotiations Files, NRA Papers.

35. Interview with Thomas, Las Vegas, June 15, 1998. Also, "Minutes, Contract Negotiations Committee," folder: Miscellaneous, in Teamsters Backend Negotiations Files," NRA Papers.

36. *Valley Times*, May 1, 1983.

37. Interview with Dick Thomas, June 15, 1998.

38. *Sun*, May 11, 1983.

39. The Supreme Court case involved eleven striking workers at a San Francisco company engaged in the transmission of foreign and interstate communications. See *NLRB v. Mackay Radio & Telegraph*, 1938. On the effectiveness of permanent replacements in the 1980s, see Jonathan D. Rosenblum, *Copper Crucible: How the Arizona Miners' Strike of 1983 Recast Labor-Management Relations in America* (Ithaca, N.Y.: Cornell University Press, 1995); and Stephen Franklin, *Three Strikes: Labor's Heartland Losses and What They Mean for Working Americans* (New York: The Guilford Press, 2001).

40. Julius Getman, *The Betrayal of Local 14: Paperworkers, Politics, and Permanent Replacements* (Ithaca, N.Y.: Cornell University Press, 1998); Timothy J. Minchin, "Permanent Replacements and the Breakdown of the 'Social Accord' in Calera, Alabama, 1974–2000," *Labor History* 42 (November 2001): 371–96; Daniel J. B. Mitchell, "A Decade of Concession Bargaining," in *Labor Economics and Industrial Relations: Markets and Institutions*, ed. Clark Kerr and Paul D. Staudohar (Cambridge, Mass.: Harvard University Press, 1994), 435–74.

41. See Labor Commissioner Notes, 1983 Strike, box 0952, folder: Labor, Papers of Governor Robert List, NSMA Special Collections.

42. Claude Evans to Mr. Murray Seeger, May 23, 1983, box: Misc. 5-A, Correspondence and Accounting Records, file: Labor March 5/9/83, Federation Papers, NSHS. Also, *Valley Times*, May 10, 1983.

43. *Review-Journal*, May 17, 1983.

44. *Nevada State Journal*, May 16, 1983.

45. Labor Commissioner Notes, 1983 Strike.

46. Vincent Helm to Jeff McColl and Jack Stafford, March 7, 1983, in folder: Correspondence to/from Unions (1983), in Teamsters Backend Negotiations Files, NRA Papers.

47. Vincent Helm to Jeff McColl, March 23, 1983, folder: Correspondence to/from Unions (1983), in Teamsters Backend Negotiations Files, NRA Papers. In same folder and file, see also Vincent Helm to Mark Tully Massagli, March 29, 1983.

48. Labor Commissioner Notes, 1983 Strike.

49. Ibid.

50. Interview with Dick Thomas, Las Vegas, June 15, 1998; *Valley Times*, May 13, 1983.

51. *Review-Journal*, May 18, 1983.

52. *Valley Times*, June 2, 1983. Union members voted for the contracts on June 1, in shifts at the Riviera.

53. "Study of Financial Results and Reporting Trends in the Gaming Industry, 1984," 20, brochure, folder: Gambling Management, in Vertical Files, UNLV Library Special Collections. This study by the accounting firm of Laventhol and Horwath examined seventeen corporations in the gaming industry. The words are those of Mark Manson of Donaldson, Lufkin and Jenrette accounting firm.

54. Barron Hilton to Stockholders, February 29, 1984, in Hilton Hotels Corporation *1983 Annual Report*, 2–4, brochure, folder: Gambling Management, in Vertical Files, UNLV Library Special Collections.

55. *Study of Financial Results and Reporting Trends in the Gaming Industry*, 10, 20. The words are again those of Mark Manson.

56. Ibid., 19–21.

57. On gaming in Atlantic City, see George Sternlieb and James W. Hughes, *The Atlantic City Gamble* (Cambridge, Mass.: Harvard University Press, 1983). Also, David G. Schwartz, *Suburban Xanadu: The Casino Resort on the Las Vegas Strip and Beyond* (New York: Routledge Press, 2003), 175–82.

58. See Tom Pilkington to Vincent Helm, January 13, 1984, Correspondence to Employees, in 1984 Culinary/Bartender Negotiations, NRA Papers. See also "Report #4 on Negotiations," n.d., folder: Correspondence to Employees by Union, in Culinary Bartender Negotiations Files, NRA Papers; and Joseph Buckley to William Campbell, January 30, 1980, folder: Membership Correspondence, in Culinary Bartender Negotiations Files (1980), NRA Papers. *Sun*, May 4; May 17, 1984.

59. "Minutes of Negotiating Sessions," February 22, 1984, 4, folder: Culinary Negotiations, in 1984 Culinary/Bartender Negotiations Files, NRA Papers. See also, Rothman, *Neon Metropolis*, 77.

60. *New York Times*, May 5, 1984.

61. See F. T. MacDonald to Tim Hay, February 13, 1984, box 1173, folder: 1984 Strike, Labor Commissioner Updates, Papers of Governor Richard Bryan.

62. Interview with Jeff McColl, June 23, 1998, Las Vegas. See also union letters to Willie Nelson and Frank Sinatra, n.d., box: Strike 1984, folder: Culinary Strike 1984, Federation Papers, NSHS. "Study of Financial Results and Reporting Trends in the Gaming Industry, 1984," 11–13.

63. See F. T. MacDonald to Tim Hay, February 13, 1984. See also, "Minutes of Negotiating Sessions," January 16–20, folder: Culinary Negotiations, in 1984 Culinary/Bartender Negotiations Files, NRA Papers. Also, *Nation's Restaurant News*, February 13, 1984; and *Sun*, March 9, 1984.

64. Interview with Philip Paul Bowe, San Francisco, December 19, 2004.

65. "Culinary and Bartenders Negotiations," February 22, 1984, folder: NLRB Case 31-CA-13935, Culinary v. NRA, in NLRB Files, NRA Papers.

66. Ibid.

67. "Report #4 on Negotiations," n.d., folder: Correspondence to Employees by Union, in 1984 Culinary/Bartender Negotiations Files, NRA Papers.

68. "To Hilton Hotel Guests," (n.d.), folder: LV-84-129-RDF, Nevada Resort Association v. Culinary Workers Union, Local 226, in Settled Grievances—All Unions Files, NRA Papers. In same folder and file, see Vincent M. Helm to Jeff McColl, February 28, and "To All Las Vegas Convention Organizers."

69. F. T. MacDonald to Tim Hay, February 13, 1984, box 1173, file: 1984 Strike, Labor Commissioner Updates, Papers of Governor Richard Bryan. Also, *Valley Times*, April 9, 1984.

70. "Minutes of Negotiating Sessions," March 16, 1984, folder: Culinary Negotiations, in 1984 Culinary/Bartender Negotiations Files, NRA Papers.

71. *Review-Journal*, April 1, 1984; *Valley Times*, April 1, 1984; *Sun*, March 29, 1984; and April 1, 1984. The other "Indies" included the Dunes, El Rancho, Barbary Coast, Riviera, Slots a Fun, and Silver City on the Strip; the Fremont, Sundance, and Hotel Nevada downtown; and the Silver Nugget and Jerry's Nugget in North Las Vegas. Wage hikes varied according to job classifications; nontipped employees were to receive bigger hikes than tipped employees.

72. *Sun*, March 29, 1984. "We are prepared to go as long as we can," John Chiero of the Tropicana told the press.

73. Vincent Helm to All Member Hotels, March 29, 1984, folder: Correspondence to/from Members, in 1984 Culinary/Bartender Negotiations Files, NRA Papers. In same folder and file, see "Vegas 1984 Strike Prep Data," and "Strike Preparation Checklist."

74. On the strike funds, see Claude Evans to Thomas Donahue, May 8, 1984, and Evans to Herman Leavitt, August 7, 1984, box: Executive Board Minutes [1944–85], folder: Executive Board Meeting, August 16, 1984, Federation Papers, NSHS. The AFL-CIO set up a strike fund with an initial contribution of $20,000. See "Statement Adopted by the National AFL-CIO Executive Council," May 7, 1984, box: Strike 1984, folder: Culinary Strike 1984, Federation Papers, NSHS.

75. "Report #5 on Negotiations," n.d., folder: Correspondence to Employees by Union, in 1984 Culinary/Bartender Negotiations Files, NRA Papers.

76. "They're Still on the Line in Las Vegas," *Catering Industry Employee*, June 1984, 14.

77. *Sun*, March 29, 1984. The kitchen would make twelve hundred loaves of bread daily (including ham and cheese, bologna, or peanut butter and jelly sandwiches).

78. F. T. MacDonald to Tim Hay, February 13, 1984, box 1173, folder: 1984 Strike, Labor Commissioner Updates, Papers of Governor Richard Bryan. Also, *Review-Journal*, April 2, 1984; *Sun*, April 3, 1984.

79. On the new "managerialism," see Robert R. Locke, *The Collapse of the American Management Mystique* (Oxford: Oxford University Press, 1996). Also Howell John Harris, *The Right to Manage: Industrial Relations Policies of American Business in the 1940s* (Madison: University of Wisconsin Press, 1982).

CHAPTER 9: THE STRIKE OF 1984–1985

1. *Review-Journal*, April 2, 1984. The nonunion properties included the Imperial Palace and Palace Station.

2. In the 1970s, membership in trade unions dropped from about 23 percent of the labor force to 19 percent. On general problems of American workers since the 1970s, see Michael Goldfield, *The Decline of Organized Labor in the United States* (Chicago: University of Chicago Press, 1987); and Kim Moody, *An Injury to All: The Decline of American Unionism* (New York: Verso, 1988).

3. *Sun*, June 14, 1984.

4. *Valley Times*, April 4, 1984; *Sun*, April 4, 1984. Also, Michael Andrew Nyre, "Union Jackpot: Culinary Workers Local 226, Las Vegas Nevada, 1970–2000" (master's thesis, California State University, Fullerton), 67–68. The Stagehands and Musicians struck first. On April 2, at 12:01 a.m., members of the unions walked off their jobs at the two Hilton properties and the Desert Inn. Culinary workers and bartenders joined the strike at 6:00 a.m., at the start of the morning shift.

5. See "Affidavits of Vito Lombardo, Frank Blankenship, Don M. Creed, and Curt Thompson," folder: Case No. A228901, Hilton Hotels, et al. v. Hotel and Restaurant Employees and Bartenders International Union, in Court Cases Files—State, NRA Papers. The police eventually apprehended the picketer and charged him with felony assault.

6. *Review-Journal*, April 3, 1984.

7. See "Affidavits of Kerry Dale Winemiller, and David Charles Bauer," Case No. A228901, Hilton Hotels, et al. v. Hotel and Restaurant Employees and Bartenders International Union, in Court Cases Files—State, NRA Papers.

8. *Valley Times*, April 4, 1984. On charges against strikers, see "Billing Statement No. 1," folder: CV-LV-84-293-HEC, Hansen, et al v. Moran (1984 Strike-Related Arrests), in box 5 of 9, Local 226 Papers. Also, Claude "Blackie" Evans to Lane Kirkland, April 5, 1984, box: Strike 1984, folder: Culinary Strike, Federation Papers, NSHS.

9. *Nevada State Journal*, April 7, 1984; *Sun*, April 4, 1984. Also, interview with McColl, Las Vegas, June 23, 1998. The police made several arrests at other properties too. At Caesars Palace, for example, they arrested drivers of catering trucks who had abandoned their vehicles in front of the property, blocking the entrances to it.

10. *Review-Journal*, April 4, 1984; *Sun* April 5, 1984.

11. Lane Kirkland to Wm. French Smith, April 5, 1984, box: Strike 1984, folder: Culinary Strike 1984, Federation Papers, NSHS.

12. Lane Kirkland to William Edwards and Barron Hilton, April 5, 1984, box: Strike 1984, folder: Culinary Strike 1984, Federation Papers, NSHS. In same folder, see "Statement Adopted by the National AFL-CIO Executive Council," May 7, 1984.

13. "Temporary Restraining Order," April 5, 1984, Case No. A228901, Hilton Hotels Corporation, et al. v. Hotel and Restaurant Employees and Bartenders International Union, in Court Cases Files—State, NRA Papers.

14. On labor's view of the restraining order, see Kenneth C. Cory to Jeff McColl, November 5, 1986, folder: CV-LV-84-293-HEC, Hansen, et al. v. Moran, in box 5 of 9, Local 226 Papers. On labor's view of the role of police in strikes and of court injunctions against mass picketing, see Rick Fantasia, *Cultures of Solidarity: Consciousness, Action, and Contemporary American Workers* (Berkeley: University of California Press, 1988), 198.

15. *Valley Times*, April 5, 1984. Metropolitan Police Lieutenant Jim Chaney suggested the man intended to use the light bulbs as explosives.

16. "What Is a Scab?" box: Strike 1984, folder: Culinary Strike 1984, Federation Papers, NSHS.

17. Nyre, "Union Jackpot," 69–70; *Sun*, April 13, 1984; *Valley Times*, April 13, 1984.

18. Nyre, "Union Jackpot," 69; *Sun*, April 16, 1984; *Valley Times*, April 15, 1984.

19. *Sun*, April 17, 1984.

20. *Valley Times*, April 6, 1984.

21. On live entertainment during the strike, see *Valley Times*, April 5, 1984.

22. *Valley Times*, April 19, 1984.

23. KVBC TV-3 Editorial, delivered by James E. Rogers, April 16, 1984, box 1003, folder 7, Papers of Governor Richard Bryan, NSMA Special Collections. See also *Valley Times*, April 9, 1984; *Sun* April 11, 14, and 19, 1984. On April 10, the NRA offered to hike wages if unions accepted all other proposals. Also, "Employers' Proposal—April 13, 1984," box: Strike 1984, folder: Culinary Strike 1984, Federation Papers, NSHS.

24. Interview with Jeff McColl, June 23, 1998. The meeting was held at the home of Dr. Elias Gonnam, a local physician and friend of Barron Hilton (and also Elvis Presley's personal physician in Las Vegas).

25. Interview with Kevin Efroymson, Las Vegas, June 16, 1998.

26. Ibid.

27. Interview with Jeff McColl, June 23, 1998. Also, "Affidavit of Jeff D. McColl," Case No. CV-LV-84-439-HC, Las Vegas Club vs. Local Joint Executive Board, in Court Cases—Federal, NRA Papers. Also, *Valley Times*, April 19, 1984. See also "Union's Post Hearing Brief," Case No. CV-LV-85-262-HDM, folder: Riverboat Casino vs. Local 226, 8–9, in box 5 of 9, Local 226 Papers.

28. *Business Week*, May 7, 1984, 33. Also, *Nevada State Journal*, May 4, 1984; and *Sun*, July 1, 1984.

29. "Study of Financial Results and Reporting Trends in the Gaming Industry, 1984," 6, 10, brochure, folder: Gambling Management, in Vertical Files, UNLV Library. Also, Barron Hilton to Stockholders, February 29, 1984, in Hilton Hotels Corporation *1983 Annual Report*, 2–4, brochure, folder: Gambling Management, in Vertical Files, UNLV Library.

30. "Opinion and Award," February 1, 1985, Castaways Hotel/Casino and Local 226 and 165, in Arbitration Files, NRA Papers. See also, *Sun*, April 19, 20, 1984.

31. "Hilton Talks Suspended," April 23, folder: Publicity File, in 1984 Culinary/Bartender Negotiations Files, NRA Papers.

32. Notes of Frank MacDonald, June 6, 1984, box 1173, folder: Culinary Workers Strike, Papers of Governor Richard Bryan. Also, *Sun*, May 2, 1984. "One person can operate the synthesizer which can replace 10 musicians," the union's president explained. "Two [synthesizers] could replace a twenty-piece orchestra, one simulates the rhythm instruments and the other simulating the remaining instruments. Hell, if they do that," he said, "every musician in this town will be out of a job."

33. *Review-Journal*, April 27, 1984. The police reportedly arrested eighty-four people at the Convention Center.

34. *Sun*, May 12, 1984; Nyre, "Union Jackpot," 72–73.

35. *Sun*, April 30, 1984; *Review-Journal*, April 30, 1984.

36. *Sun*, April 30, 1984.

37. *Sun*, April 11, 1984; and May 9, 1984. Also, interview with Dennis Kist, September 8, 2003.

38. Yvonne Rainey to Ms. Hood, April 27, 1984, folder: Miscellaneous Correspondence, in 1984 Culinary/Bartender Negotiations Files, NRA Papers. See also John Sertich to 4 Queens," n.d., in same folder and file.

39. William S. Boyd to All Striking California Hotel and Casino Culinary and Bartender Employees, April 5, 1984, box: Strike 1984, folder: Culinary Strike, 1984, Federation Papers, NSHS.

40. *Sun*, April 24, 1984, and May 1, 1984.

41. *Los Angeles Times*, May 8, 1984; *Sun*, April 24, 1984; and *Valley Times*, May 7, 1984. See also "Answer to Complaint for Confirmation of Arbitration Award," folder: Case No. CV-LV-85-262-HDM, Local Joint Executive Board v. Holiday MGM & Showboat, in Court Cases Files—Federal, NRA Papers; and Fred Suwe to Jeanne Hood, June 25, 1984, folder: Miscellaneous Correspondence, in 1984 Culinary/Bartender Negotiations Files, NRA Papers.

42. *Sun*, May 8, 11, 1984.

43. *Sun*, April 24, 1984.

44. *Valley Times*, April 16, 1984.

45. Interview with Jeff McColl, June 23, 1998. Also, *New York Times*, May 5, 1984; and the *Nevada State Journal*, May 4, 1984; *Sun*, May 10, 12, 1984. The Hilton pay raises added up to $1.46 an hour over four years. The first year raise was only a $.05 an hour boost. Leaders of the International flew to Las Vegas to seal the deal.

46. *Sun*, May 4, 1984; Nyre, "Union Jackpot," 74.

47. *Sun*, May 17, 1984.

48. Interview with Sam Savalli, March 7, 2005, and August 18, 2005, Las Vegas, Nevada. At the time of the interview, Savalli was a business agent for Local 226.

49. See "Affidavit of Jeff D. McColl," folder: Case No. CV-LV-84-439-HC. Also, "Union's Post Hearing Brief," folder: Case No. CV-LV-85-262-HDM, Riverboat Casino vs. Local 226, 8, in box 5 of 9, Local 226 Papers.

50. *Sun*, May 4, 1984. Also, *Sun*, May 17, 1984. "If the union would underwrite my losses," Exber told the press, "I'd consider the Hilton contract. As it is, I can't compete with the big hotels."

51. Timothy Hay to Richard Bryan, May 3, 1984, box 1173, folder: Culinary Workers Strike, Papers of Governor Richard Bryan. The Engineers also sanctioned a strike against Caesars Palace, which was in the process of settling with the striking unions.

52. *Review-Journal*, May 4, 1984.

53. *Nevada State Journal*, May 3, 1984; *Review-Journal*, May 2, 1984; *Sun*, May 4, 1984.

54. Timothy Hay to Frank MacDonald, May 3, 1984, box 1173, folder: Culinary Workers Strike, Papers of Governor Richard Bryan. Also, interview with Dick Thomas, Las Vegas, June 15, 1998. After the Operating Engineers urged its members not to cross picket lines, Summa attorneys sued the union for not revealing whether its parent organization had sanctioned such action, as required by terms of its labor contract. Several operating engineers lost their job as a result of their walkout. See "Complaint for Damages," May 22, 1984, folder: Summa Corporation v. Operating Engineers, Local 501, Case No. 84-3892, in Court Cases Files, NRA Papers.

55. Robert J. Kenneth to All Temporary Employees, May 4, 1984, box: Strike 1984, folder: Culinary Strike 1984, Federation Papers, NSHS. Also *Sun*, May 8, 1984; *Valley Times*, May 7, 1984.

56. *Sun*, May 9, 11, 13, 1984. The arrests at the MGM followed a demonstration to protest ongoing performances by comedian Rich Little, the first major entertainer to cross union picket lines.

57. McColl took about three-fourths of the seventy-three hundred votes cast in the election. Joe Hays and Rudi Bath, his key assistants, defeated their opponents by an equally wide margin. On the election, see *Sun* May 17, 1984; and *Valley Times*, May 16, 1984. On the MGM Agreement, *Sun*, May 21, 1984; and *Valley Times*, May 17, 1984. Also, "Opinion and Award," February 1, 1985, 43, folder: Case No. CV-LV-85-262-HDM, Local Joint Executive Board v. Holiday MGM & Showboat, in Court Cases Files, NRA Papers.

58. "Affidavit of Jeff D. McColl," Case No. CV-LV-84-439-HC. See "First Amended Complaint for Confirmation of Arbitration Award," February 1, 1985, 40–41, Las Vegas

Club vs. Local Joint Executive Board, in Court Cases Files, NRA Papers. Also, *Sun*, May 23, 1984.

59. F. T. MacDonald to Tim Hay, March 19, 1984, box 1173, folder: Labor Commissioner Updates, Papers of Governor Richard Bryan.

60. Interview with Jeff McColl, June 23, 1998.

61. Ibid.

62. *Review-Journal*, June 13, 1984; Nyre, "Union Jackpot," 80.

63. See *Valley Times*, May 25, 28, 30, 1984; June 4, 12, 1984. Also, Nyre, "Union Jackpot," 77.

64. Employers agreed that full-time musicians and stagehands would work a minimum of twelve shows a week. *Valley Times*, June 3, 1984; *Sun*, May 8, 22, and 31, 1984. See also *Sun* June 16, 1984. Also, interview with Dennis Kist, September 8, 2003; and interview with Thom Pastor, September 5, 2003.

65. *Review-Journal*, June 7, 9, 10, 11, 12, 13, 14, 1984.

66. *Sun*, June 24, 26, 1984. The Four Queens was part of the Elsinore Corporation, which also owned a resort in Atlantic City. The Holiday Inns included the Holiday Inn South on the Strip and the downtown Holiday Inn International. The Marina had recently filed for bankruptcy.

67. *Sun*, June 17, 18, 25, 1984; *Review-Journal*, June 6, 1984.

68. Vincent J. Sirabella to Hyatt & Holiday Inns, n.d., box: Strike 1984, folder: Culinary Strike 1984, Federation Papers, NSHS. In same folder, see also "Release at Will," May 24, 1984. The Elsinore Corporation owned the Four Queens.

69. "Release at Will," publicity release by Hotel Employees & Restaurant Employees International Union, May 24, 1984, box 0956, folder 7, Papers of Governor Richard Bryan.

70. *Review-Journal*, June 9, 1984.

71. *Review-Journal*, June 2, 1984.

72. "Release at Will," publicity release by Hotel Employees & Restaurant Employees International Union, May 24.

73. F. T. MacDonald to Richard H. Bryan, June 22, 1984, box 0986, folder 7, Papers of Governor Richard Bryan. Also, Nyre, "Union Jackpot, 81–82. By 1984, union-busting was big business. Consulting firms helped employers in roughly two-thirds of all NLRB supervised elections that year, providing employers with detailed ways of influencing the vote.

74. Kevin Efroymson to Gregory Smith, December 10, 1984, folder 31-RD-894, Sam's Town, in NLRB Files, NRA Papers. Also, Goldfield, *The Decline of Organized Labor*, 193–95. Union attorneys used their own tactics to thwart management initiatives, such as filing frivolous charges against resorts to block the processing of decertification petitions.

75. Jeff McColl to Sam's Town Employees, n.d., folder 31-RD-894, Sam's Town, in NLRB Files, NRA Papers.

76. Vincent J. Sirabella to All State Central Bodies, July 13, 1984, box: Strike 1984, folder: Culinary Strike 1984, Federation Papers, NSHS. Also, William S. Boyd to Terry Adrian, September 28, 1984, folder: 31-RD-894, Sam's Town, in NLRB Files, NRA Papers. In same folder and files, see Gregory Smith to Roger Goubeaux, October 24, 1984.

77. The sixth property that closed was the downtown Holiday Inn. *Sun*, July 26, 1984. On the decertification process, see Arthur A. Sloane and Fred Witney, *Labor Relations*, 5th ed. (Englewood Cliffs, N.J.: Prentice-Hall, 1985), 107. Also, "Opinion," United States Court of Appeals for the Ninth Circuit, folder: CV-LV-85-262-HDM, in box 5 of 9, Local 226 Papers.

78. Interview with Jeff McColl, June 23, 1998.

79. Hal Rothman, *Neon Metropolis: How Las Vegas Started the Twenty-First Century* (New York: Routledge, 2002), 77–78.

80. *Sun*, July 16, 1984; and July 27, 1984. Resorts lost approximately $40 million at gaming tables during the strike. According to industry analysts, the gaming revenues paid to Clark County declined by 5 percent in the second quarter of 1984 instead of increasing an expected 7 percent.

81. Workers lost perhaps $35 million in wages and tips during the 1984 strike, which took most of them years to make up. *Sun*, June 14, 1984; *Nevada Appeal*, May 24, 1984.

AFTERWORD

1. *Sun*, June 28, 1984.

2. Interview with Jeff McColl, June 23, 1998, Las Vegas; *Sun*, May 13, 1984.

3. Interview with Mark Massagli, June 12, 1998, Las Vegas.

4. *Las Vegas Perspective, 1991*, 20–25, UNLV Special Collections. In 1985 the median household income in Las Vegas was still higher than the national average, and nearly two-thirds of the population owned their own homes.

5. *Las Vegas Perspective, 1981*, 50–53, UNLV Special Collections.

6. *Las Vegas Perspective, 1985*, 3, UNLV Special Collections. About six thousand people a month poured into the area in the early 1990s, at roughly six times the national growth rate. See *New York Times*, September 17, 1990. Also, *Honolulu Advertiser*, July 20, 1998; and March 31, 2007.

7. *New York Times*, April 28, 1991. On the Las Vegas area in these years, see Eugene Moehring, "Growth, Services, and the Political Economy of Gambling in Las Vegas, 1970–2000," in *The Grit Beneath the Glitter: Tales from the Real Las Vegas*, ed. Hal K. Rothman and Mike Davis (Berkeley: University of California Press, 2002), 73–98.

8. In the early 1990s, less than 15 percent of the local population had more than a high school education; see *Las Vegas Perspective, 1991*, 24; and *Las Vegas Perspective, 1993*, 24, UNLV Special Collections.

9. In general, Hispanics had left parts of Southern California and the Southwest, not Central America. In 1990s the percentage of children with Spanish surnames in the area's school system jumped from 13 to 23 percent; see Rothman and Davis, *The Grit Beneath the Glitter*, 11. Males slightly outnumbered females in Las Vegas until the late 1990s. In 1997 about 53 percent of the population was female. For a better look at such social and economic statistics, see U.S. Census Bureau figures for 1990 available online at factfinder .census.gov. See also M. Gottdiener, Claudia C. Collins, and David R. Dickens, *Las Vegas: The Social Production of an All-American City* (Malden, Mass.: Blackwell Publishers, 1999), 93–95, 113–14.

10. *Las Vegas Perspective, 1991*, 72; *Las Vegas Perspective, 1993*, 51. See also "Historical Las Vegas Visitor Statistics," available from Las Vegas Convention and Visitors Authority, 3150 Paradise Road, Las Vegas. See too, Gottdiener et al., *Las Vegas*, 113–14.

11. On mega-resorts of the late 1990s, see Simran S. Sethi, "Reinventing the Neon Jungle: Ramifications of the Las Vegas Strip's Mega-Resort Developments on Class Hierarchy," 2000, unpublished manuscript, UNLV Special Collections. Also, Gregory W. Goussak, "An Estimate of the Impact that Mega-Resort Casino/Hotels Have on Existing Las Vegas Strip Casino/Hotels," 1994, unpublished manuscript, UNLV Special Collections. Also, *Review-Journal*, July 23, 1989; Robert D. McCracken, *Las Vegas: The Great American Playground* (Reno: University of Nevada Press, 1997). On the Bellagio, see *Business Week*, October 12, 1998.

12. Valerie S. Burmester, "Themed Architecture and Interior Design Now the Rule Rather Than the Exception," *Indian Gaming*, March 1997, 12–14. Barbara Land and Myrick Land, *A Short History of Las Vegas* (Reno: University of Las Vegas Press, 1999).

13. In 2007 the Transport Workers Union of America succeeded in organizing dealers at the new Wynn Las Vegas and Caesars Palace. Dealers at the Wynn voted 149 to 44 to unionize. The vote at Caesars Palace was 380 in favor, 128 against. *Honolulu Advertiser*, December 24, 2007; *Sun*, September 23, 1990; and *Review-Journal*, May 5, 1991.

14. Interview with Mark Massagli, Las Vegas, June 12, 1997. Also, *Sun*, September 23, 1990.

15. *Sun*, January 30, 1990; August 14, 1990; and November 8, 1990; *Review-Journal*, November 5, 1990. On the Culinary since 1985, see Courtney Alexander, "Rise to Power: The Recent History of the Culinary Union in Las Vegas," in Rothman and Davis, *The Grit Beneath the Glitter*, 145–75.

16. Interview with Jim Arnold, May 23, 1998. Arnold headed the Culinary during the Frontier strike. For an overview of the strike, see Hal Rothman, *Neon Metropolis: How Las Vegas Started the Twenty-First Century* (New York: Routledge, 2002), 82–84; and Alexander, "Rise to Power," 156–61, 173–74. The Elardis had previously owned a small nonunion hotel and casino in Laughlin, Nevada, where wages and working conditions were notoriously low.

17. *Sun*, May 1, 1994; Alexander, "Rise to Power," 169–70.

18. The Mandalay Bay hired five thousand employees, and the Venetian about four thousand. See Dave Berns, "Recruitment Drive Begins at the Bellagio," *Review-Journal*, March 31, 1998.

19. Ibid. On the labor shortage, see also John G. Edwards, "Casino Workers Soon to Be Hot Commodity," *Review-Journal*, June 6, 1993; and Alana Roberts, "Survey Qualified Workers Scarce in Nevada," *Sun*, February 4, 2005.

20. Roughly half of the Culinary's new members were African American, Hispanic, or Asian, most of whom had never belonged to a labor organization. Perhaps a fifth of the new members worked as maids, many of whom were the daughters of Mexican migrant farm workers. On the Culinary's recent success, see "Organized Labor in the 21st Century: The Las Vegas Hotel and Culinary Workers Union Local 226," at www.blackpast.org/?q= perspectives/organized-labor-21st-century-las-vegas-hotel-and-culinary-workers-union-local-226. Also, Alexander, "Rise to Power, 145–75; and Dorothee Benz, "Labor's Ace in the

Hole: Casino Organizing in Las Vegas," paper presented at the 2004 annual meeting of the American Political Science Association, Chicago, September 5, 2004, at www.ingen taconnect.com.

21. On new approaches to unionism, see Charles C. Heckscher, *The New Unionism: Employee Involvement in the Changing Corporation* (New York: Basic Books, 1988). On new approaches of the Culinary, Alexander, "Rise to Power," 150–51.

22. Steven Greenhouse, "Labor Rolls On in Las Vegas, Where Hotel Union Is a National Model," *New York Times*, May 3, 2008; Alexander, "Rise to Power," 155–56. Also, interview with Terry Greenwald, secretary-treasurer of the Las Vegas Bartenders Union, May 23, 2008.

23. Interview with Mike Magnani of Teamsters Local 995, June 24, 1998. Forty-one resorts had labor contracts with the Culinary in 1998; twenty-eight had deals with the Operating Engineers, and twenty had agreements with Teamsters Local 995. Fourteen resorts had contracts with the Stagehands, and nine with the Musicians.

24. John Wilhelm to Frank Hanley, March 29, 1994, folder: Frontier File, Papers of Operating Engineers 501, Las Vegas.

25. *Review-Journal*, May 27, 1994. See Mike Davis, "Class Struggle in Oz," in Rothman and Davis, *The Grit Beneath the Glitter*, 176–84.

26. *Review-Journal*, July 30, 1997. In October 1993, some fifteen hundred union members picketed the Santa Fe to protest management's refusal to recognize the results of union representation elections, which labor had won. On the Santa Fe protests, see *Sun*, July 7, 1995. See also Benz, "Labor's Ace in the Hole"; Alexander, "Rise to Power," 145–75; and *Review-Journal*, July 30, 1997.

27. See Harold Meyerson, "Las Vegas as a Workers' Paradise: The Hotel Workers' Union Boosted Wages and Transformed Dead-End Jobs into Middle-Class Careers in the Very Belly of the Casino Economy," *American Prospect* 15 (January 2004): 38–44, at www .prospect.org/cs/articles?article-las_vegas_as_a_workers_paradise.

Essay on Sources

Information concerning the history of work, workers, and labor relations in the Las Vegas resort industry is scattered in a variety of historical records and archives. This essay identifies materials of importance in the preparation of this study, including primary sources and secondary literature that influenced my understanding of the subject. The notes to the text chapters provide further references to the historiography.

♠ ♣ ♥ ♦

Archival sources on the history of labor relations in the resort industry in Las Vegas are concentrated in several holdings. The Special Collections Department in the Lied Library at the University of Nevada, Las Vegas (UNLV) contains the largest of these holdings. The department has materials donated by individual resorts, for example, and papers of civil rights activists and city officials. It also houses a rich collection of photographs that depict changes in the resort industry and in the urban area. The Nevada State Museum and Archives (NSMA) in Carson City is the depository of the papers of a large number of relevant political figures and state agencies. In nearby Reno, I found many useful sources at the Nevada State Historical Society (NSHS), including records of the Nevada AFL-CIO, and at the archives at the University of Nevada in Reno (UNR).

Researchers interested in labor relations in Las Vegas should contact local unions in the city, but should be warned that those organizations are not in the business of preserving records, to say nothing of maintaining archives for the convenience of historians. The locations of the headquarters of all of the unions have changed since World War II, in some cases several times, and most of the papers that would constitute the records of their history during the period of this study have been lost or destroyed in the process. No union of relevance to this study seems to have had an official record keeper, much less an archivist interested in the preservation of its historical record. I was fortunate to locate records of the

Nevada Resort Association, which include minutes of collective bargaining sessions and correspondence between the association's members as well as other materials relevant to my subject. These records are currently stored at the law firm of Armstrong Teasdale LLP, at 317 South 6th Street in Las Vegas. I made photocopies of most of the documents cited in this manuscript, which are presently in my possession. In citing a document from this collection, I have referred to its title and to the folder and cabinet in which it is filed, in that order.

Oral histories are major supplements to these contemporary sources. The UNLV Special Collections Department has an especially useful collection of transcribed interviews with former resort workers, casino owners, and labor leaders that speak pointedly to the matters central to the history of Las Vegas resorts and their employees. So, too, does the University of Nevada Oral History Program in Reno. I also interviewed scores of individuals for this project, including wage earners, management figures, and union officials. The interviewees were always generous with their time and offered valuable insights into aspects of the subject of my inquiries. They also provided insights into their own work experiences and careers. Tapes and notes from those interviews are currently in my possession.

This study also relies on newspapers and trade journals; copies of most can be found in the archives at UNLV or UNR. Because the resort industry was central to the Las Vegas economy, the city's leading newspapers—the *Sun* and the *Review-Journal*—trace its evolution in great detail. Both papers typically took management's side in labor disputes. The *Valley Times*, which circulated in the city's northern neighborhoods, was also useful, as were the *Reno State Journal* and the *Carson City Appeal*. Regional and even national newspapers such as the *Los Angeles Times*, the *San Francisco Chronicle*, the *Sacramento Bee*, and the *Wall Street Journal* published articles on Las Vegas and its tourist economy that proved helpful. *Las Vegas Today* and the *Las Vegas Report* were other publications I found useful. The former published interviews with leading figures in the resort industry, including corporate executives as well as labor leaders. The latter, published by the Las Vegas Chamber of Commerce, provided business and economic data. Trade journals like *Variety* and the *Hollywood Reporter* also carry news about industrial developments as well as entertainment in Las Vegas.

Government records and documents were also vital to my research, especially those at the NSMA in Carson City. In addition to governors' papers, the NSMA houses the records of the Nevada Labor Commissioner's Office, the Nevada Gaming Commission, and the State Gaming Control Board. The records of those organizations throw light on subjects ranging from the mediation of labor disputes and rising gambling revenue in Nevada to the politics of gaming. The records of federal agencies proved just as valuable. Decisions and orders of the National Labor Relations Board, for example, which I read at the board's Las Vegas office, help one to see how the federal government asserted its authority over labor disputes in casinos. Occupational statistics of the U.S. Census Bureau helped me to know the number of wage earners in the resort industry and to understand the demographics of the group, as did records of the U.S. Justice Department concerning the enforcement of the civil rights laws of the 1960s. Federal records are sprinkled throughout the archival sources and collections mentioned in this essay. Relevant documents of the Equal Employment Opportunity Commission, for example, are located in papers of Charles Rusco, a former history professor at UNLV who donated his personal papers to UNLV and UNR.

Published reports of congressional investigations into the role of organized crime in Las Vegas help one understand the structure of the resort industry as well as important relationships within it. A 1951 report by a special U.S. Senate committee established to investigate crime in interstate commerce, headed by Senator Estes Kefauver of Tennessee, claimed (but never proved) that an "interlocking group of gangsters, racketeers, and hoodlums" controlled several Las Vegas resorts. A 1984 report by the Senate Permanent Subcommittee on Investigations suggested (but again never proved) that Chicago crime figures handpicked leaders of the International Culinary and used the union's assets to enrich themselves. The Federal Bureau of Investigation (FBI), whose files are in Washington, D.C., kept several prominent people in Las Vegas under constant surveillance during the postwar period. Most of these records cited in this study can be viewed online at www.foia.fbi.gov; the remainder can be requested and purchased from the agency.

♠ ♣ ♥ ♦

The secondary literature on the subject of work and labor relations in Las Vegas is sketchy. Historians have only begun to understand the phenomenon of modern Las Vegas. Their studies of the American West have not ignored urban and industrial developments in Nevada and other Rocky Mountain states, but they have generally focused on more representative cities and such traditional sectors of the economy as mining, transportation, and agriculture. They have also concentrated on developments before 1960, when Las Vegas was still emerging as a major tourist destination.

My own efforts at understanding the history of Las Vegas began with a review of the secondary literature on tourism. For a good overview on that literature, see Mansel G. Blackford, "Historians Approach Tourism in the American West: A

Review Essay," *Business History Review* 75 (Autumn 2001): 579–585. A classic book on tourism in the American West is Earl Pomeroy, *In Search of the Golden West: The Tourist in Western America* (Lincoln: University of Nebraska Press, 1957). Hal Rothman's *Devil's Bargains: Tourism in the Twentieth Century American West* (Lawrence: University Press of Kansas, 1998) has more to say about the rise of tourism in Southern Nevada. More recent studies of tourism include Ovar Lofgren, *On Holiday: A History of Vacationing* (Berkeley: University of California Press, 1999); and Cindy S. Aron, *Working at Play: A History of Vacations in the United States* (New York: Oxford University Press, 1999).

One of the best books on the rise of modern Las Vegas is still Eugene P. Moehring's *Resort City in the Sunbelt: Las Vegas, 1930–1970* (Las Vegas: University of Nevada Press, 1989), though the book limits itself to the period from 1930 to 1970. On Las Vegas since 1970, the best places to begin are David G. Schwartz, *Suburban Xanadu: The Casino Resort on the Las Vegas Strip and Beyond* (New York: Routledge, 2003); and Hal Rothman, *Neon Metropolis: How Las Vegas Started the Twenty-First Century* (New York: Routledge, 2002). Also useful are Hal K. Rothman and Mike Davis, eds., *The Grit Beneath the Glitter: Tales from the Real Las Vegas* (Berkeley: University of California Press, 2002); and M. Gottdiener, Claudia C. Collins, and David R. Dickens, *Las Vegas: The Social Production of an All-American City* (Malden, Mass.: Blackwell Publishers, 1999).

Popular views of Las Vegas include Robert D. McCracken, *Las Vegas: The Great American Playground* (Reno: University of Nevada Press, 1997), which portrays the city as an exhilarating vacation spot for families; and Sally Denton and Roger Morris, *The Money and the Power: The Making of Las Vegas and Its Hold on America, 1947–2000* (New York: Alfred A. Knopf, 2001), which suggests local power-brokers created many of the city's pressing problems. For a recent view of organized crime in postwar Las Vegas, see Steve Fisher, *When the Mob Ran Las Vegas: Stories of Money, Mayhem and Murder* (Omaha, Neb.: Berkline Press, 2006). For a concise, recent overview of the city's history, see Barbara Land and Myrick Land, *A Short History of Las Vegas* (Reno: University of Nevada Press, 1999). A useful work on entrepreneurs in Las Vegas is Jack Sheehan, ed., *The Players: The Men Who Made Las Vegas* (Las Vegas: University of Nevada Press, 1997), though it suggests that workers and their unions played little if any role in the city's history. John L. Smith, *Sharks in the Desert: The Founding Fathers and the Current Kings of Las Vegas* (Fort Lee, N.J.: Barricade Books, 2005), also gives the impression that larger-than-life entrepreneurs built the city without much help from workers and unions.

Though no previous book has focused specifically on labor relations in Las Vegas, several published and unpublished articles have made important contributions to the subject. A good example is Courtney Alexander's "Rise to Power: The Recent History of the Culinary Union in Las Vegas," 145–75, in Rothman and Davis, *The Grit Beneath the Glitter*. In the same book, see Mike Davis, "Class Struggle in Oz," 176–84; Kit Miller, "Inside the Glitter: The Lives of Casino Workers," 214–39; and Joanne L. Goodwin's "She Works Hard for Her Money: A Reassessment of Las Vegas Women Workers, 1945–85," 243–59. Other useful studies that fall into this category include Michael Andrew Nyre, "Union Jackpot: Culinary Workers Local 226, Las Vegas Nevada, 1970–2000," master's thesis, California State University, Fullerton; Terri Gilbert, "Divided We Fall: The Unionization of Casino Card Dealers," unpublished manuscript, UNLV Special Collections; and Ronald W. Smith, Frederick Preston, and Harry L. Humphries, "Alienation from Work: A Study of Casino Card Dealers," in *Gambling and Society: Interdisciplinary Studies on the Subject of Gambling*, ed. William R. Eadington (Springfield, Ill.: Charles C. Thomas, 1976), 229–43. A useful paper on the recent history of the Culinary is Dorothee Benz, "Labor's Ace in the Hole: Casino Organizing in Las Vegas," paper presented at the 2004 annual meeting of the American Political Science Association, Chicago, September 5, 2004, available on-line at www.ingentaconnect.com. On the experience of African Americans in the resort industry, readers should consult Claytee D. White, "The Roles of African American Women in the Las Vegas Gaming Industry, 1940–1980," master's thesis, UNLV Special Collections.

Studies of wage earners in other service industries bring the experiences of Las Vegas resort workers into focus. Susan Porter Benson, *Counter Cultures: Saleswomen, Managers, and Customers in American Department Stores, 1890–1940* (Urbana: University of Illinois Press, 1986), helps one see that service workers exercise a considerable measure of control in their work environment, even those who are unorganized. Dorothy Sue Cobble, *Dishing It Out: Waitresses and Their Unions in the Twentieth Century* (Urbana: University of Illinois Press, 1991), and Leon Fink and Brian Greenberg, *Upheaval in the Quiet Zone: A History of Hospital Workers Union, Local 1199* (Urbana: University of Illinois Press, 1989), shed light on labor organizations of service workers. One of the best recent books on low-wage service workers is Barbara Ehrenreich, *Nickel and Dimed: On (Not) Getting By in America* (New York: Metropolitan Books, 2001), which places waitresses, maids, and other such groups at the center of contemporary working-class life. Readers interested in mechanization in the service industries should see Harry

Braverman, *Labor and Monopoly Capital: The Degradation of Work in the Twentieth Century* (New York: Monthly Review Press, 1974), which demonstrates that service workers are not immune to forces of automation.

A different body of literature inspired me to explore the nuanced nature of labor conflict. Some of the first works I read on this subject, such as Jeremy Breecher's *Strike!* (Boston: South End Press, 1972), focused exclusively on work stoppages. David Montgomery's *Workers' Control in America: Studies in the History of Work, Technology, and Labor Struggles* (Cambridge: Cambridge University Press, 1979) provided new insights into the subject by investigating "silent and oblique" manifestations of conflict. Richard Edwards, *Contested Terrain: The Transformation of the Workplace in the Twentieth Century* (New York: Basic Books, 1979), drew my attention to "bureaucratic contests" that shaped industrial relations. Steven J. Ross, *Workers on the Edge: Work, Leisure, and Politics in Industrializing Cincinnati, 1788–1850* (New York: Oxford University Press, 1984), and I. A. Newby, *Plain Folk in the New South: Social Change and Cultural Persistence, 1880–1915* (Baton Rouge: Louisiana State University Press, 1989), also expanded the meaning of labor conflict.

Studies that focused on labor conflicts of the 1970s and 1980s helped me connect the problems of resort workers in Las Vegas to those of their contemporaries in other parts of the country. Of particular value were those that spoke of postwar "social accords" in the realm of manufacturing, such as Timothy J. Minchin, "Permanent Replacements and the Breakdown of the 'Social Accord' in Calera, Alabama, 1974–2000," *Labor History* 42 (November 2001): 371–96; Julius Getman, *The Betrayal of Local 14: Paperworkers, Politics, and Permanent Replacements* (Ithaca, N.Y.: Cornell University Press, 1998); Jonathan D. Rosenblum, *Copper Crucible: How the Arizona Miners' Strike of 1983 Recast Labor-Management Relations in America* (Ithaca, N.Y.: Cornell University Press, 1995); and Stephen Franklin, *Three Strikes: Labor's Heartland Losses and What They Mean for Working Americans* (New York: Guilford Press, 2001). An important study that put this topic into broader context is Michael Goldfield, *The Decline of Organized Labor in the United States* (Chicago: University of Chicago Press, 1987), which suggests that changing class relations helps to explain the shrinking power of trade unions. A related study is Kim Moody, *An Injury to All: The Decline of American Unionism* (New York: Verso, 1988), which explores the painful effects of antiunionism on contemporary workers.

The study of union organizing campaigns is a relatively neglected topic in labor history. The historical literature on this subject is the topic of Sam Luebke and Jennifer Luff, "Organizing: A Secret History," *Labor History* 44 (November 2003): 421–32. On the significance of failed organizing drives, see Randall L. Patton, "Textile Organizing in a Sunbelt South Community: Northwest Georgia's Carpet Industry in the Early 1960s," *Labor History* 39 (August 1998): 291–309; and Bruce E. Baker, "The 'Hoover Scare' in South Carolina, 1887: An Attempt to Organize Black Farm Labor," *Labor History* 40 (August 1999): 261–82. Book-length studies of organizing campaigns include Joshua B. Freeman, *In Transit: the Transport Workers Union in New York City, 1933–1966* (New York: Oxford University Press, 1989); John P. Hoerr, *We Can't Eat Prestige: The Women Who Organized Harvard* (Philadelphia: Temple University Press, 1997); and David Palmer, *Organizing the Shipyards: Union Strategy in Three Northeast Ports* (Ithaca, N.Y.: ILR Press of Cornell University Press, 1998). On the federal government and labor organizing, see Steven Tolliday and Jonathan Zeitlin, eds., *Shop Floor Bargaining and the State* (Cambridge: Cambridge University Press, 1985).

Several recent studies have traced struggles over discriminatory employment practices. Robert H. Zieger, "Recent Historical Scholarship on Public Policy in Relation to Race and Labor in the Post-Title-VII Period," *Labor History* 46 (February 2005): 3–14, offers an overview of this literature. Readers interested in the question of how federal policy and grass-roots activism worked together to desegregate work environments should see Thomas J. Sugrue, "Affirmative Action from Below: Civil Rights, the Building Trades, and the Politics of Racial Equality in the Urban North, 1945–1969," *Journal of American History* 91, no. 1 (2004): 145–73; and Timothy J. Minchin, *Hiring the Black Worker: The Racial Integration of the Southern Textile Industry, 1960–80* (Chapel Hill: University of North Carolina Press, 1999). One of the best works on the role of courts in these struggles is Hugh Davis Graham, *The Civil Rights Era: Origins and Development of National Policy, 1960–72* (New York: Oxford University Press, 1990). A book that has generated considerable interest in this area of inquiry is Paul Moreno, *From Direct Action to Affirmative Action: Fair Employment Law and Policy in America, 1933–1972* (Baton Rouge: Louisiana State University Press, 1997), which portrays unions as job trusts that restrict opportunities for women and minorities. On the book's merits, see the symposium in *Labor History* 48 (May 2007): 209–47.

The question of how attitudes and values shape workplace relations is the subject of many historical studies, including classic works by the likes of Herbert Gutman and Sean Wilentz. Rick Fantasia, *Cultures of Solidarity: Consciousness,*

Action, and Contemporary American Workers (Berkeley: University of California Press, 1988), explores the topic as it applies to the 1970s and 1980s. Howell John Harris, *The Right to Manage: Industrial Relations Policies of American Business in the 1940s* (Madison: University of Wisconsin Press, 1982), argues convincingly that ideological perspectives of corporate managers underpin attacks on organized labor. Harris extends this argument in *Bloodless Victories: The Rise and Fall of the Open Shop in the Philadelphia Metal Trades* (New York: Cambridge University Press, 2000). Robert R. Locke, *The Collapse of the American Management Mystique* (Oxford: Oxford University Press, 1996), also shows how corporate culture affects industrial relations.

Index

Page numbers preceded by a "G" refer to illustrations in the gallery.

African Americans: and population, 36, 119, 124, 131; as public employees, 130; in resort industry, 44–45, 127–28, 130–31, 134–35, 137, 234n13; and state politics, 122–24; and trade unions, 127–29, 193, 254n20; in Westside, 118–19, 126, 131, G4; during World War II, 119. *See also* Black Consent Decree; Civil rights movement; Discrimination

Aladdin Hotel and Casino, 18, 82, 147

American Federation of Casino and Gaming Employees (ACFGE): founded, 79–80; growth of, 81–84; weakening of, 84–86

Arbitration issues: customer relations, 114–15; insubordination, 96, 103–6, 203; loafing, 29, 108–10; theft, 100–101; wildcat strikes, 101–2

Arbitration process: judicial review of, 115–16; origins and nature of, 49, 96–98; value of, 96, 116

Arnold, Jim, 205, 254n16

Ashleman, Renny, 145

Ashworth, Don, 63

Atlantic City, 140, 146, 172–73

Barbary Coast, 247n71

Barron, Charlie "Babe," 7

Bartenders: affirmative action, 134, in arbitration case, 100–101, in "holdout" properties, 195–96; and technology, 37, and women, 36. *See also* Bartenders Local 165

Bartenders Local 165: strike of 1967, 62–63; strike of 1970, 67–69, 71; strike of 1976, 143, 146–47, 157; strike of 1980, 166; strike of 1983, 170–71; strike of 1984–85, 171, 175–78, 190, 192–98

Basic Magnesium, Inc., 211n9

Basile, Richard, 114

Bayley, Judy, 44, 55

Bayley, Warren, 23–24, 25, 44, 55

Bell, Freddie, and the Bellboys, G3

Bellagio Hotel and Casino, 202, 204

Bellhops and porters, 36, 45, 109, 115, 134–35, 148

Benedict, Alvin: early career, 223n38; and dealers, 91–92; on MGM's objectives and philosophy, 31; strike of 1970, 224n61; strike of 1976, 155, 241n71; strike of 1984–85, 173

Bennett, William, 148, 239n37

Benninger, Fred, 152–53, 155, 241n71

Bernstein, Irving, 105

Binion, Benny, 22

Binion, Jack, 203

Bishop, Joey, 103

Black Book, 19, 214n37

Black Consent Decree: efforts to comply with, 133–34, G12; impact of, 134–35, 137; origins of, 132–33; provisions of, 133; refusal to dissolve, 136, 237n75

Block, Howard, 109

Bonanza Club, 84

Bourbon Street, 159

Bowe, Philip, 175–76, 177, 191

Boyd, Bill, 188, 196

Boyd, Sam, 22

Boyd Group, 188, 196–97

Bramlet, Elmer "Al": background of, 56–57; influence of, 162–63; murder of, 160–62, 238n12; on "no-strike" agreements, 143; portrayed as hero, 128, 163; portrayed as villain, 154–55, 158; strike of 1970, 69, 71; strike of 1976, 150, 155–56

Bray, Bill, 188–89

Brooke, Robert, 189

Brotherhood of Railway, Airline and Steamship Clerks, Freight Handlers, Express and Station Employees (BRAC), 90–94

Bryan, Richard, 179

Buckley, Joe, 173

Bureaucratization, 32, 99

Burke, Mae, 40

Buskin, Herman, 96–97

Caesars Palace: financing of, 18; Lum's Corporation purchases, 69, 224n52; management of, 140; in early 1980s, 172; after 1985, 1, 204; opening of, 24; and organized crime, 19; size of workforce in 1955, 34; strike of 1970, 69; strike of 1976, 148, 150–51, 153–54; strike of 1984–85, 180, 181, 184–85, 187, 191, 194

Cahill, Robbins, 21, 65–66, 67, 68, 131–32

California Hotel and Casino, 22, 82, 86, 173, 188

Callahan, M. R. "Mushy," 87, 228n54

Campbell, William: and dealers, 87–88, 92–95; death of, 164–65; hired by NRA, 65; strike of 1970, 68–69, 69; strike of 1976, 143–45

Cannon, Howard, 70

Cannon, Robert, 224n61

"Card check" strategy, 205

Carter, Frieda, 106

Casino de Paris, G15

Casino Employees Local 7, 87

Casino Employees of Nevada, 90

Castaways Hotel and Casino, 27, 82, 87, 142, 193. See also Summa Corporation

Cau, Maurice, 104–5, G11

Central Labor Council, Clark County, 51, 57, 67, 143

Central Labor Council, Nevada, 188, 194

Central States Pension Fund, Teamsters, 18, 24, 58, 213n35

Change girls and cashiers, 37, 80, 112–13, 134, 136

Chavez, Caesar, 184

Chefs and kitchen workers, 34, 43, 47, 57, 103–4, G11

Chuck Kovacs Trio, 110

Circus Circus Hotel and Casino, 18, 148, 177, 239n37

Civil Rights Act of 1964, 117, 126, 133, 137, 138

Civil rights movement in Las Vegas: language of, 124–26, 137; 182–83, leaders of, 122–25; march on Strip, 126; rioting, 131; role of grass-roots activism, 117–18, 138

Clark, Rev. Donald, 123–24

Clark, Wilbur, 17

Class consciousness: among dealers, 90, 95; and race relations, 121; in strike of 1984–85, 184

Clerks and secretaries, 34, 48, 134–35, 181

Cocktail waitresses, 44, 55, 57, 100, 110–12, 134–35, G12. See also Waiters and waitresses

Coffey, Langley A., 108

Cohen, Sanford, 105–6

Collective bargaining patterns: in 1950s and 1960s, 53–55, 57, 58–59, 66; in 1970, 67–68, 70–71; in 1976, 143–47, 152–53, 156–57; in early 1980s, 163–64, 167, 169–71; in 1984–85, 175–79, 185–87, 191, 193; after 1985, 204

Collins, Pat, 110

Concessionary bargaining, 7, 160

Control of workplace, management commitment to: dealer organizing campaigns, 74, 88; as pattern and theme, 5; strike of 1976, 139–42; strike of 1983, 165; strike of 1984–85, 173, 191, 198–99. See also Right to manage

Cooper, Irene, 101–2

"Copa Girls," 23

Copa Room, 103–4

Corporate campaigns, 186–87, 196

Corporate Gaming Acts of 1967 and 1969, 26, 215n62

Corporatization, 3, 26–31

Corrow, Gail, 107

Culinary health and welfare funds, 162, 164, 174, 177, 238n6, 244n12

Culinary, Local 226: in arbitration cases, 103–12, 115; and dealers, 86, 91; leadership in early 1980s, 163–64; membership of, 55, 174, 205; murder of Bramlet, 162–63; after 1985, 204–5, 254n20, 255n26; origins and structure of, 55; race relations, 127–29, 130–31, 133, 136; relations with HERE, 155–56, 193–94; strength and importance of, 56, 147; and workplace grievances, 99. *See also specific strikes and names of individual union leaders*

Culture of solidarity, 149–50, 184, 240n45

Dalitz, "Moe," 18

Dancers, 38–39, 145–46, G15

Davis, Roland, 176

Dealers: attitudes toward unions, 78–79, 95; attitudes toward work, 75–76; monitored and disciplined, 76, G7; photos of, G4, G6, G12; race and ethnicity, 37, 134; skills of, 42, 74–75; strike of 1976, 148–49, 154; strike of 1984–85, 181; wages of, 42, 73–74, 77, 80, 82, 84, 88–95; working conditions of, 75–77. *See also* Dealer organizing campaigns

Dealer Organizing Campaigns: AFCGE, 79–86; BRAC, 90–91; Casino Employees Local 7, 86, 91; Culinary Union, 86, 91; Dealers Protection Association, 78; International Seafarers Union, 86; MGM Crap Dealers Association, 89; after 1985, 203; and Operating Engineers, 88; Sahara Dealers Association, 89–90; Teamsters, 91; United Casino Employees Union, 6

Decertification of unions, 197–98, 203

De Jarnette, Ruth, 106

Del Webb Corporation, 26, 172–73

Desert Inn Hotel and Casino: in arbitration, 107; dealers, 91, 94; financing of, 17–18; after 1985, 204; purchased by Hughes, 27; race relations, 127; size of workforce in 1975, 34; strike of 1976, 142; strike of 1984–85, 193–95. *See also* Summa Corporation

Devine, Virginia, G16

Dial, William, 126

Dickerson, Harvey, 80

Dignity and respect, workers desire for, 90, 102, 177

Discrimination: examples of, 121, 125, 135–36; federal government involvement, 117–18, 126, 135, 137; general patterns, 36, 127; grievance process, 99; after 1985, 203; at union hiring halls, 127. *See also* African Americans; Black Consent Decree; Latinos; Women and gender

Divisions: among employers, 147, 175, 185–87; among unions, 155–56, 163–64, 171, 194, 206; among workers, 101–2, 107, 192, 194–95, 197

Downtown, Las Vegas: and African Americans, 119, 121; before 1960s, 11–13, G1; after 1985, 1, 202; strike of 1967, 62–63; and working conditions, 77

Downtown Casino Association, 67

Dreyer, Albert, 227n31

Duca, Margie, 112–13

Dunes Hotel and Casino: in arbitration cases, 106, 110; financing and ownership of, 18, 148, 213n33; new construction projects, 159; in 1984, 175, 177, 247n71; strike of 1976, 148, 154; strike of 1983, 159. *See also* Independent resorts

Duram, Howard, 100

Durant, Noel, 103–4

Eaton, Clark, 153

Efroymson, Kevin: hired by NRA, 166; in strike of 1983, 167, 169; and strike of 1984–85, 176, 186, 192–94

Elardi, Margaret, 204

El Cortez Hotel and Casino, 22, 187, 191, 204

Electrical Workers Union Local 88, 127

El Rancho Vegas Hotel and Casino, 12, 16, 120, 247n71, G2. *See also* Independent resorts

Entertainers and entertainment, 23, 37, 109–10

Entratter, Jack, 23, 215n50

Equal Employment Opportunity Commission (EEOC): and arbitration 99; and Black Consent Decree, 135–37; in early 1980s, 166; established, 117

Ethnicity, 37

Evans, Claude "Blackie," 188, 194, 197

Exber, Mel, 22, 191

Excalibur, 202

Federal Bureau of Investigation (FBI): and gambling, 15–18; and Korshak, 59–60; murder of Bramlet, 160–61

Federal Mediation and Conciliation Service, 98

Feldman, Bob, 227n42

Feller, David, 112

Fiesta Hotel, 202

Filizzola, John, 100–101

Flamingo: affirmative action, 137; early history, 15–17; purchased by Hilton Corporation, 28; in strike of 1984–85, 181, 183, 194; after 1985, 202, 204

Flippin, Roy, 57–58, 64, 221n9

Folies Bergere, 39 , G13

Four Queens Hotel and Casino: financing and ownership of, 18, 252n68; security guards, 46; strike of 1984–85, 173, 185, 188–89, 196–97

Fox, Bob, 167, 171

Franklin, George, 70

Fremont Hotel and Casino: construction of, 13; after 1985, 204; strike of 1976, 147; strike of 1984–85, 178, 247n71. See also Independent resorts

Fremont Street, 1, 13, 180, 202

Frontier Hotel and Casino: in arbitration cases, 101–2; dealers, 82; management of, 29; after 1985, 202, 204; purchased by Hughes, 27; strike of 1984–85, 194–95. See also Summa Corporation

Fyhen, Ragnald, 79, 85, 226n27, 227n47

Gambling: legalization of, 10; outside Nevada, 15, 17, 37, 87, 140, 172; regulation of, 11, 15–16, 19–21, 47–48, 82–83; revenue generated by, 14, 172, 211n5, 227n40, 243n3, 253n80. See also Dealers; Organized crime; "Skimming" operations

Gaughan, Jackie, 22, 180, 187, 191, 199

Ghelfi, Italo, 63

Giancana, Sam, 19, 214n39

Gill, Frank, 87

Gilley, Mickey, 185

Gold Coast, 202

Golden Gate, 83, 227n42

Golden Nail, 1

Golden Nugget: early history, 13; race relations, 120; strike of 1967, 63, 223n29; strike of 1983, 167–71, 173; strike of 1984–85, 175; Wynn gains control of, 28

Gonnam, Elias, 249n24

Gordon, Jerry, 15–16

Gorsuch, John, 111

Government: dealer organizing campaigns, 80–86, 91, 93; strike of 1976, 151–53, 156–57, 170; strike of 1984–85, 179, 183, 193; struggle for equal rights, 117–18, 122–24, 126–27, 129–38; workplace incidents, 97–100, 115–16. See also Federal Bureau of Investigation (FBI)

Gragson, Oran, 102

Greenspun, Hank, 71, 216n65

Hacienda Hotel and Casino, 23–24, 25, 83, 147, 175, 181

Hallusco, Elaine, 108

Hamamura, Billie Jo, 112

Hanley, Edward T., 155–56, 179, 193, 241n70, 242n79

Hanley, Gramby, 161–63, 226n29

Hanley, Thomas: arrested, 85–86, 161; background of, 79, 226n28; efforts to organize dealers, 79–86, 227n42; murder of Bramlet , 161–62, 244n11

Hanley, Wendy, 162, 244n15

Harkness, Harold, 135–36

Hartley, James, 79

Hays, Joe, 235n42, 251n57

Helm, Vincent: hired by NRA, 165; strike of 1983, 169–70; strike of 1984–85, 173, 184, 187

Herman, Stuart, 134

Herron, Glen, 85–86

Hilton, Barron: and corporatization, 27–29, 62, 216n69; on Korshak, 59; strike of 1976, 156; strike of 1984–85, 172, 186–87

Hilton, Conrad, 27–28

Hilton Corporation: and Atlantic City, 173; enters Las Vegas gaming business, 27–28, 62; management of, 140–41; strike of 1976, 140–41, 144, 151; strike of 1984–85, 185–87, 190–91

Hilton Hotel and Casino, Las Vegas: aerial photo of, G12; and International Hotel, 28;

after 1985, 204; services offered, 34; strike
    of 1976, 151; strike of 1984–85, 180–81, 184,
    185, 194
Hispanics. See Latinos
Hoffa, James, 18–19
Hoggard, David, 122
Holiday Inn Corporation, 28, 173, 252n66,
    253n77
Holt, George, 163
Hood, Jeanne, 196
Hoover Dam, 10, 12, 122
Hoover, J. Edgar, 16
Horseshoe, Binion's, 203–4
Hotel and Casino Employees Union, 227n42
Hotel Employees and Restaurant Employees
    International Union (HERE): and investiga-
    tions of union racketeering, 224n12;
    membership in early 1980s, 174; on murder
    of Bramlet, 162; after 1985, 206; origins of,
    221n5; parent of Local 226, 55; strike of 1976,
    155–56; strike of 1984–85, 177, 193–94, 196
House rules, 31, 35, 75–76, 96–97, 105, 107–9,
    111–15. See also Work rules, union
Hughes, Howard: and corporatization, 26–27,
    29–30, 62, 64, 200; recollections of, 75; and
    strike of 1976, 150; and Teamsters Union,
    213n35
Hughes, Sarah, 128
Hyatt Corporation, 196

Ideology, irreconcilable positions, 6–7, 116,
    141, 170, 196
Imperial Palace Hotel and Casino, 159, 166
Independent resorts: strike of 1970, 70; strike
    of 1976, 147; strike of 1984–85, 175, 177, 181,
    189, 247n71
Inflation: from 1967 to 1970, 60, 67–68; from
    1970 to 1976, 141–42, 144; from 1976 to 1981,
    160
International Hotel and Casino, 28, 30
International Seafarer's Union, 86–87
Italian Americans, 37, 218n11

Jacobs, Essie Shelton, 128
Jerry's Nugget, 86, 247n71
Job mobility. See Work
Job satisfaction. See Work
Johnson, Lubertha, 122, 234n11

Johnson, Viola, 120–21
Jones, Stanley, 156
"Jubilee" (MGM stage show), 185

Kefauver, Estes, 20
Kellar, Charles, 124–25, 130–32
Kenneth, Robert, 192
Kerkorian, Kirk, 33, 156
King Jr., Martin Luther, 123
Kirkland, Lane, 183, 196–97
Kist, Dennis, 182, 188, 195
Kist, Virgil, 41, 219n22
Knapp, George, 243n9
Korshak, Sidney, 59–60, 61, 64, 222n17
Kotkin, Leo, 110
Kozloff, Jacob, 23

Labor relations, general patterns in
    Las Vegas: in 1950s and early 1960s, 53–55,
    57–58; in late 1960s, 64–67; in late 1970s,
    160; in early 1980s, 139, 141; present
    day, 206
Labor relations, general patterns nationwide,
    7, 53, 60, 160, 168, 248n2
Laird, Stanley, 114–15
Landmark Hotel and Casino, 18, 19,
    35, 110, 114–15, 193. See also Summa
    Corporation
Language and rhetoric, 154, 182–83, 206
Lansky, Meyer, 17, 213n31
Last Frontier Hotel and Casino, 12, 16
Las Vegas: image of, 146; in literature and
    film, 2–3, 210n2; and popular culture, 25;
    population of, 8, 12, 14, 159, 201; in
    poststructural terms, 3; as union town,
    8, 48
Las Vegas Club, 173, 191, 193
Latinos: and affirmative action, 136–37; and
    population, 201, 237n71, 253n9, 254n20
Laxalt, Paul, 61, 70, 129, 131
Leonard, Jerris, 132–33
Lewin, Henri, 29, 141, 155–56, 216n72
Lido de Paris, 184
Lieber, Perry, 153
List, Robert, 168, 170
Little, Rich, 251n56
Lockouts, 66–67, 70, 143, 151–53, 169–70
Loomis, Walter, 155

"Loyal" employees: management's view, 87, 188–89; workers' view, 102, 196
Lucky Casino, 85
Luxor Hotel and Casino, 202

MacDonald, Frank, 168–70
Maheu, Robert, 27
Maids and housekeepers: as category of employment, 35; race and gender, 36, 130, 193, 254n20; in strike of 1976, 147; and unions, 48, 127–28, 193; wages of, 37, 60–141; work experiences of, 44–45, 120–21
Mandalay Bay, 1, 202, 204
Marathon, Mike, 85
Marina Hotel and Casino, 159, 189, 252n66
Marshall, Thurgood, 124
Marx, Karl, 207
Massagli, Mark, 38, 58, 165, 182, 200, 218n13
Mattes, Yvonne, 43
McColl, Jeff: elected to office, 164; on eve of 1984 strike, 174, 175, 177–78; re-elected to office, 193, 251n57; in strike of 1976, 143, 150, 154; in strike of 1984–85, 182, 186, 190–91, 193–98; after 1985, 200, 205
McClellan, John, 18
McGinty, Dave, 127
McMillan, James, 123
McQueen, John, 86–87
Mead, Jenny, 43–44, 54–55
Meadows Club, 12, 23
Menard, Julie, 39
"Me too" agreements, 169, 175, 178, 187, 190, 193–94
MGM Crap Dealers Association, 89
MGM Grand (new), 1, 202, 204, 206
MGM Grand Hotel and Casino: discrimination, 135; fire of 1980, 172; opening in 1973, 30; and personnel policies, 30–31, 113, 140–41; size of workforce in 1975, 34; strike of 1976, 152, 155, 173; strike of 1984–85, 180–81, 184–85, 188–89, 190–91, 193, 194–95
Militancy of workers: after 1985, 206; in strike of 1976, 150–51, 153–54, G14; in strike of 1983, 169; in strike of 1984–1985, 180–84, 187, 192–93, 195, 249n9, G15, G16
Miller, Denise, 38
Miller, E. R. "Boots," 122

Mint Casino, 22
Mirage Hotel and Casino, 202, 205–6
Moll, Joe, 41
Monte Carlo Hotel and Casino, 202, 206
Moulin Rouge Casino, 39, 123
Mooney, Frank, 63
Moore, Turner, 109
Musicians: as lounge entertainers, 109–110, 147, G3; as occupational group, 34. See also Musicians Local 369
Musicians Local 369: in early 1980s, 165; and mechanization, 146, 157, 174, 187, 203; after 1985, 203, 255n23; organization of, 48; status of lounge musicians, 145, 157, 242n81; strike of 1976, 144–46, 147–48, 157; strike of 1984–85, 185, 194–95, 248n4, 252n64

National Association for the Advancement of Colored People (NAACP): Las Vegas chapter, 123, 125, 130, 132; and workplace grievances, 99–100
National Labor Relations Board (NLRB): dealer organizing campaigns, 73, 80, 83–84, 86, 88–89, 93; Laxalt's view of, 62; after 1985, 204; strike of 1984–85, 197; and workplace incidents, 49, 97
Nevada Equal Rights Commission, 99, 123, 125, 130–32
Nevada Gaming Commission, 81, 130
Nevada Gaming Control Board, 19
Nevada Industrial Council, 57–58, 67
Nevada Resort Association (NRA): and courts, 153; and dealer organizing, 74, 86, 91–93; early history of, 64–67; new leadership in early 1980s, 163–66, 173; after 1985, 204; proposals in 1970, 67–68; proposals in 1976, 142–144, 151–52; proposals in 1983, 166–67; proposals in 1984, 173, 175, 179; and race relations, 131–34, 137–38; strategies in 1984, 177–78, 181, 184; in strike of 1983, 168–69
Nevada State Federation of Labor, 52
Nevada Tax Commission, 19
New Pioneer Hotel and Casino, 86
Newton, Wayne, 196–97
New York–New York Hotel and Casino, 202, 206

Non-union workers: compared to union workers, 74–77; nationally, 160; strike of 1976, 148, 153; strike of 1984–85, 185. *See also* Replacement workers

No-strike agreements: court interpretations of, 238n9; dealers affected by, 87–88; in early 1980s, 164, 166–67, 169–70, 171, 245n22; after 1985, 206; strike of 1970, 68–69; strike of 1976, 142, 139, 142–43, 146, 151–52, 157, 224n61; strike of 1984–85, 170, 174, 181, 191, 193. *See also* Sympathy strikes

O'Callaghan, Mike, 56–57, 151, 153, 156, 242n77

Operating Engineers Local 501: and dealers, 88; jurisdiction over slot mechanics, 80; after 1985, 206, 255n23; origins of, 66, 224n42; strike of 1969, 66–67; strike of 1980, 166–68; strike of 1983, 166–71; strike of 1984–85, 181, 191–92, 251n54

Organized crime, 14–18, 80, 259. *See also* Federal Bureau of Investigation (FBI); "Skimming" operations

Outsourcing, 7, 144, 200. *See also* Subcontracting

Palms Hotel and Casino, 202

Paris Hotel and Casino, 1, 202, 204

Park, Robert, 127

Parker, Billy, 63

Parking attendants, 35, 113–14, 134

Parvin, Albert, 215n60

Pennington, William, 148, 239n37

Permanent replacements. *See* Replacement workers

Petersen, Cary, 43

Peterson, Charlie, 145

Picket-line clause, 56. *See also* No-strike agreements

Pieper, Jack, 29

Pilkington, Tom, 173

Pit bosses and supervisors, 22, 42, 76–77, 87–92, 95, 148

Plumbers and Pipefitters Union Local 525, 127

Pottinger, Stanley J., 135

Prell, Milton, 215n61

Prentiss, William, 115

Presley, Elvis, 29, 249n24

Race relations. *See* African Americans; Civil rights movement; Discrimination

Rahas, George, 47

Ramada Corporation, 28, 159, 173

"Rat Pack," 103, G7

Ray, Clarence, 122

Reagan, Ronald, 168

Rentfro, William E., 107

Replacement workers: and dealers, 88; and management tactics, 168, 246n39; in strike of 1983, 167–68; in strike of 1984–85, 181, 184, 188–89, 192, 195–96

Right to manage, 97, 101, 180, 198–99. *See also* Control of workplace

Right-to-work laws, 50, 61, 220n43

Riviera Hotel and Casino: financing of 18; after 1985, 202; opening in 1955, 13; strike of 1976, 147; strike of 1984–85, 175, 185, 247n71. *See also* Independent resorts

Rothman, Hal, 8

Russell, Charles, 122

Ruthe, Chuck, 196

Sahara Dealers Association (SDA), 89–90

Sahara Hotel and Casino: in arbitration, 105; and dealers, 83, 89–91; financing of, 18; after 1985, 202, 204; non-union workers, 74; and strike of 1984–85, 181. *See also* Independent resorts

Sam's Town, 180, 188, 192

Sands Hotel and Casino, 17–18, 103, 142, 159, 193

Santa Fe Station Hotel and Casino, 203

Sarmiento, Antonio, 105–6

Sarno, Jay, 24, 148

Savalli, Sam, 190–91

Savoy Room, 106

Sawyer, Grant, 14, 61, 78, 82, 122–27

Schmoutey, Ben, 163–64, 193

Scott, Arlone, 121

Scott, Frank, 144, 152, 155, 240n55, 241n71

Scott, Truman, 86

Security departments, 46

Security guards: background and training of, 46–47; as category of employees, 34; duties of, 46; essentialness of, 45; and house rules, 35; strike of 1976, 150; strike of 1984–85,

Security guards (*cont.*)
178, 182–83; turnover of, 36; and unions, 81, 224n53
Shock, Eva, 107
Shoofey, Alex, 224n61
Showboat Hotel and Casino, 82, 114, 166, 180, 193
Showgirls, 23, 39, 181, G13
"Side letters" to contracts, 156, 221n10
Siegel, Benjamin "Bugsy," 16–17
Silver Nugget Casino, 83, 247n71
Silver Slipper Hotel and Casino, 27, 142, 153, 193. *See also* Summa Corporation
Sinatra, Frank, 19–20
Sirabella, Vincent, 177, 196
"Skimming" operations, 11, 15–16, 19, 212n24
Slattery, James, 125
Slot mechanics, 34, 80–81, 88, 181, G9
Smith, Adam, 207
Smith, William French, 183
Social accords, 7, 53–54, 72–74, 179, 180
Solidarity, labor: dealers, 87, 95; after 1985, 203–4, 206; as pattern and theme, 5; strike of 1967, 63; strike of 1970, 69; strike of 1976, 139, 147; strike of 1983, 171; strike of 1984–85, 180–81, 194–95, 197
Solutions Conference, 130
Sommers, Rick, 86
Spilotro, Tony, 162
Stafford, Jack, 143, 175, 177, 178
Stagehands, 41, 56, 147. *See also* Stagehands Local 720
Stagehands Local 720: after 1985, 255n23; organization of, 48; race relations, 132; strike of 1976, 146, 157; strike of 1984–85, 174, 185, 248n4, 252n64
Stardust Hotel and Casino: affirmative action, 130; financing of 18–19; opening of, 13; strike of 1976, 147; strike of 1984–85, 175 178. *See also* Independent resorts
Stratosphere Tower Hotel and Casino, 202, 206
Strikebreakers, 153, 184, 189–90, 197. *See also* Replacement workers
Strike of 1967, 62–64
Strike of 1969, 66–67
Strike of 1970, 67–72
Strike of 1976: beginning of, 147; costs of, 157–58; employer proposals and strategies,

143–44, 151–52; settlement of, 156–57; union proposals and strategies, 144, 156. *See also* Culture of solidarity; Militancy of workers; No-strike agreements
Strike of 1983, 166–71
Strike of 1984–85: beginning of, 180; costs of, 191, 199, 253nn80, 81; employer proposals and strategies, 173, 175, 178, 252; final agreement, 193–84; Hilton settlement, 186–87, 190–91; significance of, 180, 198, 201; union concessions, 190; union proposals and strategies, 176–77, 181–83, 186–87, 192, 196–98; Wynn's offer, 175. *See also* Decertification of unions; Militancy of workers; No-strike agreements
Strikes: selective, 66–69, 167–69; as source of union power, 51; statewide in 1960s, 61. *See also under individual strikes*
Strip, Las Vegas: compared to downtown area, 12, 165; early developments on, 12–14, G10
Subcontracting, 151–52. *See also* Outsourcing
Summa Corporation: and dealer organizing campaigns, 90; established, 30; strike of 1976, 140, 142, 153, 158; strike of 1984–85, 191–92, 193, 251n54
Surveillance systems and spying, 47–48, 86–87, 93, 178, G7
Switchboard operators, 34–35, 43, 101–2, 134, 181, G8
Sympathy strikes, 56, 69, 72, 166. *See also* No-strike agreements

Taft-Hartley Act, 98, 182–83, 191
Teamsters Local 995: and arbitration, 101–2, 112–15; and dealers, 91; after 1985, 206, 255n23; race relations, 131, 135; relations with Culinary in 1980, 163–64, 166; strike of 1969, 66–67; strike of 1983, 166–71; strike of 1984–85, 181, 191–92. *See also* Central States Pension Fund, Teamsters
Technological changes, 37–38, 47–48
Telles, Raymond, 136
Telles charges, 136–37
Texas Station Gambling Hall and Hotel, 203
Thomas, Dick: background of, 225n65; on collective bargaining in 1960s, 58; on corporatization, 72; in early 1980s, 163–64, 167, 171

Thomas, E. Parry, 18, 213n33

Thompson, J. Charles, 183, 193

Thunderbird Hotel and Casino, 12–13, 81, 84, 100, 211n14

Tips and tipping, 42, 44, 77, 88, 92, 228n58

Tourism: and strikes, 69, 158, 184, 188; visitor and spending patterns, 2, 14, 32, 39, 140, 158, 159, 172, 202

Tourists and strikers: in strike of 1976, 148; in strike of 1983, 170–71; in strike of 1984–85, 181, 184–85, 188, 195

Trade unions: nature and structure of, 33–34, 48–51; and race relations, 127, 132–33, 136, 138; reasons for joining, 7, 51, 74, 76–77, 116, 141, 205. *See also individual unions*

Treasure Island Hotel and Casino, 1, 202, 206

Tropicana Hotel and Casino: affirmative action, 134; and dealer organizing, 74, 81, 88; opening of, 13; purchased by Ramada, 159; security guards, 142; and strike of 1984–84, 180, 184, 191, 193–95; working at, 39, 40–42

Turnover. *See* Work

Ullom, George, 64

Uniforms and appearance of workers, 39, 44, 108, 110–14

Union Plaza Hotel and Casino, 1, 22, 193

United Casino Employees Union (UCEU), 86

U.S. Justice Department, 99, 117, 132–35, 183

U.S. Supreme Court: on arbitration, 97, 115; race relations, 117; and replacement workers, 168

Vallone, Marvin, 42–43

Vaughn, Clem, 162

Venetian Hotel and Casino, 1, 202, 204

Vickers, Walter, 226n28

Wages: arbitration cases, 105, 112; in Las Vegas vs. other cities, 60; in 1950s and 1960s, 37–38, 41–42, 57, 60–63, 65, 67–68; after 1985, 201, 204–6; relevance in collective bargaining, 49, 55, 58, 61; strike of 1967, 62; strike of 1970, 68–69, 71, 224n48; strike of 1976, 139, 141, 144–45, 151; strike of 1983,

164–65, 167, 169, 171; strike of 1984–85, 173, 175, 177–78, 190–91, 193–95, 253n81; on Strip vs. downtown, 62–63, 165, 191. *See also individual occupational groups*

Wagner, Timothy, 121

Wagner Act, 81, 97

Waiters and waitresses: and affirmative action, 134; as category of employment, 35; in strike of 1984–85, 190–91; unionization of, 48; work experiences of, 43–44, 110–11, G4, G5; workplace relations, 106–8

Walker, Rev. Prentiss, 123

Wardrobe workers, 40, 147, 218n19, G5

Webb, Del, 26, 28, 215n61

West, Charles, 126

Western Hotel and Casino, 187, 191

Westside, 119–20, 122, 126, 131, G1

Whitney, Alma, 44–45, 127–28

Wilhelm, John, 206

Wilson, Woodrow, 122, 130

Winter, Alfred, 26

Women and gender: and arbitration process, 99–100; clothing and footwear, 39–40, 110–12; as factor in employment, 31, 36; in marketing campaigns, 23; struggle for employment rights, 117–18, 126, 136–37; and unions, 80, 128–29; working conditions of, 44; workplace relations, 101–2, 106–7

Woodward, Clemmie, 136

Work: conditions of, 39–40, 44, 75–77; job mobility, 36–37, 42, 44, 77; job satisfaction; 33, 39–41, 43–45, 75–76, 120–21; in service sector, 4–5, 8, 33–35, 37, 52; turnover, 36, 40, 46–47, 52. *See individual job categories*

Work culture, 36, 39, 102, 109, 113–14

Workplace grievances: number of annual, 99; procedures for resolving, 98; and union contracts, 97–98, value of, 103

Workplace violence, 106–7

Work rules, union: and collective bargaining patterns, 55, 72; after 1985, 204, 206, 204; strike of 1976, 141, 144; strike of 1984–85, 173–76, 178–79; traveling musicians, 218n13. *See also* No-strike agreements; Sympathy strikes

Work stoppages. *See individual strikes*

Wynn, Steve, 28, 167–68, 175